D1377973

Jesus of Nazareth.

Jesus of Nazareth

MOST REV.

HILARIN FELDER

S.T.D., O.F.M.CAP.

TRANSLATED BY

BERCHMANS BITTLE, O.F.M.Cap.

14882

HOLY GHOST FATHERS
FERNDALE
NORWALK, CONN.

THE BRUCE PUBLISHING COMPANY
MILWAUKEE

NIHIL OBSTAT:
Celestine Bittle, O.F.M.Cap.
Nerius Semmler, O.F.M.Cap.

IMPRIMI POTEST:
Cyprian Abler, O.F.M.Cap.
Minister Provincialis
John A. Schulien, S.T.D.
Censor librorum

IMPRIMATUR:
✠ Albert G. Meyer
Archiepiscopus Milwauchiensis

die 20ª octobris, 1953

BT201
F37
1953

COPYRIGHT, 1953, BERCHMANS BITTLE, O.F.M.CAP.
MADE IN THE UNITED STATES OF AMERICA

Translator's Note

AN ENGLISH version of JESUS OF NAZARETH by Bishop Hilarin Felder, O.F.M.Cap., appeared in 1938, the publisher being Ferdinand Schöningh of Paderborn, Germany, and the English agent Geo. E. J. Coldwell of London, England. However, the book hardly reached the English market before World War II broke out, and in the course of the war all the books in stock, in Paderborn and in London, were destroyed. Mr. Schöningh visited Bishop Felder after the war and the question of reissuing the English version of JESUS OF NAZARETH was discussed. The translator, therefore, was asked to arrange with an American publisher for a reissue, and all rights were granted for a new publication. As a result, some minor revisions were made, and references were added to the latest books on the phase of apologetics treated in the book, that is, Christology.

The reader will surely agree with the statement of the author in his Preface that he has written the pages of this book from his heart. Its theological solidity, joined to a warmth and liveliness of presentation, is its best recommendation. The Most Reverend author did not live to see this reissue, having gone to his well-earned reward on November 27, 1951. Christ and His Church, St. Francis and his Order, were the focal points around which the heart and mind of Bishop Felder centered, and to which he dedicated his rich gifts of nature and grace. He was the confidant of Pope Pius XI, who appointed him Apostolic Visitator in 1927 and raised him to the episcopal dignity in 1938 in recognition of his successful labors in the

AUG 3 1982

various tasks entrusted to him. When Bishop Felder died at the age of 84 years, he could look back on a life spent in arduous labors for Christ and His Church, in the prolific writing of books and in the no less arduous work of teaching. Truly, a great son of the Church and of St. Francis!

THE TRANSLATOR

Preface

IN THE first decade of the present century the preliminary
studies were begun for my two-volume work on Christ: *Jesus
Christus, Apologie seiner Messianität und Gottheit gegenüber
der neuesten ungläubigen Jesusforschung* (Paderborn: Ferdinand Schöningh, 1911, dritte Auflage, 1923/1924; translated by John L. Stoddard, *Christ and the Critics*, London:
Burns, Oates and Washburne, 1924). Since then I have had
occasion to deliver lectures on this particular phase of apologetics, most recently at the university of Freiburg (Switzerland).
The audience, university students from all departments as well
as other educated groups, manifested an extraordinarily lively
interest in the subjects treated in these lectures, and at the close
a prominent professor of natural science remarked: "We educated people hunger for Christ and know so little about Him;
give us another book on Christ which is written more from
the positive angle and which is not too extensive." In response
to this request, other lectures were added to those already
delivered, the whole then rounded out and brought into book
form.

This explains the relation which the present book has to my
previous work on Christ. It is based to a great extent on the
research made for the latter, but differs in content, structure,
and method of presentation.

Regarding the content, the scope of each work is different:
in the former the messiasship and divinity of Jesus was considered; in the present it is the entire person of Jesus of Naza-

reth, regarded in its fundamental features. Thus it happens that some parts were taken over in substance from the previous work, some were recast, and others were added.

Compared to the main work, the structure of the present book is also different. In the former the messiasship and divinity of Jesus was to be established in the face of negative criticism, whereas, in the present work, the person of the divine Saviour is to be examined from the positive side in the light of the New Testament sources of history. In the former the treatment of the various problems was determined by the hostile position, while here it will be outlined and defined by ancient Christian tradition.

This change in structure made a different method of presentation necessary. In the former work the different positions of the antagonists were always expressly marked and refuted; in this they are considered only objectively and attacked. Accordingly, the scaffolding of the previous work, if we may use this term, is now removed, that is, references to relevant literature have almost completely disappeared. An exception is found only in the first three chapters. Those desiring references to controversial questions are asked to consult my first work on Christ, mentioned above. Except for the preceding work, the following chapters could not have been written, at least not in the form in which they now appear.

The author candidly admits that he has written the pages of this book from his heart. After delving through the almost incalculable mass of modern works on Jesus and having witnessed the collapse of so many rationalistic bulwarks, it is with unspeakable joy that he points to the fact that human cleverness and human science have not been able to efface even one feature of the New Testament portrait of Jesus.

The author presents this book as a small token of gratitude for the signal grace that he was permitted to believe all his life in our Lord Jesus Christ and to confess him before men: "To the king of ages, immortal, invisible, the only God, be honour and glory for ever and ever. Amen" (1 Tim. 1:17).

The English edition of this book affords me the welcome opportunity of paying tribute to two of my American friends and co-workers.

The first is John L. Stoddard, one of the noblest and most cultured men whom I have met in my long life. Born and raised a Puritan, he lost his faith while studying Protestant theology. As philosopher, writer, politician, and lecturer he expounded the rationalistic-agnostic philosophy or *Weltanschauung* for forty years, until in 1918 he returned to the bosom of the Catholic Church. From that time on until his death (1936) he became an apostle of Christian truth and charity by word and pen and example. In order to offset the effects of "Stoddard's Library," which was written in the period of his agnosticism, the various volumes of which had a circulation of millions of copies, there now appeared the magnificent works, *Rebuilding a Lost Faith* and *Twelve Years in the Catholic Church,* as well as English versions of various French and German works. Among the latter is my two-volume apology of the messiasship and divinity of Jesus, which Stoddard published under the title: *Christ and the Critics.* He often said of this work: "If I had been acquainted with it in my younger years, I should never have lost the faith!" How often — surely I may mention this in my admiration for this unforgettable friend — did Stoddard speak of this work, in his idyllic home in Merano, with such flaming enthusiasm for Christ that the author himself was most deeply edified! The picture of this valiant comrade-in-arms — this was Stoddard's own expression — even today stands as a lasting inspiration on my desk and will remain engraved on my soul until death.

The other comrade-in-arms is Father Berchmans Bittle, a noted writer of the American Province of St. Joseph (Mt. Calvary) of the Capuchin Order, which was established almost one hundred years ago by two Swiss priests and which today is in its full prime. Father Berchmans is personally unknown to me and will be astonished to see his name mentioned here. However, gratitude and a community of ideas demand that he

be mentioned. Thirteen years ago he helped to spread the veneration of "The Little Poor Man of God" among wide circles
in English speaking countries by translating my work *The
Ideals of St. Francis* (New York: Benziger Brothers, 1925).
Now he offers the likewise excellent translation of this new
work on Christ, JESUS OF NAZARETH. This English version,
with the original German and the French and Italian editions
already published and the Dutch translation now in preparation,
will work effectively in the cause of him in whose "name . . .
every knee should bow, of those that are in heaven, on earth,
and under the earth" (Phil. 2:10).

May the Lord reward these two American friends for having
"laboured with me in the gospel, with . . . the rest of my
fellow-labourers, whose names are in the book of life" (Phil.
4:3).

✝ HILARIN FELDER, S.T.D., O.F.M.Cap.
Titular Bishop of Gerrha

Freiburg, Switzerland

Contents

CONTENTS

PART V

THE DIVINITY OF CHRIST

PART VI

JESUS IN THE EARLY CHURCH

Jesus of Nazareth

Part I
Preliminary Considerations

JESUS OF NAZARETH is the greatest figure in history, regardless of the position which is taken toward him, whether that of belief or unbelief.

We believers are convinced that he is true man as we are, flesh of our flesh and bone of our bone, substantially united, however, to God in one Person, God-Man, God the Son, God the Redeemer. In him rests the whole of Christianity, the entire plan of salvation and sole redemption, according to the words of the apostle: "Neither is there salvation in any other. For there is no other name under heaven given to men, whereby we must be saved" (Acts 4:12). This belief was laid into our cradle as a blessed gift from heaven; it grew with us; we bear it as our supreme treasure through life and death, and hope for our future resurrection and eternal glory through it. For this very reason we must be concerned with strengthening our belief in Jesus and deepening our knowledge about him. To all of us is directed the admonition of the apostle: "Sanctify the Lord Christ in your hearts, being ready always to satisfy every one that asketh you a reason of that hope which is in you" (1 Pet. 3:15).

The unbelieving and half-believing critics of Christ deny both his divinity and his divine mission. They do, however, see in him the foremost figure of history, a paragon, the perfect man, whose influence mankind will never fathom, and before whose personality all humanity must bow. Wherever and whenever these critics encounter this man of Nazareth, they experience what Goethe experienced in himself. The sage of Weimar, who in general approved Christ and Christianity merely from an aesthetic standpoint, at times changed his attitude when in the intimate circle of his family. "He praised the glorious person of Christ ever more ardently, ever more passionately, until he broke into a flood of tears."[1] "I bow before him as the divine revelation of the supreme principle of morality," he declared on another occasion. "Let intellectual culture progress as much as it will, let natural science grow in ever greater expansion and depth, let the human mind extend itself as much as it will, it will never advance beyond the grandeur and moral sublimity of Christianity as it shines and sparkles in the gospels."[2] The greater the advances which human culture makes, the higher the pinnacle from which it scans the activities of mortals — the more it admires the one commanding figure of Christ, before which all other images vanish as mist before the noonday sun. A tremendous nostalgia, a feverish yearning for Christ has gripped even large circles of a completely negative world philosophy, all appearances to the contrary notwithstanding. "Even in the experiments that are made in and about it, the strange and abstruse answers that are given to questions, the way in which it is caricatured, the chaotic confusion which it exhibits, nay, even in the hatred [of Christ] that it excites, a real life and an earnest endeavor may be traced."[3]

The numerous and widely divergent opinions about Jesus of Nazareth are due to the fact that his person and his life are not studied in the full light of historical sources. The personality

---

[1] Ottilie von Goethe, *Goethes Gesprächen*, Leipzig, 1890, 203 f.

[2] *Gespräche mit Eckermann*, loc. cit., 148 f.

[3] Adolf Harnack, *Das Wesen des Christentums*, Leipzig, 3; translated by Thomas Bailey Saunders, *What Is Christianity?* (New York: G. P. Putnam's Sons, 1902), 5. This work will henceforth be referred to under its English title.

of Jesus is neither complicated nor problematical, much less enigmatic. Whoever takes the genuine records as a guide will recognize the greatest figure of history with ease and certainty. On the other hand, it will become a sphinx to him who attempts to fashion it according to his own ideas and to interpret it arbitrarily.

Chapter 1. The Sources of the Life of Jesus

IT IS, indeed, fortunate that we possess historical sources which furnish competent and adequate information regarding Jesus. Just as he is the greatest figure in history, so also do we possess more and better authenticated records regarding Jesus than regarding any other person of ancient times. These records are partly *Christian*, partly *non-Christian*.

The non-Christian records, it is true, are very sparse. This, however, is not surprising when we consider that "Christ crucified, [was] unto the Jews indeed a stumbling block, and unto the Gentiles foolishness" (1 Cor. 1:23). To the pagan Romans Christianity appeared to be merely a Jewish sect, and for such they naturally had little interest, since in the vast empire there were to be found countless cults and religious beliefs. Furthermore, the founder of this sect had lived in a mere corner of the world, had labored but for a short time, and had caused no political upheaval. It was not to be expected, therefore, that the Roman writers would occupy themselves with him. If we add to this that the majority of the literature of the imperial Roman era has been lost, we must marvel if only the one or the other notice about Christ is found in it.

Suetonius makes passing mention of Jesus in his biography of the Emperor Claudius.[1] Tacitus, the only consul of the year 97, speaks of the execution of Christ under Pontius Pilate,

---

[1] *Vita Claudii,* c. 25.

of the rapid expansion as well as of the persecution of Christianity.[2] Plinius, governor of Bithynia, attests in a letter to Emperor Trajan that the believers adored Christ as God and were held by him to the strictest moral code.[3] Phlegon, the manumitted slave of Hadrian, tells of the eclipse of the sun at the death of Jesus, and mentions that the latter had foretold various future events, which had actually happened.[4] Phlegon's statements, however, must be received with caution, since he confuses Jesus with Peter. Celsus, the Voltaire of the second century, undertook the task of thoroughly studying and refuting Christianity during the reign of Marcus Aurelius. He boasted of having knowledge of hitherto entirely unknown sources for the life of Jesus, but in reality not a single record, outside of the gospels, was at his disposal.[5] No matter how skeptical and sarcastic his attitude was, he was forced to admit the fact of the life of Jesus, even though he attempted to explain it as superstition and devilish machination in accordance with the senseless talk then current among the Jews.[6]

The Jews, as can be seen especially from Matthew and John, from the beginning made every effort to fashion the life of Jesus according to their own ideas. Even before the oldest gospel was written they had woven a tangle of legends about the hated Nazarene.[7] In the course of the first and in the beginning of the second century these slanderous misrepresentations increased. We learn this from Justin,[8] Tertullian,[9] and Hegesip-

---

[2] Annales, XV, 44.
[3] Epist. X, 96.
[4] Origenes, Contra Celsum, II, 13, 33, 59.
[5] Ibid., II, 13.
[6] Cf. Seitz, Christuszeugnisse aus dem klassischen Altertum von ungläubiger Seite, Köln, 1906; H. Windisch, "Das Problem der Geschichtlichkeit Jesu," Theol. Rundschau, 1929, 266–288; Pierre de Labríolle, La Réaction païenne, Étude sur le Polémique antichrétienne du 1er au 4me siècle, Paris, 1934, 19–54; G. Ricciotti, The Life of Christ (Milwaukee: The Bruce Publishing Co., 1947), §§ 82–84; K. Adam, The Son of God (New York: Sheed & Ward, 1935), 49–53.
[7] Mt. 28:15.
[8] Dialogus cum Tryphone Judaeo, 17, 108, 117.
[9] Ad nationes, I, 14; De spectaculis, c. 30.

pus,[10] as well as from the scoffer Celsus.[11] Shortly thereafter some of these pseudo-legends regarding Jesus were written into the *Talmud*, the great organ of the post-Christian Rabbis, and thus were introduced into official Jewish theology. Since the fourth century this oral and written web of lies gradually thickened into a caricatured "Life of Jesus" (*Toledoth Jeschu*), which even today is found in the hands of many of the children of Israel.[12]

According to the admission of Jewish scholars, this "Life of Jesus" does not, however, represent the truth regarding the Saviour, but merely the subjective views, desires, and feelings of post-Christian Judaism. This is certainly the mildest judgment that one could pass on it. The Christians, beginning with Matthew (28:15), have always branded the Jewish blasphemies against Jesus as open-faced lies and intentional calumnies.

There is but one passage in Josephus Flavius, the Jewish patriot and subsequent renegade, which deserves historical notice in regard to Jesus. In his *Jewish Antiquities*, written about the year 93–94, we read the remarkable sentences:

> There was about this time Jesus, a wise man, if it be lawful to call him a man; for he was a doer of wonderful works, a teacher of such men as receive the truth with pleasure. He drew over to him many of the Jews and many of the Gentiles. He was [the] Christ. And when Pilate, at the suggestion of the principal men amongst us, had condemned him to the cross, those that loved him at the first did not forsake him; for he appeared to them alive again the third day; as the divine prophets had foretold these and ten thousand other wonderful things concerning him. And the tribe of Christians, so named from him, are not extinct at this day.[13]

While formerly the genuineness of this testimony was uni-

---

[10] Eusebius, *Hist. Eccl.*, II, 23.

[11] Origenes, *op. cit.*, II, 13 ff.

[12] Samuel Krauss, *Das Leben Jesu nach jüdischen Quellen*, Berlin, 1902, 22. Cf. Ricciotti, *op. cit.*, §§ 78–81; F. Prat, *Jesus Christ* (Milwaukee: The Bruce Publishing Co., 1950), I, 7–10; K. Adam, *op. cit.*, 53–57.

[13] *Antiquities*, XVIII, 3, 3. Tr. by Wm. Whiston, The John C. Winston Co., Philadelphia, p. 535.

versally attacked, it is definitely accepted in our day by authoritative liberal critics, such as F. C. Burkitt, Kurt Linck, K. G. Goetz, W. E. Barnes, J. Phackeray, and Adolf Harnack. Harnack rightly stresses the fact that previous negative criticism had fallen into the same error which it had made regarding many other points of ancient tradition, "the old mistake of regarding as spurious what it does not as yet understand." Liberal criticism was not able to comprehend how the Jew Josephus could say something so sublime and laudatory about Jesus. It therefore attributed this testimony to a loyal Christian falsifier. In fact, however, it is found in all copies of the *Antiquities* and is attributed to Josephus by the ecclesiastical historians of early times. To this unanimous, external attestation must be added an equally important internal consideration. The *Antiquities* were to be a monument which Josephus dedicated to his politically destroyed people, a mirror of memorable events in the history of his race which he holds up before the eyes of the Romans. All the Jewish sects and all the factional leaders from the time of Augustus down to the destruction of the city of Jerusalem find their place in this gallery. It would be simply unintelligible if Jesus were not mentioned in a corresponding manner, all the more so since Josephus expressly mentions John the Baptist[14] and even names "James, the brother of Jesus, who is called the Christ."[15] Josephus must therefore also have spoken of Christ. That he does so in a manner so laudatory should not surprise us. Even if he had not said such extraordinary things about him for the sake of the truth, he certainly would have done so for the sake of glorifying his own people and of flattering the Christian members of the imperial Flavian family, so adored by him. It is indeed questionable whether the remark: "He was the Christ," was not interpolated by a Christian, for a Jew, even if he were half a renegade like Josephus, would hardly be able to make such a candid confession

---

[14] *Ibid.*, XVIII, 5, 2.
[15] *Ibid.*, XX, 9, 1.

of the messiasship of Jesus. In fact, Origen[16] makes the statement that Josephus "did not recognize Jesus as the Christ."[17]

Be that as it may, the Jewish and pagan records regarding Jesus fade into insignificance before the picture of the Master which the Christian writers have painted in the New Testament. The majority of the New Testament books are indeed doctrinal. They express the truth as revealed by Jesus, but only here and there do they refer to the facts of his life. We hear in them the heartbeat of Jesus, we feel his blood coursing in them; his earthly countenance, however, glows but faintly through the veil of these books.

The Pauline epistles especially are a good source of historical information. That they were written by the apostle of the Gentiles is admitted today by the majority of liberal critics. The extreme liberal, Otto Schmiedel, establishes this with the words: "It is therefore agreed: the genuineness of the principal Pauline epistles and with it the basic facts of the life of Jesus are assured."[18] "Of course," adds Harnack, "just as the ancient history of Christianity has not yet surmounted the extremes of radical criticism up to the present time, so there are still a few authorities who declare all of Paul's epistles as spurious."[19] The epistle to the Hebrews in particular and the pastoral epistles, that is, the two letters to Timothy and the one to Titus, are questioned by some hypercritics. They admit, however, that even these writings are attributable to Paul as to content and that they originated during the lifetime of Paul or shortly after his death. Consequently they are very important as documentary evidence for Christian belief as regards the Pauline period.

---

[16] *Comment. in Mt.*, X, c. 17; *Contra Celsum*, I, 47; II, 3, ed. Lommatzsch, III, 46; XVIII, 87, 161.

[17] Concerning this passage in the *Antiquitates* as well as the essentially identical testimony in the original Aramaic text (origin about A.D. 75) of the *Bellum Judaicum* of Josephus Flavius, compare Felder, "Josephus Flavius und Jesus Christus," *Linzer Quartalschrift*, Vol. 67 (1914), 608–620.

[18] *Die Hauptprobleme der Leben-Jesu-Forschung*, Tübingen, 1906, 16.

[19] "Über die Glaubwürdigkeit der evangelischen Geschichte," *Christliche Welt*, 19. Jahrg. (1905), 318.

Even if they were not written by the great apostle, still they would be historically important from the standpoint that they serve the Pauline epistles as independent witnesses, attesting to the Christology of those ancient days and countersigning the statements of the apostle to the Gentiles.

These statements, however, are so numerous and so accurately coined that Paul can remark in his epistle to the Galatians that he has "set forth" (Gal. 3:1) Christ Crucified, painted him, so to say, before their very eyes. In fact, he gives a detailed account of the Last Supper, of the betrayal of the Master, of his arrest on "that black night." Again and again he speaks of the suffering Christ, whose wounds he himself carries in his body. To him we owe the most detailed and most faithful account of the resurrection. In a word, the overpowering personality of Jesus stood so real and so constantly before his mind's eye that it springs into life in almost all of his letters and assumes plastic reality. In view of this Harnack rightly says:

> Taking together all that the post-Pauline Christian writers [i.e., the authors of the doctrinal writings of the New Testament] up to the beginning of the second century, as well as Paul himself, have said about Jesus, one can well speak of a fifth unwritten gospel, and in a certain sense this gospel is even more important than the four which we possess. As many and as few details as may be contained in that fifth ecumenical gospel: the main features of the character portrait, the teacher, the prophet, the Saviour, his majesty in humility, his holiness, his love of his enemies, his associating with sinners, the cross and the appearances after death are attested. But above all, it is certain that this life, no matter what its course, and this personality, whatever features it may have borne, were the basis for belief: This one is the Son of God and the Lord.[20]

The surpassing importance of the Pauline Christology increases as we consider the sources from which he drew his knowledge of Jesus. He was not, properly speaking, a disciple of the Lord in the original sense, and, therefore, not an eye-

[20] *Ibid.*, 436.

or earwitness of his message. But the remark of the apostle in the second epistle to the Corinthians that he knew Jesus "according to the flesh" (5:16) suggests the thought that he had seen and heard him at least from a distance. He gained more accurate information later on from those first Christians whom he had "persecuted . . . unto death" (Acts 22:4). "The things that are of Jesus" (Acts 18:25)²¹ he learned from the narrative of those who had become acquainted with them before him (1 Cor. 15:1-3). These bearers of the original tradition were known to Paul as the result of a most intimate association over a period of many years.

Accurate information about Jesus was first obtained by Paul during his three years at Damascus, one of the primitive churches intimately connected with the mother church at Jerusalem (Acts 9:19-25). He then sojourned a short time with Peter, James, and the brethren in Jerusalem (Acts 9:26-30; Gal. 1:18-20). He spent six or seven years among the brethren of the church at Antioch, the nucleus of which was formed by the Christians who had fled from Jerusalem (Acts 11:25-30; 13:1-3). On his missionary journeys he was accompanied and assisted by the oldest members of the church of Jerusalem, namely Barnabas, Mark, and Silas. He furthermore appeals to the hundreds of still living witnesses and hearers of the Lord (1 Cor. 15:5-7). Finally, in order not to go astray in his gospel of Jesus, he once more betook himself to Jerusalem to visit the original disciples (Gal. 2:1 ff.), regarding whom he himself says: "I . . . communicated to them the gospel, which I preach among the Gentiles, but apart to them who seemed to be something: lest perhaps I should run, or had run in vain" (Gal. 2:2). By reason of this concatenation of witnesses, Paul feels himself so securely joined to the life and doctrine of Jesus that he is able to designate his gospel as having been received

---

²¹ The expression "the things that are of Jesus" must be understood both grammatically as well as according to the usage of Paul and Luke as the personal life history of Jesus (cf. Eph. 6:22; Col. 4:8; Phil. 1:27; Lk. 7:3, 17; 9:9; 24:14).

from Jesus himself: "I have received of the Lord that which also I delivered unto you."[22] If we add to this that Paul had once been a hater and persecutor of Christ, that he was converted only by the overwhelming power of his experience with Christ, and that he sealed his testimony with his own heart's blood, then we must admit that his statements regarding the Saviour evince the highest degree of historical credibility.[23]

The main epistles of St. Paul, the first of which date from about the year 50, are, from a purely literary standpoint, the earliest documents dealing with Jesus. There may have been some earlier attempts at a formal narration of the life of Jesus, and a few years later the synoptics Matthew, Mark, and Luke wrote their gospels. The key to the proper evaluation of these earliest attempts and of the synoptic gospels is furnished by Luke in the preface to his work: "Forasmuch as many have taken in hand to set forth in order a narration of the things that have been accomplished among us: according as they have delivered them unto us, who from the beginning were eye-witnesses and ministers of the word: it seemed good to me also, having diligently attained to all things from the beginning, to write to thee in order, most excellent Theophilus, that thou mayest know the verity of those words in which thou hast been instructed" (Lk. 1:1–4).

When, therefore, Luke took up his pen there already existed "many" writings, in which an orderly narration of the life of Jesus had been attempted. Their authors had been content with simply recording the oral traditions of the apostles and of the other personal disciples of the Lord, who from the beginning had been eye- and earwitnesses of Jesus and authorized ministers

---

[22] 1 Cor. 11:23. With these words, as Theod. Zahn (*Einleitung in das N. Test.*, II, Leipzig, 1891, 171) proves, is not meant a personal revelation made to Paul, be that the one of Damascus or a later one, but the mediate revelation by means of the apostolic tradition.

[23] Concerning Pauline Christology, cf. Ricciotti, *op. cit.*, §§ 90–92; K. Adam, *op. cit.*, 58–62; F. Prat, *The Theology of St. Paul* (Westminster, Md.: Newman Book Shop, 1927), II, 111–223; C. J. Callan, *The Epistles of St. Paul* (New York: J. Wagner, 1931), 2 vols.

of his word. Some of these ancient writings probably originated a few years after the death of the Saviour. Some scholars even are of the opinion that the so-called "word-source," that is, the original gospel of Matthew written in Aramaic, was composed during the lifetime of Jesus, because it makes no mention of the story of the passion, and because everything points to the fact that it was already known to Paul and used by him. Be that as it may, these oldest records, including the "word-source," have only hypothetic value, because they are not accessible from a literary standpoint, that is, they are no longer extant. The Church was concerned only with those gospels which she held as divinely inspired. But even the science of history, which does not take the inspired character of the bible into account, is, as Oscar Holtzmann remarks, "intrinsically bound to the centuries-old tradition, namely, that the truth concerning Jesus is to be found only in the New Testament."[24]

Nevertheless, Luke's statement is of extraordinary value in so far as it attests to the fact that all the oldest records of Christ adhered scrupulously to the primitive witnesses, apostles, and preachers of the life of Jesus, and that the synoptics likewise had but one aim, namely, to order and compile these original traditions concerning Jesus. The apposite statement of the physician and evangelist Luke excludes every doubt. That the same is true of the gospels of Matthew and Mark, which have the same character as Luke's, is evident.

Matthew was acquainted with the pertinent fact-matter partly from personal experience and partly from the Jewish-Christian tradition. This is evident from the strong emphasis which he places on the Messianic prophecies of the Old Testament. Thereby his account became specifically the gospel of the Jewish-Christians, as St. Irenaeus (c. A.D. 80) attests: "Matthew edited a gospel for the Hebrews and in their language."[25] The Hebrew, respectively Aramaic original, which disappeared early, became known only somewhat later in a Greek translation. At

---

[24] *Christus*, Leipzig, 1907, 27.
[25] *Adversus haer.*, III, 1, 1.

first "everyone translated it as he was able," according to the expression of Papias of Hierapolis.[26]

Of the other two synoptics Irenaeus reports, in company with the entire ancient tradition: "After the death of Peter and Paul, *Mark*, the disciple and interpreter of Peter, has delivered unto us in writing what was preached by Peter. But *Luke* also, the companion of Paul, has put down in a book the gospel preached by the latter."[27]

The Petrine-Roman character of Mark's gospel is evident. Jewish customs and practices are explained for the reason that they were unknown to its readers; Jewish currency is given in Roman coinage; Latin terms occur in some places instead of Greek. Everywhere Peter and his mission to the Gentiles is placed in the foreground. Without doubt Mark's gospel contains the sermons which the prince of apostles delivered in the capital of the Roman empire.

The gospel of Luke carefully develops the universalistic program of St. Paul: the gospel "the power of God unto salvation to every one that believeth, to the Jew first, and to the Greek [Gentile]" (Rom. 1:16). According to content, expression, and structure this gospel is altogether Pauline. Considering the technically medical terms, observations, and opinions, the author clearly proves himself to be a physician. "Luke, our most dear physician" (Col. 4:14), and companion of Paul, has written down in his gospel the instructions of the teacher of the Gentiles. Clearly he at the same time, as evidently also the other synoptics, "diligently attained to all things from the beginning" (Lk. 1:3).

Thus the catechesis of Matthew, Peter, and Paul, proper to each of the synoptics, has been supplemented by the accounts of the Mother of Jesus and of the other primitive witnesses, as well as probably also by the "word-source" and early written records. However, all the sources used by them flowed from the one, unadulterated tradition.

---

[26] Eusebius, *Hist. Eccl.*, III, 39.
[27] *Adversus haer.*, III, 1, 1.

Therein also lies the solution to the unnecessarily exaggerated synoptic problem arising from the similarity and divergence of the three first gospels. All synoptics adhere to the common tradition; but each presents the factual material in the particular catechesis utilized by him. Hence the essential unity and the accidental difference in the synoptic texts. Liberal critics today boast of having rediscovered this explanatory fact, which has been adhered to by all Christian ages, after they themselves had doubted the synoptics on account of this alleged "synoptic puzzle."

It is only by reason of this adherence to tradition by the synoptics that it can be explained how they are able to give us such accurate information regarding the life and country of Jesus. The personality of the Saviour, his appearance, his words and deeds are carved directly from reality and preserved with astonishing freshness. The evangelists lead us on all the roads and paths on which the Saviour walked; they accompany us into the towns and villages where he preached, into the solitary places and mountains where he prayed, into the houses and market-places where he healed the sick and raised the dead to life. The gospel story is told with sureness as well as touching candor and simplicity. Nowhere does the narrator push himself forward; never does he set forth his own personal opinions; he barely mentions now and then the successes of the Saviour and the impression which his words and wonders made. The synoptics simply put on record what happened and what was related by the immediate eye- and earwitnesses.

The outward framework of the history of Jesus, likewise, that is, the political, economic, social, and religious conditions of Judaism of that time, is painted by the synoptics with bright, sparkling, true colors. The relations between the pagan governor and the Jewish vassals; the tension between the foreign officials and the native Great Council; the fine lines of demarcation separating the rights of the Roman judges and those of the Sanhedrin at Jerusalem — all this presupposes that the evangelists wrote in the atmosphere of the Palestine in the time of

Christ. They give information even unto minutest details about those days. The census under Emperor Augustus and the Governor Quirinus of Syria; the Greek and Roman coins which circulated side by side with the previous Hebrew currency; the coin of tribute and the wage-penny of the laborer; the famine under Claudius; the expulsion of the Jews from Rome under the same emperor; the tragic end of Herod Agrippa I; the members of the Herodian dynasty, as well as other personal conditions, are familiar to the synoptics. They are also familiar with the turbulent goings-on of the religious and political parties of the time, of the Pharisees, Sadducees, and Herodians, as well as of the philosophical schools of the Epicureans and Stoics. The glorious capital still stands before their eyes with its monumental circular wall and its temple buildings, its priests and scribes, its pompous cult and complicated service. Only men who lived in Palestine before the decisive war with Rome — men who adhered to the facts regarding Jesus on the basis of the oldest traditions prior to the final catastrophe of the year 70 — could write in such a way.[28]

The gospel of John is of an entirely different character. Although its origin must doubtlessly be placed toward the end of the first century, nevertheless it gives proof throughout to be the work of a companion of Jesus. The personal incidents regarding the Saviour stand out so real, lifelike, and concrete that only an eyewitness could have described them. The evangelist introduces the Master at the moment when the precursor pointed him out: "These things were done in Bethania, beyond the Jordan, where John was baptizing. The next day, John saw Jesus coming to him, and he saith: Behold the Lamb of God, behold him who taketh away the sin of the world. . . . The next day again John stood, and two of his disciples. And

---

[28] Concerning the synoptics, see also K. Adam, *op. cit.*, 62–68; Ricciotti, *op. cit.*, §§ 92–134; F. Prat, *op. cit.*, I, 14–26; J. Steinmueller and K. Sullivan, *A Companion to the New Testament* (New York: J. Wagner, 1944), 32–53; also P. J. Arendzen, *The Gospels — Fact, Myth or Legend* (London, 1923); M. J. Lagrange, *The Gospel of Jesus Christ* (London, 1938).

beholding Jesus walking, he saith: Behold the Lamb of God.
. . . Now it was about the tenth hour. . . . The third
day, there was a marriage in Cana of Galilee: and the
mother of Jesus was there. And Jesus also was invited, and his
disciples, to the marriage. . . . After this he went down to
Capharnaum, he and his mother, and his brethren, and his
disciples: and they remained there not many days. And the
pasch of the Jews was at hand, and Jesus went up to Jerusalem. . . . After these things Jesus and his disciples came
into the land of Judea: and there he abode with them, and
baptized. And John also was baptizing in Ennon near Salim;
because there was much water there. . . . He left Judea
and went again to Galilee. And he was of necessity to pass
through Samaria. He cometh therefore to a city of Samaria,
which is called Sichar, near the land which Jacob gave to his
son Joseph. Now Jacob's well was there. Jesus therefore being
wearied with his journey, sat thus on the well. It was about
the sixth hour. There cometh a woman of Samaria, to draw
water."[29] Then follows the entire lifelike scene at the well of
Jacob.

Thus the story runs on from chapter to chapter, from incident
to incident, covering the entire activity of Jesus up to the days
of his passion.[30] Everywhere bright, radiant colors, the sharpest
lines — snapshots as it were, a speaking likeness, active, living
memoirs, such as can flow only from the pen of an eyewitness.

And then the days of the passion of Jesus! Almost with the
accuracy of a statistician and with the deep emotion of the
disciple who was a most intimate witness of them, the incidents
of these days are described by John with detailed minuteness.
"Jesus . . . went forth with his disciples over the brook Cedron,
where there was a garden, into which he entered with his
disciples. . . . Then they led Jesus from Caiphas to the governor's hall. And it was morning; and they went not into the

---

[29] Jn. 1:28–29, 35–36, 39; 2:1–2, 12–13; 3:22–23; 4:3–7.
[30] For a complete compilation see Knabenbauer, "Der geschichtliche Charakter des 4. Evangeliums," *Stimmen aus Maria-Laach*, Freiburg, 1904, 365 f.

hall, that they might not be defiled, but that they might eat the pasch. Pilate therefore went out to them. . . . Pilate therefore went into the hall again. . . . Pilate therefore went forth again. . . . And he entered into the hall again. . . . He brought Jesus forth, and sat down in the judgment seat, in the place that is called Lithostrotos, and in Hebrew Gabbatha. . . . It was the parasceve of the pasch, about the sixth hour. . . . The place where Jesus was crucified was nigh to the city. . . . Then the Jews, (because it was the parasceve,) that the bodies might not remain upon the cross on the sabbath day, (for that was a great sabbath day,) besought Pilate that their legs might be broken, and that they might be taken away. . . . Now there was in the place where he was crucified, a garden; and in the garden a new sepulchre, wherein no man had yet been laid. There, therefore, because of the parasceve of the Jews, they laid Jesus, because the sepulchre was nigh at hand. . . . On the first day of the week, Mary Magdalen cometh early, when it was yet dark, unto the sepulchre. . . . Mary stood at the sepulchre without, weeping. . . . When it was late that same day, the first of the week, and the doors were shut, where the disciples were gathered together, for fear of the Jews, Jesus came and stood in the midst. . . . After eight days again his disciples were within, and Thomas with them. Jesus cometh, the doors being shut, and stood in the midst, and said: Peace be to you."[31]

In every verse and in every remark it is the eyewitness who speaks. The evangelist John must be the same person as the apostle and beloved disciple of this name. His character is stamped upon the entire fourth gospel. The absolute sureness, the majestic composure, the loving, flaming enthusiasm with which the picture of the Saviour is presented, the depth of feeling, the soaring flight of thought, the content and the manner of presentation, all are undoubtedly Johannine. Besides, the gospel itself claims John as author in these express and clear terms: "This is that disciple who giveth testimony of these things, and hath written these things. . . . That disciple whom

---

[31] Jn. 18:1, 28–29, 33; 19:4, 9, 13, 14, 20, 31, 41–42; 20:1, 11, 19, 26.

Jesus loved, who also leaned on his breast at supper, and said: Lord, who is he that shall betray thee?" (Jn. 21:24, 20), the disciple who stood under the cross and to whom the Saviour commended his Mother (cf. Jn. 19:26 f.). If some rationalistic know-alls nevertheless doubt the Johannine origin of this gospel, they rely, as the Protestant scholar Theodore Zahn emphasizes, not on "positive observations of the text and positive knowledge which goes beyond tradition . . . but the champions of such hypotheses were only united in the negative opinion that a personal disciple [of Jesus] could not have written the book, because its content is — incredible."[32]

It is solely in the name of unbelief that rationalism has denied the genuineness of the gospels. In order to be able to represent the life of Jesus as a myth, David Frederick Strauss (1834) repudiated the evangelists, saying that their writings originated 150 years after Christ. For the purpose of unmasking ancient Christianity as a witches' cauldron of discord, Ferdinand Christian Baur soon after (1845–1847) declared the gospels to be fabrications of swindlers who accomplished their handiwork 140–170 years after Christ. These and similar allegations were possible in the period of uncontrolled rationalism, which had as little sense for history as it had for belief.

Gradually, however, they again turned their attention to early Christian literature, and by means of it endeavored to establish the age and the origin of the gospels. Thus liberal research, in the second half of the nineteenth century, approached closer and closer to the traditional position. According to Keim, the first three gospels originated about 70–117; according to Hilgenfeld, about 70–100; according to Holtzmann, about 68–100; according to Bernard Weiss, about 69–95; according to Harnack, about 65–93.[33] Later on, however, the leader

---

[32] *Realenzyklopädie für protestant. Theologie*, 3 ed., IX, 280. For a fuller treatment, see Ricciotti, *op. cit.*, §§ 135–153; Prat, *op. cit.*, I, 26–29; K. Adam, *op. cit.*, 69–75; Steinmueller-Sullivan, *op. cit.*, 53 ff., 219–226; J. Donovan, *The Authorship of St. John's Gospel* (London: Burns and Oates, 1936).

[33] *Chronologie der altchristlichen Literatur* (Leipzig, 1897), I, 651 ff.

of the liberal school admitted that the dates must be set earlier,[34] and he finally declared that the gospel of Matthew must be "placed in close proximity with the destruction of Jerusalem (A.D. 70)," and even that its "composition before the catastrophe cannot be excluded with absolute certainty," and that various reasons "are rather in favour of the composition before the catastrophe";[35] that the gospel of Luke, however, was written "while St. Paul was still alive" (therefore, before A.D. 67); and the gospel of Mark, which was used by Luke, at the very latest in the sixth decade after Christ.[36] In the same way the fourth gospel was gradually moved to the end of the first century. "They have gone back from 160–170 (Baur, Bruno Bauer) to 150–160 (Schwegler), 155 (Volkmar), 150 (Zeller), about 150 (Bretschneider, Scholten, Mathes), between 135 and 163 (Tayler), about 140 (Hilgenfeld, Hausrath, Thoma), 130–135 (Lützelberger), 130 (Keim), 110–115 (Nicolas, Renan, Schenkel), 100 (Aube)."[37] Today the date of the origin of the fourth gospel is again placed at the end of the first Christian century.

Together with this dating the classic accounts of the life of Jesus were again attributed to the "quadrumvirate": Matthew, Mark, Luke, and John. The fight about the Johannine origin of the gospel of the same name has not yet subsided, just because of its "incredibility." But the resistance is crumbling more and more in the face of the unanimous testimony of the ancient Christian tradition[38] and will finally have to cease, just as all

---

[34] *Die Apostelgeschichte* (Leipzig, 1908), 217 ff. English by J. R. Wilkinson, *The Acts of the Apostles* (New York: G. P. Putnam's Sons, 1909), 290 ff.

[35] *Neue Untersuchungen zur Apostelgeschichte und zur Abfassungszeit der synoptischen Evangelien* (Leipzig, 1911), 93 f., 94, *n.* 1. English by J. R. Wilkinson, *The Date of the Acts and of the Synoptic Gospels* (New York: G. P. Putnam's Sons, 1911), 133 f., 134, *n.* 2.

[36] Harnack-Wilkinson, *The Date of the Acts*, 124, 126–135.

[37] H. J. Holtzmann, *Einleitung in das N. Test.* (Freiburg, 1886), 476.

[38] For a complete compilation, see P. Lagrange, *Évangile selon Saint Jean*, 2 ed. (Paris, 1925), XXII to LXVI. See also J. Donovan, *The Authorship of St. John's Gospel* (London: Burns and Oates, 1935).

the other positions held by a prejudiced criticism had to be surrendered.

An extraordinarily important supplement to the gospels, to be exact, especially to the third, are the Acts of the Apostles. For intrinsic and extrinsic reasons they were attributed to St. Luke from the beginning, and the date of their origin was placed in the period of the first imprisonment of the teacher of the Gentiles at Rome (61–63). In them we become acquainted with the victorious march of Christianity from the Feast of Pentecost to the imprisonment of St. Paul. In the first part the author describes the Jewish-Christian period of the Church (chaps. 1–9); in the second, the origin and development of the mission to the Gentiles (chaps. 10–28). It is only from this invaluable source that we learn what the most ancient preachers taught of Christ and what the first Christians believed of him.

Because of its content and particularly because of its Christology, liberal critics, up to a short time ago, have attacked this book with extreme vehemence. First the authorship of Luke was impugned, although not a single reason against it could be brought forward. Then it was arbitrarily assumed that its writing dated only from the end of the first or even the beginning of the second century. On the basis of these fantastic assertions they then alleged that the author had drawn from entirely unreliable sources, and, furthermore, that he had distorted his material. Thus these critics arrived at the monstrous charges which Harnack aptly castigates with the words:

> With them the book passes as a comparatively late patchwork compilation, in which the part taken by the editor is insignificant, yet in all cases detrimental; the "we"-sections are not the property of the author, but an extract from a source, or even a literary fiction; historical errors are as numerous as gaps and ill-disguised joinings; the portrait of St. Paul is drawn with bias, or in ignorance; the description given in the first chapters is scarcely anywhere other than pure fancy — Peter is Pauline, Paul is Petrine; but who can number the objections that have been raised against this book! If they were only objections that one could take hold of! But after no small number of these has been refuted, one has

to deal not so much with definite objections, as with an attitude of general mistrust in the book, with airy conceits and lofty contempt; most of all, however, with the fruits of that vicious method wherein great masses of theory are hung upon the spider's thread of a single observation, wherein a writer of the New Testament is allowed no weakness, no possibility of ignorance, wherein instances of such failing are used as powder to blow the whole book into the air.[39]

Harnack has the great merit of having unmasked the vagaries of his own liberal-minded colleagues. In three masterly monographs[40] he again assigns to the Acts of the Apostles the place which they had occupied in early Christian literature. The Berlin savant did not arrive at his later conclusions at the start of his researches in this field. He designates them as the result of a "slow evolution," which he experienced step by step during the period of more than fifteen years.[41] The first result of this development was the volume which appeared in 1906: *Lukas der Arzt, der Verfasser des dritten Evangeliums und der Apostelgeschichte.* The outcome of his splendid researches is expressed in the title of this volume. But while Luke the Physician is therein proved to be the author of the Acts, Harnack nevertheless adheres to the assumption that it originated only about the year 80.[42] In the book which appeared in 1908, *Die Apostelgeschichte,* he begins to waver about fixing this date at so late a period, indeed so much so that he penned these sentences: "What, then, is to be said in favour of the Acts (and therefore also of the gospel) having been already written at the beginning of the seventh decade of the first century? There are, in

---

[39] Harnack-Wilkinson, *The Acts of the Apostles,* Introduction, XII f.

[40] *Lukas der Arzt* (Leipzig, 1906). English by J. R. Wilkinson, *Luke the Physician* (New York: G. P. Putnam's Sons, 1907); *Die Apostelgeschichte,* English by J. R. Wilkinson, *The Acts of the Apostles; Neue Untersuchungen zur Apostelgeschichte und zur Abfassungszeit der synoptischen Evangelien,* English by Wilkinson, *The Date of the Acts and of the Synoptic Gospels.* These works are Vols. I, II, and IV of Harnack's *Beiträge zur Einleitung in das Neue Testament.*

[41] Harnack-Wilkinson, *The Date of the Acts,* 93.

[42] *Ibid., Luke the Physician,* 163.

my opinion, the following very weighty considerations."[43] The
conclusive discussion, however, is found in his third work,
published in 1911: *Neue Untersuchungen zur Apostelgeschichte und zur Abfassungszeit der synoptischen Evangelien.*
It reaches its climax in the proof that the Acts originated "before the destruction of Jerusalem, and before the death of Paul,"
consequently in the first years of the sixties.[44]

If the Acts were written at a time when many witnesses to
the facts therein related still lived, witnesses who were able to
investigate the truth of the statements contained in the writing,
then the charge that Luke had drawn from entirely unreliable
sources, or even fabricated ones, is also without basis. On the
contrary, it can be proved with certainty that he relied on excellent oral traditions, and no doubt also on written sources for
the first part of his book, while the entire second part was
written by him partly as eyewitness, partly on the solid ground
of the accounts given by eyewitnesses who co-operated with
him.[45]

This material, self-witnessed as well as drawn from oral and
written sources, was elaborated by Luke with historical fidelity.
This is warranted not only by his own protestation and his
proved conscientiousness as historian, but also by the content
and structure of the book. In no wise does Luke give the impression of being "a physician turned into a wild enthusiast,"
such as liberal critics describe him; he is, writes Harnack,

> neither credulous nor uncritical. Credulous and uncritical writers
> of those days produced works of a character entirely different
> from his! Again, for the larger half of the work we possess in
> the epistles of St. Paul a stringent test of the accuracy of the
> historian. That these epistles were the creations of the moment,
> the offspring of a personality of the most marked subjectivity,
> only increases the stringency of the test. And yet it is only the
> overscrupulous and those who split hairs who cannot recognize
> that in dozens of important and unimportant passages the Acts

---

43 *Ibid., The Acts of the Apostles,* 293.
44 *Ibid., The Date of the Acts,* 124.
45 *Ibid., Luke the Physician,* 121–145; *The Acts of the Apostles,* 162–202.

of the Apostles has stood the test imposed upon it by the Pauline epistles. Leaving out of account a few minute details, the description of the Council of Jerusalem and of St. Paul's apology in the last speeches, in fact the whole account of his attitude toward the Jews at his last visit to Jerusalem, alone remain questionable.[46]

But these parts, likewise, though they cannot be put to the test by means of the Pauline epistles, are impregnable. Yes, just those things which the critics have attacked the most bitterly in Luke "bear the stamp of historical reality," and these critics cast doubt upon them only because they "treat their own conceits in regard to the book with more respect than the grand lines of the work, which they either take as a matter of course, or criticize from the standpoint of their own superior knowledge."[47]

Harnack sums up his final judgment on the Acts, based on the most penetrating analysis and painfully exact investigation, in the words: "Judged from almost every possible standpoint, it is a solid, respectable, in many respects an extraordinary work";[48] it "shows an amount of historical insight which claims the highest appreciation,"[49] and "St. Luke has produced a splendid piece of work."[50]

In but one point does Harnack take a stand against the author of the Acts, and that is in regard to "experiences, if these admit of a miraculous interpretation."[51] To him Luke is "trustworthy so long as his faith in the miraculous, and his interest in his own 'spiritual' gift of healing, do not come into play."[52] Harnack cannot share the "prejudice" of believing scholars who take miracles into account.[53] Yet whoever studies the arguments of the Berlin critic with open eyes will find that Harnack him-

---

[46] Ibid., The Acts of the Apostles, Introd., XXXVIII.
[47] Ibid., Introd., XXVI.
[48] Ibid., 299.
[49] Ibid., Introd., XXVII.
[50] Ibid., Luke the Physician, 165.
[51] Ibid., 123.
[52] Ibid., 125.
[53] Ibid., The Acts of the Apostles, 296.

self proceeds to judge this work of Luke with a "prejudice," that is, with the aprioristic, philosophic postulate that real and genuine miracles are impossible, and that there cannot exist a divinely revealed, supernatural religion. The student will find that this prejudice injects a flagrantly dissonant note into Harnack's otherwise excellent work; that his argumentation immediately becomes threadbare and naïve whenever he attempts to get around the miraculous; and that in the end he cannot deny the account of miracles as given by Luke, nor prove them to be an almost incredibly fast-growing "legend,"[54] nor is he able to explain them in any natural way. Thus liberal critics will find themselves forced to return to the traditional positions, not only in all other points, as Harnack points out, but also in regard to the miracles of the Acts, and to accept the work of Luke as the uniformly exact account of the earliest period of Christianity.[55]

At the end of the nineteenth century Harnack flung into the world the words which caused such a sensation: "The criticism of the sources of early Christianity is gradually returning to the traditional standpoints."[56] At first there was loud contradiction on the part of the smaller minds in the ranks of liberalism. But ten years later the leader of the liberal school of criticism was able to confirm his candid statement as having been proved by the facts.[57] Liberal critics had to surrender one position after the other to the historical tradition of the Church. The one or other outsider is still poking around the ruins of rationalism for potsherds from the days of Strauss and Baur; the enemy still perseveres stubbornly, as we have just seen from the example of Harnack, and as we shall further

---

[54] Ibid.

[55] See Steinmueller-Sullivan, op. cit., 143 f.; C. J. Callan, The Four Gospels and the Acts of the Apostles (New York, 1942); C. Fouard, St. Peter and the First Years of Christianity (New York, 1915).

[56] Harnack, Geschichte der altchristlichen Literatur, II, 1 (Leipzig, 1907), X.

[57] Harnack-Wilkinson, Luke the Physician, Preface, VI.

explain in the next chapter, in a negative criticism of the facts of the New Testament; regarding the literary-historical criticism of the sources, however, they utter a decisive *yes*. That is the most important event of present-day research regarding Jesus and the earliest history of Christianity.

Chapter 2. The Credibility of the Gospel Portrait of Jesus

THUS far we have determined that the belief in Christ and the research regarding Christ rest on trustworthy records. The four gospels in particular originated only a few decades after the death of Jesus. They were written by the apostles Matthew and John and the apostolic disciples Mark and Luke, and they conform to the tradition of the entire ancient Church. Even liberal critics today are willing to concede this point.

They endeavor, however, to escape the conclusion as to the credibility of the gospel portrait of Jesus by advancing the so-called evolutionary or legendary hypothesis. In their generous love and ardent veneration the first Christians are supposed to have woven ever new legends about the historical person of Jesus, until the Christ of faith had been completed, and the evangelists thereupon fixed this portrait with a devout pen. Thus the gospel portrait of Christ is said to be no more than a distorted image of the man of Nazareth, this image having been intensified into the supernatural, the miraculous, the divine.

A historical life of Jesus or a devout legend of Christ? That is the decisive question. We put this question first of all to the evangelists themselves, then to the gospels, and lastly to the early disciples as the final guarantors of the evangelists and their gospels.

1. First of all we put the question to the evangelists, that is, whether they could, and wanted to, represent the life of Jesus with historical accuracy and fidelity.

The evangelists certainly were not historians after the manner of Thucydides or Tacitus, much less according to the demands of the modern professional science of history. They lacked the method, the higher scientific training, and the critical discernment. They were not, however, in need of these. There was no question of solving deep problems, nor of gleaning facts from dusty bundles of reports and sifting them with a critical eye. The work of the evangelists was simply to write down wholly concrete incidents which occurred mostly in public and were of the simplest nature. The miraculous works and the sublime doctrine of Jesus were no exception to this. Their extraordinary character does not change or modify the natural phenomena in the least. Furthermore, the evangelists were not called upon to pass judgment on the preternatural character of the miracles of Jesus nor on the supernatural character of his doctrine. They simply report what the Master had said or done. They state, for instance, the simple fact that he made the blind to see, that he calmed wind and waves in an instant, raised the dead to life, and the like. For this neither critical training nor higher culture of the mind is needed. Sound senses, a sure eye, unbiased judgment, common sense — those are the important things.

The evangelists possessed these qualities in a high degree. Nothing is more unjust than the charge that they were eccentric, credulous, and had a mania for miracles. There is not a trace of the visionary in them; everywhere there is calm, sober, and dispassionate perception. Even where one could undoubtedly expect a mixture of personal temperament and judgment, nothing is found but the bare recording of facts. The evangelists narrate the healing of the sick, the raising of the dead, physical miracles, without the least expression of astonishment. They report the mistreatment, the slandering and condemnation of the Master without a word of indignation or disapproval. Even the death and resurrection of the Saviour is recorded with an unemotional pen, as if they had no further interest in it than that of an observer and reporter. Thereby they establish most decidedly their *fitness* to record the gospel events in accordance with the truth.

That this was their express and sole purpose is equally as certain. The gospels, from the first to the last line, from the most profound basic idea to the final structure, are of such a character that no doubt remains: these men want to be regarded as recording history, and their works are to be considered as historically true presentations. Luke in particular, whose critical aptitude is appraised most highly by the enemy, and also John, to whom the smallest measure of historical importance is conceded, state this in plain words.

We are acquainted with the literary preface to the gospel of Luke: "Forasmuch as many have taken in hand to set forth in order a narration of the things that have been accomplished among us; according as they have delivered them unto us, who from the beginning were eyewitnesses and ministers of the word: it seemed good to me also, having diligently attained to all things from the beginning, to write to thee in order, most excellent Theophilus, that thou mayest know the verity of those words in which thou hast been instructed" (1:1–4). The sole object of the evangelists, therefore, is to fix accurately the portrait of Jesus in the light of the true facts, of the historical events, and of undeniable happenings. It is exactly this essential concordance of the synoptics among themselves together with the diversity of presentation, so much objected to by some antagonists, which proves with what touching fidelity and accuracy they relate the original life of Jesus.

Even more emphatically does John assert toward the end of his gospel: "He that saw it, hath given testimony; and his testimony is true. And he knoweth that he saith true; that you also may believe" (19:35). In his first epistle he stresses with like emphasis that it is the unadulterated echo of the life of Jesus witnessed by himself: "That which was from the beginning, which we have heard, which we have seen with our eyes, which we have looked upon, and our hands have handled, of the word of life . . . we do bear witness. . . . That which we have seen and have heard, we declare unto you, that you also may have fellowship with us, and our fellowship may be with the Father, and with his Son Jesus Christ" (1 Jn. 1:1-3). The disciples of John expressly affirm that their master has drawn purely the self-witnessed and faithfully preserved portrait of Jesus: "This is that disciple who giveth testimony of these things, and hath written these things; and we know that his testimony is true" (Jn. 21:24). Hence it is absolutely clear that the last of the evangelists is to be regarded as a historian and not as a novelist.

The evangelists therefore desire to record the events of the life of Jesus to the best of their ability and knowledge. Not a line is written by them which they do not regard as true. Not an episode is related by them in the actuality of which they do not believe. They do not place a single doctrine in the mouth of the Master which they did not consider with fullest conviction to be his doctrine. It would be a waste of time to say more about this.

2. Let us now examine the gospels themselves, in order to ascertain whether they mirror the original portrait of Jesus, or whether they stabilize later legends about Christ.

Because of the difference between the first three gospels and the fourth as to time, content, and form, it is necessary to consider the Christology of the synoptics and of John separately.

The synoptic gospels give the definite impression of presenting the original story of Jesus as it actually happened, not a later remodeling or embellishment of the facts. The synoptics have drawn even the external framework of the gospels, that is, the religious, political, economic, and social conditions of Judaism as it accurately fitted the time of Jesus but which was no longer true a few decades later when the evangelists composed their writings. In like manner, primitive Christianity is pictured in their writings in that archaistic form as it existed in the days of the Lord, while it already had entered upon entirely different conditions at the time when the synoptic books originated. Of course, the entire gospel story cannot be examined as to these earlier and later conditions within the limits of a single chapter.

Therefore, we have selected just one point for consideration. This point, however, is of utmost importance, for everything hinges upon it, not only from our own standpoint, but also from that of the antagonists: the synoptic views regarding the messiasship and divinity of Jesus.

At the time when the synoptics wrote their gospels the belief in the messiasship and divinity of Jesus was the unquestioned common property of all true Christians, as it had been ever since the resurrection. This fact cannot be denied and will be demonstrated later in detail (Chapters 16 and 17). It could therefore be expected that the evangelists would have selected this final belief as their starting point. They could have been tempted, and quite easily, to build up their narrative in such a way as to depict the apostles and disciples believing in the messiasship and divinity of Jesus in the very beginning of their calling and of their acquaintance with him. Or they could, since this would have been equivalent to patent deception or dishonesty, have intimated that the Saviour, from the beginning to the end of his life, had declared his Messianic mission and his divine-human essence with positive emphasis. Or, because this portrait of Jesus was likewise far removed from historical truth and actual reality, they could and might have followed the tendency of emphasizing or giving preference to and elaborating the instances whenever the messiasship and divinity of the Master manifested itself in the course of his life. If the synoptic portrait of Jesus, as liberal research so definitely asserts, were but a devout touching-up of the historical figure of the Saviour, then all three mentioned possibilities would have to be possible of proof as actually present in the synoptic gospels.

The opposite is true. Instead of seeing the subsequent belief of the apostles and disciples presented as previously or even originally present, we witness the totally indocile apprenticeship of the first companions, until they finally wrest themselves free from the Jewish-Rabbinical spell and arrive at the recognition and confession of the messiasship and divinity of Christ after

a long, arduous ascent and after many relapses. Instead of forc-
ing the ways of Providence and thereby falling into the error of
having the great secret of the person of Christ bursting suddenly
upon mankind, which was still unprepared for it, and blinding
it with its splendor, there is, according to the synoptics, first
the dawn of it on the morning of Good Friday, then chastely
and wisely one ray of the eternal light after the other breaks
through, until on Easter Day the bright sun of God beams upon
the world, and on the day of Ascension it stands high in the
heavens. And instead of giving particular emphasis to the actual
revelation of Jesus regarding his messiasship and divinity, the
synoptics weave them so naturally, so harmoniously, and with
such artless simplicity into the natural course of the life of
Jesus that one is almost equally amazed at the human fidelity
and unaffected veracity of the presentation as at the divine
happenings themselves. This sincere character of the synoptic
writings alone affords the strongest possible refutation of skeptical
criticism, as well as the most objective and unassailable defense
of the synoptic portrait of Jesus.

To these general remarks we must add, however, several
observations which have reference partly to the messiasship
and partly to the divinity of Jesus.

In the synoptic gospels we encounter the Messianic conceptions which the disciples harbored solely before the resurrection of the Saviour. They expected, just as the popular opinion
of the Jews conceived him, the son of David to be a worldly
potentate and conqueror of the Romans; they reveled in the
expectation of his royal splendor and eagerly endeavored to
secure for themselves the best places and positions of honor in
his realm. All this not without petty jealousy, despite the
constant instructions on the part of the Master.

The death of Jesus, the resurrection, the sending of the
Holy Ghost, and all the things that followed until the time
when the synoptics wrote, had drastically run counter to this
conception of the messiasship; everything had happened differently, everything had been contrary to what they had hoped,

expected, and enjoyed with such avid anticipation. Instead of the flesh, there was spirit; instead of the earth, a heavenly kingdom; instead of a national hero, a world-redeeming Saviour of sinners. If the evangelists had wanted to accommodate themselves to the belief of those days in which they wrote, the former Messianic portrait, which they now decisively rejected by force of actual facts, would never have appeared again. If regarding any point, then certainly in this, the previous history would of necessity have to have been glossed over with the common theology of that later date. How easy it would have been to surrender the old Messianic dreams to oblivion, not only for practical pastoral reasons, but also out of indulgent consideration for the apostles! But no, black on white, just as it corresponded with historical facts, the Messianic expectations of those first days are strongly marked. And then the synoptic gospels are supposed to be the portrait of a legendary Christ from the sixties and seventies!

The absurdity of such an assumption is all the more obvious if the teaching of the synoptics regarding the divinity of Christ is placed beside that of his messiasship. The former recedes so far into the background in the first gospels that until recently the antagonists asserted that it is not found in them at all. In contrast to this the leaders of liberal research, such as W. Wrede, J. Weiss, W. Bousset, W. von Schnehen, and others, today admit that even in the eyes of Mark, whose gospel is regarded as the oldest, Jesus is not only the Messias, but the eternal Son of God. It is true, however, that the synoptics allow us to recognize the splendor and divinity of Christ only in a dusky light and as if through a veil. His human nature, on the other hand, comes out in strong relief on every page.

The synoptic Christ is a being of flesh and bone, who associates with men as one of them, in spite of, or rather as a result of, the consciousness of his exalted mission; he speaks and acts as man; he sits at table with the Pharisees and publicans; he allows himself to be touched by the sinful woman; he converses as a friend with his disciples; he is tempted by the demon; he is sorrowful in the garden of Gethsemani; he works miracles out of compassion, and conceals them rather than uses them as proofs of his mission; he is calm and dignified in the presence of his judges and allows himself to be smitten and insulted; the cry which he utters before his death is one of anguish of heart and of agony; even if we discover everywhere, in his discourses, in his actions, his sufferings, the breath of the divine which raises him above common humanity — even at its best — yet it remains nonetheless true that everything which he does and everything which he says is profoundly human, deeply impenetrated with human reality, if we may so express ourselves.[1]

Now it is precisely our adversaries who declare that at the time when the synoptic gospels came into existence theological speculation had already forced the *man* Jesus almost entirely into the background and had stressed solely his divinity, and that formerly, especially at the beginning, it had been entirely different. If that be the case, then the synoptic gospels cannot be a mere reproduction of the later belief of the Church in contrast to actual history, since their portrait of the Saviour exhibits throughout those characteristics which are pointed out by liberal critics as perfectly genuine, in contrast to the portrait of Christ of later decades.

Just as the synoptic gospels are alleged to reflect the belief of their time in a legendary Christ, so also the gospel of John is said to represent in an even higher degree the Christological ideas of the end of the first century, in contradiction, however, to historical fact. As proof of this we are reminded that the gospel of John does not agree with the synoptics as to content, and that in particular the figure of Christ is radically different in the one and in the others. As to substance, according to the synoptics, it is a genuinely human person; according to John, a positively divine person. Also as to the external plan, according to the synoptics Jesus labored principally in Galilee and for the Jews, while according to John the theater of his labors was mostly Judea and Jerusalem, although at the same time Jesus

---

[1] Alfred Loisy, Le quatrième Évangile, Paris, 1903, 72.

offered salvation also to the Gentiles. These are the differences to which the liberal critics point.

However, far from justifying the cry: "Here synoptics, here John!" — all four gospels become peacefully harmonious when studied calmly. The mere reference to the aim and purpose of the gospel of John will, after all, clarify everything.

In the first place, the last evangelist wishes to supply what the first three had omitted or merely touched on. This explains his silence about the synoptic parables, about some of the miracles, and about the institution of the Eucharist; this accounts, too, for the recording of the words and deeds of Jesus omitted by the synoptics, in particular of the eucharistic and high-priestly discourses, and of the washing of the disciples' feet, as supplementary to the description of the Last Supper as given by the synoptics. The detailed account also of the activity of Jesus in Judea and Jerusalem, which is given in abbreviated form by the synoptics, as well as the concise summary of his Galilean activity, which had been already recounted in detail in the first gospels, are all comprehensible from this point of view.

A further aim is to be considered in the gospel of John. The synoptics wrote before the downfall of the Jewish nation; they still hoped to win over the chosen people to the kingdom of God. They therefore stressed as much as possible the lines of transition from the Old to the New Testament, the genuine humanity in Christ, things which united Jew and Christian. John takes up his pen after God's judgment had fallen upon Jerusalem, and after the Church had fortunately wrested herself from the arms of the synagogue. Accordingly, he accentuates the points of separation between them, the thoroughly non-Jewish element in Christianity, the very thing whereby the Church stood out in the splendor of its spiritual independence and thus became attractive to the pagans. Even in the wording and the presentation of Christian doctrine, John, writing in Asia Minor, makes the greatest possible concessions to Hellenic ways of thinking, feeling, and speaking. He even adopts the

Hellenic idea and terminology regarding the Logos, because both seemed to him admirably suited to serve as a vessel for the doctrine of the incarnate Son of God.

The incarnate Son of God — that was the great thesis of this prophet among the evangelists. While the synoptics, out of consideration for the Jews, had to stress the human side and the Messianic conception of the Saviour as presented in the Old Testament, John, in opposition to the Jewish-Christian heresy which declared Christ to be a mere man, had to emphasize the supernatural grandeur and the essential divinity of the Lord.

This was surely one more reason why John prefers the later period of Judea and Jerusalem, during which the divine-human manifestations had made further progress than in the Galilean period, when the Lord made known to his disciples only the basic ideas regarding the plan of salvation. The beloved disciple, furthermore, fully conscious of his purpose, selects those episodes which furnish the most striking proofs for his thesis. Even the miracles are chosen from the "point of view of the self-revelation and manifestation of the glory of the Son of God."[2]

The Christ of John is the true Son of God, who out of love for men has come down to this earth from the glory of the Father, and has become flesh in order to live with men and for men, as man himself; the Christ of the synoptics is the true Son of man, flesh of our flesh and blood of our blood, but elevated by his Messianic dignity and thoroughly imbued with divine power and essence, in order to lift us up to God.

Thus the alleged contradictions between John and the synoptics are solved by the higher unity of the gospel.[3] It is therefore out of the question that the Christ and the Christology of John differs essentially in character from that of the synoptic gospels. Harnack admits this expressly:

---

[2] Julius Grill, *Die Entstehung des vierten Evangeliums*, I, Tübingen, 45.
[3] Cf. Worsley, *The Fourth Gospel and the Synoptics*, Edinburgh, 1909.

If we have called St. John a glorified Matthew, because his aim also is didactic and apologetic, we may with equal justice call him a glorified St. Mark and St. Luke, for he shares in the aims which dominate both these evangelists. By means of the historic narrative he strives, like St. Mark, to show that Jesus is the Son of God, and, like St. Luke, to prove that he is the Saviour of the world, in opposition to the unbelieving Jews and the disciples of St. John the Baptist.[4]

Still more emphatically does Harnack's colleague express himself: "It must be acknowledged that *all* our gospels occupy in principle the same standpoint and that the difference between Mark and the other two synoptics on the one hand and John on the other, is only a relative difference of degree."[5]

The gospel of John, therefore, does not present a later Christ-legend any more than the synoptics; all four stand on the historical ground of the genuine and unfalsified life of Jesus.

3. The primitive disciples confirm the conclusions hitherto obtained. It will not be out of place to mention again that the gospel accounts are based throughout on the testimony of the companions of Jesus. St. Luke says briefly and clearly: "They have delivered them unto us, who from the beginning were eyewitnesses and ministers of the word" (1:2). The groundwork of the gospels was furnished by the catecheses of Matthew, Peter, Paul, and John. The individual evangelists, furthermore, according to the remark of Luke, "diligently attained to all things from the beginning," in order to supplement all pertinent material by means of the depositions of other disciples of the Lord. But no matter how numerous the individual testimonies which were at the disposal of the evangelists for the gospels as such, the unanimous tradition of the apostolic college and of the apostolic Church was decisive. With it was bound up the entire "paleontologic" period of Christianity. Even the individual testimony of the primitive disciples, even that of

[4] Harnack-Wilkinson, *Luke the Physician*, 168 *n.*

[5] Otto Pfleiderer, *Das Urchristentum, seine Schriften und Lehren*, 2 ed., Berlin, 1902, I, 666.

John, is of no moment as independent, purely personal testimony, but only as the expression of the faith of the entire primitive Church.

On this point all are in agreement, those who plead the cause of positive Christian, as well as those who represent rationalistic research. The conclusions, however, which are drawn from this fact by the different advocates differ basically. We behold in the harmony of the gospels with the belief of the primitive Church *the strongest proof* for the dependability of the gospel portrait of Jesus; our adversaries, however, base their legend-hypothesis on this harmony between the gospel and the primitive Church. The latter is alleged to have passed through a constant evolution, and with it the belief regarding Jesus is said to have changed also, up to the moment when it was fixed in writing, first by Paul, shortly after by the synoptics, and lastly by John.

But how is it possible that the "young artisan and peasant of Nazareth," as the liberal scholars describe Jesus, could be transformed by the disciples shortly after his death into that supernatural Christ? How can it be explained that the same men who shortly before had eaten and drunk with him, and had convinced themselves of his being a mere man, having associated with him for years, should now regard him as a superman, as the pre-existent Saviour of the world and consubstantial Son of God? How is it conceivable that the law-observant Jews, to whom the idolization of a creature was an abomination, should fold their hands to that Jesus whom they had heard pray always and solely to the Father, and should adore the one whom they had seen live and die as a man? How could it happen that all the Christians of the primitive era, the first disciples as well as Paul, the synoptics as well as John, approved this blasphemous deification of a human being and took part in it, and that not one sound of protest and censure was raised against it in the entire Christian Church? How can it be explained that everyone fashioned his portrait of Jesus on his own responsibility, and that all these so diverse and alien elements nevertheless blend together into *one* definite and harmonious portrait, which was approved by the entire body of the apostles and disciples, and fixed in writing by the evangelists? How is it psychologically imaginable, to use the words of Kalthoff, that a "liberal-Protestant" Jesus was laid in the grave and a "Catholic" Jesus arose from it? How can the legend-theorists even think of cutting so deeply into their own flesh by assuming such an unpsychological hypothesis?

Liberal critics who champion the evolution theory can give at best the one answer which is intelligible: this extremely rapid transformation of the Man Jesus into the God-Man Jesus Christ was brought about by the tremendous impression which Jesus made on his disciples during his lifetime, and which was recalled by them after his death. This explanation does not solve the puzzle, but renders it completely unsolvable. They raise the exact point in question: how could the disciples have borne witness to their Master and adored him after his death as the risen Messias and God, if he had not previously impressed them as being the God-Messias while he lived among them? The mere attempt of wishing to explain the origin of the faith of the disciples in the God-Messias by means of this psychological monstrosity is a clear-cut confession that skeptical historical research and psychology of religion have reached their limits in this matter.

The alleged building up of legends was impossible for this reason also: *the Christology of the primitive Church was controlled by contemporaries.* Liberal critics overlook this circumstance completely. They assume that the wild growth of legends could overrun the field of the primitive Christian world unnoticed and unchecked up to the time when historical and legendary elements were forged together into the gospel. That could have happened only if the entire generation of contemporaries had died out with Christ and had made room for another generation which knew hardly anything certain about him. But this is not the case. A large number of those who knew the Saviour from daily contact lived through the subsequent period down to the writing and publication of the gospels.

Hegesippus, in his *Memorabilia* (written about A.D. 180), relates that "Simeon, the son of Cleophas, who was of the tribe of David," suffered martyrdom at the age of 120 years in the beginning of the second century. Up to this time, Hegesippus adds, the Church of Jerusalem had been guided by men "who had been privileged to hear with their own ears the divine truth."[6] The apologist Quadratus[7] and Papias of Hierapolis[8] relate that some of those who were healed by Christ and raised by him from the dead lived until the time of Adrian (117–138). When, therefore, the gospel of John appeared, the generation of contemporaries of Jesus had not yet died out. When the synoptics wrote, some decades before, the survivors who were of the same age as Jesus were in their sixties. The somewhat younger contemporaries and hearers of the Saviour had not yet outgrown manhood; considering the vitality of the Jewish race, one can reasonably estimate that about half of them were still living when the gospels appeared.

How could the real portrait of Jesus have been disfigured by such grotesque legends in the presence of these witnesses? How could the mere Man Jesus, before the very eyes of his contemporaries, spring at a bound into the position of a wonder-worker, of the Lord of life and death, of a supernatural being and true Son of God? And how could this legendary mummery have been believed by his contemporaries as sacred truth and accepted as the actual history of Jesus?

If it had been merely the case of pure introspection, of some phantastic transformation and deification of the portrait of Jesus on the ground of inward sentiments, impressions, feelings, and soul-experiences, then all would be more comprehensible. But, as has been already remarked, the evolution of interior belief

---

[6] Eusebius, *Hist. Eccl.*, III, 32.

[7] *Ibid.*, IV, 3.

[8] *Neue Fragmente des Papias*, Hegesippus and Pierius, published by C. de Boor, in *Texte und Untersuchungen*, published by Gebhardt and Harnack, V, 2, Leipzig, 1889, 170. Cf. Giuseppe Ricciotti, *The Life of Christ* (Milwaukee: The Bruce Publishing Co., 1947), §§ 138–139; F. Prat, *Jesus Christ* (Milwaukee: The Bruce Publishing Co., 1950), 14, 17 ff.

would have to have been effected by reason of, and in company with, external facts, with tangible, manifold, and well-known historical reality. The time, the scene, the circumstances of the superhuman life and activity of Jesus are minutely characterized in the gospel. It was, for instance, in Corozain, in Bethsaida, and Capharnaum that his divine power of working miracles was proved in broad daylight and before all the people. In the synagogue at Capharnaum, still used by the Jews, he drove out devils; in the house of Simon, whose inmates were still there, he cured the mother-in-law of Peter of her fever; to this house, on the sabbath day, the people brought their sick and he healed them; under minutely described circumstances he also healed the man sick of the palsy and the servant of the centurion, and raised from the dead the daughter of Jairus, the ruler of the synagogue.[9]

Would it have occurred to the community of the Christians to invent these and similar details, and would the evangelists have been bold enough to record them, if they had been invented? Would not the persons called upon as witnesses have unmasked these legends? There were among them not only believers in Christ, but also enemies of Jesus — individuals, groups, and entire villages. Capharnaum and its neighboring towns are reminded of the miracles wrought in them and the severest accusations, reproaches, and condemnations are based thereon.[10] The country towns and country people in Galilee no less than the leaders of the nation in Jerusalem, the scribes and Pharisees, are upbraided by the gospels for their unbelief and for the judicial murder committed against Jesus, although he had proved himself to be the Messias by his miracles. That, however, would have been madness, if these reports of miracles and other accounts had been based on nothing but mystification. The accused party leaders, who were well acquainted with the life and the deeds of the hated Nazarene, and who scru-

---

9 Cf. Mt. 8:5-17; 9:1-8, 18-26; Mk. 1:21-34; 2:1-12; 5:21-43; Lk. 4:31-41; 5:17-26; 7:1-10; 8:40-56.
10 Cf. Mt. 11:20-24; Lk. 10:12-16.

tinized every account about him with argus-eyed vigilance, would have needed but to point out this deception to be able to strike down these annoying accusers and their followers with one blow. Instead, they were forced to hear this gospel preached day after day, before and after its commitment to writing, in the streets and squares, and daily listen to the accusation of the judicial murder of the Messias and Son of God.[11] Not one of the leaders of the Pharisees dared to give the lie to these preachers and thus save his own honor and that of his party and nation. The apostles were indeed summoned from time to time before the tribunal and commanded to be silent regarding Jesus,[12] but never was the charge brought against them that their preaching and their gospel did not agree with the actual history of Jesus. This silence on the part of the contemporaneous adversaries is the most eloquent condemnation of the legend theory.

The absurdity of the latter is made manifest by the inexorable steadfastness of the primitive disciples and of the primitive Church in clinging to the portrait of Jesus as handed down by tradition. It is a wanton offense against ancient Christianity to speak of a "creative Church-dogmatism" (Harnack) and to assume that the faithful of the first decades had quietly looked on while certain legendary exaggerations and disfigurements were added to the true portrait of Jesus or that they had promoted them. The very opposite is true. Whoever has studied the New Testament knows that the Christian message was intent from the very beginning on nothing more than the most faithful conservation of the deposit of faith, which had come down from Christ through the primitive disciples, and on the determined repudiation of every innovation. "Remember the word of the Lord Jesus" (Acts 20:35); "Let that which you have heard from the beginning, abide in you" (1 Jn. 2:24); "The holy commandment which was delivered to them. . . . Be mindful of those words which I told you before from the holy

---

[11] Cf. Acts 2:22–24; 3:14–16.
[12] Cf. Acts 4; 5:27; 24:5; 2 Tim. 4:9.

prophets, and of your apostles, of the precepts of the Lord and Saviour" (2 Pet. 2:21; 3:2). "If any man teach otherwise, and consent not to the sound words of our Lord Jesus Christ, and to that doctrine which is according to godliness, he is proud, knowing nothing" (1 Tim. 6:3). In this and similar vein runs the constant admonition of the apostolic era.[13] The entire Christian profession of faith for this reason is called simply *paradosis,* tradition, and the entire ministry of the faith is condensed in one word: "Stand fast, and hold the traditions" (2 Thess. 2:14) of the primitive Christian era and of the primitive apostolic witnesses.

Thus the ancient faith remained unshaken on the firm ground of the actual history of Jesus. Both faith and history are one in the gospels, just as and because they were one in the preliterary period and on the day when our Lord and Saviour passed from this earth. The protestation of Luke is true of every evangelist: "The former treatise I made . . . of all things which Jesus began to do and to teach, until the day on which, giving commandments by the Holy Ghost to the apostles whom he had chosen, he was taken up" (Acts 1:1–2).

It is with deep emotion that we recall the message and the words of farewell which Jesus addressed to his own immediately before his ascension into heaven: "All power is given to me in heaven and in earth. Going therefore, teach ye all nations; baptizing them in the name of the Father, and of the Son, and of the Holy Ghost. Teaching them to observe all things whatsoever I have commanded you: and behold I am with you all days even to the consummation of the world" (Mt. 28:18–20).

That is what comforts and sustains the disciples of all times and all nations, even though Jesus passed to heaven: "Behold I am with you all days even to the consummation of the world." All the days unto the consummation of the world Jesus remains with us in a mystical, eucharistic, and historical manner. Mystically he is ever with us as the head of the Church, which is his

---

13 Cf. Th. Zahn, *Einleitung in das N. Test.,* II, 158–172.

body and whose members we are: "He hath subjected all things under his feet, and hath made him head over all the Church, which is his body. . . . Christ is the head of the Church. . . . We are members of his body" (Eph. 1:22; 5:23, 30). Eucharistically he abides with us in his sacrifice and his sacrament: "This is my body, this is my blood" (Mt. 26:26–28; Mk. 14: 22–24; Lk. 22:19 f.; 1 Cor. 11:23–25). "He that eateth my flesh and drinketh my blood, abideth in me, and I in him" (Jn. 6:57). Historically he remains ever with us in the holy gospels. In these is revealed his spirit, in these his heart beats, his word resounds, his truth shines forth, his power operates, his sanctity edifies and attracts. Whosoever reads the gospels with an unbiased mind and an upright heart will experience that the Lord lives for us in them, speaks to us and abides with us "all days to the consummation of the world" (Mt. 28:20).[14]

---

[14] Cf. Ricciotti, *op. cit.*, §§ 129–216; P. J. Arendzen, *The Gospels — Fact, Myth, or Legend* (London, 1923); C. J. Callan, *The Four Gospels and the Acts of the Apostles* (New York, 1942); P. Batiffol, *The Credibility of the Gospel*, trans. G. C. Pollen (New York: Longmans, Green and Co., 1912). French Title: *Orpheus et L'Evangile.*

Chapter 3. The Collapse of Rationalistic Criticism

WE ARE firmly convinced, then, after studying the previous chapter, that even the most severe criticism, presupposing that its researches are unbiased, must acknowledge the reliability of the gospel portrait of Jesus. We say advisedly, "presuming that its researches are *unbiased,*" not, "presuming that they are *honest.*" It would be an offense against truth, justice, and charity if we were to affirm offhand that our adversaries lack the intention of being honest in their research, or if we were to impugn in any way the sincerity of their scientific endeavors or of their world philosophy. It is, however, often a difficult matter not to question it. Albert Schweitzer, the outspoken partisan as well as the brilliant historian of liberal research, remarks: "Modern theology will some day become completely honest. However," he adds cautiously, "this prophecy concerns the future."[1] Arthur Drews, a lay theologian who upholds the extreme left, comments sardonically: "Quousque tandem, Catilina!"[2]

But as determined as we may be in our endeavor to avoid the accusation of dishonesty regarding our adversaries, just as strongly must we accuse them of prejudice. The rationalistic mind proceeds not only actually, but on principle, from the prejudicial, unproved, and undemonstrable assertion that every religious happening and every religious belief must be confined

---

[1] Von Reimarus zu Wrede, *Geschichte der Leben-Jesu-Forschung,* Tübingen, 1906, 249.
[2] "How much longer, O Catiline!" *Die Christusmythe,* Jena, 1909, ix.

within the limits of pure reason, and that consequently super-natural revelation must be negated as a matter of course, that miracles and inspiration must be critically destroyed, that the person of Jesus must be divested of its character as the Messianic Saviour and a divine-human Being, and that the gospels be so trimmed and shorn that a mere extract of modern *Kultur* remains.

Against this rationalistic, biased position even the strongest proofs for the credibility of the gospel portrait of Jesus and of positive Christianity recoil. The nemesis of this prejudiced stand is the collapse of rationalistic criticism of the gospels and of their portrait of Jesus. All its phases and all its theories have ended in a complete fiasco.

I. THE THEORY OF DECEPTION. The first to apply the incendiary torch of rationalism to the gospels was the Hamburg professor, Herman Samuel Reimarus (1694–1768). Besides other works, he wrote a volume of 4000 pages entitled, *A Vindication of the Rational Worshippers of God* (*Schutzschrift für die vernünftigen Verehrer Gottes*). He died, however, before he could publish it. Soon thereafter Lessing obtained the manuscript and published the most important parts under the title of *Wolfenbütteler Fragmente*.[3] As the *Wandsbecker Bote* wittily remarks, Lessing did "place muzzles on them, but the dogs have frightened many people with their barking and their viciousness." The most incisive of these Fragments is the third, in which the impossibility of any revelation is asserted, and the seventh, in which the entire gospel is roundly stigmatized as a fraud. Christ is alleged to have had merely the intention of liberating his country from a foreign power by plotting a popular insurrection. When this "systema" of his had been frustrated, and the disciples had seen themselves betrayed, they tried to extricate themselves from their dilemma by attributing to their Master another purpose, a second "systema," and alleging that in reality he had not wanted to be a political liberator,

---

[3] Braunschweig, 1774–1778.

but a spiritual Redeemer. In accordance with this new "systema," they changed the entire history of Jesus and finally made of him the Son of God. They then propagated the swindle thus perpetrated in the four gospels. The Christians were "mere parrots, who did not fail to repeat what had been said to them." Thus the fraud theory of Reimarus-Lessing.

This was, however, too much of an absurdity. Even Semler, a contemporary of Reimarus and Lessing, himself a rationalist and the father of "critical-historical research," refuted the Fragmentist sentence for sentence.[4] David Frederick Strauss, the biographer of Reimarus, found it disgusting that the writer of the Fragments "at times pronounced the [gospel] facts, at times the narratives themselves, to be impostures and clumsy fabrications of swindlers."[5] Albert Schweitzer, who otherwise wields a mighty cudgel for Reimarus, calls the latter's Fragments "a polemical piece of writing, not an objective, historical study. . . . It was merely a hypothesis on his part, born of desperation, when he attributed the origin of primitive Christianity to a fraud."[6] According to Pfleiderer, this example is "significant of that lack of a true historical sense and psychological understanding in religious matters which is generally characteristic of that sort of rationalism."[7] All attempts, often repeated since Reimarus, to stamp Jesus as the standard-bearer of a political messiasship, respectively as a nationalistic revolutionary against Roman domination, have miscarried completely. Robert Eisler rehashed this wholly impossible theory in a two-volume work.[8] At first the critics were struck by the display of great erudition and by the blatant ostentation which characterized the book. Soon, however, even extremely liberal critics recognized it to be merely a piece of romantic fiction, born of an uncontrolled

---

[4] Johann Salomo Semler, *Beantwortung der Fragmente eines Unbekannten, insbesondere vom Zweck Jesu und seiner Jünger*, Halle, 1779.

[5] *Ulrich von Hutten* III, Leipzig, 1860, Preface.

[6] Von Reimarus zu Wrede, Tübingen, 1906, 22 f.

[7] *Die Entstehung des Christentums*, Munich, 1905, 4.

[8] It appeared in an English translation under the title, *The Messiah. Jesus and John the Baptist*, trans. by Alexander Krappe, London, 1930.

fancy, and played up with unpardonable levity. The motto of the work, coined by the author himself, is to the point: "From Reimarus to Reimarus." This *Reimarus redivivus* sank into oblivion just as rapidly as his predecessor and father of the eighteenth century.

2. THE "NATURAL" EXPLANATION OF THE GOSPELS. The problem before which rationalism saw itself placed, meanwhile demanded, always more loudly, a satisfactory solution. The Heidelberg professor Gottlob Paulus attempted it.[9] Mindful of the pitiable fiasco of the *Wolfenbütteler Fragmente* and yet true to his own rationalistic position of the denial of revelation, Paulus apparently allowed the gospel to pass as history, but interpreted it "naturally," "rationally." All miraculous events and all supernatural truths in general, whether feasible or not, were reduced to the level of purely natural occurrences, and the gospel text was so strained, shortened and enlarged, interpreted and misinterpreted, until not a trace of the supernatural was left in it.

This "natural" explanation of the gospels, however, turned out to be so unnatural, so inane, and so forced that it was an easy matter for the equally rationalistic Strauss to give it the deathblow shortly after, as far as science was concerned.

Later on, however, this "natural" explanation became the pet theory of the romanticized biographies of Christ. It was this hypothesis, for instance, which alone made possible the *Life of Jesus* by Ernest Renan. This romance lacks not only all scientific value but all "moral consciousness" as well, as Luthardt remarks.[10] It is a book in which the description of the topography of Palestine, which the author had toured, is exact and the language beautiful, but all the rest offends the expert as well as the Christian by its superficiality and impiety. The book owes its unheard-of success, aside from its fascinating form and manner of presentation, above all to the sentimental, frivolous,

---

[9] *Kommentar über das N. Test.*, Lübeck, 1800–1804.

[10] *Die modernen Darstellungen des Lebens Jesu. Eine Besprechung der Schriften von Strauss, Renan, usw.*, Leipzig, 1864.

and lascivious style of the French society novel. Renan, under the mask of assumed piety, has become a modern Judas, with the sole difference that he did a correspondingly better piece of business. While Judas had to content himself with thirty pieces of silver, Renan, as Dumas the younger informs us, received a million francs for his work from the Jew Rothschild.

Renan had passed into oblivion long before his death (1892), and today nobody would have the courage to declare himself an adherent of the "natural" explanation devised by Paulus. In fact, however, it is precisely the so-called critical "Lives of Jesus" of modern times which have retained much of Renan's romanticism, and if necessary they do not hesitate to explain everything "naturally," just as Gottlob Paulus did, in order to eliminate miracles and revelation from the gospels and from the life of Jesus.[11]

3. THE MYTHICAL HYPOTHESIS. The irony of fate decreed that Strauss (1808–1874), who condemned Paulus, the father of "naturalism," later on greeted the son, Renan, as a kindred spirit and stretched out to him "his hand across the Rhine."[12] In fact, he practically returned to the views of Reimarus, but with this difference, that in his theory of mythical evolution Strauss replaced intentional fraud by the delusive "unintentionally poetizing legend." According to Strauss, the Christian legend simply developed the equally legendary Messianic expectations of the Old Testament still further, and wove out of the Old and New Testament legends or myths a motley cloak which it threw about the Jesus of history, in order to make of him the Jesus of the gospels.

We need not expatiate here on the falsity of the assumptions and the extreme shoddiness of the structure of Strauss's myth theory; it is sufficient to note its complete bankruptcy. The myth theory is in fact repudiated not only by positive, but also

---

[11] Cf. Ricciotti, The Life of Christ (Milwaukee: The Bruce Publishing Co., 1947), §§ 193–196.
[12] Leben Jesu für das deutsche Volk, Leipzig, 1864, Preface, trans. M. Evans (New York: Blanchard, 1860).

by rationalistic critics. Harnack dismisses it with the words: "Strauss' contention that the gospels contain a very great deal that is mythical has not been borne out, even if the indefinite, defective conception of what 'mythical' means in Strauss' application of the word, be allowed to pass."[13] Chamberlain, however, remarks:

> At the beginning of the nineteenth century . . . it had become fashionable to explain everything "mythically." In the year 1835 David Strauss, following the example proffered on all sides, presented as a key to the gospels "the idea of the myth"! Every one now recognizes that this so-called key was nothing more than a new, mistily vague paraphrase of a still-unsolved problem, and that not an "idea," but only actually lived existence, only the unique impression of a personality, whose like the world had never before known, supplies the "key" to the origin of Christianity. . . . Strauss never had the least notion what a myth is, what mythology means, how it is produced by the confusion and mingling of popular myths, poetry, and legends. That, however, is another story. Posterity will really not be able to understand the reception given to such dreary productions as those of Strauss: they are learned, but destitute of all deeper insight and of any trace of genius. . . . The progress of historico-critical research . . . causes one to look upon the mythological standpoint of Strauss as so unintelligent that one cannot turn over the leaves of this honest man's writings without yawning.[14]

The contemporaries and colleagues of Strauss, especially his teacher Baur, already saw that no undesigned, poetical legend could create Christianity, and that there was no other escape than to return either to the historical credibility of the gospels, or to intentional fraud on the part of the evangelists.

4. THE TENDENCY HYPOTHESIS. Ferdinand Christian Baur[15] dug up once more the rusty battle-ax of Reimarus. He thought that he could grind down its ragged edges by imput-

---

[13] Harnack-Saunders, *What Is Christianity?*, 26.

[14] *Die Grundlagen des 19. Jahrhunderts*, München, 1907, 227 f.; trans. John Lees, *The Foundations of the Nineteenth Century* (London: John Lane Co., 1911), I, 181 *n.* Cf. Ricciotti, *op. cit.*, § 185 ff.

[15] *Kritische Untersuchungen über die kanonischen Evangelien, ihr Verhältnis zueinander, ihren Charakter und Ursprung*, Tübingen, 1847.

ing the intention of fraud to the evangelists of the second century instead of to those of the first, and by declaring that the gospels were produced in the post-apostolic period as intentional deceptions.

Appealing to "higher criticism," he asserted that primitive Christianity had passed through a period of constant conflict between the so-called pagan-Christian tendency of Paul, on the one hand, and the party of Peter and of the other apostles, which was more friendly to the Jews, on the other. The factious brethren finally became reconciled and, in order to patch up the previous breach and to allow Catholic dogmatism to emerge victorious, the four gospels were then fabricated as a compromise. According to Baur's computation, the gospel of Matthew appeared as the first one about 130; then, about 150, the gospel of the heretic Marcion was enriched by parts from Matthew and the writing thus produced was christened the gospel of Luke; out of Matthew and Luke the gospel of Mark was soon after hammered together; finally, about 170, John's gospel was ushered into the world. All New Testament writings were accordingly nothing but a single, extremely shameless piece of deceit, a fabrication of history and falsification of facts on a grand scale, all of which, however, was swallowed without hesitation by the blindly credulous Christians. By his discovery of the "tendency theory," Baur became the founder of the "younger Tübingen school," and Köstlich, Zeller, Schwegler, and Holsten swung over completely into his camp, while Keim, Hilgenfeld, Volmar, and others joined him only to a degree.

Soon, however, the proponents returned to their senses and the collapse followed. All those arguments which had already crushed Reimarus arose against the *tendency theory* of Baur. Whether it was a fraud perpetrated in the first or in the second century, Christianity and the gospels cannot be the result of a fraud. Baur is indicted by serious scientists much more severely than Reimarus, because he was unjust both to the first century by flatly denying that it possessed the gospels, and to the second, by branding it as a tangle of quarrelsomeness and tendentious lying. "The whole critical apparatus with which Baur has impugned the old tradition today rightly passes as worthless."[16] The collapse of the historical structure of Baur is complete, and what he loved to call "higher criticism" is regarded without any restrictions as higher nonsense.

5. THE SKEPTICAL CRITICISM OF THE GOSPELS. Christian Baur was followed by Bruno Bauer (1809–1882), the *enfant terrible* of rationalistic bible criticism. This criticism had, little by little, blasted away at the entire gospel history, with the exception of the actual existence of Christ, in order to get rid of revelation and miracles. But it did not succeed, and all attempts in this direction failed miserably. In a veritable rage Bruno Bauer therefore decided to go to the extreme limit, that is, complete skepticism regarding the gospel, radical denial of all which negative research had up to that time allowed to stand.

Not only the miracles, discourses, and events, but also the very personality of Jesus was declared by Bauer to be a piece of religious fiction. Jesus was an idea, not a historical figure. Greco-Roman and oriental ideas of virtue had blended with the Jewish ideal of the Messias at the beginning of the Christian era. A crafty poet, the "original Matthew," personified this ideal and created the figure of Jesus, just as a novelist would create the characters in his story. From among the readers of this oldest gospel there subsequently arose primitive Christianity, and by means of later poetic ingenuity the four gospels were evolved. Finally, what was religious poesy and pure art was exhibited by faith and theology as history.

Goaded on by a truly pathological hatred against everything Christian, blinded by his own megalomania, furious on account of his failure, Bauer labored for forty years at his skeptical criticism of the gospels, of the Acts, and of the Pauline epistles.

---

[16] Harnack, *Chronologie der altchristl. Literatur*, I, Leipzig, 1897, 244 *n.* Concerning Baur, see Ricciotti, *loc. cit.*, § 187 f.

But when his final work appeared,[17] his lifework had already been long condemned and forgotten.

Since the beginning of the present century desperate efforts have been made to resuscitate his work. An entire page could be filled with the names of those who felt themselves called on to contribute their mite to the system of denying the existence of Jesus. Best known are the writings of the German lay theologian, Arthur Drews,[18] and of the French physician, P.-L. Couchoud,[19] which at the same time are contradictory. Serious critics, both of the positive Christian as well as of the liberal schools, are unanimous in rejecting these fantastic fabrications. These deserve, moreover, the honor of a refutation just as little as the skeptical theory of Bauer, or, more correctly, they bear the most decisive refutation within themselves, just as all the doubts cast on the existence of Jesus since the days of Bauer. Whoever must first of all deny the gospels, which were written by eye- and earwitnesses, and then is forced to patch together an artificial "pre-Christian" Christ with the help of all sorts of Greek and ancient oriental fables, so as to be able to doubt the real historical Christ, has lost every claim to be taken seriously. And even if he were able to tear the gospel into shreds and to transform his mythological patches into a dead phantom of Christ, the living, historical person of Christ would even then, in spite of all, shine forth undisputed and undisputable from the unwritten gospel of the primitive Church and from the non-Christian records of Jesus. Every attempt to undermine the complete historical reality of our Lord and to render the origin of Christianity intelligible without a personal founder, must be shattered to pieces on the wall of facts and come to ruin by its own intrinsic falsity.[20]

6. THE EVOLUTION OR LEGEND THEORY.   This

---

[17] *Christus und die Cäsaren, der Ursprung des Christentums aus dem römischen Griechentum*, Berlin, 1877.

[18] *Die Christusmythe*, Jena, 1924.

[19] *Le mystère de Jésus*, Paris, 1924.

[20] Concerning this theory, see Ricciotti, *op. cit.*, § 188 ff.

theory is the only one hostile to positive belief in the gospels and in Jesus which is to be taken seriously. This theory was put forth by A. Ritschl, found its most outstanding protagonist in A. Harnack, and its following in the entire school of liberal research, until recently it reached its culmination in the formation of the "form-critical" school (K. L. Schmidt, M. Albertz, G. Bertram, O. Cullmann, Dibelius, R. Bultmann).[21] The Ritschl-Harnack movement, as distinct from the extremely liberal systems, again shows an understanding for historical conception, and for this reason it calls itself with preference "historical-critical" theology, although it is commonly designated as modern-liberal, or radical-liberal theology. It deserves high distinction for its researches into ancient Christian literature, and it recommends itself for the acumen and the thoroughness of many of its works and for the industry of some of its adherents. In particular, it thoroughly dismissed the daydreams of a Reimarus, Christian Baur, Strauss, Renan, Bruno Bauer, and destroyed the last doubts regarding the genuineness of almost the entire New Testament.

It cannot reach, however, the full recognition of the historical value of the latter, since it considers all supernatural parts of the New Testament books as romantic infiltrations, and therefore as unhistoric, alien elements. In answer to this we have proved in the preceding chapter the credibility of the gospel portrait of Jesus and thereby of the entire gospel story. There now remains only the task of establishing the fact that the legend theory condemns itself, bringing about its own downfall by its absurdities. Its starting point, method, and ultimate results even at present portend its eventual collapse.

Modern liberal research into the gospel and life of Christ proceeds, just as the old rationalistic criticism, from the presupposition or postulate that all supernatural revelation and every kind of intervention in the affairs of the world on the

---

[21] For an excellent exposition and refutation of this school, see F. M. Braun, O.P., *Où en est le problème de Jésus,* Paris, 1932; Ricciotti, *op. cit.,* § 192.

part of God is simply impossible. It recognizes none but purely natural factors and products of an evolutionary character as regards the world and humanity. Accordingly, Jesus also is accepted by liberal critics merely as the finest flower produced by the evolution of man, as the perfect human being, excluding, of course, everything supernatural and divine from his life.

We could not blame our adversaries if they were to maintain this position after making an objective examination of the gospel text, and if they were to base their stand on a possibly negative result of this examination. But the very opposite is the case. Previous to every historical investigation, the "form-critical" school is solemnly committed to the dogma that the man of Nazareth can be no more than an aristocrat among men, a golden link, the ripe fruit of the purely natural development of humanity. Again and again one encounters this precedent bias in the writings of the liberal critics of the gospel. They themselves confess that they proceed from this standpoint and always halt before it. Thus Julius Kaftan remarks: "The portrait of Jesus of modern theology is only apparently actual history. It is not history as it is or as it was, but only as it is allowed to be."[22] Loisy expressly states that he and his colleagues do not alter the portrait of Jesus for historical reasons, but on the basis of the opinions of modern philosophy.[23] Bernard Weiss declares: "The process of demarcation is undertaken in accordance with . . . philosophical assumptions which are totally foreign to historical inquiry."[24]

The starting point, the judgment seat as it were, from which the evolution theorists pass sentence on the gospel and the person of Christ is, therefore, the rationalistic world philosophy — a previously stipulated philosophic postulate. However, it is an outrage against science to strangle a purely historical problem with the rope of a preconceived philosophic principle. Even if

---

[22] *Jesus und Paulus*, Tübingen, 1906, 16.
[23] *Autour d'un petit livre*, 128 f., 151 f. Concerning Loisy, see Ricciotti, *op. cit.*, § 198 ff.
[24] *Leben Jesu*, I, Stuttgart and Berlin, 1902, 11, trans. M. G. Hope, *The Life of Christ* (Edinburgh: T. & T. Clark, 1894), 11.

this principle were not false, the procedure of liberal criticism would be unscientific.

This unhistorical postulate naturally also influences the procedure, the method, of our adversary's research. In every phase and in respect to every problem, only that which fits in with the liberal conception of the portrait of Jesus, is always designated as historical and critical, while, on the other hand, whatever does not willingly adapt itself to this fantastic picture is declared unhistorical and uncritical. In so far as the sources contain things which lie within the borders of the natural, or which can be forced within these bounds by means of daring interpretations, "form-critical" research will agree; but as soon as there is a question of an account of the miraculous or supernatural in general, it asserts that these are impossible and, therefore, that these accounts are false. Consequently it injects a foreign element into the "form-critical" method, an element which is of an entirely disparate character, and which has nothing to do with the historical character: the aprioristic philosophic postulate that real and genuine miracles are impossible and that a divinely revealed, supernatural religion does not and cannot exist. As a rule, the liberal school endeavors to conceal very carefully the fact that it is inserting into its accounts such entries which pertain to an entirely different department, and which are a blow to "form-critical" science. Some liberal critics, however, admit candidly that they allow themselves to be guided by this extremely biased method. Otto Pfleiderer states that radical theology,

> instead of examining the entire content of the New Testament belief in Christ thoroughly and without prejudice, selects only that which suits the present-day way of thinking, in order to build up thereby — eliminating all else and dragging in much which is its own — a portrait of Christ which suits the modern taste.[25]

---

[25] *Das Christusbild des urchristlichen Glaubens in religionsgeschichtlicher Beleuchtung*, Berlin, 1903, 6.

William Wrede characterizes the procedure of this school more in detail in these words:

> Incredible features are hammered out and the sense so interpreted as to make it historically usable; that is, something of which the writer never thought is injected into the account, and this is declared to be its historical content . . . no concern being shown as to whether thereby the real substance of the account itself is destroyed or not. . . . For this reason arbitrary opinions flourish. The number of capricious psychologic interpretations of facts, words, and contexts of the gospel in literature is legion. . . . Every researcher ultimately proceeds in such a way that he preserves of the transmitted accounts only that which allows itself to be fitted into his own construction of facts and into his own conception of historical possibilities, and repudiates the rest.[26]

H. J. Holtzmann makes the relevant observation:

> There is no doubt that such a complaint is justified. Psychologic conjecture, amateurish poetizing, and adventurous guesswork play a part in the entire literature which is almost as fatal as the harmonization and violation of the sources motivated by dogmatism.[27]

According to Albrecht Kalthoff, the purpose of the entire school of liberal research into the gospel and the person of Jesus is

> to treat all features of ancient Christianity, which do not suit our moderns, as spurious nonessentials of the Bible, or as additions and revisions of a later period, and accordingly to eject them from the content of primitive Christianity. . . . The numerous passages in the gospels which must be deleted by this school of theology are, from a literary standpoint, exactly as important as those from which theology constructs its historical Jesus. . . . Most of the representative leaders of so-called modern theology, in making their deletions, use the shears according to the critical method so favored by David Strauss: the mythical parts of the gospel are cut out, what remains is supposed to be the historical kernel.[28]

---

26 *Das Messiasgeheimnis*, Göttingen, 1901, 2 f., 85 f.
27 *Das messianische Bewusstsein Jesu*, Tübingen, 1907, 44.
28 *Das Christusproblem*, Leipzig, 1903, 27.

It is readily understandable that such an arbitrary and brutal method, actually savoring of legerdemain, is a mockery of science.

What the results of the "form-critical" research must be after employing this method can be easily imagined. Since each individual critic rejects whatever does not suit him and substitutes his own ideas, Jesus is made a constantly changing representative, a kaleidoscopic image, of modern religious individualism. Edward von Hartmann observes rightly that modern Protestant theology has become entirely

> involved in one thought, to project its religious ideals upon Jesus. . . . Each one transports his own more or less finished picture of the ideal religion and of the ideal founder, and endeavors to interpret this out of the gospels. Thus Jesus appears to the one as a poet, to another as a mystic enthusiast, to the third as a valiant fighter for the freedom and dignity of man, to the fourth as an organizer of a new church and church morals, to the fifth as a rationalistic enlightener, to the sixth as a moralist of common sense, to the seventh as a preacher of the Essenic world philosophy with its contempt of the mundane and its unresisting submission to injury, to the eighth as a stern preacher of penance and prophet of retribution, to the ninth as a harbinger of the communistic and socialistic gospel, to the tenth as a bearer of the Hindu doctrine of reincarnation to the Mediterranean races, to the eleventh as a naturalistic pantheist after the manner of Giordano Bruno, to the twelfth as a superman after the manner of Nietzsche's Zarathustra who usurps the place of God, to the thirteenth as a conquering king of battles, to the fourteenth as a prince of peace who banishes all strife and discord from the world, to the fifteenth as a heavenly spouse, that is, the personification of sensual-supersensual eroticism, and so forth *ad infinitum.*[29]

As numerous as are the research scholars on the side of liberalism, who occupy themselves with Jesus, so numerous are the metamorphoses which the portrait of Jesus must undergo, so numerous the contradictions which it must perforce embody.

If one were to ask whether liberal research had nevertheless

---

[29] *Das Christentum des Neuen Testamentes,* Sachsa im Harz, 1905, 13.

not produced some positive knowledge in spite of all these contradictions, the answer would have to be a categorical denial. As often and as determinedly as the "form-critical" scholars assure us that they have thrown away only the ancient Christian shell, and have preserved the genuine kernel, just as evidently has the fear expressed by Harnack been justified: "We must not be like the child who, wanting to get at the kernel of the bulb, went on picking off the leaves until there was nothing left, and then could not help seeing that it was just the leaves that made the bulb."[30] Today this pedantic stripping of the gospel, as perpetrated by "form-history," has arrived at absolute skepticism. Its leading exponents declare that "we know as much as nothing"[31] of the life and person of Jesus, yes, that the figure of Jesus "is not directly accessible to research."[32] In the entire gospel there is not a word, not a single doctrine, not a single fact, which has not been designated as having been painted over by faith, and accordingly has been eliminated from the historical content of the gospel. To liberal theologians Christ and Christianity are the unknown quantity of history. Outwardly indeed they still cling to the New Testament; inwardly, however, and objectively, all values are altered according to their own pleasure, all gospel ideas are falsified and replaced with modern, incommensurable quantities.

In reality this kind of theology becomes enthusiastic about Christ and Christianity only in so far as it believes to see embodied in them the absence of dogma, contempt of Church organization, modern humanitarian ideals, and modern Kultur. Ed. von Hartmann flatly declares that the "Christianity of Christ" in liberal Protestantism is even more irreligious than Islam, and that it does not essentially differ from reformed Judaism; modern ideas of Kultur, sailing under the Christian flag, are decked out with the mere name of Christianity, and

[30] Harnack-Saunders, What Is Christianity?, 16.
[31] R. Bultmann, Jesus (Die Unsterblichen. Die geistigen Heroen der Menschheit in ihrem Leben und Wirken), Berlin, 1926, 12.
[32] C. Bertram, Neues Testament und historische Methode, Tübingen, 1928, 41.

held up for praise as genuine Christianity.[33] Therefore it is undeniable that liberal Protestantism "can in no sense claim the right to wish to stand within the bounds of Christianity, in one word, that it is as irreligious as it is un-Christian."[34]

Thus the collapse of contemporary criticism of the gospels and of Jesus is evident, and this is admitted, willingly or unwillingly, by these critics themselves. After Harnack had dissected the jumble of modern ideas about Jesus and his gospel, and endeavored to palliate it, he added: "When taken together, the impression made by the contradictory opinions is disheartening: the confusion seems hopeless."[35] Jülicher states resentfully: "An adroit opponent can place together the results of the critical labors of the last years, especially those of Wrede, Wellhausen, and Harnack, in such a way that a pure nothing of certain tradition seems to remain."[36] Fr. Lipsius also admits with his well-known candor:

> The portrait of Jesus, such as liberal theology has painted for us, was in fact a prodigious illusion. Far from being the result of sober "form-critical" research, it is rather merely the reflection of modern ideas. . . . In this sense the penetrating and candid work of Albert Schweitzer of Strassburg: 'From Reimarus to Reimarus,' has of late established the collapse of modern research into the life of Jesus.[37]

In fact, Schweitzer sums up his opinion regarding the entire modern critical school:

> This book cannot but ultimately give expression to bewilderment regarding the historical Jesus, such as modern theology paints him, because this bewilderment is the result of observing the entire course of research into the life of Jesus. There is nothing more negative than the result of this research. The

---

[33] *Die Selbstzersetzung des Christentums und die Religion der Zukunft*, Berlin, 1874, 11, 57, 60, 64.

[34] *Das Christentum des Neuen Testaments*, Sachsa im Harz, 1905, xiii.

[35] *Op. cit.*, 3.

[36] *Neue Linien in der Kritik der evangelischen Überlieferung*, Giessen, 1906, 67.

[37] In *Protestantenblatt*, Berlin-Bremen, 1906, 702.

[liberal] Jesus of Nazareth . . . has never existed. It is a figure which has been drawn by rationalism, quickened by liberalism, and dressed up by modern theology with historical science. This figure has not been destroyed from without, it has collapsed from within. [Liberal research] went forth to find the historical Jesus and thought it could place him as he is into our times as teacher and Saviour. It loosed the bonds with which he had been bound for centuries to the rock of dogmatism and rejoiced when . . . it beheld the historical man Jesus approaching. But he did not stop, he walked past our times and returned to his own. It was just this which surprised and terrified the theology of the past forty years, that it could not hold him to our times in spite of all subtle and violent efforts, but had to let him go. He returned to his own times, not because of historical ingeniousness, but because of that same necessity with which the liberated pendulum returns to its original position. The historical foundation of Christianity, such as the rationalistic, the liberal, and the modern theologians had built up, exists no longer.[38]

This fact is overwhelmingly shocking. For two hundred years unbelieving science has endeavored to interpret the person and religion of Jesus Christ as purely human, and for this purpose to rob the gospels of their historical character, or at least of their theological content. Every method which seemed practicable was tried, and every imaginable means employed in order to accomplish this end. There was not a single possibility which was not taken advantage of to the very extremes of the impossible.

And with what success? A complete fiasco, which is admitted even by liberal scholars. All attempts to discover a purely natural gospel and a portrait of Jesus of purely human lines have failed. The critical tower of Babel, in the building of which many generations of rationalistic researchers have exhausted their strength, has fallen into ruins. From the "fraud hypothesis" of Reimarus down to the "legend theory" of "form-critical" theologians of our day, the entire structure of the opponents of Christ has been buried in ruins.

---

[38] *Op. cit.*, VIII, 396, 397. Concerning this school, see Ricciotti, *op. cit.*, §§ 206–216.

There has come upon them the judgment of God which Jesus, the cornerstone of the gospel and of Christianity, foretold to the Jews: "Have you never read in the Scriptures: The stone which the builders rejected, the same is become the head of the corner? . . . Whosoever shall fall on this stone, shall be broken: but on whomsoever it shall fall, it shall grind him to powder" (Mt. 21:42, 44).

In the entire history of the intellectual development of man there is hardly a disaster more tragic than the collapse of the rationalistic criticism of the gospel and of Jesus.

Part II
The Personality of Jesus

ON THE basis of the preceding chapters we may henceforth draw unhesitatingly from the sources of the life of Jesus, for every doubt regarding their historical credibility is baseless. It is our next task to examine the accounts and records of the New Testament conscientiously and to present them in all their unclouded purity.

In the first place we shall endeavor to point out the characteristic features which distinguish the Man of Nazareth from all other men, which determine his uniqueness, and which constitute his personality in the stricter sense of the word. For the time being we shall pass over the fullness of virtue, the messiasship, and the divinity of Jesus, and direct our attention solely to his human personality, his prophetic spirit, and his sinless life.

Chapter 4. *The Human Personality of Jesus*

IT WOULD be of considerable value to us in describing the character of Jesus if his physical appearance were known to us, for this must have been indeed the mirror of his rich inner life. But at this point the evangelists desert us. Their entire interest is directed to pointing out the spiritual significance of the Saviour of the world and Son of God, in accordance with the program enunciated by John: "The Word was made flesh, and dwelt among us, (and we saw his glory, the glory as it were of the only begotten of the Father) full of grace and truth" (1:14).

As far as the bodily form and physical features of the Master are concerned, we are dependent on mere conjecture. This is evident from the varying and manifold history of the representations of Jesus. None of them may lay claim to being an original likeness of Jesus, for an authentic portrait has never existed. Such a portrait could not be expected from his Jewish contemporaries, for they were bound by the law: "Thou shalt not make to thyself a graven thing, nor the likeness of any thing that is in heaven above, or in the earth beneath, nor of those things that are in the water or under the earth" (Exod. 20:4). The representations of Abgar, Luke, and Veronica do not merit historical consideration. Even in the days of St. Augustine attention was called to the extraordinary variety and fancifulness of the portraits of Christ, and he says that most likely not one of them corresponded with actuality, and that the Lord perhaps looked very unlike what all the artists together have imagined.[1]

Later generations, relying on passages of the Old Testament, sometimes represented the Saviour as a contemptible, woe-begone figure of misery, sometimes as the epitome of supreme manly beauty. Isaias indeed prophesied: "There is no beauty in him, nor comeliness: and we have seen him, and there was no sightliness, that we should be desirous of him: despised and the most abject of men, a man of sorrows and acquainted with in-firmity" (53:2). However, the prophetic seer of the passion is speaking here of the servant of God, tortured to death on the cross in unspeakable agony. On the other hand, the psalmist describes the beauty of the Saviour in a burst of rhapsody: "Thou art beautiful above the sons of men: grace is poured abroad in thy lips; therefore hath God blessed thee forever. Gird thy sword upon thy thigh, O thou most mighty! With thy comeliness and thy beauty, proceed prosperously and reign" (Ps. 44:3 f.). This song, on the other hand, is raised to the conquering King-Messias, to the glorified Son of Man. What we learn directly from Scripture about the physical appearance of Jesus does not go beyond the words of the apostle: "[He] emptied himself, taking the form of a servant, being made in the likeness of men, and in habit found as man" (Phil. 2:7).

But whatever his human appearance, he possessed an over-whelmingly impressive personality. The fullness of indescribable charm and gentleness of benevolence and love, of power and superiority, of seriousness and majesty, of winning sympathy and real dignity emanated from him. When meeting him for the first time Philip is forced to the conviction: "We have found him of whom Moses in the law, and the prophets did write, Jesus the son of Joseph of Nazareth" (Jn. 1:45). This conviction was not based on long instruction, but on the soul-stirring force of the moment: "Come and see!" (Jn. 1:46.) So spontaneous was the effect produced by the appearance of Jesus that it needed only the words: "Follow me!" and the one called

---

[1] De Trinitate, lib. 8, c. 4, 7.

leaves his handicraft, his trade, his boat, family, and kindred, and joins the company of the unknown leader. Not only plain men, but scribes also, leaders of the intellectual aristocracy, overwhelmed by the majesty of his personality, exclaim: "Master, I will follow thee whithersoever thou shalt go!" (Mt. 8:19.)

The effect of his person and of his words upon the masses was the same: "The people were in admiration at his doctrine, for he was teaching them as one having power" (Mt. 7:28). No age, sex, social position, or class distinction can escape the impression which Jesus makes upon them. Children of tender age wrest themselves from the arms of their mothers and nestle on his bosom, drawn by his amiability and captivating charm (cf. Mt. 19:14; Mk. 10:14; Lk. 18:16). Public sinners, the outcasts of Jewish society, read in his countenance the language of mercy and pardon (cf. Mt. 9:9; Lk. 15:1; 19:7; Jn. 8:4–11). The profaners of the temple take to precipitate flight before the flaming zeal which flashes from his eyes and pours from his lips (cf. Jn. 2:15–17). Those who were about to cast him down from the precipice scatter like dust before the power of his mere presence, while he quietly goes his way (cf. Lk. 4:30). Men and women, rich and poor, lettered and unlettered — all are brought under the spell of his irresistible personality.[2]

There is no doubt that the physical appearance of Jesus was an important factor in conveying this impression; however, it was an appearance which was spiritualized, lighted up and permeated through and through by his interior, psychic personality. Our task now is to study this personality in its most important characteristics, and to let it impress itself upon our mind and heart.

First of all, we are captivated by the absolute clarity which Jesus had regarding his life's purpose and the implicit determination to accomplish it. His unique mission was the messiasship,

---

[2] Concerning the physical appearance of Jesus, see also Ricciotti, *The Life of Christ*, §§ 174–178; F. Prat, *Jesus Christ*, I, 494–496; K. Adam, *The Son of God* (London: Sheed and Ward, 1935), 87–93.

the founding of the kingdom of heaven, and with it the redemption of the human race. If we do not take his pre-existent and
divine Being into consideration, it is psychologically impossible
to conceive how he could have become conscious at any time
of his life of this astounding mission and of the obligations
which it entailed. This is all the more true since he came from
a small corner of the world, a Galilean village, grew up in the
simplest environments, and was the son of a poor carpenter.
Despite this, the first word which is reported as coming from
his lips proves that he was perfectly clear, even as a twelve-
year-old boy, regarding his life's mission: "How is it that you
sought me? did you not know that I must be about my father's
business?" That sounded so mysterious even to his parents,
that the evangelist adds: "They understood not the word that
he spoke unto them" (Lk. 2:49 f.). We hear nothing further
about him until the time of his public appearance. The account
which the four evangelists give regarding this event, shows that
he had a most far-reaching view of the road which lay before
him, and of all that it implied, and that he fully comprehended
his task as Redeemer of the world. Later on, too, there was not
the least hesitation or irresolution. He knows at all times what
is demanded of him. He is master of even the most difficult
situations without having need of reflection or consultation.
Motive and guiding star of all his actions is the absolute comprehension of, and trust in, his mission. "I am come to cast fire
on the earth: and what will I, but that it be kindled? . . . The
Son of man is come to seek and save that which was lost. . . . I
am not come to call the just, but sinners. . . . Do not think
that I came to send peace upon earth: I am come not to send
peace, but the sword. . . . The Son of man is not come to be
ministered unto, but to minister, and to give his life a redemption for many. . . . Do not think that I am come to destroy the
law, or the prophets. I am not come to destroy, but to ful-
fil."[3] In these and similar words Jesus reveals more and

---

[3] Lk. 12:49; 19:10; Mt. 9:13; 10:34; 20:28; Mk. 10:45; Mt. 5:17.

more that his Messianic purpose stood before his soul with the clearness of the noonday sun, with certitude and constancy.

He endeavored to accomplish it likewise with an unbending determination. Although he was subject to his parents as a boy (Lk. 2:51), he let it be known when he sat among the doctors in the temple that the task entrusted to him by the Father was the supreme and sole law of his life. As soon as the moment arrived to undertake this task, he left family, home, and trade in Nazareth, destroyed all bridges behind him, and expended himself henceforth in his mission as Redeemer. Honor and esteem, money and goods, comfort and luxury, yes, even the claim to a minimum of earthly possession and enjoyment was relinquished forever. His public activity took place almost without exception, day and night, under the open sky. He said in truth: "The foxes have holes, and the birds of the air nests: but the son of man hath not where to lay his head" (Mt. 8:20). "But one thing is necessary" (Lk. 10:42) — that is his axiom, and this one great purpose he pursued with all his physical and mental powers. He gave himself, his entire being, to every word and deed. There is nothing without purpose, nothing by mere habit. The least as well as the greatest was done with finished completeness, with astounding energy, and with fullest devotion to his Messianic mission. He himself experienced what he described in the parable of the pearl of great price and of the hidden treasure: "The kingdom of heaven is like unto a treasure hidden in a field. Which a man having found, hid it, and for joy thereof he goeth, and selleth all that he hath, and buyeth that field. Again the kingdom of heaven is like to a merchant seeking good pearls. Who when he had found one pearl of great price, went his way, and sold all that he had, and bought it" (Mt. 13:44-46).

No obstacle, however great, could daunt him. He overcame all opposition with an astounding ease, as if it were a matter of course. When for the first time he spoke clearly of his impending passion to his disciples, Peter remonstrated: "Lord, be it far from thee, this shall not be unto thee!" But he turned and rebuked Peter, saying: "Go behind me, Satan, thou art a scandal unto me: because thou savourest not the things that are of God, but the things that are of men" (Mt. 16:21–23). He then went directly to meet his tragic fate, up to Jerusalem, the city which killed its prophets; forward to that gigantic battle with the powers of darkness, to that most horrible death for the life of the world. He declared. "No man taketh it [my life] away from me: but I lay it down of myself" (Jn. 10:18). It would have been an easy matter for him to escape, even up to the last moment, but he surrendered himself, chose the most terrible form of death, and died only when he was ready to exclaim: "It is consummated!" (Jn. 19:30.) He was a man of incomparable determination, of purposeful intentness, of iron strength of will.

For his apostles he chose men who were of a like disposition. His main companions in this battle for the kingdom of heaven were Simon, whom he named Cephas, man of rock; the two sons of Zebedee, to whom he gave the surname of Boanerges, the sons of thunder; Andrew, the valiant, the manly one; Simon Zelotes, the man of zeal; Jude Thaddeus, the courageous one. No matter how much effort and labor it may have cost him to train these contentious, quick-tempered, and hot-blooded characters, only determined, strong-willed associates were of use to him in his Messianic mission. He constantly spurred on their zeal and their energy. "If any man come to me, and hate not his father, and mother, and wife, and children, and brethren, and sisters, yea and his own life also, he cannot be my disciple. . . . Whosoever doth not carry his cross and come after me, cannot be my disciple. . . . Which of you having a mind to build a tower, doth not first sit down, and reckon the charges that are necessary, whether he have wherewithal to finish it. . . . No man putting his hand to the plough, and looking back, is fit for the kingdom of God. . . . Whosoever will save his life, shall lose it; for he that shall lose his life for my sake, shall save it."[4] In these and similar demands made upon his disciples, Jesus

---

[4] Lk. 14:26, 27, 28; 9:62; 9:24.

simply mirrors his own clarity of purpose and determination.

From the standpoint of psychology it is striking that Jesus, despite his complete devotion to his super-human mission, yet manifests an incomparable prudence and an extraordinary sense of reality. Rationalistic and rationalizing critics cannot understand this. Because they will accept the Man of Nazareth as man only, with a purely human purpose of life, they are forced to interpret his clear and determined avowal of, and devotion to, his Messianic mission as ecstatic exaltation.[5] However, the portrait of Jesus, even the rationalistic one, rebels most decisively against this sort of diagnosis.

The fanatic is by nature eccentric, the opposite of a calm, deliberate, circumspect character. His monomania never allows him to arrive at sober reflection, unbiased judgment, and mental balance. He can do but one thing — drive recklessly forward on his erratic course, using the most despicable means and the most devious methods to attain his end. With force and violence, with fire and sword he smites down everything which stands in his way. Ruthless and irreconcilable toward dissenters and enemies, he has for them but hatred and persecution. Shameless and unreasonable toward friends and partisans, he exploits them for the furtherance of his cause with cold, devilish selfishness.

How entirely different is Jesus! In him was lofty, serene deliberation, an imperturbable calmness of mind, complete harmony of thought and will, of word and deed, unfathomable divine peace, which no passion could becloud, a freedom and serenity of the soul even under the greatest stress, such as no prophet before him ever possessed. Although he pledges all his powers to the fulfillment of his Messianic mission, nevertheless he does not wish to establish his kingdom by means of ruthless violence and fanatical despotism. Little by little, from within outward, by organic evolution and of its own power,

---

[5] Concerning the criticism of Jesus from the viewpoint of psychiatry and psychopathology, see Felder, *Christ and the Critics*, II, 18–72; K. Adam, *The Son of God*, 93–112.

the kingdom of God is to develop, like the mustard seed which quietly and silently grows into a great tree. He indignantly rejects all forceful methods. "Put up thy sword into the scabbard!" (Jn. 18:11) he cries out to Peter at a critical moment, and he sharply puts in their places the "sons of thunder," who wished to call down fire from heaven upon his enemies: "You know not of what spirit you are! The Son of man came not to destroy souls, but to save" (Lk. 9:55). "Blessed the meek . . . Blessed the merciful . . . Blessed the peacemakers . . . Blessed they that suffer persecution . . . blessed . . . blessed . . . blessed!" (Cf. Mt. 5:4–11.) Meekness, love, peaceableness, gentleness, mercy, forgiveness, devotion, self-denial, self-sacrifice unto the most grievous suffering, yes, even unto death for friend and foe — those are the underlying principles of his life and of his gospel. Thus he is able to recommend for imitation his meekness and humility — the personal opposite of and living contrast to fanaticism: "Learn of me, for I am meek and humble of heart!" (Mt. 11:29.)

The ideas of a religious enthusiast are fantastic. A fanatic is so very truly the man with a single idea, which is the product of his unbridled imagination — a monomania. In this lies the pith and essence of fanaticism, that it stands in contradiction to actual reality and lives only for a confused dream, the realization of which is simply impossible. For everything else in heaven and on earth it has no eyes to see, no ears to hear, and no heart to feel.

But who does not admire the sense of reality, the warmhearted understanding of human affairs which Jesus manifested! Whatever he has observed and felt himself, he depicted so graphically in his discourses and parables. How his interest was caught by the things about him! Home, hearth, and country; the playing and the banter of children, whom he caresses and blesses; the solicitude of the woman for her wheaten meal, its leavening and baking, for house cleaning, in her search for the lost groat; the son who wanders off into a far country, and the father, bowed down with grief, awaiting his return; the happiness and the peace of the friendly circle, which he knew how to enjoy to the fullest; the bridal procession and the nuptial customs, the wedding banquet in which he took part; joyous feasting of the living and mournful tears for the dead. Agriculture and wine growing, trade and commerce; the preparation of the soil and the teams of oxen in the field; the sowing of the seed, the growth and swelling of the grain, harrowing and watering, the withering of the stalks and the grain trodden on, the cutting of the sickle, storing in barns, the winnowing of the grain, and the burning of the cockle; the vintner among his vines, his labors and his cares; the laborers who stand idle in the market places; the steward who pays the daily wages; the shepherd in the field who seeks the lost sheep and carries it back to the fold on his shoulders; the pearl merchant on the sea; the fisherman in his boat and mending his nets on the shore. Life in all its gradations and in all its conditions: family relations, social conditions, and political institutions; mourning and tears, laughter and joy; wealth and poverty; hunger and thirst, health and sickness; the extravagance of the rich and the misery of beggars; the caste system of the upper classes and the political intrigues of parties; the pupil and the teacher; the tax gatherer in the customhouse, the money changer at his table, the dealer in doves and cattle, the magistrate in the courtroom, and the judge in the forum. Nature also, with all its beauty and rhythmic harmony: clouds and sunshine, rain and snow, flood and drought, the nearness of spring, harvest time and the approach of autumn; the trees as they burst into leaf, as they bear fruit each after its kind, as they are cut down and used for fuel; the lily of the field, which in its adornment surpasses the fine raiment of Solomon; the brood hen which gathers the chickens under her wings and shields them; the birds of the air and the sparrow on the roof. These and a thousand other things Jesus has seen, felt, and experienced. What a contrast between him and the religious *exalté* who dreams in his home in the clouds, without the faintest idea of the realities of the world and of life!

To this sober reflection and keen sense of reality manifested by Jesus is joined a harmonious completeness, which fascinates us by its majesty and charm. All other personalities lack this quality, they suffer from one-sidedness and incongruities. One-sided endowment, one-sided development, and one-sided activity is the mark of everything human. Each one has his peculiar temperament, his own character, his own individuality. It is based on the fact that in every individual certain qualities, faculties, and gifts are predominant, while others fall into the background, or are lacking altogether. Even the greatest and best of men cannot escape this rigid law which dominates all human life and existence. Those indeed have accomplished much who succeed, by dint of relentless self-training and self-correction, in divesting themselves of the most flagrant weaknesses and in repairing the greatest flaws of their character. No one succeeds in developing a character in which all noble qualities are equally conspicuous and in perfect harmony.

It is only in Jesus that all lofty qualities are found in perfect symmetry, completeness, and in fullest harmony: flaming zeal and inexhaustible patience, noble passion and sympathetic leniency, solemn gravity and serene cheerfulness, love of solitude and understanding of the things of the world, majestic greatness and deepest humility, unbending determination and the most engaging meekness, stupendous energy and calm deliberation, most tender love for sinners and invincible hatred for sin, all-merciful compassion and severest justice, captivating charm and undaunted candor, incorruptible truthfulness and extreme forbearance, meekness and might, resignation and energy, granite strength and motherly tenderness, indefatigable labor and loftiest contemplation, childlike trust in God and manly self-reliance. In all things he is equally great and perfect — in thought and will, in speech and action, in theory and practice, in doing and in suffering, in life and in death. In him everything blends in wondrous harmony — the higher and lower faculties of the soul, feelings and sentiment, reason and will, idealism and realism, a keen sense of reality regarding the things of life, and unceasing effort for the things of heaven.

It has been asserted more than once that the character of Jesus was not devoid of contrasts. This is true, if considered from a one-sided and superficial point of view. Whoever proceeds to estimate only this or that quality in the personality of Jesus will find it so highly developed, that it seems to tower above all other qualities, or to dwarf them. But as soon as this one feature is inserted into the framework of the whole, line after line blends into the uniform and complete picture, and all alleged contrasts and dissonant elements are resolved into a higher concordant harmony.

From this point of view those who say that Jesus did not possess a distinct individuality are absolutely right, since every individuality is based on one-sidedness and inequality. This is true in so far as we apply the idea of individuality to Jesus in the sense in which it is true of other human beings, that is, as a preponderance of certain qualities, or the lack of them. In Jesus, however, there is found only supreme symmetry of all eminent qualities and perfections. No genuinely human quality is lacking in his sublime personality, not one rises discordantly above the marvelous unity and completeness of his being: that is *his* individuality.

We can readily understand that the universality of Jesus can be combined with his individuality, or rather that the former is demanded by the latter. Just as Jesus is superior to the individual peculiarities of men, so also is he free from every limitation as to time and nationality.

History cannot say this of any other man. It is simply impossible that any individual, in so far as he is purely man, could acquire a completely universal character. With the very air that surrounds him he inhales to a certain extent the ideas and peculiarities of his age, of his country, and of his race. It was said of Socrates that he overcame these limitations. He actually "answered the question as to what country he belonged, with the proud words: 'I am a citizen of the world,' for he regarded himself as an inhabitant and citizen of the whole world."[6] Considered strictly, however, these words of Socrates simply define that denationalized cosmopolitanism which later on became common both in Greece and in Rome, and as it is popular today perhaps among socialists and communists. In his mentality and in his life, however, Socrates is "through and through a Greek and an Athenian, a man from the innermost core of his nation." His character is in every respect identical with that of the Greek people.[7]

With Jesus it was entirely different. In his outward manner of life he was, it is true, a child of his country and of his age. He was strongly attached to his native soil, and the weal or woe of his people affected him so deeply that he wept tears at the thought of the destruction of Jerusalem. His preaching also and his miracles were limited almost exclusively to his homeland: he had been sent for the lost sheep of the house of Israel (cf. Mt. 15:24). Nothing in him suggests unpatriotic cosmopolitanism. He was rather the most genuine and most perfect of the sons of Abraham.

Yet withal he clung to the national and Jewish ideas only so far as these did not come in conflict with human nature in general, only so far as they did not obscure his world-wide range of vision. He condemned Pharisaic exclusiveness; he abhorred Rabbinical chauvinism; he broke the bonds of narrow Talmudic nomism; all his life he battled against the political and national conception of the messiasship, and finally conquered it by his death and in his gospel. No, he was not only a Jew; his spirit cannot be confined to the narrow horizon of his people, his country, and his times. When Renan asserted that the personality of Jesus bears an exclusively Jewish stamp,[8] it was easy for Strauss to demonstrate that one could just as well point out the qualities of the Hellenic character in Christ. "This serenity, this optimism, this acting from the sheer delight and joy of a

---

[6] Cicero, *Tuscul., Quaest.,* lib. V, 37.
[7] Zeller, *Philosophie der Griechen,* 4 ed., II, 68–71.
[8] *Vie de Jésus,* ed. 49, 36 ss. 471.

sunny disposition, can be called the Hellenic element in Jesus."[9]
Other critics, with Loosten, have made the nonsensical assertion
in all seriousness: "Jesus may have been a cross between a purely
Jewish and probably Greek, or Greco-Asiatic stock."[10] Houston
Stewart Chamberlain has stamped him as of Aryan or Indo-
Germanic origin,[11] while Frenssen, in company with other
"homeland" novelists among German Christologists, attempts
to represent him as genuinely Teutonic. In all these conceptions
there is the truth that Jesus belongs exclusively to no one
people and to no one age; that he possesses the superior qualities
of all, without sharing their weaknesses and faults; in a word,
that he is not national, but supranational. In him not one
nationality, but humanity — common, concrete humanity — has
appeared in substance and entered personally into history.

When we compare Christ's portrait with other figures of
history we are impressed by a further characteristic of Jesus:
his uniqueness.

This comparison has often been made in the past in an
effort to substitute for Jesus' uniqueness a mere classification
of a certain type. The age of rationalism exhausted itself in
drawing countless parallels between Jesus and the intellectual
leaders of Jewish, Grecian, and Roman classicism. At that time
it was the fashion to place Socrates beside the Saviour. For
a whole century German poets, philosophers, and rationalistic
theologians labored over this problem. Hamann, Mendelssohn
and Eberhard, Mathias Claudius, Wieland, and Klopstock, and
many others, prided themselves on having contributed their
share toward making the world believe that Christ and Socrates
were two stars of equal magnitude and brilliancy. Serious
scientists today, as well as even light-footed poets, have at most
a compassionate smile for all these clever little essays of
rationalistic memory.

---

[9] *Leben Jesu für das deutsche Volk,* 1864, 208.
[10] *Jesus Christus vom Standpunkte des Psychiaters,* Bamberg, 21.
[11] Chamberlain-Lees, *The Foundations of the Nineteenth Century,* I,
221–238.

In their place the evolutionary critics evaluate the Saviour according to the standards of the "history of religions." They still allow him to rank perhaps as the greatest religious hero, but as a hero who has found his equals in the founders of religion outside of Christianity — in Moses, Gautama-Buddha, Kongtse (Confucius), Zoroaster, and whatever their names may be. Each is said to bear some striking resemblance to him. For every feature in the portrait of Jesus a search is made for parallels and illustrations in the outer, and especially the pre-Christian, world. But even if all these could be brought together, the wonder would still be that they are all concretely present in Jesus, and in Jesus only. The difference, moreover, between the above-mentioned men and the founder of Christianity is in every respect immense. To place these non-Christian men on a plane with Christ in regard to their character and their mental individuality — and here that is precisely the point — is sheer absurdity. The closer they are placed together, the greater and the more glorious the unique personality of Jesus stands forth, and the more these much-lauded heroes, who had been trumped up as his counterparts, if not actually as his models, fade away and vanish. Jesus has no equal, nor can there be found outside of the history of Christianity either his counterpart or, still less, his model.

On the other hand, the saints and heroes of Christianity, however manifold their resemblance to Jesus, not only stand immeasurably below the Saviour, but should not even be compared to him. Their holiness is not original, but is a copy, an imitation, a following of Jesus. They owe everything to him. By means of loving contemplation they have become immersed in his example; with the application of all their powers they have endeavored to portray his life in theirs, and even the first and best of them confess in shame and humility that they have succeeded only in the smallest measure, that the perfection of the Master is unattained and unattainable. Just as Jesus has no model, so he has also no perfect counterpart.

Yet he is not inimitable. That is the most remarkable thing

about his uniqueness. Although his greatness has never been completely attained in any one point, or by any one person in the history of the world, and cannot be attained, yet when contemplating the portrait of Jesus one cannot help but feel that everything in it is, as it were, destined for imitation. To all great and holy men the saying can be applied in more than one sense: "They are to be admired, but cannot be imitated." Jesus, however, greater and holier than all, possesses no characteristic which could not serve as an example. There is nothing heroic and gigantic in his fate, there is nothing deterrent or exaggerated in the rigor of his life. Children and adults, youths and maidens, the man in his daily toil, the mother in her quiet family cares, rich and poor, learned and unlearned, the sick and the healthy, servants and masters and lords — all can imitate him in every respect and in every way. He alone is the absolute prototype and original model for all humanity. The subsequent section on his fullness of virtue will strengthen this conviction.

For this very reason Jesus cannot be merely one in the sum total of human beings. His uniqueness rises to a peak in that we recognize him not only as an extraordinary man, but as the ideal man. Hettinger truly and beautifully remarks:

> Every human being bears of necessity upon his brow the mark of the finite, the imperfect, the relative, and the partial. It is stamped upon his soul, it appears in all his works and in all his activity. He is only a fractional part of the real, universal human nature, and represents only one tendency, one endowment, one peculiarity, and one type of mind. The individual man is not humanity; the latter pours out its wealth of gifts and its entire content only into the sum total of individuals. Man may indeed strive for complete moral development and perfection, but he will always demonstrate it in himself only approximately, will cultivate only the one or the other sphere of the spiritual world, will find himself more or less perfect only in one direction. Just as his outward appearance and his mental endowment is peculiar to him and differs from that of another, so also the moral character of his life. Ideal humanity appears to be divided and split up among separate individuals. . . . Everything great, noble, and holy which has ever existed on this earth proves,

precisely by the manifold beauty of its manifestation, this fundamental law of all purely human development. They are the
various rays of the one Light, but they are not the Light Itself;
they are the various colors of the Sun of all minds, refracted in
finite manifestations and brightly reflected in its mirror, which is
the free and conscious creature, but they are not the Sun Itself.
They are the individual, scattered notes from the Symphony of
absolute holiness and perfection, but they are not the Symphony
Itself. The pure, undimmed ideal is present only where the *idea
presents itself in absolute completeness,* where not only *one*
word, *one* divine thought, reveals itself in man, but the *Word,*
who is *God Himself.*[12]

------

[12] *Apologie des Christentums,* II, 8 ed. Freiburg i.Br., 474 f. See also K.
Adam, *The Son of God,* 93–133; A. Goodier, *Jesus Christ, The Model of
Manhood,* New York, 1928; M. Meschler, *The Humanity of Jesus,* St. Louis,
1926; A. Vonier, *The Personality of Christ,* London, 1939.

Chapter 5. The Prophetic Spirit of Jesus

AS SUBLIME as the human personality of Jesus is, it does not constitute the whole of his uniqueness. This ideal Man of Nazareth reveals himself also as a historical person to whom not only the gift but the spirit of prophecy is essentially inherent.

The prophetic figure of Jesus stands out in towering prominence throughout the entire history of revelation. The pre-Christian, Old Testament revelation speaks exclusively of him, the Messias and King of the heavenly kingdom so ardently longed for. Immediately after the fall in paradise, the first prophetic ray of light concerning the redeeming Messias pierces the darkness of the misery of man's sin. From then on, light upon light, star upon star, rise in rich promise in the firmament of Scripture. Always more brightly, always more clearly do they point to the great day of redemption, to the Sun of Justice, which is to rise upon all nations. Jesus of Nazareth proved to be this Sun. He himself attests that all things would be fulfilled in himself "which are written in the law of Moses, and in the prophets, and in the psalms," concerning him (Lk. 24:44). His disciples can appeal to this fulfillment as to an undeniable fact before Jew and Gentile: "Those things which God before had showed by the mouth of the prophets . . . he hath so fulfilled" (Acts 3:18). With one penetrating glance of his mind's eye Jesus surveyed the numerous prophecies which had been vouchsafed the prophets in the course of the centuries (cf. Lk. 24:27); he let all the threads of this manifold prophecy come together in his hands, embodied their content in his person, and fulfilled them to the last iota in his life, in his death, in his glorification, and in his kingdom. Thus Jesus is the bearer, the soul, the beginning, central point, and fulfillment of pre-Christian prophecy, the Prophet of all those prophets who had prophesied before him and of him.[1]

Jesus, furthermore, carried on this spirit of prophecy himself, and manifested a prophetic knowledge such as had not been given to any other of the prophets. To these the gift of supernatural vision was imparted only as a passing ray of light. It springs suddenly into flame, lights up the object which the Lord wishes to illumine, disappears again and leaves the prophet to the darkness of his shortsighted, natural perception. The prophets themselves indicate this again and again in varying phrases: "And the word of the Lord came to me. . . . And the word of the Lord came to me, saying. . . . And the Lord said to me. . . . And I turned and lifted up my eyes: and I saw, and behold. . . . Now it came to pass in the thirtieth year, in the fourth month, in the fifth day of the month . . . the heavens were opened, and I saw the visions of God."[2] As the pupil stands before his teacher and attends to what is said, so that he might learn thereby, thus also the prophet before the Lord (cf. Isa. 50:4). Very often he waits in vain for instruction and enlightenment, and must confess: "The Lord hath hid it from me, and hath not told me" (4 Kings 4:27).

How unlike these was Jesus! The most hidden things lay before him like an open book; even the loftiest mysteries of God are always and fully clear to him. He did not wait for the hour of mental illumination and thought communication. Not only occasionally was it given to him to behold a prophetic vision, to stammer a word of sublime prophecy. The spirit of prophecy sprang up in him in a constant, steady, and quiet stream; the superhuman flow of thought poured out from his inner being as from its native source, and whenever an occasion

---

[1] Cf. W. Devivier, S.J., *Christian Apologetics* (New York: Jos. Wagner, 1924), 433–443.

[2] Jer. 1:4, 13; 2:1; Ezech. 12:1; 13:1; 14:2; Jer. 1:12 ff.; Zach. 5:1; 6:1; Ezech. 1:1 ff.

presented itself, the words of prophecy flowed from his lips as spontaneously as if it were the most natural thing in the world.

Witness hereto is the knowledge of hearts which Jesus possessed. Whoever reads the gospels with studious attention cannot escape the impression that the Saviour was able to read the most secret thoughts of men, and that he fathomed their inner being with an unfailing certainty.

At a glance he knew all about Peter, fully estimated his innermost character, and accordingly changed his name from Simon to Cephas, "the Rock" (cf. Jn. 1:42). The following day he saw Nathaniel coming to him for the first time and said of him: "Behold an Israelite indeed, in whom there is no guile." Nathaniel replied: "Whence knowest thou me?" Jesus answered: "Before that Philip called thee, when thou wast under the fig tree, I saw thee." Recognizing the fact that Jesus possessed the knowledge of hearts, Nathaniel cried out: "Rabbi, thou art the Son of God, thou art the king of Israel!" (Jn. 1:45–49.)

At Jacob's well Jesus entered into a conversation with the Samaritan woman, saying to her: "Go, call thy husband." The woman replied: "I have no husband." Jesus confirmed this: "Thou hast said well, I have no husband: for thou hast had five husbands: and he whom thou now hast, is not thy husband. This thou hast said truly." He then revealed to her all things whatsoever she had done, so that the woman cried out in wonderment: "Sir, I perceive that thou art a prophet!" (Jn. 4:16–19, 28 f.)

Jesus dined in the house of Simon the Pharisee, and a sinful woman entered and cast herself weeping at his feet. "This man, if he were a prophet, would know surely who and what manner of woman that is that toucheth him, that she is a sinner." Hardly had Simon formed these thoughts in his mind, when they became known to Jesus with the same certainty as if they had been spoken aloud by the host (cf. Lk. 7:36–50).

On the way to Capharnaum the disciples busied themselves conjecturing about who would be the greater in the kingdom of heaven, and eventually a bitter dispute broke out among them. "But Jesus saw the thoughts of their heart" (Lk. 9:47). As soon as they were in the house with him, he asked them the question: "What did you treat of in the way?" But they fell silent before the penetrating glance of their Master. He himself then gave the answer and rebuked them: "If any man desire to be the first, he shall be the last of all, and the minister of all." Then, taking a child into his arms, he said: "Amen I say to you, unless you be converted, and become as little children, you shall not enter into the kingdom of heaven. Whosoever therefore shall humble himself as this little child, he is the greater in the kingdom of heaven" (Mt. 18:1–5).

Jesus proved himself to be a reader of hearts not only with his disciples, but also in his clashes with his adversaries. He saw through all their plots, he foreknew the snares which they planned to lay for him, he met their contentious questions with telling blows even before they had the chance to ask them. The scribes were prepared to accuse him as a profaner of the Sabbath, because he had cured the man with a withered hand on the day of the Lord. But Jesus "knew their thoughts," and he met their unspoken charge with a crushing refutation (cf. Lk. 6:6–11). The Pharisees were talking covertly among themselves about his casting out devils, intimating that it was done by the power of Beelzebub. But Jesus, "knowing their thoughts," brought confusion upon them by an irrefutable argument (cf. Lk. 11:14–23; Mt. 12:22–30). The rabbis were scandalized because Jesus attributed to himself the power of forgiving sins. But Jesus, "seeing their thoughts, said: Why do you think evil in your hearts?" He then silenced them and justified himself by means of a sudden miracle. "And all were astonished; and they glorified God. And they were filled with fear, saying: We have seen wonderful things to-day" (Mt. 9:2–8; Lk. 5:18–26).

With greater clearness than they themselves possessed Jesus knew the stand which friend and foe took toward him, and

what was going on in their minds: "Jesus knew from the beginning, who they were that did not believe, and who he was,
that would betray him" (Jn. 6:65). He never allowed himself
to be deceived by appearances, never to be misled by hypocrisy:
"When he was at Jerusalem, at the pasch, upon the festival
day, many believed in his name. . . . But Jesus did not trust
himself unto them, for he knew all men, and because he needed
not that any should give testimony of man: for he knew what
was in man" (Jn. 2:23–25).

He knew their sentiments; he understood everyone fully;
he knew even the secrets of hearts — that is the impression
which Jesus made upon his contemporaries, and makes upon
us. As our bodily eye perceives the external world of the
senses, and reflects it within itself, thus does the mental eye
of the Saviour penetrate into the hidden world of the hearts
of men, thus is the world of the spirit caught in the mirror of
his perception, without distortion, without a shadow, down
to the last thought and to the most profound secret. This is
brought out by all the gospels with a spontaneous certitude and
a touching candor. It would mean to destroy the best traditions
of ancient Christianity, if one were to doubt that Jesus possessed
the absolute knowledge of hearts, or cardiognosis.

A natural explanation of this cardiognosis fails completely.
Attempts have been made to compare it with the occult phenomena of telepathy, of mind reading, and of thought transference. In recent times frequent experiments have been made
to discover whether, and under what conditions, one could
perceive a thought of another person in a way different from
the ordinary and well-known way of sense perception.

If we consider the results of thought transference with an
unbiased judgment, we cannot escape the assumption that impressions of a different nature from those caused by the ordinary
senses were active in the receiver. Whence do they arise? The
nearest thing to assume is: from the sender through the medium
of the body, in particular of the brain. The sender concentrates
his attention on sensual images, sensations, and feelings, and in

like manner sensual images and sensations arise in the receiver, and then only does the mental elaboration set in. The experiments often demand a great length of time in order to succeed; pronounced nervous fatigue is present in both sender and receiver; bodily contact between the two affects the results in a most favorable manner. All of which are signs that the body is a factor. . . . As far as the experiments in thought transference allow us to form an opinion, telepathic thought communication from one human being to another is very limited. The experiments succeeded only within a short distance, mostly always only in the same room. A conclusive judgment as to the possibility of distant communication in the strict sense of the word cannot therefore be formed. Furthermore, the experiments place such a heavy demand on the nerve forces of both sender and receiver, that for hygienic reasons they cannot be long continued. The enormous length of time alone necessary to produce a single image in this way, according to the experiments made, does not allow the hope to arise that any sort of connective thought transference can be achieved. The fear that at any time one might be able to read the secret thoughts of another against his will by means of telepathy, is entirely groundless.[3]

Telepathic experiments are, therefore, by no means a counterpart of the cardiognosis manifested by Jesus. The former are purely natural, and, in fact, confirm the supernatural character of the latter. It is undeniable, and will always remain so: no mortal being can read heart to heart and mind to mind in the soul of his fellow man. God alone "knoweth the secrets of the heart. . . . [Only] the Lord searcheth all hearts, and understandeth all the thoughts of minds . . . [who] is the searcher of hearts and reins . . . [and who] understood . . . thoughts afar off. . . . The eyes of the Lord are far brighter than the sun, beholding round about all the ways of men . . . and looking into the hearts of men, into the most hidden parts."[4] The knowledge of hearts is reserved to the divine Being and springs from his omnipresence and omniscience. Since Jesus

---

[3] Julius Bessmer, "Telepathie," Stimmen aus Maria-Laach, LXXVII (1908), 161, 162.

[4] Ps. 43:22; 1 Par. 28:9; Ps. 7:10; Jer. 17:10; Ps. 138:3; Ecclus. 23:28.

knows the secrets of men and reveals them without limitation as well as without effort, he proves that he constantly partakes of divine knowledge, and therefore is a prophet in the highest sense of the word.

The prophetic knowledge of Jesus is not restricted, however, to bringing to light what is hidden for the moment in the heart of man; it penetrates into the realm of the future and unveils what at present is not in any way actual, but known only to the One for whom there is no earlier and later, no yesterday and tomorrow, but only an eternal now and today. The prophecies of the Saviour regarding future events concern principally his passion and death, his resurrection and glorification, the fate of Jerusalem and of the Jewish nation, and the end of the world.

The prophecies of his future passion run through his entire public life like a blood-red thread. Already during the first period of his public life he had spoken, using his own body as a figure, of the destruction of the temple (cf. Jn. 2:19–21), and had proclaimed that the Son of man must be lifted up like the serpent in the desert, so that whosoever believed in him, might have life everlasting (cf. Jn. 3:14 f.). From the time when he concluded his activity in Galilee, he repeated with ever greater precision the predictions of his death. "From that time," writes the eyewitness Matthew, "Jesus began to show to his disciples, that he must go to Jerusalem, and suffer many things from the ancients and scribes and chief priests, and be put to death, and the third day rise again" (16:21). His discourses end again and again with these and similar words: "Behold we go to Jerusalem; there the Son of man shall be betrayed to the chief priests and the scribes. They shall condemn him to death and deliver him to the gentiles, to be mocked and scourged and crucified. But on the third day he will rise again" (Mt. 20:18 f.; Mk. 10:33 f.; Lk. 18:32–34).

Thus Jesus not only foretold the fact of his future death as well as the manner of his suffering, he also mentioned exactly the various circumstances connected with it. Those who would plot the death of the Messias would be the hierarchs of the Jewish people; they would take him captive and condemn him in a session of the Sanhedrin, and would deliver him to the Gentiles, the pagan Romans, in order to obtain the confirmation and execution of the death sentence. The latter would subject him to the vilest mockery and physical violence, would carry out the sentence of scourging and finally that of crucifixion. More than this; Jesus also foretold definitely the fateful role which two of his disciples would play in the enactment of the passion: Judas Iscariot by his betrayal[5] and Simon Peter by his denial.[6]

These prophecies, which were fulfilled to the last letter, bear a thoroughly supernatural character. Of course, it would be quite natural to assume that Jesus derived the certain knowledge of his future passion from the Messianic prophecies of the Old Testament. Therein was written clearly that the Messias would have to suffer and die for our sake.[7] The Saviour actually recalled these prophecies when he prefaced the prediction of his passion with the words: "Behold, we go up to Jerusalem, and all things shall be accomplished which were written by the prophets concerning the Son of man" (Lk. 18:31). The prophets, however, foretold only the fact and the general outlines of the death of the Messias, not all its details, which, however, Jesus foresaw. Of this even liberal critics are well aware, but they venture the assertion that Jesus could have based his prognosis on the enmity of the Jewish hierarchy toward himself.

But this is not true regarding even the fact of his death. Already in the first period of his activity he alluded to his cruel suffering, and completed his definite prediction before the end of the Galilean springtime, at a time, therefore, when the hierarchs had not yet declared war against him, and when

---

[5] Mt. 26:21–25, 46–50; Jn. 6:65, 71 f; 13:21–32.

[6] Mt. 26:31–35, 69–75; Mk. 14:27–31; 14:66–72; Lk. 22:33 f., 54–62; Jn. 13:38; 18:17 f., 25–27.

[7] Ps. 21 and 68; Isa. 42:1–16; 49:1–9; 50:4–10; 52:12–13; 53:12; 61:1 f.

no one surmised that his activity and life would end so abruptly. Furthermore, Jesus knew well that the Jews had no right to carry out a legally valid death sentence imposed upon him. Only the Roman governor, in whose eyes Jesus knew himself to be innocent, could exercise the *jus capitis*. Finally, the mass of the people, before whom the dastardly leaders were in constant fear (cf. Mt. 26:5; Mk. 14:1 f.), had always shown resistance whenever the latter attempted to take measures against him (cf. Lk. 19:47; 22:2). Especially was this true immediately before his passion when the enthusiasm for Jesus manifested itself in the most outspoken and magnificent manner.[8] How could the hierarchs have dared to take steps against him under these circumstances? At any rate, he needed but to return to his native province of Galilee in order to escape the plots of the Jewish chiefs and to remain completely unmolested.

Still less could Jesus have foreseen by natural means the manner of his death. It seemed entirely beyond the limits of possibility that he should be condemned to the cross after juridical proceedings before the highest Jewish and Roman courts, and on the basis of a formal sentence. Since judicial guilt was lacking, which alone would have justified any sort of juridical procedure and this manner of death, his condemnation to the death on the cross was unthinkable from a legal standpoint. If, nevertheless, he were to become the victim of a sudden crisis, according to human reckoning, it could have happened only during a popular uprising, and then by being stoned to death. Stoning to death by a mob could be justified before Jewish and Roman law, at least for the sake of appearances. If Jesus were to fall a victim to mob justice during a riot, then the plotters would escape the charge of having executed the death penalty in violation of Roman law. The Mosaic law, however, which inflicted death by stoning on blasphemers (cf. Lev. 24:13–16), could have been invoked, at least on false pretenses, against Jesus. From ancient times those prophets who proved annoying were decried by the mob as

---

[8] Cf. Mt. 21:8–11; Mk. 11:8–11; Lk. 19:36–38; Jn. 12:12 f.

pseudo-prophets and stoned to death. That this form of death was the fate of the prophets Jesus declared when he uttered his woe over the city: "Jerusalem, Jerusalem, thou killest the prophets, and stonest them that are sent unto thee!" (Mt. 23:37; Lk. 13:32–34.) Stephen also suffered this form of death (cf. Acts 7:57 ff.). On various occasions the Jews had attempted to stone the Saviour himself under the pretext that he had blasphemed (cf. Jn. 8:59; 10:31 ff.; 11:8). Only this form of death, therefore, would have been his fate according to human expectation.

Least of all would Jesus have been able to foresee, according to purely natural factors, the circumstances of his death. That the Roman soldiery would make a mockery of him and spit upon him, was humanly speaking, not to be foreseen. The penalty of scourging was never inflicted in other cases upon those condemned to death. The betrayal of Judas, despite the bad character of this "thief," was totally unexpected on the part of the disciples. How, otherwise, could one after the other have asked: "Is it I, Lord?" (Mt. 26:22.) How, otherwise, could Judas have dared to be present at the Last Supper? That Peter, of all men, should deny the Lord certainly seemed incredible. Was he not the stanchest and most loyal of all the apostles, and for this reason chosen as the pillar of the Church? Did he not, in the very face of the prophetic words of Jesus, protest that he was ready to go into prison and to death with the Master? If the Saviour, nevertheless, did make the very definite statement that Peter was to deny him that very same night and before the cockcrow, it is because he alone, who reads in the future and in the hearts of men as in an open book, could know it.

Immediately upon the prediction of his death follows the prophecy of his resurrection with the further detail that it is to take place on the third day. As often as the Saviour spoke of his coming death, he would add directly "that on the third day he must rise again. . . . The Son of man shall be betrayed into the hands of men: and they shall kill him, and the third

day he shall rise again. . . . The Son of man must suffer many
things, and be rejected by the ancients, and by the high priests,
and the scribes, and be killed: and after three days rise again.
. . . The Son of man shall be betrayed to the chief priests and
the scribes, and they shall condemn him to death. And shall
deliver him to the Gentiles to be mocked, and scourged, and
crucified, and the third day he shall rise again."[9] Jesus had
informed even the Pharisees about this on more than one occasion. When they asked of him a sign from heaven, he said:
"An evil and adulterous generation seeketh a sign: and a sign
shall not be given it, but the sign of Jonas the prophet. For
as Jonas was in the whale's belly three days and three nights:
so shall the Son of man be in the heart of the earth three days
and three nights" (Mt. 12:39 f.). When he drove the traders
out of the temple, the Jews said to him: "What sign dost thou
show unto us, seeing thou dost these things? Jesus answered,
and said to them: Destroy this temple, and in three days I will
raise it up. The Jews then said: Six and forty years was this
temple in building; and wilt thou raise it up in three days?"
(Jn. 2:18–20.) "But he spoke of the temple of his body,"
the evangelist adds. The Jews, nevertheless, understood these
words in this sense, despite their hypocritical charge that
Jesus wished to destroy the temple, for they came together
before Pilate with the request: "Sir, we have remembered that
that seducer said, while he was yet alive: After three days I will
rise again. Command therefore the sepulchre to be guarded
until the third day: lest perhaps his disciples come and steal
him away, and say to the people: He is risen from the dead"
(Mt. 27:63 f.).

From all this it is clear that Jesus foretold, in the presence
of friend and foe, at various times and in the most definite
manner, that he would rise from the dead on the third day.
Even if the Pharisees ridiculed this prophecy, and even if the
disciples remained skeptical until his Easter appearances the

---

[9] Mt. 16:21; 17:21–22; Mk. 9:30; 8:31; Lk. 9:22; Mt. 20:18–19; Mk.
10:32–34; Lk. 18:32–33.

prophecy concerning his resurrection nevertheless proves that
it is above all human calculation. According to all natural experience and presumption Jesus would have to have foreseen that
his body was to decay in the grave. There was, indeed, an inti-
mation of the resurrection of the Messias in the Old Testament
(cf. Ps. 3:6; 15:10 f.), but Jewish theology found this prophecy
nowhere in the prophets, and even the disciples recognized it
there only after it had been fulfilled (cf. Jn. 2:22; 20:9; Acts
2:25–31). By the mere fact that Jesus alone unveiled this
prophecy (cf. Lk. 24:46), he manifested unique and exceptional
knowledge. To this prophecy of the resurrection as found in
the Old Testament he added, however, an entirely new circumstance, that of his rising again on the third day. This
detail is mentioned nowhere in the Old Testament, not even
obscurely. Taken with this added circumstance, the resurrection
of the Saviour was known to God alone. By foretelling it clearly
and definitely, and by coming forth gloriously from the grave on
the third day, Jesus proved irrefutably that he not only shares
in God's knowledge of the future, but is cognizant even of the
most wondrous mysteries of God's omnipotence.[10]

If the resurrection was the one sign which Jesus proposed
to give to the unbelieving Jews, he prophesied another which
was to become the most terrible punishment for this unbelief:
the destruction of Jerusalem and of the temple.

On various occasions the Saviour pointed out the final, horrible fate of the holy city.[11] His most deeply affecting words, however, concerning the downfall of Jerusalem and of the national
sanctuary, were uttered a few days before his passion: "When
he drew near, seeing the city, he wept over it saying: If thou
also hadst known, and that in this thy day, the things that are
to thy peace; but now they are hidden from thy eyes. For the
days shall come upon thee: and thy enemies shall cast a trench

---

[10] Cf. W. Devivier, op. cit., I, 449 f.

[11] Cf. Mt. 16:28; 23:31–39; Lk. 23:28–31. Concerning the destruction
of Jerusalem, see Ricciotti, The Life of Christ, § 523 f.; F. Prat, Jesus Christ,
II, 236–239.

about thee, and compass thee round, and straiten thee in every side, and beat thee flat to the ground, and thy children who are in thee: and they shall not leave in thee a stone upon a stone: because thou hast not known the time of thy visitation." Standing before the magnificent temple buildings, he added: "The days will come in which there shall not be left a stone upon a stone that shall not be thrown down. And they asked him, saying: Master, when shall these things be? What shall be the sign when they shall begin to come to pass? Who said: Take heed you be not seduced; for many will come in my name, saying: I am he; and: The time is at hand: go yet not therefore after them. And when you shall hear of wars and seditions, be not terrified: these things must first come to pass; but the end is not yet presently. . . . Nation shall rise against nation, and kingdom against kingdom. And there shall be great earthquakes in divers places, and pestilences, and famines, and terrors from heaven; and there shall be great signs. . . . When you shall see Jerusalem compassed about with an army; then know that the desolation thereof is at hand. Then let those who are in Judea, flee to the mountains; and those who are in the midst thereof, depart out: and those who are in the countries, not enter into it. For these are the days of vengeance, that all things may be fulfilled, that are written. But woe to them that are with child, and give suck in those days; for there shall be great distress in the land, and wrath upon this people. And they shall fall by the edge of the sword; and shall be led away captive into all nations; and Jerusalem shall be trodden down by the Gentiles; till the times of the nations be fulfilled. . . . Amen, I say to you, this generation shall not pass away, till all things be fulfilled."[12]

This prophecy transcends all natural foreknowledge, whether we consider the main event which is foretold, or the accurately predicted circumstances, or the fixing of the time of the fall of Jerusalem and its temple. How accurately Jesus foresaw all this,

---

[12] Lk. 19:41–44; 21:6–12, 20–24, 32; cf. Mt. 24:3–28, 34; Mk. 13:3–23, 30.

however, is proved by the history of the fateful cataclysm, as Josephus Flavius describes it in his *Jewish War*. Eusebius of Caesarea truly observes: "Whoever compares the words of the Saviour with the description which the historian gives of the entire war, cannot but admire the foreknowledge and the prophetic spirit of the Saviour, and to acknowledge it as truly divine and supremely miraculous."[13]

To this prophecy of the destruction of Jerusalem is joined another, in part even closely interwoven, of the destruction of the world, and of the coming again (parousia) of the Son of man at the end of time. It is not difficult to understand why Jesus links these two prophecies together. The prophets are accustomed to place side by side those future events which have a logical and objective point of contact, without any consideration whatever of the time element as to earlier and later, that is, of their chronological happening. Now the destruction of Jerusalem has an intimate relation to the destruction of the world. The former is a symbol of, and a step leading up to, the latter. The destruction of Jerusalem is the judgment of God coming upon the Jewish nation, and at the same time the decisive event by which the Old Covenant was dissolved and the kingdom of God on earth freed from the confining embrace of the synagogue. The end of the world brings God's judgment upon all nations, and leads God's kingdom to final victory and eternal triumph. It is, therefore, not only by accident that both catastrophes are placed side by side in this prophecy. On the contrary, the parousia is connected by Jesus most intimately with the Jewish cataclysm, because the latter itself was a first coming of the Son of man, and the appearance of his kingdom, in might and power.

The difficult point, however, is this, that at first glance the coming again of the Son of man at the destruction of Jerusalem seems to be coincident as to time with his appearance, or parousia, at the end of the world. Hostile critics declare outright that Jesus had foretold definitely that he would appear at the

---

[13] *Hist. Eccl.*, III, 7.

final catastrophe of Jerusalem, and this even before the generation then living would have passed away. They assert that he
was in error on this point, and that he thereby furnished proof
that his prophetic knowledge was not perfect and complete. We
therefore face the question of whether Jesus had definitely set
the time of his coming again as coincident with the destruction
of Jerusalem, or whether he had left it undetermined.

The decisive gospel passage regarding this point is the great
eschatological discourse which Jesus delivered to his disciples
shortly before his passion. It concerns in part the fall of Jerusalem, in part the consummation of the world. Its twofold
content corresponds to the twofold question of the disciples:
"Tell us when shall these things [the destruction of Jerusalem]
be? and what shall be the sign of thy coming, and of the
consummation of the world?" (Mt. 24:3.) Jesus answered by
foretelling both catastrophes in two successive passages. He
prophesied the destruction of Jerusalem in the manner known
to us,[14] and then added: "There shall be signs in the sun, and
in the moon, and in the stars; and upon the earth distress of
nations, by reason of the confusion of the roaring of the sea
and of the waves; men withering away for fear and expectation
of what shall come upon the whole world. For the powers of
heaven shall be moved; and then they shall see the Son of
man coming in a cloud, with great power and majesty. But
when these things begin to come to pass, look up, and lift up
your heads, because your redemption is at hand."[15]

After both catastrophes have been thus described, two illus-
trative parables are added. The one is the parable of the fig
tree shooting forth its leaves, with the remark: "So you also,
when you shall see these things come to pass, know that the
kingdom of God is at hand. Amen, I say to you, this generation
shall not pass away, till all things be fulfilled."[16] The other is a
reference to the heedlessness of the people at the time of the

---

14 Cf. Mt. 24:4–20; Mk. 13:1–18; Lk. 21:5–27.
15 Lk. 21:25–28; cf. Mt. 24:21–31; Mk. 13:19–27.
16 Lk. 21:29–33; Mt. 24:32–35; Mk. 13:28–31.

deluge, and the parable of the watchful goodman of the house, with the added admonition: "Of that day or hour no man knoweth, neither the angels in heaven, nor the Son, but the Father. Take ye heed, watch and pray. For ye know not when the time is. . . . Watch ye, therefore, (for you know not when the lord of the house cometh: at even, or at midnight, or at the cockcrowing, or in the morning,) lest coming on a sudden, he find you sleeping. And what I say to you, I say to all: Watch!"[17]

In this eschatological discourse the prophecy of the fall of Jerusalem at first glance seems to be inextricably bound up and interwoven with that of the parousia. One is inclined to assume without further ado that both events are to happen at the same time, or at least soon after each other.

Upon closer scrutiny, however, insuperable difficulties stand in the way of this assumption. There is no doubt whatever of the fact that the time of the destruction of Jerusalem is definite. It will be preceded by a number of easily recognizable portents; it will finally come to pass in the lifetime of some of the contemporaries of Jesus, even then standing before him. But side by side with this event another is foretold in the eschatological discourse — naturally it can be no other than the final catastrophe, the end of the world — which is most uncertain as to time, and which cannot be computed beforehand from previously occurring signs. Only a few days of tribulation, and "immediately" (cf. Mt. 24:29) the earth will be shaken in its foundations, the sea in its depths, the firmament with its heavenly bodies, and at the same moment will the Son of man appear. We are never certain of the time of this parousia, and must, therefore, watch constantly and be prepared for it.

Thus there follows, despite the linking together of both prophecies regarding the end of Jerusalem and the end of the world, the definite conclusion that between the historical events of which some contemporaries will be witnesses, and

---

[17] Mk. 13:32–37; cf. Mt. 24:36–42; Lk. 21:34–36.

the last moments of the human race there is no necessary connecting link. One thing is certain: Jesus foretold in clearest terms the destruction of Jerusalem as occurring during the lifetime of the then living generation; but just as unmistakably did he decline to set a similarly definite time for his appearance at the end of the world.

The parousia passage of the gospel, then, raises no obstacle to the absolute foreknowledge of Jesus. His psychic life is an almost uninterrupted succession of prophetic visions, and all his prophecies are in effect an outstanding and overwhelming manifestation of his infallibility.[18]

No man ever walked this earth who was not fallible. As old as the world itself is the saying: "To err is human." The history of civilization and the cultural efforts of all times have their bases in this common-sense truth. Nothing therefore is more superhuman, more divine, than infallibility. To even the mightiest geniuses and the greatest savants it has been granted to penetrate to the light through the darkness of night, to come to the truth only through error. The poet Rückert has expressed this in the simple yet profound words: "Those who abide in error are fools forsooth. Wise are they who proceed from error to the truth."

Jesus alone does not proceed from error to the truth. He is Truth. "I am the truth" (Jn. 14:6) — with this one word he has characterized his entire psychic life. We not only vainly seek error in him; we seek vainly in him a striving for truth, a striving for mental superiority. He does not study; he does not speculate; he does not develop. He never deliberates; he never hesitates, never doubts, never fears to make a mistake. Nowhere does he give the impression of a student or scientist; his most sublime thoughts come forth with absolute directness, like water springing from the lowest depths of the earth, like the stars

---

[18] Concerning the eschatological discourse, see F. Prat, *op. cit.*, II, 228–249; Devivier, *op. cit.*, I, 450–454; C. Fouard, *Christ the Son of God* (New York: Longmans, Green and Co., 1919), 201–211.

piercing the blue firmament of heaven. His wisdom springs from the interior, divine fountain of truth, which flows unto life everlasting (cf. Jn. 4:14), and his prophetic spirit is only a partial unveiling of his divine knowledge, in which all eternal happenings as well as all temporal events shine forth in unquenchable light like the stars in the heavens.

Chapter 6. The Sinlessness of Jesus

AS THE human personality and the prophetic spirit of Jesus, so also his sinlessness is a part of that personal uniqueness which distinguishes him from all other men. An absolutely sinless man is not only a magnificent, but a unique figure in the history of mortal man. History knows no man before Jesus and none after him of whom it could dare to claim this.

The greatest and most virtuous men of classical antiquity again and again express the conviction that man cannot live a faultless life. "Can it be possible to be without sin?" asks Epictetus, and his answer is: "It is impossible. The only thing possible is that you should strive continuously not to sin. It already means to strive for the good, if we refrain at least from some sins by means of this unremitting effort."[1] "We have all sinned, some more, some less grievously," remarks Seneca. "We have not only committed faults, but shall continue committing faults to the end of time."[2] Crates declared that "it is impossible to find a human being who has not fallen. Rather, as in every pomegranate there is hidden in every man a foul core."[3] Philo lauds Epimarchus for having made the statement: "He is the best man who has committed the least faults; for no one is guiltless, no one blameless."[4] "Not to sin is divine, and proper to God alone," stresses Libanius.[5]

---

[1] *Epicteti Dissertationes*, IV, 12, 19, ed. Dübner, Paris, 1878, 218.

[2] *De Clementia*, lib. I, 6, 3, ed. Haase, Leipzig, 1862, Vol. I, 282.

[3] Crates ap. Diogen. Laertium, *De clarorum philosophorum vitis*, IV, c. 5, ed. Cobet, Paris, 1862, 150.

[4] *Quaest. in Genesim*, IV, n. 407, 203, ed. Haase, *Opera Omnia*, VII, Leipzig, 1830, 188.

[5] *Epist. 1554.* Similarly Petronius, *Satyr.* 75, 1.

The Old Testament ideal of morality rose as far above the pagan ideal as it stands below the Christian. Throughout the entire text, however, runs the conviction that no man can reach this ideal in sinless perfection. "There is no man who sinneth not. . . . Who can say: My heart is clean, I am pure from sin? . . . A just man shall fall seven times. . . . There is no just man upon earth, that doth good, and sinneth not. . . . Who can make him clean, that is conceived of unclean seed?"[6] In these and similar passages the revelation of the Old Testament precludes the sinlessness of man.

That was the state of things before Christ. The apostle Paul summarizes it succinctly in the words: "We have charged both Jew and Greeks, that they are all under sin" (Rom. 3:9). Not even the wholly perfect idea of sinless holiness is found before Christ, and where this idea begins to dawn, it is clouded by the conviction of the impossibility of its being realized. If, therefore, Christ is a sinless man, and if he has kept himself free from every fault by his own innate power, then he stands apart from all other men in history, a solitary giant, who towers above all, yes, who immeasurably towers above them, so that it is a colossal mistake to try to measure him by ordinary human standards.

Thus the question of the sinlessness of Jesus becomes the touchstone of his personality in general. We direct this question first of all to the contemporaries who knew him. Do we know their verdict? Is it possible to determine accurately what they thought of him, closely associated as they were with him, and in the bright daylight of actuality? Do we know positively what friend and foe testified of him?

The Pharisees and the scribes, the official representatives of the Jewish Church, dogged his footsteps unremittingly and scrutinized every act and every word of his in order to seize upon a reason for condemning him to death. Neither did they shrink from employing the most despicable means to accomplish this end: cunning and subtlety, dissimulation and deceit, incite-

---

[6] 3 Kings 8:46; Prov. 20:9; 24:16; Eccles. 7:21; Job 14:4.

ment of popular riots and appeals to the state, false witnesses, and even the seduction of an apostle. Jesus submitted quietly to everything. He did not avoid his accusers and tempters; he entered into disputes with them; he could appeal to the fact that his life and words were open to all, thus exposing them to the judgment of his mortal enemies. Not one word did he speak in secret, but all was spoken in the presence of the people, in public places, in the synagogues and in the temple, "whither all the Jews resort" (Jn. 18:20 f.). Supported by this publicity of his actions and words, he even challenged the Jews: "Which of you shall convince me of sin?" (Jn. 8:46.) No one was able to do this, no matter how many and varied were the accusations raised against him.

We know the "offenses" with which he was charged: This man receives publicans and sinners, and eats with them;[7] he blasphemes God in that he forgives sins;[8] he casts out devils by Beelzebub;[9] he desecrates the Sabbath by healing the sick,[10] and by permitting the hungry disciples to pluck ears of corn on the Lord's day;[11] he eats bread without washing his hands;[12] he threatens to tear down the temple;[13] he stirs up the people, teaching throughout Judea, beginning from Galilee to this place;[14] he asserts that he is Christ, the Son of God.[15]

All this represents but one thing — the charge, made in various forms and indeed well grounded, that Jesus was an enemy of carping, hypocritical Pharisaism, together with the consciously and patently false pretext that he resisted the laws of the state and fomented political intrigues; and, finally, the charge of his miraculous deeds, of his Messianic and divine consciousness, and the confession of this divine messiasship

[7] Cf. Mt. 9:11; Mk. 2:16; Lk. 5:30.
[8] Cf. Mt. 9:4–8; Mk. 2:6 ff.; Lk. 5:21.
[9] Cf. Mt. 12:24; Mk. 3:22; Lk. 11:15.
[10] Cf. Lk. 6:7 ff.
[11] Cf. Mt. 12:1 ff.; Mk. 2:23 ff.; Lk. 6:1 ff.
[12] Cf. Mt. 15:2, 20; Mk. 7:2 ff.
[13] Cf. Mt. 26:61; Mk. 14:58.
[14] Cf. Jn. 7:12; Lk. 23:5.
[15] Cf. Mt. 26:64; Mk. 14:62; Lk. 22:70.

were the only charges which could be brought against Jesus! But not one shady spot in his life could be pointed out and proved, not even during his trial before the Sanhedrin. "The chief priests and the whole council sought false witnesses against Jesus . . . and they found not, whereas many false witnesses had come in" (Mt. 26:59). How spotless must have been the innocence of Jesus that it could remain intact before such a murderous pack of haters and traducers!

Pilate resumed the examination, and with Argus eyes searched for some pretext, however minute, in order to be able to extenuate the condemnation of Jesus, if once decided on. The same lack of success! After the most penetrating and pains-taking investigation, he, too, was forced to admit: "I find no cause in him" (Jn. 19:4). The wife of the governor, Claudia Procula, adjured her husband not to stain himself with the blood of this just man, in order not to draw down upon himself the wrath of heaven (cf. Mt. 27:19). The malefactor who was crucified with him is so moved by the innocence of Jesus, that he exclaimed: "This man hath done no evil!" (Lk. 23:41.)

This, then, is the unqualified verdict which Jesus' enemies arrived at regarding his whole life. They must all admit that it bore nothing worthy of blame, nothing that could have cast a shadow of sin upon it, even under the strictest observation. It could, of course, be objected that the enemies of Jesus had not been admitted to a more confidential association with Christ, and that their scrutiny had to pause precisely before those most important, because most intimate, expressions of his life which were accessible only to the innermost and trusted circle of friends, before whom alone a man reveals his real and entire character.

But this does not apply to Judas Iscariot, whom the Jewish leaders had obtained as their instrument to betray Jesus and deliver him up to death. In his years of friendly association with the Master, Judas had been able to observe him closely, to hear every word he uttered, to feel, as it were, every beat of his heart. It must have been all-important to him to justify his base treachery and to quiet his conscience by pointing out a possible fault in the Lord. How he must have tormented himself, how he must have searched all the memories of his years of discipleship in order to discover at least some fault in the conduct of Jesus! In vain! Seized with the remorse of despair, he cried out: "I have sinned, in that I have betrayed innocent blood!" He then threw the price of his treachery at the feet of the high priests, and hanged himself (cf. Mt. 27:4). What an overpowering testimony to the sinless holiness of Jesus!

The other disciples also enjoyed the same intimate acquaintance and friendship with the Master. They had the opportunity, day after day, to compare the charges of the Pharisees with his real life. They were deemed worthy to penetrate into all the mysteries of his sublime personality, from the first moment of their discipleship to that of the Last Supper, when Jesus poured out before them all the tenderness of his soul. It would be ridiculous to assert that they had not come to know the outward and inner life of Jesus in its essentially true light. Still less can it be assumed that they have represented it in an idealized form, for in support of their representation and their convictions they suffered persecution and death. Thus they are and remain the real and principal witnesses of the life of Jesus, of his actions, his words, his most secret purposes and motives. And what do they tell us of these?

It is not necessary for our purpose to give a thorough and detailed answer to this question. The apostles believed in Jesus as the Saviour and Redeemer who, endowed with all the gifts of the Holy Ghost, has redeemed the world from sin; they saw in him the true, the only and eternal Son of God. How, then, could there be any question of sin! Jesus, therefore, appears in their writings and utterances in the most radiant and glorious raiment of absolute sinlessness.

It is significant that it is precisely Peter, James, and John, the apostles of the first and the last hour, those who stood nearest to him, who speak with the greatest enthusiasm of his holiness. They came before the Jewish authorities and the people, acknowledged Jesus as "the holy child" of God (cf. Acts 4:27), and uttered the reproach: "You have denied the Holy One and the Just" (Acts 3:14). They enjoined the faithful to imitate the exalted example of him "who did no sin, neither was guile found in his mouth . . . who his own self bore our sins in his body on the tree, that we, being dead to sins, should live to justice" (1 Pet. 2:22, 24). They point triumphantly to the fact that in the blood and death of the Most Holy One the full ransom for our sins has been paid: "Knowing that you were not redeemed with corruptible things, as gold or silver . . . but with the precious blood of Christ, as of a lamb unspotted and undefiled. . . . Christ also died once for our sins, the just for the unjust" (1 Pet. 1:18 f.; 3:18). They were lifted above all misery of the world and of sin by the invincible confidence that mercy and forgiveness will be ours for evermore through the sinless holiness of Jesus: "If any man sin, we have an advocate with the Father, Jesus Christ, the just . . . [who] appeared to take away our sins, and in him there is no sin" (1 Jn. 2:1; 3:5).

As the first disciples thought, so thought also their greatest teacher, Paul, and with them the entire apostolic Church, built up on their teaching. In Christ's sinless holiness they beheld the foundation of his High Priesthood, of his entire work of redemption, and of the Christian religion in general. "Him, who knew no sin, he hath made sin for us: that we might be made the justice of God in him" (2 Cor. 5:21; Rom. 5:18). "For we have not a high priest, who cannot have compassion on our infirmities, but one tempted in all things like as we are, without sin . . . whereby he is able also to save for ever them that come to God by him, always living to make intercession for us. For it was fitting that we should have such a high priest, holy, innocent, undefiled, separated from sinners, and made higher than the heavens" (Hebr. 4:15; 7:25, 26).

The testimony of Jesus to himself completes and intensifies all that has been thus far said of his sinlessness. Even the last doubt disappears when the infallible Saviour himself asserts his absolute innocence.

One cannot object to this testimony on the ground that a statement in favor of oneself is of no value. The exact opposite is true; when we have to do with a truthful and intelligent man, his own declaration as to his inner self is evidently superior to the judgment of those about him. Whoever objects to the personal testimony of Jesus regarding his own sinlessness thoughtlessly carries over into the realm of morals a principle which is applicable only to the practice of law; he applies, as K. Hase rightly observes, a presumption derived from the most unpleasant practical experience, "which among men of honor even in ordinary social intercourse is regarded as an insult, to him who called himself a king of truth, and in whose mouth no falsehood was found."[16] The truthfulness of Jesus is so heroic and his humility so infinitely profound that we cannot assume either that he overrated himself or that he has deceived us. The most humble and truthful of men could not assert of himself that he possessed precisely the highest quality of all, absolute sinlessness, unless that assertion were based on a certainty superior to any other certainty. His subjective testimony to himself thus becomes an objectively verified proof of truth.

To this must be added a twofold verification from another source, as we have seen: his own testimony to his sinlessness is confirmed by all the actions and words of his life as well as by the testimony of friend and foe, based on their own experience. Hence his personal moral estimate of himself is corroborated even according to the principle otherwise applicable only in legal matters: "In the mouth of two or three witnesses every word may stand."[17]

It remains, therefore, but to examine whether he attributed to himself absolute sinlessness. In the first place, it is most striking that we find no confession of sin on his part. His whole life was dedicated to delivering mankind from sin. He tracked down sin everywhere, even into its most secret hiding places. He condemned even the most hidden sins of thought with a

---

[16] *Theol. Streitfragen*, III, Leipzig, 1837, 109 f.
[17] Mt. 18:16; cf. Jn. 8:17; Deut. 19:15.

hitherto unheard-of severity. He valued the confession of sins and conversion from sin so highly that even the angels in heaven rejoice over them (cf. Lk. 15:7, 10). His high moral sense discovered something sinful in all men. However mild his judgment, and however kind his whole attitude, he nevertheless presupposed that all men are evil by nature (cf. Mt. 7:11), and that no one can declare himself free from guilt (cf. Jn. 8:7). He demands of all men contrition and works of penance (cf. Mk. 1:15), and declares that limitless guilt will be forgiven to all (cf. Mt. 18:24, 35). Only he himself nowhere allowed a thought of his own guilt to arise. He never bowed humbly before God the Father on account of sin, nowhere is there a trace of a confession of sinfulness.

Evidently, this is comprehensible only from the standpoint of his absolute sinlessness.

> If he had developed a perfect, interior harmony between himself and God despite the presence of actual cause for inner disharmony; if he had, as his sermon on the Mount shows, traced sin in others into the innermost recesses of the heart, and accounted even hidden anger as murder and secret lust as adultery, but nevertheless had never scrutinized himself with this eagle eye and had never applied this absolute standard of morality to sins of which he himself were guilty, then he would, as far as his own character is concerned, by no means be the most beautiful of the children of men, as Strauss feels himself compelled to acknowledge him — he would on the contrary be a morally contradictory and abhorrent phenomenon, since he himself would have out-pharisced the Pharisaism which he had justly excoriated on account of its self-justification and its sitting in judgment upon others.[18]

Moreover, nowhere do we find Jesus praying for the forgiveness of sin. He taught others to pray: "Forgive us our debts, as we also forgive our debtors" (Mt. 6:12), "forgive us our sins, for we also forgive everyone that is indebted to us" (Lk. 11:4). He alone did not pray thus. He taught his disciples to offer this petition, but he himself did not pray the *Our Father*

---

[18] Beyschlag, *Das Leben Jesu*, I, 3 ed., Halle a. S., 1893, 194.

with them. The disciples had expressly asked: "Lord, teach us to pray" (Lk. 11:1), and Jesus answered just as definitely: "Thus therefore shall you pray" (Mt. 6:9); "when you pray, say" (Lk. 11:2). It is, therefore, contradictory to his own definite words to assert that the *Our Father* is the expression "of the humble power of his own prayer."[19] He expressly excludes himself from the petition for forgiveness of sins in the *Our Father* by the words: "For if you will forgive men their offences, your heavenly Father will forgive you also your offences" (Mt. 6:14).

Nowhere else do we come upon a petition for the forgiveness of sins in Jesus' rich, yet humble life of prayer. He knelt down in adoration before his Father; he addressed to him prayers of gratitude and praise; he prayed for the apostles, for the sick, for all the faithful; he prayed for his own glorification, and implored the Father for aid in his own terrible agony in the Garden of Olives, but in all his supplications we seek in vain for one passage which would even distantly imply a petition for the forgiveness of his own sins. If at any moment of his life, then surely at least in the hour of his death on the cross one could expect such a prayer from him. Had he not spoken most emphatically of the account which every man must render to God (cf. Mk. 4:22)? Had he not said that even every idle word (cf. Mt. 12:36) would one day be weighed in the balance of him who searches hearts and reins? But he himself had nothing to repent of and manifested no need of forgiveness. On the threshold of eternity he begged only for forgiveness of the sins of his enemies (cf. Lk. 23:34), and he was perfectly certain of his own eternal blessedness, so certain indeed, that he was able to grant it also to the malefactor crucified with him: "This day thou shalt be with me in paradise!" (Lk. 23:43.)

The absence of any remorse is, in general, a further indication of Christ's consciousness of absolute innocence. In another place we shall show how extraordinarily tender and sensitive his

---

[19] Deissmann, "Evangelium und Urchristentum," *Beiträge zur Weiterentwicklung der christlichen Religion*, München, 1905, 101.

conscience was whenever there was a question of fulfilling the will of his heavenly Father. The solicitude to fulfill the will of God to the last iota and to the last moment dominated all his thought, speech, and action; in a word, his whole life. So much the more remarkable is it, therefore, that in view of this unique fear of God not a trace of repentance ever reveals itself, never the least apprehension that he has possibly deviated from the will of the Father as the sole rule and guide of his life. Had even a shadow come between him and the Father, even a tiny cloud "as large as a man's hand," it would, by reason of his most exalted moral sentiment and his childlike love of God, have thrown a gigantic shadow, which would have dimmed his frank, trustful gaze into the face of the Father. But there is not the least question of this. Endless sunshine rests upon his soul; the whole life of Jesus, as we know it, gives us the impression of a constantly undisturbed intimacy with God.

On this we base our conviction that in that period also of his earthly pilgrimage which is unknown to us, nothing is to be found of which he had to repent. If at any time before his public activity he had not been united to God in complete sinlessness, some traces and aftereffects of that previous condition must have been found in his later consciousness of intimate communion with God. The more perfect the later portion of his life, the more deeply would he of necessity have regretted and repented the former. Even David Strauss admits this: "In all those natures which have become purified only through conflicts and a violent conversion, the scars of these remain forever, and something hard, severe, and gloomy adheres to them their whole life long. There is in Jesus no trace of this. Jesus appears as an innately beautiful nature, which needed but to develop from within itself to become more clearly conscious of itself, to become more solidly fixed within itself, but not to be converted and to begin a new life."[20] Adolf Harnack wrote in the same strain: "Where shall we find the man who at the age of thirty can so speak, if he has gone through bitter

[20] *Leben Jesu für das deutsche Volk*, Leipzig, 1864, 208.

struggles — struggles of the soul, in which he has ended by burning what he once adored, and adoring what he burned? Where shall we find the man who has broken with his past in order to summon others to repentance, but through it all never speaks of his own repentance? This consideration makes it impossible that his life could have been spent in inner conflict."[21] The only man who is without a trace of remorse is one who is either conscienceless or godless, or the sinless one — Jesus.

He does, in fact, expressly claim sinlessness for himself, in contrast to all other men. He spoke the words: "If you then, being evil, know how to give good gifts to your children. . . . The Son of man shall be betrayed into the hands of sinners" (Mt. 7:11; 26:45). "If I shall say to you that I know not the Father, I shall be like to you, a liar. But I do know him, and do keep his word" (Jn. 8:55). Whoever speaks in this manner puts himself in sharp contrast to sinners.

Jesus, however, made still plainer declarations on this point. He proclaimed that there is no injustice in him; that the fulfillment of the divine will has become for him so much the greatest necessity of his soul, as food is for the life of the body; that he unceasingly and without exception does what is pleasing to God; that Satan, the prince of this world, had nothing in him[22] — all literal and objective utterances in favor of his own personal faultlessness.

To these he added the decisive challenge to the Pharisees: "Which of you shall convince me of sin?" (Jn. 8:46.) This cannot possibly be merely the claim to public blamelessness of life. Complete external and internal spotlessness alone could put such an unheard-of question. Even the most perfect man, yes, precisely he, feels that he cannot repeat these words without making himself guilty of the most execrable hypocrisy and unsufferable arrogance, and without precisely thereby answering his question to his own detriment. This is all the more true in the light of the teaching of Christ, who raised both objective

[21] Harnack-Saunders, *What Is Christianity?*, 36.
[22] Cf. Jn. 7:18; 4:34; 8:29; 14:30.

moral law and subjective conscientiousness to the highest degree, so that the beloved disciple of Jesus writes: "If we say that we have no sin, we deceive ourselves, and the truth is not in us" (1 Jn. 1:8). Only in the mouth of the all-holy One is such a statement admissible and true. He alone hurls the thrilling challenge into the face of his enemies: "Which of you shall convince me of sin?" And his enemies are dumb, while the prince of the apostles falls upon his knees and implores: "Lord, depart from me, for I am a sinful man" (Lk. 5:8).

As the finest crystal appears dull beside a genuine diamond, so even the best of men feels, in the presence of Jesus, that his own virtue is imperfection. Richard Wagner observes no less profoundly than truly:

> One might think, there have been so many martyrs and saints, why should precisely Jesus be the divine one among them? But all those saintly men and women became so through divine grace, an illumination, an experience, an inward conversion, which caused them to be transformed from sinful men into supermen, who almost strike us as not being human. . . . In Jesus, on the contrary, there is from the very beginning complete sinlessness without any passion, most divine innate purity, and yet withal it does not appear — as might be expected — as something "interesting" or even not entirely human; this purest divinity is wholly characterized by purest humanity, which must affect us in its suffering and compassion in a universally human way — an incomparably unique phenomenon. All others *have need* of the Saviour. He *is* the Saviour.[23]

We have thus far briefly pointed out the direct utterances regarding the sinless consciousness of Jesus. These, however, do not form the principal proof. Of much greater importance is the proof drawn from the external, indirect testimony to his absolute sinlessness. This follows as the natural, and therefore undeniable, inference based on the vocation of the Saviour. His redemptive work is in its essence opposition to sin: forgiveness of sin, deliverance from sin, judgment of sinners —

[23] From Hans v. Wolzogen's *Erinnerungen an Richard Wagner*, in Gustav Pfannmüller, *Jesus im Urteil der Jahrhunderte*, Leipzig, 1908, 428 f.

this is the threefold purpose of his activity. All this, however, excludes sinfulness in himself as day excludes night and light excludes darkness.

FORGIVENESS OF SIN. Jesus remitted sin according to his own free judgment.[24] He expressly ascribed to himself the right to forgive sins, and proved by means of miracles that he personally possessed this absolute power.[25] He even delegated the divine right to forgive sins in his name to his disciples.[26]

But that is evidently not proper for one who is himself burdened with sin and guilt. No prophet had ever dared do that. At most, the prophets proclaimed forgiveness in the name of Jahweh (cf. 2 Kings 12:13). The power to forgive sins was not ascribed by Judaism even to the expected Messias. The Pharisees of the time of Jesus thought no differently, and characterized the presumption of a man forgiving sins as outright blasphemy.[27] Jesus silently confirmed this view. God alone can forgive sins, because he alone is the absolutely Holy One, who is offended by sin. Since the Saviour claimed for himself the same power of remitting sins and exercised it, he put himself above the entire sinful race of mankind and declared himself to be the All-Holy God.

DELIVERANCE FROM SIN. The power to forgive sins, furthermore, belongs directly to the Saviour, because he is the deliverer from sin. Jesus came to seek and to save that which was lost (cf. Lk. 19:10). The saving consists in bringing man out of the state of eternal reprobation in which he finds himself in consequence of the guilt of sin. This is accomplished, however, not merely by God's promise of forgiveness to the sinner and actual pardon, but rather this forgiveness and remission of sin is bound up with the sacrifice of Jesus. Jesus expressly stated that his life is a "redemption for many," that his blood is the means unto the "remission of sins."[28] Jesus, therefore, was

---

[24] Cf. Mt. 9:2 ff.; Mk. 2:3 ff.; Lk. 5:18 ff.; 7:47 ff.; 23:43; Jn. 5:14; 8:11.
[25] Cf. Mt. 9:5–7; Mk. 2:10–12; Lk. 5:24 f.
[26] Cf. Jn. 20:23; Mt. 18:18.
[27] Cf. Mt. 9:3; Mk. 2:7; Lk. 5:21.
[28] Cf. Mt. 20:28; 26:28; Mk. 10:45; 14:24; Lk. 22:20.

conscious of the fact that his life, his blood, and his person had such a value that their sacrifice formed an amply sufficient atonement for the insult done to the majesty of God by sin. It would be madness and blasphemy if a sinful man, and for that matter, if any creature should ascribe to himself such importance. Only the spotless, sacrificial Lamb, who has no share in human sin, can deliver man from sin. He alone who stands above humanity and whose essence is absolute, divine holiness can pay the full price of redemption for the whole human race.

THE JUDGMENT OF SINNERS is most closely bound up with deliverance from sin. We can easily understand that Jesus, as Redeemer of the world, ascribes to himself also the right to pass sentence upon the living and the dead, as the Judge of the whole world. He appeared in humility and poverty to redeem the world; he will come again at the end of time in divine majesty, "in the glory of himself, of the Father, and of the angels,"[29] to judge mankind. He will judge them all; he alone will not be judged by anyone, not even by the Father. How is this thinkable, if he himself bore the guilt of sin in his heart?

The circumstances under which he exercises his office as Judge presuppose in him the most exalted, divine holiness, for he conducts the judgment of the world not merely as God's representative, but by virtue of his own personal, absolute sovereignty.[30] Judgment and the final sentence are so exclusively his prerogative that the heavenly Father will take no part in it whatever: "Neither doth the Father judge any man, but hath given all judgment to the Son, that all men may honor the Son, as they honor the Father" (Jn. 5:22).

Thoroughly divine also is his procedure at the Last Judgment. He will search out the actions of all men and pass

---

[29] Cf. Lk. 9:26; Mt. 13:41; 16:27; 24:31; 25:31; Mk. 13:27.

[30] Cf. Mt. 7:23; 10:32; 16:27; 24:30 f.; 25:34 ff.; 26:64; Mk. 8:38; 13:26 ff.; 14:62; Lk. 9:26; 12:8 f.; 21:27; 22:69.

sentence upon them with omniscient precision;[31] he will judge men not alone by outward works, but by their most secret thoughts and intentions, known to God alone[32] and he will, as an independent sovereign, award to everyone eternal life or eternal punishment according to the measure of his merit or his guilt.[33]

In Jesus the sinlessness of God has lived among us and manifested itself. Such is the result of the foregoing investigations. Among all sinful men Christ stands out as the only sinless one. The spotlessness of the most Blessed Virgin Mary, as enunciated by Catholic dogma, is no exception, for it is based exclusively on the sinlessness of Jesus himself and is merged in it. More than this, Jesus is sinless in an absolute sense and degree such as no man could ever be or become, even if God favored him with exceptional gifts of grace. The sinlessness of Jesus must be characterized as a personal "quality, which by its very nature cannot be conferred and cannot be acquired, but must be an eternal possession, and which betokens divine Being."[34]

This is a historical fact which cannot be denied by even the sharpest critic. Every attempt to overthrow this fact breaks down inevitably under the force of the conclusions which are established with absolute certainty: that he testified to himself as being an absolutely sinless person, and that he proved this assertion by a sinless life before God and man. Were that testimony not true, then this sinless life would not have been possible. If he had arrogated to himself that holiness in blasphemous madness and unprecedented pride, he would forthwith have to be regarded as the most unholy of men. History raises an emphatic protest against the latter supposition, logic and psychology against the former; the holiness of Jesus triumphs over both suppositions.

---

[31] Cf. Mt. 10:26; Mk. 4:22; Lk. 8:17.

[32] Cf. Mt. 7:21–23; 12:36; Lk. 13:25 ff.

[33] Cf. Mt. 7:23; 16:27; 25:32–46; 26:64; Mk. 14:62; Lk. 13:27.

[34] Steinbeck, Das göttliche Selbstbewusstsein Jesu, Leipzig, 1908, 24. See Devivier, Christian Apologetics, I, 534–542.

Part III
His Fullness of Virtue

THE personality of Jesus is placed in the fullest light only when we endeavor to obtain a more detailed knowledge of the fullness of his virtue. Therefore we shall first of all consider those qualities which refer to the inner life of Jesus, and which for this reason have been designated as ipsistic, or strictly personal virtues; to these are joined those perfections which give distinction to the association of Jesus with his fellow men, as well as those sublime qualities in which is expressed the relation of Jesus to his heavenly Father.

Chapter 7. The Interior Life of Jesus

IF WE direct our attention to the golden background of the inner, personal character of Jesus, it is especially the virtues of truthfulness, fortitude, and humility which stand out in brilliant relief.

1. THE TRUTHFULNESS OF JESUS. This is the first and perhaps most striking trait in the character portrait of Jesus. He himself points to truthfulness as to one of his essential qualities. "I am the truth," he declares (Jn. 14:6). His most intimate friends are thoroughly imbued with the inexhaustible fullness of truth and the incorruptible love of truth which shed such splendor over his life, his works, and his whole personality: "The Word was made flesh, and dwelt among us, (and we saw his glory, a glory as of the only begotten of the Father), full of grace and truth. . . . The law was given by Moses, grace and truth came by Jesus Christ" (Jn. 1:14, 17). "Neither was guile found in his mouth" (1 Pet. 2:22). Such is the jubilant testimony which pours from the grateful hearts of the first disciples. But even his enemies must likewise, willingly or unwillingly, render him tribute: "Master, we know that thou art a true speaker, and carest not for any man. For thou regardest not the person of men, but teachest the way of God in truth" (Mk. 12:14).

In these words the teaching office of Jesus is characterized sharply and correctly. Every word, every action, his whole conduct, the entire gospel of Jesus, "the tidings of great joy," are a single, brilliant revelation of truthfulness — truthfulness even unto the minutest details and unto the remotest consequences,[1] truthfulness without palliation or intrigue, without deception or artifice: "Let your speech be, Yea, yea, and no, no" (Mt. 5:37); truthfulness toward everyone, incorruptible truthfulness;[2] truthfulness at any price, even if the rabbinical casuists cry out and the synagogical nomists are beside themselves with rage,[3] even if his most beloved disciples threaten to lose faith in him[4] and his whole lifework seems doomed to failure on that account; truthfulness with uncompromising severity, with the keenness of fire and sword.

Jesus inveighs against nothing with such incisiveness and persistence as against hypocrisy, lying, and pretense, in all their forms and consequences. One need but think of his denunciations of the Pharisees, these typical representatives of external formalism, sanctimoniousness, and carping criticism! A soul-stirring, manifold "Woe!" over their deceitful conduct breaks forth from the breast of this divine lover of truth: "Woe to you, scribes and Pharisees, hypocrites! Woe to you, ye foolish and blind! Woe to you, blind guides! Woe to you, who outwardly indeed appear to men just, but inwardly you are full of hypocrisy and iniquity! Woe to you, serpents, generation of vipers, how will you flee from the judgment of hell?" (Mt. 23:1–33; Lk. 13:15.)

It is this incisive truthfulness which draws down upon him the hatred of the great and the persecution of the masses. He is in a position to appeal to this fact even at the moment when they take up stones to kill him for his bold and candid speech: "Now you seek to kill me, a man who have spoken the truth to you, which I have heard of God. . . . But if I say the truth, you believe me not" (Jn. 8:40, 45). It is truthfulness also which forms the unqualified condition for becoming his disciple: "If you continue in my word, you shall be my disciples indeed. And you shall know the truth, and the truth shall make you free" (Jn. 8:31 f.).

---

[1] Cf. Mt. 23:25; Lk. 13:15.
[2] Cf. Mt. 22:16–21; Lk. 13:32.
[3] Cf. Mt. 7:3; 9:10, 14; 15:2 ff.; Lk. 7:39; 13:10 ff.; 14:3 ff.; 15:2; 19:7.
[4] Cf. Jn. 6:65 f.

Truth is the legacy, such as no one had ever made before, which Jesus bequeathed to his disciples when he left this world: "I will ask the Father, and he shall give you . . . the Spirit of truth. But when he, the Spirit of truth, is come, he will teach you all truth" (Jn. 14:16 f.; 16:13). The burden of his last high priestly prayer is an imploring, urgent, touching petition for truth on behalf of his disciples and the faithful: "Sanctify them in truth. Thy word is truth" (Jn. 17:17).

Before his earthly judge, on the threshold of eternity, Jesus once more sums up the aim and work of his life in the words: "For this was I born, and for this came I into the world; that I should give testimony to the truth. Every one that is of the truth, heareth my voice" (Jn. 18:37). And while Pilate asks the question with a sneer: "What is truth?" Jesus allows himself to be condemned to death in order not to become unfaithful to the truth; he gives his life and his blood as a martyr to truth.

The history of the world knows of no other man who was so consumed with a passion for truth, no one who so hated falsehood. A passion for truth and the right is the mark of every prophet and man of God; they all inveigh against duplicity and hypocrisy, lying and fraud, injustice and tyranny. But not one of them is in his whole being, in life and in death, so heroically truthful as the prophet of Nazareth, who is able to identify himself with the truth so tersely and so irrefutably with the words: "I am the truth."

2. THE FORTITUDE OF JESUS. This flamingly ardent love of truth points to another, not less characteristic trait of Jesus: his determination, courage, self-sacrificing spirit and tireless energy, carried to the point of heroism — in a word, to his fortitude.

Since the rise of religious indifferentism, all imaginable efforts have been made to divest the personality of the Saviour of its energetic, strong, and virile features. From Tiedge, the poet of sighs and tears, and Voss, the most intolerant preacher of universal tolerance, down to the Congresses of Religion at Chicago and Berlin, the portrait of Christ has been more and more revamped into a figure so sugary, weak, unmanly, impotent, and so indistinct, that it could easily serve as the prototype of the most lachrymose and doleful conception of religion.

Against this conception all the ancient Christian writers raise a vigorous protest. They behold in the personality of Jesus the embodiment of force, power, might, and courage. Matthew declares emphatically: "The multitude seeing it, feared and glorified God, that gave such power to men" (9:8). Mark testifies: "He was teaching as one having power" (1:22). Luke writes: "They were astonished at his doctrine, for his speech was with power" (4:32). "He gave them power to be made the sons of God," John writes jubilantly (1:12). The disciples on the way to Emmaus declared: "Jesus of Nazareth was a prophet mighty in work and word before God and all the people" (Lk. 24:19). "Jesus of Nazareth . . . God anointed with the Holy Ghost and with power," add the Acts of the Apostles (10:38), and Paul preaches "Christ, the power of God and the wisdom of God" (1 Cor. 1:24), while Peter also boasts: "We have not by following artificial fables made known to you the power and the presence of our Lord Jesus Christ; but we were eyewitnesses of his majesty" (2 Pet. 1:16).

What he demands of his disciples reflects, in fact, most clearly his own energetic, self-sacrificing, resolute personality. Not without reason did he gather about himself a circle of determined and courageous men and christen Simon the "Rock," while John and James were preferably called the "Sons of Thunder." They were to be heroes, the shock troops, who should take the kingdom of heaven by assault.[5] It is not halfway action, not mediocrity, but heroism which he demands of them: "Let the dead bury their dead, but do thou follow me, and preach the kingdom of God. . . . Go, sell what thou hast, and give to the poor, and come, follow me. . . . If any man come to me and hate not his father, and mother, and wife, and

---

[5] Cf. Mt. 11:12; Lk. 13:24; 16:16.

children, and brethren, and sisters, yea, and his own life also, he cannot be my disciple. And whosoever doth not carry his cross and come after me, cannot be my disciple. Every one that doth not renounce all that he possesseth, cannot be my disciple. . . . No man putting his hand to the plough, and looking back, is fit for the kingdom of God. . . . Do not think that I came to send peace upon earth; I came not to send peace, but the sword."[6] The sword, war, battle against Satan, against the world and against self for God and his kingdom — that is the battle cry of Christ. For this reason he sounded those trumpet blasts of victory which are comprehensible only to heroic hearts: "Blessed are they who suffer persecution! . . . Blessed are ye when they shall revile you, and persecute you, and speak all that is evil against you! . . . Be glad and rejoice, for your reward is very great in heaven!" (Mt. 5:10–12.)

The whole life of Jesus is a sublime development and fulfillment of this heroic program. The claim of his messiasship and of his divine sonship placed him in the most decisive and lasting opposition to the existing state of things. The mere preaching of the kingdom of God, so strongly in opposition to all earthly, political, and national hopes of the Jews, was an act of supreme daring and an attempt to achieve the seemingly impossible. And in what manner did he win that kingdom of God which he had proclaimed! He himself is the first and most courageous among those "heroes" who "from the days of John the Baptist" have taken the kingdom of God by violence. He is that merchant of pearls and that treasure seeker who sells all that he has in order to secure the pearl and the treasure of the kingdom of heaven.[7] From the first moment of his appearance to the days of the final crisis his prayers, thoughts, words, and actions, his whole life is a single gigantic battle, the combat of a giant for the kingdom of God. Only thus can it be

---

[6] Mt. 11:12; Lk. 13:24; 16:16; Mt. 8:22; Lk. 9:60; Mk. 10:21; Mt. 19:21; Lk. 18:22; Mt. 10:37–38; Lk. 14:26, 33; 9:62; Mt. 10:34; Lk. 12:51.

[7] Cf. Mt. 11:12; 13:44 f.

explained how he, in the short space of three years, could accomplish a work immeasurable in its nature, and world-conquering in its results.

As the life of Jesus was one of heroism, so also was its ending, the heroic drama of his passion and death. Suffering and pain tests and proves the hero, and the sharpest test of bravery and fortitude is death. History tells of men who without pain or emotion cast themselves into the arms of suffering and death, yes, even with voluptuous joy and callous eagerness: enthusiasts, fanatics, madmen! Philosophy knows of others who considered their whole wisdom and virtue as consisting of an assumed apathy to suffering and in a blasé coquetry with death: stoical egoists, unnatural pessimists, proud representatives of self-deification.

How entirely different did Christ suffer! He was neither callous to pain nor did he trifle with it. He tasted to the full the whole bitterness of the chalice of anguish, even before the terrible reality arrived.[8] The unspeakable tortures of his last days and the bloody baptism of crucifixion stood at all times clearly before his mind's eye and shook his sensitive soul to its very depths. Even in the most joyous and solemn hours they hovered like dark shadows over the inspiration of his words and feelings. The transfiguration on Mount Thabor and the profession of Peter at Caesarea closed with the sorrowful prospect, "that he must go to Jerusalem, and suffer many things from the ancients and scribes and chief priests, and be put to death" (Mt. 16:21; Mk. 8:31 f.). When finally the moment ordained by the Father arrived, his whole human nature shuddered; an indescribable sadness overwhelmed him in the garden of Gethsemani; his soul was sorrowful even unto death; he trembled, feared, and fell down in agony, and bloody drops of sweat dripped from all the pores of his body.[9] One of his last utterances on the cross was the heart-rending cry of a sufferer dying in frightful agony of soul and body: "My God,

[8] Cf. Mt. 26:39; Jn. 18:11.
[9] Cf. Mt. 26:37 f.; Mk. 14:33 f.; Lk. 22:43 f.

my God, why hast thou forsaken me?" (Mt. 27:46; Mk. 15:34.)
That is truly human!

Still there was not a moment in his life or in death in which
he did not face suffering with sublime courage, and submit
himself quietly and lovingly to the will of the heavenly Father.
To the traitor, Judas, who delivered him to the myrmidons of
the law, he offered the kiss of peace and the word "Friend"
(Mt. 26:49), while he repulsed Peter, who out of unjudicious
love wished to divert him from the thought of the cross, with
the sharp reproof: "Go behind me, Satan, because thou savourest
not the things that are of God, but that are of men" (Mk.
8:33). He longed for the hour to go to his death out of love
to the Father and to us: "I have a baptism wherewith I am to
be baptized, and how am I straitened until it be accomplished!"
(Lk. 12:50.) Now it had arrived. His human strength threatened to fail in the presence of the frightful tortures about to
begin. He lay prostrate before God upon his face, and in
fervent prayer he fought his way to gigantic fortitude and
heroic resignation: "Father, if it be possible, let this chalice
pass from me. Nevertheless, not as I will, but as thou wilt"
(Mt. 26:39, 42; Mk. 14:36; Lk. 22:42). Then like a hero
he walked the way of sorrows, drained to the dregs the divinely
ordained chalice of that martyrdom of soul and body, and in
holy, humble and childlike love to the Father, with touching
compassion and forgiveness for his torturers, he endured to the
consummation, uttering the ever memorable words: "It is
finished! Father, into thy hands I commend my spirit!" (Lk.
23:46; Jn. 19:30.) That is more than human — that is divine!

How far below Jesus stand those men who are so often
and so confidently placed beside Nazareth's "Man of Sorrows"
— Buddha, Laocoon, and Socrates. Buddha lacked precisely
that which so incomparably distinguishes the Saviour: energy
of will and power to endure suffering. Buddha chastised and
crucified himself from weariness of life, from the resignation
of despair and cowardly negation of life; in his Nirvana, the
dreamed-of return to annihilation, is offered "merely one of the

many religio-philosophical opiates against the weariness of life."[10] Christ proclaimed, as even Schopenhauer concedes, the highest affirmation of the will, and regarded suffering and death simply as the transition to, and entrance into, true and everlasting life.

Laocoon, the classical model of a man suffering and dying in the prime of life, succumbed to inevitable fate; he struggled with all his might against pain, and, as Virgil recounts, in dying uttered a horrible cry, like the bellowing of an ox which has broken away from the shambles (*Aeneid,* II, 222). Christ submitted to suffering of his own free will and was "led as a sheep to the slaughter, and opened not his mouth" (Acts 8:32).

Socrates might have been able to escape the draught of hemlock through dishonorable flight; he took it with great mental composure and sublime serenity, and ended an estimable life with the death worthy of a man. But in him was wanting not only the incomparable drama of hours of heroically endured agony, there was wanting also that childlike feeling of nearness to God and love of God, and the submission to the most holy will of God which we admire in the dying Saviour. Instead of praying for his enemies like the Saviour, Socrates mocked his, and commanded his pupil Crito to sacrifice a cock to the god of medicine.[11]

Even Rousseau indignantly rejects the comparison of the dying Socrates with the dying Christ.

> What prejudices, what blindness are necessary to induce one to compare the son of Sophroniscus with the Son of Mary! How far removed they are from one another! Socrates dies without pain, without disgrace; he boasts conceitedly of his own personality to the last, and had not this easy death done honor to his life, we should doubt, in spite of his great intelligence, whether he had been really more than a sophist. . . . The death of Socrates,

---

[10] W. Ph. Englert, *Christus und Buddha in ihrem himmlischen Vorleben,* Vienna, 1898, 120.

[11] "To Aesculapius, O Crito, we owe a cock!" Phaedo 66, *Platonis Opera,* I, rec. Hirschigius, Paris, 1856, 93. It was customary to sacrifice a cock to Aesculapius after obtaining a cure.

peaceably philosophizing with his friends, is the most agreeable that one could possibly desire; that of Jesus expiring in the agonies of crucifixion, mocked, jeered at, cursed by an entire nation, is the most horrible that could be feared. . . . Yes, if the life and death of Socrates are those of a philosopher, the life and death of Jesus are those of a God![12]

3. THE HUMILITY OF JESUS. This impression is rendered doubly strong when we consider the humility of Jesus. Supreme strength joined to deepest humility appeared to the poet Schiller as the matchless characteristic of Christianity: "Religion of the Cross, thou alone entwinest in one wreath the double palm of humility and strength!" (*Die Johanniter.*)

The religion of the cross inherited this from Jesus Christ. He was the first to unite littleness and greatness, "the double palm of humility and strength." He did not destroy strength by his humility, nor humility by his strength. Friedrich Nietzsche, the prophet of "superman" morality, ridicules the humility of Christ and of Christianity as being equivalent to denial of greatness. According to him it is "a revolt of all that crawls on the ground against that which has height: the gospel of the lowly lowers man."[13] What a flaming protest against this does the life of Jesus make! Jesus maintained and steadfastly emphasized the consciousness of his superhuman Messianic dignity and of his divine nature. In accordance with this he also developed a personality full of nobility of sentiment, energetic force of action, and majesty of suffering. Nothing greater, nothing more sublime, nothing more powerful exists than the life and person of the Saviour!

Yet Jesus trod this towering height with such condescension toward others and with such unfathomable and voluntary humility that one might think him the last and the least of all.

The civilized peoples of antiquity would not have thought this possible. They knew indeed men of power and high rank

---

[12] Rousseau, *Emile,* Oeuvres II, Paris, 1905, 280.
[13] *Der Antichrist,* n. 43, *Fr. Nietzsches Werke,* Vol. X, Leipzig, 1906, 415.

who stood at the head of society and also the lowly ones who lay at the feet of the others as their servants and slaves. But a mingling of that class of "supermen" with those of the lowest rank, a combining of the pride of conscious dignity, based on personal or class distinction, with the spirit of condescension, would have been for them an absurdity. The gulf between the two classes was so great that the classical languages did not even have a word for this humble sentiment. One may, indeed, translate the words ταπεινός and *humilis* by "humble," but they mean something entirely different. In the idiom of the Romans and of the Greeks they retained always the flavor of something base, ignoble, contemptible. Only under the influence of Christianity were these words so changed in significance that the poor, the ones less favored by nature, the "lowly ones," were no longer regarded as outcasts in the eyes of the people of rank and birth.

It was, of course, better in Old Testament Judaism. The Old Testament had not only praised the union of high rank and power with lowliness and humility, but had also partly realized it in its noblest representatives. At the time of Christ, however, the theology of the Pharisees had long ago ceased to think of this. The *Mischna* is proof of this fact. However highly humility is recommended in the *Mischna* tract, "Sayings of the Fathers," just as strongly is it emphasized that the learned caste of the Rabbis is justified in looking down haughtily upon the common herd.[14] Even Hillel uttered the arrogant words: "An unlearned man does not shun sin, and a layman is not pious."[15] Still more clearly does the boastful bearing, the laughable vanity and the lust for honors manifested by the scribes and Pharisees stand out in the gospels.

Jesus Christ, on the contrary, from the first moment of his earthly existence to his death on the cross, makes every effort to break down the spirit which keeps the favored few aloof from

---

[14] Fiebig, *Pirque aboth. Der Mischna Traktat "Sprüche der Väter,"* Leipzig, 1906, 7, 43.

[15] In *Aboth* 2, 5.

the masses, and to set up a perfect example of most profound condescension and self-renunciation in his own person. Fr. Nietzsche even reproaches him for this and significantly gives to his Antichrist as a motto for his banner the words: "Main objective: Aloofness!"[16] With this condescension in view, Jesus came into this world like a homeless foundling. Cast out by human society, he was born in a stable and borrowed, as it were, a mere span of ground from the cattle in order to be able to set foot upon the earth.[17] Not content with this, he let himself be persecuted by Herod and carried by Mary and Joseph into Egypt as a fugitive.[18] Returning to the homeland, the Holy Family took up its abode in a despised corner of the least of the provinces of Palestine.[19] Later on, Jesus earned his livelihood as an artisan, and all his life he was looked at askance as the son of the carpenter of Nazareth.[20]

During the years of his public activity, likewise, he lived in such humble despoilment of all earthly things that he himself confessed: "The foxes have holes and the birds of the air nests, but the Son of man hath not where to lay his head" (Mt. 8:20).

Humble also is his manner of teaching. Far from imitating the pomposity, the quibbling, and the professional manner of the scribes and Pharisees, he clothed his profound truths in the simple language of the people, and used metaphors and parables adapted to the intellectual level of his hearers.

Humble also is his manner of working miracles. His mighty deeds were performed without the least flavor of professional and blatant ostentation. Whether he made the blind to see, the lame to walk, or the deaf to hear; whether he raised the dead to life, or commanded the elements of nature — everything proceeded so simply and unpretentiously as if it were the most

[16] *Der Antichrist*, n. 43, *loc. cit.*, 415; *Der Wille zur Macht*, n. 866, 891, *loc. cit.*, 115, 131.
[17] Cf. Lk. 2:7.
[18] Cf. Mt. 2:13–18.
[19] Cf. Mt. 2:19–23.
[20] Cf. Mk. 6:3; Mt. 13:55; Lk. 3:23; 4:22; Jn. 6:42.

ordinary thing in the world. And always was this working of
miracles directed solely to the honor of his heavenly Father and
to the documentation of his own mission from God. Whenever the gratification of vanity or the satisfaction of curiosity
sought to force him to work a miracle, he indignantly repudiated
those who asked for it,[21] and when the people wished to
confer honors upon him on account of his miracles and even
to make him a political, Messianic King, he fled into the solitude of the mountains and in fervent prayer rendered all honor
to the Father.[22]

Humility characterizes every step of his life and dominates
all his thoughts. Never did a word of self-aggrandizement pass
his lips; never did a word of flattery find him a willing hearer.
Every sort of title which served only vanity and adulation was
rejected by him.[23] He chose poor fishermen for his disciples, he
made publicans and sinners, the outcasts of Jewish society, his
friends and confidants, heedless of the reproach that he thereby
showed contempt for the class distinction of the educated elite,
to which he nevertheless seemed to belong.[24] He forbade his
disciples to strive after rank and honors, the "pathos of distance," with the decisive words which constituted, as it were,
his platform: "It shall not be so among you: but whosoever
will be the greater among you, let him be your minister: and
he that will be the first among you, shall be your servant. Even
as the Son of man is not come to be ministered unto, but to
minister, and to give his life a redemption for many" (Mt. 20:
26–28; 23:11; Mk. 9:35; 10:43–45). The Lord accordingly
washed the feet of his disciples — the usual task of slaves —
on the eve of his passion, and hence could really and truly say:
"I am in the midst of you, as he that serveth" (Lk. 22:27).

But the greatest depth of his humility is revealed by him
only in his passion and death. To take upon oneself, silently

---

21 Cf. Mt. 12:39; 16:4; Mk. 8:12; Lk. 11:29; 23:8 f.
22 Cf. Jn. 6:15.
23 Cf. Mt. 23:7; Mk. 10:18.
24 Cf. Mt. 11:19; Mk. 2:16.

and willingly, every sort of insult and injustice, unspeakable pain and a most ignominious death, is beyond question a mark of unsurpassable humility and of moral sanctity in general. Plato had already seen herein the fiery ordeal of his ideal man. He conceived his ideally just hero as "an upright and great-hearted man, who does not strive to appear good, but to be good. First of all, he must be deprived of the good opinion of others; for if he is thought to be just, honors and gifts will be bestowed upon him on that account, and it will remain doubt-ful whether he is just from a love of justice, or rather from the desire for these gifts and honors. Therefore he must be deprived of everything save justice. . . . And although he has done nothing unjust, yet he is to be held as the most unjust by mankind, and neither this slander, nor all the affliction which may result therefrom must cause him to lose his composure in any way. He must rather retain his equanimity even unto death, and allow himself to be considered all his life as an unjust man, in spite of his actual justice. . . . Moreover, he is finally to be scourged, tortured, put in chains, have his eyes gouged out, and after he has endured all these things, to be crucified and hacked to pieces."[25] Only when he has submitted willingly to all this, is it certain that he has been a perfectly just man.

Who does not think of Jesus Christ when reading this de-scription of Plato's just man? But while the "divine" philosopher of antiquity only dreams of an ideal justice, without even think-ing of the possibility of its being realized, Jesus realized that ideal fully and absolutely, and even far surpassed it. He knew that he possessed supreme virtue and perfection, yet he let himself be bound like a common criminal, accused of the worst offenses, and condemned to the cross! He had the absolute consciousness of his Messianic mission and divine Being, yet he allowed inhuman miscreants to inflict upon him the punish-ment of scourging, usually reserved for slaves, to spit upon him, to mock him in a fool's garb and to crown him with thorns!

---

[25] D. Platonis, *De rebus publicis sive de iusto*, lib. II, ed. Joannes Sozo-menus, Venice, 1926, 44.

He could as easily summon to his aid twelve legions of angels[26] as he could cast his enemies to the earth with one word and thus justify himself, but he was silent and rejected all aid![27] He is the Lord of life, and has often brilliantly proved his miraculous power in behalf of the living and the dead, and he allowed himself to be led like a lamb to the slaughter, to be trodden on like a worm, to be nailed to the cross of martyrdom with highwaymen, and he breathed forth his soul amidst unspeakable torments.[28]

How overwhelmingly true and appropriate, therefore, is the characterization of himself which Jesus gives in the words: "Learn of me, for I am meek and humble of heart!" (Mt. 11:29.) The teaching, the life and death of Jesus are a sublime model, in boldest relief, of the most profound humility — and gentleness.

---

[26] Cf. Mt. 26:53.
[27] Cf. Mt. 26:53, 63; Mk. 14:61.
[28] For further treatment, see K. Adam, *The Son of God,* 134–156; Devivier, *Christian Apologetics,* I, 535–542.

Chapter 8. Jesus in His Association With Men

AS THE interior, personal life of Jesus is characterized by truthfulness, fortitude, and humility, so his outward life, his association with his fellow men, is characterized by gentleness, compassion, and love.

I. THE GENTLENESS OF JESUS. Gentleness is nothing else than humility in the social contacts with one's neighbor. It does not consist in weakness of character, nor in the lack of principle, nor in a servile surrender to the wishes and views of others, just as little as humility consists in the denial of one's personal power or eminence. Gentleness, in the sense of meekness, is the moderation of anger, of hatred and of the desire for revenge; it is passionless composure toward those who offer insults. It is, therefore, not just composure as such, or lack of passion, or still less insensibility. The composure of the gentle has its roots in the active love of one's neighbor, its limits in personal duty, and its aim in the honor of God. Whenever one of these three things is at stake, even the most delicate gentleness must, under certain circumstances, be joined to fiery zeal and burning indignation. Moses became inflamed with holy anger at the sight of the stiff-necked, idolatrous people, and yet he was "exceeding meek above all men that dwelt upon earth" (Num. 12:3).

So it was with Jesus. His gospel and his whole person breathe the spirit of all-pervading peacefulness, of composure, patience, and conciliation. His is not the gentleness of a life secluded from the world and unacquainted with the perils of impatience, for Jesus "hath dwelt among us" (Jn. 1:14), he lived in the world and in the most active association with men; there was not in the whole country a man who was so much in the public eye, no one whom the masses of the people so "pressed upon," "thronged," and "importuned" as Jesus of Nazareth.[1] And yet Jesus constantly maintained tranquillity and gentleness. When the disciples, after the labors and burdens of the day, endeavored to send away the mothers with their children in order to guard against his complete exhaustion, he beckoned the little ones with a sweet smile: "Suffer the little children, and forbid them not to come to me: the kingdom of heaven is for such!" (Mt. 19:14 f.; Mk. 10:13 f.) Ingratitude and injustice toward him at times became so great and unbearable that the disciples cried out: "Lord, wilt thou that we command fire to come down from heaven and consume them?" But he turned and rebuked them: "You know not of what spirit you are" (Lk. 9:54 ff.). The dullness, narrow-mindedness, and lack of faith on the part of the apostles so severely and so constantly taxed the patience of the Master that he vented his feelings in the words: "O unbelieving and perverse generation, how long shall I be with you? How long shall I suffer you?" (Mt. 17:16.) Nevertheless, he manifested patience with them and suffered their weakness and perverseness with inexhaustible forbearance.

Nothing seems to have attracted Jesus more powerfully and to have afforded him more pleasure than the things that are characteristically mild, quiet, and gentle. His eye feasted constantly on peaceful scenes, on the silent, noiseless wonders of God in nature. His heart was drawn to men of gentle disposition, to children, to the fishermen on the shore, to the bitter misery of patient sufferers. His constant and dearest wish was for peace and unity, and whenever he entered a house, peace entered with him.[2] His words, so forceful and commanding, nevertheless bore the joyful message of gentleness and peaceful-

---

[1] Cf. Mk. 3:10; 5:24; Lk. 5:1; 8:43, 45.
[2] Cf. Mt. 10:13; Mk. 5:34; Lk. 10:5 f.; 24:36; Jn. 14:27; 16:33.

ness: "Blessed are the meek: for they shall possess the land! Blessed are the peacemakers: for they shall be called the children of God! Blessed are they that suffer persecution for justice' sake: for theirs is the kingdom of heaven!" (Mt. 5:4, 9.) "His spirit ever moves on a height whereon the sun of the divine never sets, and which towers above the gloomy mists and dark clouds of passionate excitement. He is agitated by no inordinate emotion, nor carried away by stormy passion — so exalted is he that passion seems to touch not even the outermost fringe of his inner life."[3]

And yet, despite this serenity and meekness, Jesus could act with great decisiveness, yes, reprove severely and display indignation majestically. To the agents of the crafty despot, Herod, he gave the answer: "Go and tell that fox: Behold, I cast out devils, and do cures today and tomorrow, and the third day I am consummated" (Lk. 13:32). To Peter he gave the unusually sharp rebuke: "Go behind me, Satan, thou art a scandal unto me: because thou savourest not the things that are of God, but the things that are of men" (Mt. 16:23). Upon the Pharisees his words fell like blows from a club: "Hypocrites! Serpents! Generation of vipers! Whited sepulchres! Foolish and blind guides!" (Mt. 23:13–33; Lk. 13:15.) An oft repeated "Woe!" was uttered by him upon the cities of Corozain, Bethsaida, Capharnaum, and Jerusalem.[4] When purging the temple he made a scourge of cords and drove out the sellers of oxen and sheep, together with their animals, scattered the coins of the money-changers, overturned their tables, and cried out to the sellers of doves: "Take these things hence, and make not the house of my Father a house of traffic!"[5] These are certainly stirring, even severe words.

But they are all dictated by the purest altruism, by love for God and man, by his Messianic consciousness — they do not spring from a sense of personal wrong, or from passionate excite-

---

[3] Franz Hettinger, *Apologie des Christentums*, II, Freiburg, 1899, 456.
[4] Cf. Mt. 11:21–24; Lk. 19:41 ff.
[5] Jn. 2:14 ff.; Mt. 21:12 ff.; Mk. 11:15 ff.; Lk. 19:45 ff.

ment. Jesus is indignant over the evil, but not because that evil is done to him personally. The well-meaning disciple who would save him from death received just as sharp, and even a sharper reproof than did the princely barbarian who sought to intimidate him with threats of death and to restrain him from his work of redemption in Judea, for both promoted the plans of his infernal adversary and opposed the ways of God. He reprimanded the Pharisees because they falsified the law of God and kept the people from the kingdom of God; he charged them with all their wickedness and depravity in order to alarm and convert them, even though he may have thereby exposed himself to the bitterest persecution and to death. His heart-rending "Woe!" resounded over the cities, not because they disappointed and despised him, but because they had not done penance and had not reformed, because they did "not know the things that were to their peace." And where his own person did not come into question, even in the remotest degree, he nevertheless executed judgment upon the desecrators of the temple solely out of zeal for the house of God. "The zeal of thine house hath eaten me up," the Psalmist had prophesied concerning him.[6] Zeal for the house and kingdom of God is the only rule of conduct in the life of Jesus. And this is the unique and astonishing thing about his conduct: even when he must pass judgment, when he is moved to anger, or must punish, even in the moments of the deepest moral indignation, there is nowhere a trace of personal hurt, or desire for revenge, of egoism. Thus even the sad and apparently harsh words and actions of Jesus, at which injudicious or malevolent critics take offense, become a confirmation of his gentle disposition.

Concerning the real, crucial test of his meekness, that is, his personal conduct toward his defamers, his enemies, and the barbarous soldiers, what astounding and truly divine kindness confronts us! With what superhuman composure he endured the wounds of disappointed friendship! With tireless, heavenly patience Jesus had trained the twelve disciples, initiated them

---

[6] Ps. 68:10; cf. Jn. 2:17.

into the innermost secrets of his heart, and had made them his most intimate friends. And so, at the Last Supper, while he gave them the highest proof of his love, there poured from his gentle heart the overpowering lament that he had nourished a viper in his bosom: "One of you shall betray me."[7] Yet not one word of reproof for the traitor Judas who was present; indeed, in order to protect him from possible injury, he did not even say openly who the wretch was. He let him join in celebrating this love feast, and only hinted in an unobtrusive manner, so that "no man at table knew to what purpose he said this unto him. . . . That which thou dost, do quickly" (Jn. 13:27). Some hours later Judas came at the head of an armed band, approached the Master, and said: "Hail, Rabbi. And he kissed him."[8] Even for this hellish crime Jesus had no word of reproof, only a cry of disappointed friendship: "Judas, dost thou betray the Son of man with a kiss?" (Lk. 22:48.)

Peter, who was the most indignant over this act of treachery, whom Jesus had to restrain from violent excesses at the time of his arrest;[9] Peter, whom Jesus had distinguished before all the other disciples, shamefully denied his Lord with oaths and curses after the events in Gethsemani: "I know not the man. . . . And the Lord turning looked on Peter," with a look of infinite sadness, kindness, and forgiveness which pierced the prince of apostles to the very depths of his soul, and moved him at once to tears of repentance.[10]

Jesus stood before his accusers and judges, the Lamb of God before ravening wolves. A soul-stirring spectacle, a spectacle of sublime beauty! His humble attitude, his calm countenance, serene with the composure of patient suffering, his closed lips, his holy silence — everything breathed the beauty of heavenly patience and gentleness. He spoke only when duty and love of truth compelled him to speak; but in the whole history of the passion he scarcely uttered a word in self-defense. Depraved

---

[7] Mt. 26:21; Mk. 14:18; Lk. 22:21; Jn. 13:21.

[8] Mt. 26:47 ff.; Mk. 14:43 ff.; Lk. 22:47 ff.

[9] Cf. Jn. 13:24; 18:10; Mt. 26:51 ff.; Mk. 14:47; Lk. 22:49 f.

[10] Cf. Mt. 26:69 ff.; Mk. 14:66 ff.; Lk. 22:56 ff.; Jn. 18:17 ff.

and suborned scoundrels brought false witness against the innocent one: he was silent. The high-priest Caiphas stepped forth
and cried out: "Answerest thou nothing to the things that are
laid to thy charge by these men?" But Jesus "held his peace,
and answered nothing."[11] The Roman governor could not understand why the accused man did not defend himself, though it
had been said of him that "he spoke with power." He asked the
accused: "Dost not thou hear how great testimonies they allege
against thee?" But Jesus "answered him never a word; so that
the governor wondered exceedingly" (Mt. 27:13, 14). The
Tetrarch Herod listened to the impassioned charges which the
priests and scribes made against Jesus: but Jesus was silent.
Herod sought "in many words" to elicit from him some words
of self-defense, "but he answered him nothing. . . . And Herod
with his army set him at nought, and mocked him" (Lk.
23:9–11).

The meek, divine Saviour then became the prey of the
minions of the law, a band of brutal, pagan soldiers. They
stripped and scourged him in order to satisfy their boundless
hate for the condemned man. Every nerve of Christ's body
quivered with agonizing pain; he was silent and endured
all; he, who with a breath could strike down his torturers. They then put on him a fool's garb, pressed a crown of
thorns deep down upon his head, thrust a reed as scepter into
his right hand in order to ridicule him as a pseudo-king; then
they snatched the reed from his hand, beat his thorn-pierced
head with it, mocked him by bending their knees before him,
and spat in his face.[12] Like a red-hot brand their filthy spittle
burned in his soul; every word of mockery was felt by him as a
cruel stab; the shameful degradation and derision was the most
shocking insult which could be offered to the Messias-King and
Son of God. Yet, despite all this, not a word of complaint fell
from his divine lips, not a syllable of self-defense and vindication

---

[11] Mk. 14:56–61; Mt. 26:59–63.
[12] Cf. Mt. 27:27–30; Mk. 15:16–20; Jn. 19:2 ff.

of his honor, not one utterance of vengeance against his tormentors.

He had hung for hours upon the cross, but the mockery still continued: "If thou be the Son of God, come down from the cross! . . . He saved others, himself he cannot save! . . . This man calleth Elias!" So railed the soldiers, the priests and scribes, as well as the rabble who looked on and passed by. Jesus, however, prayed: "Father, forgive them, for they know not what they do!"[13]

That is simply overpowering — a patience and meekness which no human strength can imitate, no human mind can comprehend, no human tongue can express. This meekness made such an impression upon those about him that many years later Paul adjured the Corinthians by the "mildness and modesty of Christ" (2 Cor. 10:1), and Peter, full of admiration, reminded his hearers that Jesus "when he was reviled, did not revile; when he suffered, he threatened not" (1 Pet. 2:23).

The gentleness of Jesus becomes the more astounding when we consider his delicacy of feeling. If only his heart had been hardened by apathy and insensible to mockery and derision, to pain and suffering! If only he had, like the Stoics, at least pretended to face suffering and injustice coldly, without pain, without interest or emotion![14] But the very opposite was the case. No heart more tender, no nature more richly endowed and sensitive ever existed than his. The pain and injustice suffered by him agonized every fiber of his delicately attuned and lofty soul, and this suffering revealed itself outwardly in a touchingly sincere, frank, and affecting manner. We have only to think of Gethsemani, of the meeting with the traitor Judas and with Peter in the latter's hour of weakness, and of his words on the cross!

And just as he felt, and felt deeply, his own anguish, so was

---

13 Mt. 27:39–50; Mk. 15:29–37; Lk. 23:34–39.
14 As regards stoical apathy, cf. Cicero, *Quaest. Tuscul.*, II, 2, 29; III, 10, 21; Seneca, *De const. sap.*, XIV, 123; Horatius, *Ep.* I, 1.

he also full of compassion, of pity, and of mercy toward his suffering fellow men.

2. THE COMPASSION OF JESUS. Pity and compassion is just as much a fundamental trait of his character as is gentleness and meekness. In several passages of the gospel it is stressed that he was filled with deep compassion for the distress of the people in general or of individuals: "He had compassion on them."[15] This was plainly noticeable, for his countenance changed, his words were fraught with tender sympathy, his eyes grew dim, and even filled with tears.[16] He forgot everything else, his sole thought being how he could alleviate and help: "He had compassion."

He felt compassion for those who were burdened with grief and sorrow. He could not see affliction of any kind without being affected, and without thinking of practical assistance, or at least of consolation. He calls blessed both those that mourn as well as those that assuage sorrow (cf. Mt. 5:24; 25:35 ff.). He was most deeply touched by the grief of those who stood at the bier of their beloved dead. When he beheld the disconsolateness of the widow of Naim, whose only son was being borne to the grave, "being moved with mercy towards her, he said: Weep not!" Then he stepped to the bier, awakened the young man to life by his omnipotent word, and led him to his mother (cf. Lk. 7:13 f.). The chief of the synagogue, Jairus, fell at the feet of the Saviour in the open street and implored his aid in behalf of his little daughter, who was dying. Jesus forthwith left the crowd which was waiting for him, and hastened to the deathbed, where death had already claimed its victim. "Weep not!" he said compassionately to the relatives, then he caused the mourning women and the musicians to leave the room, and called the maiden back to life.[17] Still more touching is his profound grief over his dead friend, Lazarus, and his compassion for the sorrowing sisters, Mary and Martha

---

[15] Cf. Mt. 9:36; 14:14; 15:32; 20:34; Mk. 1:41; 6:34; 8:2; Lk. 7:13.
[16] Cf. Lk. 19:41; Jn. 11:33, 35.
[17] Cf. Mk. 5:22 f., 35–43; Mt. 9:18 f., 23–26; Lk. 8:41 f., 49–56.

of Bethania. "Jesus, therefore, when he saw her weeping, and the Jews that were come with her, weeping, groaned in the spirit, and troubled himself . . . and Jesus wept. The Jews therefore said: Behold how he loved him . . . Jesus therefore again groaning in himself, cometh to the sepulchre," called the dead man back to life and dried his tears and those of the others (Jn. 11:33-36).

He felt the keenest commiseration for the sick and the suffering. Those who witnessed his almighty power cannot repeat this often enough: "Jesus having compassion on them, touched their eyes. And immediately they saw" (Mt. 20:34). "Jesus having compassion on him [the leper], stretched forth his hand; and touching him, saith to him: I will. Be thou made clean" (Mk. 1:41). "He coming forth saw a great multitude, and had compassion on them, and healed their sick" (Mt. 14:14). "Jesus went about all the cities, and towns . . . healing every disease, and every infirmity" (Mt. 9:35). In the dining hall he could not eat until he healed the man afflicted with dropsy, unmindful of the fact that it was the Sabbath, and unaffected by the scandal taken by the Pharisees who were present (cf. Lk. 14:2-4). Even in the synagogue he stopped in the middle of his discourse to heal the man with the withered hand (cf. Mk. 3:1-5), and also the woman suffering from infirmity (cf. Lk. 13:10 ff.).

He did not shrink even from lepers. He did not consider leprosy, as the Jews did, as a type of and punishment for sin. He did not, as was the custom of the law, make outcasts of even the poorest who were afflicted with this frightful disease. It was with preference that he healed the lepers; he was solicitous for them with a special love and recommended them to the special care of the apostles (cf. Mt. 10:8). Hence the lepers, in the mind and language of the Middle Ages, came to be known through him as "the sick of the good God." "He healed them all," the evangelists remark, no matter how numerous they might be who came to him or were brought to him — the infirm, the fever stricken, the lame, the wretched, and the lepers.

He manifested in fact such heartfelt kindness toward the sick that the disciples saw fulfilled in him the prophetic word: "He took our infirmities and bore our diseases" (Mt. 8:17; cf. Isa. 53:4). In the parable of the good Samaritan Jesus elevated the care of the sick to a genuine service of God and to a token of perfect love for one's neighbor (cf. Lk. 10:30–37).

He was deeply grieved by the suffering of the poor and needy. We can but marvel when we see how keen his eye, how open his hand and his heart were for all who were in want. "Seeing the multitude, he had compassion on them: because they were distressed, and lying like sheep that have no shepherd" (Mt. 9:36). For days at a time he preached in the desert without food or rest, without a thought that he was more in need of food and refreshment than his hearers. Yet he did not forget the hungry masses: "I have compassion on the multitudes, because they have not what to eat, and I will not send them away fasting, lest they faint in the way" (Mt. 15:32).

Then, again, he remembered the debtors, and especially those hopelessly imprisoned for debt (cf. Mt. 18:21 ff.). Their cry of distress and the cruel sentence of their judges rang painfully in his ears and became for him an eloquent illustration of sin and its misery, and even furnished him with a pathetic petition in the "Our Father": "Forgive us our debts, as we forgive our debtors" (Mt. 6:12).

The poor in general were the object of his affection. He called the poor blessed (cf. Lk. 6:21) and demanded of the rich that they become poor at least in spirit and by disposition (cf. Mt. 5:3). He came to preach the gospel to the poor (cf. Lk. 4:18). To the poor before all others he will apportion the kingdom of heaven (cf. Lk. 6:20; 14:13 ff.). The widow's mite was of greater value to him than the richest bounties (cf. Lk. 21:3 ff.). Whosoever gives to the poor lays up treasure in heaven (cf. Mt. 19:21). He placed almsgiving above the observance of all ritual regulations; indeed, he even suspended the latter in order to promote the former (cf. Lk. 11:38–41). He could not bear to see riches and poverty, luxury and want side by side. He pitied the rich, since many of them will be lost on account of their hardheartedness and greed: "Woe to the rich! It is easier for a camel to pass through the eye of a needle, than for a rich man to enter the kingdom of heaven" (Mt. 19:24). On the hardhearted wealthy reveler he pronounced the sentence of condemnation, while the poor Lazarus was made an heir of heaven for his privations (cf. Lk. 16:23 ff.). Yes, the poor Saviour, who himself had not where to lay his head, nevertheless gave alms from the little which was offered to him in charity (cf. Jn. 12:6, 8; 13:29).

He pities the sinners, the spiritually poor, more than those who suffer physical want. On this point there is a yawning gulf separating the Saviour from the official doctors of the law and their legally righteous followers. The sinners, foremost among whom were considered the fornicators and the publicans, or tax collectors, were either formally excommunicated, or at least regarded by public opinion as renegades. The strict Jew kept himself scrupulously aloof from them, because he regarded them as unclean and every sort of communication with them as defiling. Isolation, social outlawry, contempt, hostility, damnation for the sinners — that was the fundamental creed of Pharisaical justice and of a Pharisaically righteous manner of life.

Jesus, on the contrary, mingled with sinners and publicans, and summoned these as well as the rest of the people to a change of heart and invited them into the kingdom of God. He even proclaimed as the hitherto-unheard-of leading principle of his work, that the divine plan of salvation was directed first and above all to sinners; that he was not sent to quench the smoking flax and to break completely the bruised reed, but to raise up, to save, to redeem that which was lost.[18] "For God so loved the world, as to give his only begotten Son; that whosoever believeth in him, may not perish, but may have life everlasting. For God sent not his Son into the world, to judge the world, but that the world may be saved by him" (Jn. 3:16 f.). His sympathy for sinners and his kindness to them

---

[18] Cf. Mk. 2:17; Mt. 12:20; cf. Isa. 42:3.

went so far, in fact, that the words became almost proverbial and passed from mouth to mouth: "Behold, he is a friend of publicans and sinners!" (Mt. 11:19.)

Nothing more was needed to make him a stumbling block to every partisan of the scribes and Pharisees. His friendship and forgiving compassion for the publican Levi (cf. Mt. 9:9–13) and the chief of the publicans as well as "chief sinner" Zacheus (cf. Lk. 19:1–10); his eating with sinners and their coming in crowds to the discourses of the Master (cf. Lk. 15:1 ff.) evoked a veritable storm of Pharisaical indignation. Jesus reproved and admonished them with a reference to divine mercy: "Go then and learn what this meaneth, I will have mercy and not sacrifice. For I am not come to call the just, but sinners" (Mt. 9:13). The exercise of this divine mercy was the avowed aim of his life: "They that are whole need not the physician: but they that are sick. . . . The Son of man is come to seek and to save that which was lost" (Lk. 5:31; 19:10). His compassion for sinners reached its most sublime height in the touching parables of the strayed sheep and the lost coin. As the shepherd leaves the ninety-nine sheep and goes forth into the desert to seek the hundredth at the risk of his own life and to carry it back to the sheepfold on his shoulders, and as the poor woman seeks the lost coin for days and to her great, overflowing joy finds it again, so Jesus seeks and finds sinners. "I say to you, there shall be joy in heaven upon one sinner that doth penance, more than upon ninety-nine just, who need not penance. . . . So I say to you, there shall be joy before the angels of God upon one sinner doing penance" (Lk. 15:3–10).

Not even those sinners who have fallen the lowest are excluded from his mercy. On the contrary, they are the specially favored objects of his benevolence, his compassion, and his forgiving love. The sinful woman who anointed his feet in the house of the Pharisee and dried them with her hair, heard the consoling words: "Thy sins are forgiven thee. . . . Go in peace!" (Lk. 7:36–50.) The adulterous woman who was being led away

to be stoned, was saved by Jesus: "Go, and now sin no more!"
(Jn. 8:1-11.) In the parable of the prodigal son Jesus finally
describes the almost immeasurably exuberant joy of a father
who again finds his son after he had sunk to the lowest depths
of sin and shame (cf. Lk. 15:11-32). Thus Jesus does not
refuse his mercy even to him who has degraded himself shamefully and is abandoned by all as a hopeless outcast. As the misery
of sin grows and deepens, so also the boundless joy of the
divine Friend of sinners, as often as a prodigal son returns to
his heart.

He is moved to compassion for all who appeal to his kindness, or who are in need of his help. Closest to his heart are
indeed the poor and the despised, yet his benevolence embraces
also the rich and those of high rank. He instructed the illustrious
councilor Nicodemus with special solicitude (cf. Jn. 3:1 ff.);
he honored wealthy Pharisees as well as publicans by his presence; he granted the request of the chief of the synagogue,
Jairus, and of the centurion of Capharnaum; he showed deep
affection for the rich young man because he had inquired after
the way to eternal life (cf. Mk. 10:17-22). He is sent indeed
first of all to the children of the house of Israel, but he does not
confine his benevolence to those of his race or nation: with
great compassion he came to the aid of the sinful Samaritan
woman (cf. Jn. 4:7 ff.) and listened to the pleading of the
pagan Syro-Phoenician woman who begged for a miracle (cf.
Mt. 15:21-28). He had compassion for all his fellow men without distinction, that is, for every needy one whom he met (cf.
Lk. 10:30 ff.).

No doubt, at times Jesus rejected petitions (cf. Mk. 5:19;
Lk. 12:14); but at no time and to no person did he refuse a
plea for mercy and help. The limit of his compassion is solely
the limit of the need of it. All those who are oppressed and
who groan under a grievous burden are invited by him to
come to him and be refreshed and be relieved of their burden,
or to find at least alleviation (cf. Mt. 11:28-30). He designates
this compassionate assistance as the characteristic function of his

life: "The Spirit of the Lord is upon me, wherefore he hath anointed me to preach the gospel to the poor; he hath sent me to heal the contrite of heart, to preach deliverance to the captives, and sight to the blind, to set at liberty them that are bruised, to preach the acceptable year of the Lord, and the day of reward" (Lk. 4:18 f.). Everything in his life served this mission of mercy, all his strength, all his thought, prayer, and labor, his words, his hands (cf. Mt. 8:3; 20:34), even his spittle (cf. Jn. 9:6) and the hem of his garment (cf. Mt. 9:20).

Moreover, he impressed on his disciples the need of this all-surpassing compassion: "Be ye therefore merciful, as your Father also is merciful" (Lk. 6:36). The works of mercy will be a deciding factor at the judgment, for the merciful will hear the verdict from the lips of Jesus: "Come, ye blessed of my Father, possess you the kingdom prepared for you from the foundation of the world. For I was hungry, and you gave me to eat: I was thirsty, and you gave me to drink: I was a stranger, and you took me in: naked, and you covered me: sick, and you visited me: I was in prison, and you came to me. . . . Amen I say to you, as long as you did it to one of these my least brethren, you did it to me" (Mt. 25:34 ff.). The infinitely merciful Saviour accordingly puts himself in the position of suffering humanity; he feels all its sufferings as if they were his own; he accepts mercy shown to the poorest of his brethren as shown unto himself: "I was hungry, thirsty, a stranger, naked, sick, and in prison; and you have fed, given to drink, sheltered, clothed, and visited me." Even the mercy of God can go no further. Such compassion as that of Jesus the world will never be able to fathom.

3. HIS LOVE OF HIS FELLOW MAN. We have, however, said too little in speaking heretofore of the compassion of Jesus. The term "compassion" is not sufficiently comprehensive, since it does not express plainly enough the disposition and motive with which the divine Saviour exercised his merciful beneficence. The verb σπαλαγχνίζεσθαι, which the evangelists almost always use and which in this sense is not customary in

classical Greek or in the Old Testament, means much more than "he was moved to compassion," or "he had pity." It denotes commiserating with someone with every fiber of his being, with his whole heart and soul, out of purest goodness and deepest sentiment of love. A better expression than mere compassion would be: "he was deeply grieved" for those who were sorrowful and troubled, for the sick and the suffering, the poor, the needy, the sinners — for all the people.

Far from merely coming to their aid outwardly, his compassionate beneficence proceeds rather from heartfelt force of love and from the pain which love suffers at the sight of the misery of others. The motive of love is the source from which his beneficent deeds spring, and these bear at all times the character of love put into practice, of active charity, of compassion in the noblest sense of the word. Hence it is said of Jesus not merely that "he *did* good, he went about doing good" (Acts 10:38), but also that "he *was* good" (Jn. 7:12). It was "the goodness and kindness of God our Saviour" (Titus 3:4) which rendered his life a continuous, well-nigh unbroken chain of good deeds. Wherever we come in contact with the mighty deeds of the Lord, we actually feel the warmth of this living and life-giving love. There is not an instance when he rendered assistance in which we fail to sense the pulsation of loving affection. Love is the secret and the solution of his humble patience and of his compassionate beneficence. His life is simply the embodiment of love, an uninterrupted flaming and glowing of that fire of love which consumes him. On a thousand occasions the flames of this hidden fire burst forth from his heart as from a sun. The whole gospel becomes, as St. Paul says, the manifestation of "the goodness and kindness of God our Saviour."

At the Last Supper, however, during his last loving discourse, this sun breaks through the gathering clouds and reveals its infinite beauty and warmth (cf. Jn. chaps. 15–17). Love to the end, thus John inscribes the account of that love feast: "Before the festival day of the pasch, Jesus knowing that his hour was come, that he should pass out of this world to the

Father, having loved his own who were in the world, he loved them unto the end" (Jn. 13:1).

In that one small, but mighty word "love" the evangelist sums up all that the Lord said and did on that evening; in that one word he gives us the key to the mysteries of the Last Supper. All of it forms the last and supreme proof of love, which the Lord had reserved for this evening, and which "with desire he had desired" to give (Lk. 22:15) when the approach of the hour of supreme sacrifice had made his heart beat with a mightier pulse. Love moved him to celebrate this quiet, sacred family feast; love was the soul of the humble act of washing his disciples' feet; love above all was the soul of that most holy institution which was introduced by this act — the institution of the Pasch of the New Covenant. . . . Love, too, is the only speaker on that evening. It bids farewell to the disciples in the most touching manner, and after it had enjoined everything upon them, and had comforted, encouraged and strengthened them in the faith, it folds its hands and addresses to the Father in heaven its evening orison and death prayer. Love draws the curtain before the dark future in which loving ones are to be separated; grim death approaches, murder lurks in waiting, weakness denies and flees: love points upward to the glory of heaven with the Father, to the glory of an eternal re-union. In short, love is the fragrant sentiment which pervades all the acts and words, all the comfort and sorrow and anguish of this evening.[19]

The commandment of love, which is the ever enduring glow of the fire of love emanating from Jesus, is characterized by the Saviour himself as the end and aim of all that he has brought to mankind and enjoined upon it: "This is my commandment . . . these things I command you, that you love one another. . . . A new commandment I give unto you: That you love one another, as I have loved you, that you also love one another" (Jn. 15:12, 17; 13:34).[20]

If we consider the qualities of this love of Jesus, we are impressed by the astounding warmth and tenderness with which

[19] Paul Keppler, *Unseres Herrn Trost*, Freiburg, 1887, 1 f.

[20] Concerning the last discourse, see Ricciotti, *The Life of Christ*, §§ 580–585; F. Prat, *Jesus Christ*, II, 278–298; Fouard, *Christ the Son of God*, II, 237–257.

he loved both friend and foe, the just and the sinners, in short, all mankind.

He condescended to the lowliest, and endeavored to bring joy to the least of men. He loved children, and caressed them with such fondness that all crowded around him (cf. Mt. 19:14; Mk. 10:16). He folded them in his arms, blessed them and uttered those wonderful words which have become the inspiration for the love of children: "Whosoever shall receive one such child as this in my name, receiveth me; and whosoever shall receive me, receiveth not me, but him that sent me" (Mk. 9:36 f.). The purest and heartiest affection of friendship united him to the brother and sisters, Lazarus, Martha, and Mary, of Bethania (cf. Jn. 11:1 ff.), and also to his disciples (cf. Jn. 15:15). He received even the traitor with the word "Friend!" and with the kiss of a friend (cf. Mt. 26:50), and regarded all who believe in him as his "brothers" (cf. Jn. 20:17). He called the unknown paralytic "son" and the woman with an issue of blood "daughter" (cf. Mt. 9:2, 22). He shed tears of compassion over the ungrateful city of Jerusalem which delivered him to death, and with an aching heart he bewailed its present blindness and its future destruction: "Jerusalem, Jerusalem, that killest the prophets, and stonest them that are sent to thee, how often would I have gathered thy children as the bird doth her brood under her wings, and thou wouldst not! . . . If thou also hadst known, and that in this thy day, the things that are to thy peace!" (Lk. 13:34; 19:42.) Forgetful of his own frightful anguish, he said to the women who wept over him on the way to Calvary: "Weep not over me, but weep for yourselves and for your children!" (Lk. 23:28.)

The hours of martyrdom on the cross are a revelation of such tender love that we cannot but be carried away with deep emotion. At his feet, in unutterable grief, he beheld his own mother and the disciple John, whom he loved above all others, and he bequeathed to them the dearest and the last which remained at his disposal: "Behold thy son!" he said to Mary, and to the disciple: "Behold thy mother!" (Jn. 19:26.) He heard the death rattle of the thief crucified with him and gave him the sweetly comforting assurance: "This day thou shalt be with me in paradise!" (Lk. 23:43.) He heard round about him the blasphemies of the mockers, who a few hours before had cried: "Crucify him, crucify him!" and who now sought to satisfy their devilish hatred by their ribald jeers, and he used his last moments for a word and a deed of the most tender love, for a forgiving plea for pardon (cf. Lk. 23:24).

Yet, despite all this warmth and tenderness, the love of Jesus is never weak and sentimental, but strong and forceful, and, when necessary, even relentless to the point of an unyielding demand: "If any man . . . hate not his father, and mother, and wife, and children, and brethren, and sisters, yea and his own life also, he cannot be my disciple" (Lk. 14:26). The sole consideration and the sole motive of his love is the welfare, not only the eternal but also the temporal, of those whom he loves. That is indeed the most sublime and divine thing about his love: he has elevated and ennobled it to the purest loving benevolence, to disinterested, unselfish devotion, to heroic self-sacrifice for mankind.

Natural love can never rid itself entirely of self-interest and self-seeking. It loves because it derives enjoyment and gratification in the object loved, or, at all events, because it hopes for a return of love and gratitude. Jesus loves solely for the sake of loving, of doing good. He seeks to become the eye for the blind, the ear for the deaf, the cry for help on the lips of those whose tongue is bound. He seeks to radiate love even where there is no prospect either of thanks or reward: "If you lend to them of whom you hope to receive, what thanks are to you? For sinners also lend to sinners, for to receive as much" (Lk. 6:34). In a thousand ways and by countless sacrifices he seeks to meet our needs and to serve us (Mt. 20:28), to spend himself and to despoil himself for us (cf. Phil. 2:7).

Whoever reads the gospels is filled with awe at the revelation of this most unselfish love in the life of the Saviour. Even the bitterest enemies of Jesus, the high priests and the scribes, standing beneath the cross, acknowledged his complete sacrifice of self, albeit unwillingly: "He saved others, himself he cannot save!" (Mt. 27:42.) The beloved disciple and evangelist, however, stood overwhelmed at the feet of the Crucified on Calvary, and with tear-dimmed eyes repeated the words of the Master: "God so loved the world, as to give his only-begotten Son" (Jn. 3:16).

To us he gave the great commandment that we should love our neighbor as ourselves; he, however, loved us more than he loved himself: he "loved me, and delivered himself for me" (Gal. 2:20). He demands of us only that we should follow his precepts in order to assure ourselves of his love and friendship; yet he wished to gain our friendship at the price of his own most heroic love: "Greater love than this no man hath, that a man lay down his life for his friends" (Jn. 15:13). To us he gave the admonition that we should love one another as brothers (cf. Mt. 23:8); but his love to us is like that of a mother, a love greater than which there is none among mortals, and which is itself the counterpart of the love of God for man (cf. Isa. 49:15; Mt. 23:37). Jesus, finally, declared that his love for us is like that love which he has for the Father and which the Father has for him: "As the Father hath loved me, I also have loved you; abide in my love!" (Jn. 15:9.)

This alone makes the unexampled love of Jesus toward us comprehensible: the love of Jesus is the love of the Son of God; it flows out from the heart of the Father, pours itself into the heart of the Son, and overflows thence upon humanity. Its primary source, its fountainhead, is the love of the Saviour for God the Father.

Chapter 9. The Relation of Jesus to the Father

WHEN we consider the relation of Jesus to his heavenly Father we enter into the innermost sanctuary of his personal holiness. This relation can be summed up in three considerations: the love of Jesus for the Father, his self-surrender to the Father, and his communion with the Father in prayer.

I. THE LOVE OF JESUS TO THE FATHER. The love of Jesus for humanity not only flows out from God, but also streams back again to God. He loves men out of love for his Father in heaven. He loves them because God loves them as his children (cf. Mt. 5:45). He ministers to them and works his miracles in their behalf in order "that the works of God should be made manifest" in them (cf. Jn. 9:3), that through them God "may be glorified" (cf. Jn. 11:4), that they might praise God (cf. Mk. 2:12). He loves them all and sacrifices himself for all, in order that he might gain them all for God and lead them all to God (cf. Mt. 18:11; Mk. 10:45).

Herein lies the exalted sublimity and the unique character of the love of Jesus for mankind. Even Friedrich Nietzsche felt this:

> To love man out of love to God — that has been until now the noblest and almost unattainable sentiment which has been reached among men. That the love for human beings, if it lacks some sort of sanctifying purpose, is just one more act of stupidity and bestiality, that the inclination to this love for mankind has first to receive from a higher inclination its measure, its refinement, its grain of salt and its particle of amber — whoever it

was who first felt and "experienced" this, no matter how his tongue may have stumbled when it attempted to express such a tender sentiment, he shall remain for us sacred and venerable for all time.[1]

It is only because Christ raised the love for man to this celestial height of the love of God that it became possible to place the second commandment of love directly beside the first and to merge both into one. It is only because he loves the heavenly Father in every child of this earth that he could say: "The first commandment of all is: Thou shalt love the Lord thy God with thy whole heart, and with thy whole soul, and with thy whole mind, and with thy whole strength. This is the first commandment. And the second is like to this: Thou shalt love thy neighbor as thyself" (cf. Mt. 22:37–40; Mk. 12:29–32). It is only because he does good unto men for the love of God that he could declare: "All things therefore whatsoever you would that men should do to you, do you also to them. For this is the law and the prophets" (Mt. 7:12). It is only because he makes service to men a service to God that he could put the love of one's neighbor above the observance of the Sabbath, mercy above sacrifice in the temple, almsgiving and readiness to help above ritual regulations.[2] Love for God and love for fellow man, which otherwise stand side by side, are merged by Jesus into one. These two poles of his nature are in reality its axis. His boundless compassion with humanity, his beneficence which knows neither measure nor restriction, his entire life, full of the most comprehensive, the most tender and most unselfish charity, his whole association with mankind — all this becomes a sublime monument, visible to all the world, of the love of Jesus for the Father in heaven.

His conduct toward unconscious creation likewise breathes the spirit of the love of God and is diffused throughout with it. He cannot turn his gaze upon the wonders of nature without

---

[1] *Jenseits von Gut und Böse.*
[2] Cf. Mt. 9:13; 12:9–14; 15:2–11; 23:23–25; Mk. 2:27 f.; Lk. 6:5–11; 14:1–6.

having his thoughts soar to the Father in heaven and his heart vibrate with the sweetest harmonies of love. The least and commonest objects and phenomena of nature evoke in him the most tender sentiments of admiration for the providence of the heavenly Father, and become the advocates of trust in God and attachment to God.

He beheld the sower cultivating his field, and the seed as well as the grain of mustard became for him symbols of the kingdom of God: "So is the kingdom of God, as if a man should cast seed into the earth. . . . To what shall we liken the kingdom of God? It is as a grain of mustard seed . . . it groweth up, and becometh greater than all herbs, and shooteth out great branches, so that the birds of the air may dwell under the shadow thereof" (Mk. 4:26, 30 ff.). He observed the song birds in the air, the flowers in the field, and his heart swelled with grateful love for the Father in heaven who provides for all: "Are not five sparrows sold for two farthings, and not one of them is forgotten before God? Yea, the very hairs of your head are numbered. Fear not therefore: you are of more value than many sparrows" (Lk. 12:6 f.). "Behold the birds of the air, for they neither sow, nor do they reap, nor gather into barns: and your heavenly Father feedeth them. Are not you of much more value than they? . . . Consider the lilies of the field, how they grow: they labour not, neither do they spin. But I say to you, that not even Solomon in all his glory was arrayed as one of these. And if the grass of the field, which is to-day, and to-morrow is cast into the oven, God doth so clothe: how much more you, O ye of little faith!" (Mt. 6:26 ff.)

Jesus admired the flood of sunlight which pours itself in a golden sheen over the world, the rain which refreshes the earth, and they became to him symbols and eloquent witnesses of the love and goodness of the Father: "But I say to you . . . that you may be the children of your Father who is in heaven, who maketh his sun to rise upon the good and bad, and raineth upon the just and unjust. . . . Be you therefore perfect, as also your heavenly Father is perfect!" (Mt. 5:44 f., 48.) Jesus regards all creatures who serve God and love him as his brothers and sisters: "Whosoever shall do the will of my Father that is in heaven, he is my brother, and sister, and mother" (Mt. 12:50). All creatures are to him the children of the fatherly love of God; he beholds them all clothed in the magic light of his love for God.

Like his relation to nature and his love for mankind, so also is his whole interior life pure love for God, joy in God, intimacy with God, and happiness in God. It is true, the commandment to love God with one's whole soul, whole mind, and with all one's strength, was not first proclaimed by him. Not even the name of God as "Father," in which this love is expressed with greatest tenderness, was new.[3] Yet in the Old Testament the fear of Jahweh was especially stressed, and in the synagogue the servile observance of the Law replaced love to such an extent that the rabbis hardly dared to utter the name of the Most High. Jesus, however, knows, demands, and exercises only a childlike feeling toward God — the purest and the most intimate heartfelt love for the Father in heaven.

The Father in heaven, his Father! No name was so often on his lips as the sweet name: "My Father, your Father, our Father!" Never has this name been spoken so tenderly, so trustfully, so reverentially, and so lovingly, as by Jesus. At times it became for him the collective name of the thousand-fold revelation of the love of God: the Father who loves us all (cf. Jn. 16:27); the Father who cares for all; the Father who listens to our most secret pleas; the Father to whom our most hidden needs are known; the Father who rewards the most insignificant act of charity; the Father who enlightens all, and reveals himself to the smallest and humblest (cf. Mt. 6:6, 8, 18, 25 ff.; 11:25); the Father who gives for us his most dearly beloved and only begotten Son, that we may not perish; the Father who sends us the Holy Ghost, the Comforter, the Spirit of truth and love, that he may remain with us forever (cf. Jn.

---

[3] Cf. 2 Kings 7:14; Ps. 88:27; Book of Jubilees 1, 25; Sotah 9, 15.

3:16; 14:16 f.). It is always boundless love which is associated with the name "Father."

Furthermore, whenever he portrayed God in parables he usually described love. Wherever the human love of a father shone forth brightly, it became a symbol and a reflection of the fatherly love of God. The owner of the vineyard, who from the dawn of day until the eleventh hour goes out to hire the idle, and pays to the last the same as to the first from pure benevolence (Mt. 20:1–16); the king who invites to the marriage feast of his son the blind, the halt, the cripples and beggars from the streets (Mt. 22:2–10); the creditor who remits the enormous debt of ten thousand talents in favor of the debtor servant (Mt. 18:23 ff.); the compassionate father, who does not cast out the unworthy son, sunk into disgrace and vice, but presses him to his heart with touching love (Lk. 15:11–32) — all these are symbols of the fatherly love of God for us. With such rich and glowing colors does Jesus depict the greatness, the goodness, and love of his Father in heaven, that the disciples were aflame with the ardor of desire to see him, and wished for nothing else: "Lord, show us the Father, and it is enough for us" (Jn. 14:8).

Such spontaneous enthusiasm could be evoked by Jesus in his disciples only because his own heart and his own words were wholly possessed by the love for the Father. He was drawn with irresistible force to the place where his Father dwells, the temple, and where his Father is the subject of discussion: "I must be about my Father's business!" (Lk. 2:49.) He worked, lived and breathed in the unity of love and essence with the Father: "I am in the Father, and the Father in me" (Jn. 14:11). In joy and in sorrow, in hours of devotion and of labor, from earliest youth to the days of his greatest successes, his only comfort and his sole delight was in the thought of his heavenly Father. Having come to the evening before his death, all the fibers of his heart thrilled with the blissful thought: "I go to the Father! . . . Father, the hour is come! . . . Holy Father, now I come to thee!" (Jn. 16:16; 17:1, 11, 13.) His last words on the cross were an outcry of love for the Father: "Father, into thy hands I commend my spirit!" (Lk. 23:46.)

2. HIS SELF-SURRENDER TO THE FATHER. The love of Jesus for the Father was not restricted to sentiments of joy and intimate communing. On the contrary, to this sentiment of love was added action motivated by love: the resolute self-surrender to the Father, willingness and readiness for every sacrifice.

There is no doubt but that the complete surrender to the divine will is the supreme law of moral conduct and the infallible standard of holiness on the part of a creature. It brings the entire man into the service of the Most High and makes the greatest demands on the heroism of love. For this reason it is at the same time the most difficult duty imposed on man.

This difficulty was by no means lessened in the case of Jesus; on the contrary, it was heightened for him in proportion to his superiority over mankind. The consciousness of his supernatural mission as Messias, of his divine sonship and true divinity must have made that dependence and zealous service, humanly speaking, immensely difficult for the Saviour. He was God-Man and God-Messias, and yet there was the self-abasement and the submission of the creature under God! What sublimity, on the one hand, and what abysmal depth on the other! Yet Jesus bridged the chasm, and united to his Messianic consciousness such a complete surrender to the will of the Father as had never before been accomplished by a creature.

It was a surrender to the will of the Father with every particle of his strength, an unreserved, unwearied, most zealous surrender. The will of the Father, as it concerned him, was that he establish and extend the kingdom of heaven. This lifework was bound up with the very being of Jesus, and was laid upon him directly by the Father. That was sufficient to make it the basic thought and sole purpose of his whole life. Everything was directed to the one thing — the fulfillment of the will of the Father in obedience and with love.

And with what enthusiasm and fervent zeal! Words, deeds,

prayers, his whole life, everything in him was directed by him
to that supreme ideal and sole ideal: to proclaim the kingdom
of heaven, to gain souls for the kingdom of heaven, to increase
the honor of his Father in the kingdom of heaven.[4] He sought
to inflame everyone with fervor to work with him in the vineyard of the Father.[5] To all he gave the admonition: "Let your
light shine before men, that they may see your good works, and
glorify your Father who is in heaven" (Mt. 5:16). He himself
lights up the way as the sun of truth and holiness, which comes
from heaven and shows the way to the Father.[6] Indefatigable
in his Messianic activity, he knew no relaxing, no trifling, no
occupying himself with unimportant matters: "I must work
the works of him that sent me, whilst it is day: the night
cometh, when no man can work" (Jn. 9:4). In one word, the
fulfillment of the will of the Father is the very essence of his
life and its sole purpose: "My meat is to do the will of him that
sent me, that I may perfect his work" (Jn. 4:34).

His surrender to the will of the Father is one of absolute
conformity. How inscrutable were not the ways of God with the
Redeemer of the world, often how complicated and devious,
how apparently ill-suited to lead to the appointed goal! Why
did he spend almost all his years in the isolation and solitude of
Nazareth, when he was, nevertheless, to advance the kingdom
of God to world-supremacy? Why did even his public activity
take place for the most part in Galilee — small and despised
Galilee? Why not in Jerusalem, in Athens, in Rome, the
centers of Jewish and Roman culture? Why did he choose for his
disciples and ambassadors fishermen and publicans, insignificant
men of no social standing, and not the great, the educated, the
princes and leaders of the people and of the synagogue, on
whose influence the success of his work apparently would
depend? Why did he not, with his apostles, make a conquest
of the courts, of the schools of philosophers, of the higher and

---

[4] Cf. Mt. 9:8; 15:31; Lk. 5:25; 7:16; 8:39; 13:13; 17:15, 18; 18:43.
[5] Cf. Mt. 9:37 f.; 10:7 f., 27; 20:1–16; 21:28–33; 25:14–30; Lk. 17:7, 10.
[6] Cf. Jn. 8:12; 9:5; 12:46.

most powerful social circles? Why are these and many other problems to be found in his Messianic career?

Such problems, however, did not exist for Jesus. To all these questions he had but one answer: obedience, submission to the will of him that sent him. Again and again he put forth the will of his Father as the sole authoritative rule of conduct of his life.[7] The majestic justification of his entire conduct lies in the utterance which may be called his motto: "I do always the things that please [the Father]" (Jn. 8:29).

He chose a little corner of the earth for the scene of his preaching, because the Father had sent him to the lost sheep of the house of Israel (Mt. 15:24). He called illiterate and insignificant men to be the pillars of God's kingdom because the Father had chosen them to be his instruments: "I confess to thee, O Father, Lord of heaven and earth, because thou hast hid these things from the wise and prudent, and hast revealed them to little ones. Yea, Father, for so it hath seemed good in thy sight" (Mt. 11:25 f.). He was concerned about the least and the lowliest, before all others, because their salvation was the special care and the express command of the Father: "It is not the will of your Father, who is in heaven, that one of these littles ones should perish" (Mt. 18:14). He devoted himself to the most debased sinner and the most disreputable publican, because the Father sent them to him: "All that the Father giveth to me shall come to me; and him that cometh to me, I will not cast out. Because I came down from heaven, not to do my own will, but the will of him that sent me" (Jn. 6:37 f.).

Not even one word from his mouth, not one thought, not one beat of his heart was without the will of his Father: "I cannot of myself do anything . . . because I seek not my own will, but the will of him that sent me" (Jn. 5:30). "I do nothing of myself, but as the Father had taught me, these things I speak" (Jn. 8:28). His gaze was fixed steadily on what he saw the Father do (cf. Jn. 5:19). Nowhere in his whole life do we

---

[7] Cf. Jn. 3:17; 4:34; 5:23, 30, 37 f.; 7:16–18, 28, etc.

perceive an opposition to the will of the Father, or even a strained relation between his will and that of the Father. The harmony is so pure, the conformity so perfect, that not one iota of that which the Father had decreed for him and revealed about him was to remain unfulfilled.[8]

His surrender to the Father was also one of complete sacrifice of self. The voluntary acceptance of the Messianic mission from the hand of the Father meant essentially a life of sacrifice in poverty, lowliness, ignominy, and pain, as well as the most cruel death of expiation for the redemption of mankind. It was with a pen dipped in blood that God had written down the destiny of the "Servant of God" in the documents of revelation.[9] With a keen eye and a trembling heart Jesus had read these decrees of the Father regarding himself. With the clearness of the noonday sun they stood constantly before his mind.[10] They lay like an oppressive weight on the most solemn and joyous moments of his life.[11] And as the frightful end drew near, what a humanly real and divinely grand conflict raged in his soul! His pulse raced; his temples became hot with fever; from all the pores of his body the anguished blood oozed; his soul was sorrowful even unto death, and his heart burst forth in the thrice-repeated, overwhelmingly touching cry of distress to the Father: "My Father, if it be possible, let this chalice pass from me. Nevertheless, not as I will, but as thou wilt. . . . My Father, if this chalice may not pass away, but I must drink it, thy will be done. . . . Abba, Father, all things are possible to thee: remove this chalice from me; but not what I will, but what thou wilt" (Mt. 26:38-42; Mk. 14:34-36).

But there was no conflict between his will and that of the Father. From the first he had submitted willingly and with childlike resignation to the Father: "Go behind me, Satan,

---

[8] Cf. Mt. 3:15; 26:54; 27:9, 35; Mk. 14:49; 15:28; Lk. 18:31; 21:22; 22:37; 24:44; Jn. 13:18; 17:12; 19:24, 36.

[9] Cf. Ps. 21 and 68; Isa. 42:1-16; 49:1-9; 50:4-10; 52:13; 53:12; 61:1 f.

[10] Cf. Mt. 8:17; 17:2 f.; 20:18 f., 28; 26:54, 56; 27:35; Mk. 9:30; Lk. 9:44; 12:50; 18:31; Jn. 18:32.

[11] Cf. Mt. 16:21-23; Mk. 8:31 ff.

thou art a scandal unto me" (Mt. 16:23), he cried to the well-meaning Peter, who wished to spare him the cup of anguish. With full consciousness of what awaited him and yet with inward exaltation he set out for Jerusalem to meet his death.[12] The conflict on the Mount of Olives was fought only between the lower nature of man, which naturally shrank back from suffering, and the higher nature, which was ready to go forth to death with full consent and resolute self-denial. "The spirit indeed is willing, but the flesh is weak. . . . Father, not as I will, but as thou wilt! Not my will, but thine be done!"[13]

Then he drained the chalice of sufferings to the dregs. Not a word of complaint escaped the sufferer on the cross. One thing alone oppressed him with an unbearable weight — that he was forced to renounce even the feeling of loving union with the Father: "My God, my God, why hast thou forsaken me?" (Mt. 27:46.) Yet he denied himself by accepting even this most bitter and extreme suffering, and placed the seal upon his service of God by the most perfect self-renunciation. He bowed his head in death only after he had avowed before heaven and earth that the will of the Father had been completely fulfilled and the sacrifice demanded of him wholly made (Jn. 19:28, 30).

Self-surrender can go no further. Jesus manifested such a singular moral union with God that everything points to his physical unity of essence with the Father. Everything resolves itself into his own divine-human attestation regarding himself: "I and the Father are one" (Jn. 10:30).

3. HIS COMMUNION WITH THE FATHER IN PRAYER. If we turn our attention to Jesus at prayer this impression is confirmed and deepened. The perfection of his own personal character, his conduct toward his fellow men, his love for the Father and his surrender to the Father in all the situations of life receive their fitting conclusion and become entirely comprehensible only in the light of that inward com-

---

[12] Cf. Mt. 20:17–20; Mk. 10:32–34; Lk. 18:31–34.
[13] Mt. 26:39; Mk. 14:32–36; Lk. 22:42–46.

munion with God, which is best designated as his life of prayer. His was truly a life of prayer, a life in prayer, a life springing from prayer — in fact, the whole life of the Saviour was a living prayer. The evangelists hardly dare to lift the veil from this most tender mystery; by only a span's breadth do they uncover the root of this divine-human manifestation. Communion with the Most High in prayer is in itself something so sacredly secret that it naturally remains as far as possible a thing between God and the one who prays. And yet, from the little which we learn of the praying of Jesus, we receive an overpowering impression. Nowhere in the history of the world do we meet a man who prayed so much and so perfectly as Jesus.

JESUS PRAYED MUCH.

And rising very early, going out, he went into a desert place: and there he prayed (Mk. 1:35).

And having dismissed the multitude, he went into a mountain alone to pray (Mt. 14:23).

And he retired into the desert, and prayed (Lk. 5:16).

And it came to pass in those days, that he went out into a mountain to pray, and he passed the whole night in the prayer of God (Lk. 6:12).

And it came to pass about eight days after these words, that he took Peter, and James, and John, and went up into a mountain to pray (Lk. 9:28).

And going out, he went, according to his custom, to the mount of Olives. And his disciples also followed him. And when he was come to the place, he said to them: Pray, lest ye enter into temptation. And he was withdrawn away from them a stone's cast; and kneeling down, he prayed (Lk. 22:39-41).

These are but a few occasional glimpses which the gospel gives us of Jesus at prayer. Prayer is the soul of his Messianic activity. "It incorporates itself with this activity as a spring, which by its tension continually brings new impetus and force into motion."[14] All important acts related to the work of redemption are set by Jesus in a framework of prayer: He prayed at

---

[14] Grimm, *Leben Jesu*, II, Regensburg, 1909, 589.

his entry into the world (Hebr. 10:5 ff.), as a twelve-year-old
boy in the temple, at his baptism (Lk. 3:21), before choosing
his apostles (6:12), before the promise of the primacy (9:18),
at his transfiguration (9:29), after the miracle of the loaves
(Mt. 14:23; Mk. 6:46), at the institution of the Eucharist (Mt.
26:26 f., *et al.*), after the Last Supper (Mt. 26:30; Jn. 17),
in the agony of Gethsemani (Mt. 26:39–44, *et al.*), during
his hours of anguish on the cross (Mt. 27:46; Mk. 15:34) and
at the moment of his death (Mt. 27:50, *et al.*), after his
resurrection (Lk. 24:30), and at his ascension (Lk. 24:50 f.).
/ He admonished all whom he met to pray (Mt. 6:5 f.); he
taught all how to pray (Lk. 11:1 ff.) and he himself prayed
for all: for the children (Mt. 19:13, 15, *et al.*), for the sick
(Mk. 7:34), for Peter (Lk. 22:31 f.), for the disciples and the
faithful of all places and all times (Jn. 17), and even for his
executioners (Lk. 23:34). All the results of his activity, all
proofs of divine love called forth fervent prayers to the
Father (Mt. 11:25 f., *et al.*). Every step he took is marked
by him with prayer. In Nazareth and Capharnaum, as well as
in Jerusalem, he selected favorite places for prayer. He prayed
in the quiet chamber (Mt. 6:6), in the desert secluded from
the world, in the temple, in solitary gardens, on the hills of
Galilee and Judea. The earliest hours of dawn (Mk. 1:35), as
well as the approaching twilight of evening (Mt. 14:23; Mk.
6:46) saw him at prayer, and after he had wearied himself
by laboring all day long for the people, he often passed the
whole night without sleep in prayerful communion with the
Father (Lk. 6:12; 21:37; Jn. 8:1; 18:2).

He thus fulfilled most perfectly and literally the precept
which he gave to us: "We ought always to pray, and not to
faint" (Lk. 18:1). Nothing could draw him away from this
secret communion with his Father; nothing could interrupt his
intimate association with his God in life and in prayer. On
the contrary, he compelled everything, even the most distracting
and mundane affairs, to come under the spell of this divine
atmosphere. Everything was referred by him to God, everything

became a service of God. This concentration of thought on the Most High was without interruption and absorbed him entirely and exclusively. His life was wholly taken up by his piety; it was a continuous prayer, a ceaseless adoration of the Father.

JESUS PRAYED PERFECTLY.

His communion with God in prayer assumed the closest and most intimate form imaginable. Far from merely entering into a closer relation with God, prayer with him became a child-like recognition of God as his Father, a touching communing of the child on earth with its Father in heaven. It is precisely here that we first become aware of the immense difference between Jesus praying to his Father and humanity as it prayed before his coming. Though the name of God as "Father" was nothing new, yet men were neither fully conscious of their relation to God as his children, nor dared to pray to him as children. For them the Father in heaven was only the Most High God, who created the world, and who was enthroned above his creation in the remote realms of heaven. Among the ancient Indo-Germanic, Hamitic, and Mongolian civilized peoples, as well as among the Semitic Assyrians, Babylonians, Arabs, Arameans, Sabeans, and Hebrews, the worship of God and prayer to him bore this character exclusively. Even the Old Testament[15] and the "Eighteen Prayers" (*Schmone Esre*) of the Rabbis, in use among the Jews at the time of Christ, give to God the name of "Father" only in this sense.[16]

According to prophecy, the Messias was to be the first to address God as the Father (Ps. 88:27). "It remains an established fact, despite the occasional pre-Christian use of the name Father, that Jesus by this form of address first clearly expressed the real relation of his own person and that of his followers

---

[15] Cf. Deut. 32:6; Job 38:28 f.; Isa. 1:2, etc.

[16] For the text, see Schürer, *Geschichte des jüdischen Volkes im Zeitalter Jesu Christi*, Leipzig, 1898, II, 461 f., English ed., *A History of the Jewish People* (New York: Scribner's Sons), Vol. II, 83 ff. The final edition of the *Schmone Esre* in which God is twice called "Father" dates from a post-Christian period.

to God."[17] The prayer of Jesus to the Father made such an
overpowering impression on primitive Christendom that for
generations among the Greek and Jewish Christians, in Jerusalem as well as in Asia Minor and Rome, the invocation used
by Christ: "Abba, Father!" was retained in its original, Aramaic
form.[18] Paul, a pupil of the Pharisees, who reports this, at
the same time adduces the reason why Christ first prayed to
the Father and why we also can pray to the Father only in
Christ: "God hath sent the Spirit of his Son into your hearts,
crying: Abba, Father" (Gal. 4:6). "You have received the spirit
of adoption of sons, whereby we cry: Abba [Father]" (Rom.
8:15). Jesus alone was the only-begotten Son of God, and
through him alone have we become partakers of the sonship
of God. He alone and his followers with him and through him
can pray thus to the Father.

For this reason all the prayers of Jesus Christ began with
the invocation of the Father. Even when he uttered Old
Testament prayers from the Psalms, he prefaced them with
the name "Father."[19] He teaches us also to pray in no other
way to the Father: "Thus therefore shall you pray: Our Father,
who art in heaven" (Mt. 6:9). A child's cry to the Father —
that is the theme and the basic sentiment of Christ's praying.
And with what harmonious purity and fullness, with what depth
and tenderness, with what trustfulness and reverence does
this basic feeling pervade his whole life of prayer!

Whether his prayer was a jubilant hymn, a joyful cry and
exaltation of the heart in God (cf. Mt. 11:25; Lk. 10:21);
whether it rose to heaven in fervent sentiments of gratitude
and expressions of utmost confidence (cf. Jn. 11:41); whether
it accompanied his wondrous works as a suppliant plea (cf. Mt.
15:36, et al.), or wrested itself from his soul as a cry of distress

---

[17] Ed. v. d. Goltz, Das Gebet in der ältesten Christenheit, Leipzig, 1901, 12.
[18] Cf. Mk. 1:36; Rom. 8:15; Gal. 4:6. Cf. Margreth, Das Gebetsleben Jesu
Christi, des Sohnes Gottes, Münster, 1902, 117 f.
[19] Cf. Lk. 23:46; Ps. 30:6.

in the darkest night of anguish (cf. 26:39–44, *et al.*); whether it was a prayer for his own and his Father's glorification (cf. Jn. 12:28), or his own death prayer (cf. Lk. 23:46), it was always permeated with the most childlike sentiment toward the Father, full of attachment, love, humility, and admiration.

When he taught his disciples how to pray, everything likewise pointed to the same spirit of childlike simplicity, submission, fervor, and trustfulness toward the Father in heaven: "When ye pray, you shall not be as the hypocrites, that love to stand and pray in the synagogues and corners of the streets, that they may be seen by men. . . . But thou when thou shalt pray, enter into thy chamber, and having shut the door, pray to thy Father in secret. . . . And when you are praying, speak not much, as the heathens. For they think that in their much speaking they may be heard. Be not you therefore like to them, for your Father knoweth what is needful for you, before you ask him" (Mt. 6:5–8). The "Lord's Prayer," which follows this exhortation, is the unsurpassed and unsurpassable model of prayer, in which all prayerful communion of men with the heavenly Father will for all time reach its highest expression.

It was surpassed only by the high-priestly prayer which Jesus himself addressed to the Father, and which no one except himself could address to the Father (cf. Jn. 17). It unveils for us the most secret and holiest mysteries of such a sublime spirit of prayer that it is comprehensible only in him who invokes the heavenly Father not only as a child of man, but as the true Son of God. In this discourse the human communing with the Father in prayer rises upward into the divine relationship of essential unity with the Father: "Father, glorify thy Son, that thy Son may glorify thee! . . . Glorify thou me, O Father, with thyself, with the glory which I had, before the world was, with thee. . . . They have known in very deed that I came out from thee. . . . All my things are thine, and thine are mine. . . . Holy Father, keep them in thy name whom thou hast given me; that they may be one, as we also are . . . that they all may be one, as thou, Father, in me, and I in thee. . . .

Father, I will that where I am, they also whom thou hast given me may be with me; that they may see my glory which thou hast given me, because thou hast loved me before the creation of the world."[20]

In the three foregoing chapters we have sought to represent Jesus as the model of virtue. Whether we consider the inner life of the Saviour in the perfection of his personal virtues, or observe him in his conduct toward his fellow men, or admire him in his relations to the Father in heaven — everywhere we meet with the same most sublime holiness, which throughout bears the stamp of superhuman quality. Not superhuman in the sense that the virtue of Jesus was not fully and genuinely human. On the contrary, we have remonstrated step by step that the personality of the Saviour is wholly rooted and grounded in humanity, and that it everywhere presents the most flourishing and fruitful development of human greatness of character. However, in no phase can it be explained entirely as being merely the evolution of a human being. The summits of the separate virtues of Jesus tower always far above the merely human and the created and reach up into the lofty realm of the divine. Such a passionate love for truth and such truthfulness emanate from him that he is justified in saying: "I am the Truth" Itself — eternal, uncreated, unclouded Truth. Such energy and fortitude ennoble him that even Rousseau exclaims in admiration: "The life and death of Jesus are indeed those of a God!" His humility and gentleness surpass all human conception; his compassion and love are the reflection of that divine mercy and power of love which are inherent in the Creator of all creatures. His love for the Father, his self-surrender to the Father, his communion in prayer with him, compel us with decisive finality to confess with Peter: "Thou art Christ, the Son of the living God!"

---

[20] Jn. 17. Regarding the relation of Jesus to the Father, see K. Adam, *The Son of God*, 134–156.

Part IV
The Messiasship of Jesus

THERE now arises the question which is really vital to Christianity, that is, whether Jesus of Nazareth is the Christ, the Messias, the Anointed of the Lord, the Saviour of the world, and whether for this very reason Christianity represents the transcendent, only true religion with an everlastingly valid claim.

All that has been said in the foregoing chapters about the personality of Jesus and his fullness of virtue points definitely and always more clearly to his messiasship. The whole appearance of Jesus, his prophetic spirit, his sinless life, the absolute perfection of his inner life, of his conduct toward his fellow men, of his prayerful communion with the Father in heaven — all these are not only in accordance with his mission as Saviour of the world, but force us to the conviction that he is truly the Messias, sent by God, the Anointed of God, yes, that he is actually the God-Messias. At the very least it is inconceivable that a man of such absolute spiritual and moral excellence should deceive himself or us when he proclaims his messiasship. It remains, therefore, only to examine what Jesus thought and made known regarding his Messianic mission. This will be accomplished best if we briefly sketch first the concept of the Messias before Christ, second, the Messianic testimony of Jesus to himself, and, finally, examine his messiasship as such.

Chapter 10. The Concept of the Messias Before Christ

IN ORDER to understand the Messianic testimony of Jesus to himself, we must first of all examine the concept of the Messias as held by the Jews. The original and genuine idea of the messiasship is put forth in the Old Testament; its later and erroneous interpretation is found in the rabbinical and apocalyptic theology.

I. THE OLD TESTAMENT CONCEPT OF THE MESSIAS. This concept and its import can be elucidated but briefly in the limited space of a chapter. Essentially it is expressed by the terms: *Son of David, Servant of God, Son of Man, God with us,* and the *Kingdom of God.*

Son of David. Immediately after the fall God promised to the misguided mother of our race a descendant who was to wage a victorious war against the seducer, and, in opposition to the latter's adherents, was to establish a kingdom of goodness: "I will put enmities between thee and the woman, and thy seed and her seed: she shall crush thy head, and thou shalt lie in wait for her heel" (Gen. 3:15). After the deluge this promise passed on to the Semites through Noe, and later to Abraham, the first progenitor of the Israelitic people. "I will bless thee . . . and magnify thy name, and thou shalt be blessed. I will bless them that bless thee, and curse them that curse thee, and in thee shall all the kindred of the earth be blessed. . . . In thy seed shall all the nations of the earth be blessed."[1]

---

[1] Gen. 12:2 f.; 22:18. Cf. also Gen. 9:25–27; 18:18 f.; 26:4 (Isaac); 28: 13–15 (Jacob).

Jacob, the grandson of Abraham, bequeathed the promise of the blessing of nations and of the Saviour of the world to the tribe of Juda: "The sceptre shall not be taken away from Juda, nor a ruler from his thigh, till he come that is to be sent, and he shall be the expectation of nations" (Gen. 49:10).

This supremacy of Juda was handed down to David and his descendants,[2] and long after David and his successors had departed this life and their power had passed, it is declared again and again that David, the Son of David, the offspring of the house of David, shall reign forever over Israel: "I will set up one shepherd over them, and he shall feed them, even my servant David: he shall feed them, and he shall be their shepherd. And I the Lord will be their God: and my servant David the prince in the midst of them."[3]

But not only Israel, the Gentile nations also are to be the heirs of this Son of David, whom God will set as an everlasting king upon Sion, the holy hill (Ps. 2:4 ff.). For he will replace the old covenant, which was made only with Israel, and the old Jewish theocracy by a new covenant and a new Messianic kingdom (cf. Jer. 31:31–34). "In that day the root of Jesse [David], who standeth for an ensign of the people, him the Gentiles shall beseech, and his sepulchre shall be glorious" (Isa. 11:10). "And many people shall go, and say: Come and let us go up to the mountain of the Lord, and to the house of the God of Jacob, and he will teach us his ways, and we will walk in his paths; for the law shall come forth from Sion, and the word of the Lord from Jerusalem" (Isa. 2:3; Mich. 4:1–3). "The earth is filled with the knowledge of the Lord, as the covering waters of the sea" (Isa. 11:9). In justice, peace, mercy, and blessing the Son of David will reign "from sea to sea, and from the river unto the ends of the earth. . . . And all the kings of the earth shall adore him: all nations

---

[2] Cf. 2 Kings 7:11–16; 1 Par. 17:10–14; Ps. 88:30 ff.

[3] Ezech. 34:23 f.; cf. also 37:21–28; Jer. 23:5 f.; 30:8 f.; 33:15–26; Osee 3:5; Amos 9:11.

shall serve him . . . and in him shall all the tribes of the earth be blessed" (Ps. 71).

While in the "Son of David" there is seen almost nothing but the brilliant and felicitous glory of the Messias, who is to rule as the head of the universal kingdom, yet, on the other hand, he is also depicted as the *Servant of God* who suffers and dies vicariously for the sins of mankind, thus acquiring Messianic sovereignty and glory. This phase of the Messianic expectation is emphasized especially in the Psalms describing the Man of Sorrows, and in the songs of Isaias concerning the Servant of God.[4]

Chosen and anointed by Jahweh and endowed with all the gifts of the Spirit of God (cf. Isa. 11:2 f.; 61:1), the Servant of God is to be teacher, prophet, worker of miracles, and Saviour in the full sense of the word. As such he is called not only for the salvation of Israel, but for "the light of the Gentiles . . . salvation even to the farthest part of the earth" (Isa. 49:6). Because of us, sufferings, distress, and death will come upon him: "Despised and the most abject of men, a man of sorrows" (53:3), he gives his body to the strikers and his cheeks to them that "plucked" them, he does not turn away his face from them that rebuke him and spit upon him (50:6). "He was wounded for our iniquities, he was bruised for our sins, and the chastisement of our peace was upon him, and by his bruises we are healed. . . . The Lord hath laid on him the iniquity of us all. . . . He was offered . . . and opened not his mouth: he shall be led as a sheep to the slaughter" (53:5–7). Under nameless tortures, deserted by heaven and rejected by the earth, pierced in his hands and feet[5] he dies between male-factors, he, who has "done no iniquity, neither was there deceit in his mouth" (Isa. 53:9). The slain Servant of God shall, however, rise to a new life, and at the right hand of God be filled with joy and delight (cf. Ps. 15:10 f.).

[4] Cf. Ps. 21, 68; Isa. 42:1–16; 49:1–9; 50:4–10; 52:13; 53:12; 61:1 ff.
[5] Cf. Ps. 21:17; 68; Zach. 12:10.

From this blissful nearness to God he will, as the *Son of Man*, one day return in the clouds of heaven for the judgment, in order to assume forever the dominion over the Messianic kingdom of God, which he has merited by his passion, death, and resurrection. That is the meaning of Daniel's prophecy of the Son of Man: "I beheld therefore in the vision of the night, and lo, one like the Son of man came with the clouds of heaven, and he came even to the Ancient of days; and they presented him before him. And he gave him power, and glory, and a kingdom: and all the peoples, tribes and tongues shall serve him: his power is an everlasting power that shall not be taken away; and his kingdom that shall not be destroyed" (7:13–14).

In view of this unheard-of dignity and these supernatural functions of the Messias, it is not surprising that he is proclaimed directly as God in human form, as Emmanuel, *God with us*.

In many passages the Old Testament gives the promise that God himself in person will come to redeem his people. It is sufficient to merely mention the relevant passages of Isaias: "God himself will come and will save you. . . . Prepare ye the way of the Lord, make straight in the wilderness the paths of our God. . . . Behold your God: behold the Lord God shall come with strength, and his arm shall rule!" (35:4; 40:3, 9 f.) In the Psalms the Redeemer is designated more exactly as the *Son of God*. The royal psalmist here places in the mouth of the Messias, constituted and anointed by God, the following words: "The Lord hath said to me: Thou art my son, this day have I begotten thee" (2:7). But most clearly does Isaias prophesy of the God-Redeemer: "The Lord himself shall give you a sign. Behold a virgin shall conceive, and bear a son, and his name shall be called Emmanuel [*God with us*]" (7:14). That by *Emmanuel*, born of the Virgin-Mother, is really meant God in the strict sense of the word is evident from the mere fact that this Emmanuel is designated immediately afterward as the supreme Lord and possessor of the land of Israel and is therefore identical with Jahweh (8:10).

Isaias then describes the Emmanuel still more definitely as the God-Messias: "The people that walked in darkness, have seen a great light: to them that dwelt in the region of the shadow of death, light is risen. . . . For a child is born to us, and a son is given to us, and the government is upon his shoulder: and his name shall be called, Wonderful, Counsellor, God the Mighty, the Father of the world to come, the Prince of Peace. His empire shall be multiplied, and there shall be no end of peace: he shall sit upon the throne of David, and upon his kingdom to establish it and strengthen it with judgment and with justice, from henceforth and for ever: the zeal of the Lord of hosts will perform this" (9:2, 6, 7).

The dominion of God over the world, or the *kingdom of God* in the world, was in general the sum total of all the hopes for the future. The entire Old Testament is replete with the idea which Jesus expresses in the words: "Thy kingdom come!" By the term *Malkuth Schamaim* or *Malkuth Jahweh* (the kingdom of heaven or kingdom of God, heaven being only a metonymic designation of God), Holy Scripture means, in line with Semitic usage, precisely the concrete, royal rights which God possesses over the world, the exercise of these rights on the part of God, and the recognition of them on the part of men — consequently a kingdom which is governed from heaven and which must be entirely subject to heaven, a heavenly dominion, a royal government of God.[6]

It is precisely this recognition of the inalienable rights of God on the part of men which the Messias is to make a reality. *Kingdom of God* and *Messias* are therefore correlative ideas. All the distinctive traits of the Messias unite here as in one

---

[6] Concerning the Old Testament conception of the kingdom of God or heaven, see Schürer, *A History of the Jewish People* (New York: Scribner's Sons), II, 170–187; Dalman, *Die Worte Jesu*, I, Leipzig, 1898, 75–79; F. Zorell, "Das Himmelreich, das Gottesreich," *Ztschr. für Katholische Theologie*, XXVII (1903), 581–583; Lagrange, "Le règne de Dieu dans l'Ancien Testament," *Revue Biblique*, 1908, 36–61; J. Steinmueller and Kathryn Sullivan, *A Companion to the New Testament*, 90–91; Ricciotti, *Life of Christ*, § 73 f.; F. Prat, *Jesus Christ*, I, 216–220, 306–307; K. Adam, *The Son of God*, 157–164.

focal point. As the suffering Servant of God he makes the founding of the kingdom possible; as the Son of David he steps at the head of it; as the Son of Man he will return one day in glory to sit in judgment over it. Since, finally, the Messias is himself "God with us," his dominion will be one with that of God, and the Messianic kingdom becomes in the highest sense God's kingdom.

It is clearly indicated in the prophetic announcements that in this kingdom the earthly aspirations of the people of the revelation will also have a part. Jerusalem is designated as the center and the capital of the new kingdom, where the throne of the Messias will be erected, whither the splendid gifts of all the nations, their silver and gold, shall flow together (cf. Isa. 60:1 ff.). Indeed, the most prominent of all the prophets had promised the children of Israel that they should eat of the riches of the Gentiles and pride themselves in their glory (61:5 f.); that they should "suck the milk of the Gentiles" and "be nursed with the breasts of kings" (60:16); that "the children of strangers shall build up" their walls, and "their kings shall minister" to them (14:2; 60:10). "And they shall be gathered together as in the gatherings of one bundle into the pit, and they shall be shut up there in prison: and after many days they shall be visited. And the moon shall blush, and the sun shall be ashamed, when the Lord of hosts shall reign in mount Sion, and in Jerusalem, and shall be glorified in the sight of his ancients. . . . And the Lord of hosts shall make unto all people in this mountain, a feast of fat things, a feast of wine, of fat things full of marrow, of wine purified from the lees. And he shall destroy in this mountain the face of the bond with which all people were tied, and the web that he began over all nations. . . . And the Lord God shall wipe away tears from every face, and the reproach of his people he shall take away from off the whole earth" (24:22–23; 25:6–8). As carefully as one must guard against a too literal interpretation of these passages, just as definite, however, are the indications that the prophetic hope also contains certain earthly, political undertones, and that it was not able to overcome entirely the nationalistic Jewish particularism. Furthermore, the assumption seems to be very strong and positive that Israel, provided it would not reject the Messias, would actually inherit that temporal and national blessing which from the beginning had been the reward of its fidelity to Jahweh.

Nevertheless, the spiritual and religious blessings form the most important and essential part, as is sufficiently evident from the foregoing exposition. The Messias will bring the perfect knowledge of God.[7] The people as a whole will be rendered happy by God's presence, and will find in him a refuge and help in every kind of distress.[8] Above all, however, the kingdom of God will be blessed by the full abundance of the remission of sins as promised by the Messias and merited by his death. "In that day there shall be a fountain open to the house of David, and to the inhabitants of Jerusalem, for the washing of the sinner" (Zach. 13:1). "In those days, and at that time, saith the Lord, the iniquity of Israel shall be sought for, and there shall be none: and the sins of Juda, and there shall none be found: for I will be merciful to them" (Jer. 50:20). "I will forgive their iniquity, and I will remember their sin no more" (31:34). "If your sins be as scarlet, they shall be made as white as snow: and if they be red as crimson, they shall be white as wool" (Isa. 1:18). "I have blotted out thy iniquities as a cloud, and thy sins as a mist: return to me, for I have redeemed thee" (44:22). Not only the Israelites, but all nations are to receive these blessings of redemption. The Messias-King, who is to reign over this kingdom of God, is given "for a covenant of the people, for a light of the Gentiles . . . salvation even to the farthest part of the earth" (42:1–7; 49:6; 55:4). "He shall rule from sea to sea, and from the river unto the ends of the earth. . . . All kings of the earth shall adore him: all nations shall serve him . . . and in him shall all the tribes of the earth be blessed" (Ps. 71:8, 11, 17). "The earth

---

[7] Cf. Isa. 2:2–4; 11:9; Mich. 4:1–3.
[8] Cf. Isa. 4:4 ff.; 25:4 ff., etc.

is filled with the knowledge of the Lord, as the covering waters of the sea" (Isa. 11:9). The Messianic kingdom, therefore, according to the Old Testament, is of an essentially spiritual and religious character, as is the Messias himself.[9]

2. THE LATER JEWISH CONCEPT OF THE MESSIASSHIP is embedded principally in the rabbinic-pharisaic theology, which developed after the return from exile, reached its height about the time of Jesus, and then was deposited in the synagogal, particularly the Talmudic, literature. Although this literature originated in the Christian era, it is nevertheless "an invaluable source for the times of Christ, for the fountain of the traditions fixed therein is to be sought away back, not merely in the times of Christ, but in yet earlier periods."[10] We may be sure that the oldest and most important synagogal writings, *Talmud, Mischna,* and *Midraschim,* accurately reflect the Jewish conception of the messiasship, prevalent at the time of Jesus, in all important points.[11]

At first glance it seems strange that the rabbinical theology was not able to maintain itself at that same high level of prophetic concept of the messiasship. In general it gave but little importance to the prophetical writings. In order to strengthen practical Jewish life against the influences of a pagan environment, the *Law,* or *Torah,* with its 613 precepts — such was the number which the scribes found in the Pentateuch —

---

[9] Concerning the Old Testament concept of the Messias, see C. Fouard, *Christ the Son of God* (New York: Longmans, 1919), I, 13–17; F. Prat, *op. cit.,* I, 15, 99, 100, 218, 219, 306, 307.

[10] Schürer, *op. cit.,* I, 118–119; cf. also Bousset, *Die Religion des Judentums im neutestamentlichen Zeitalter,* Berlin, 1903, 41.

[11] The *Talmud* will be quoted simply by treatise and folio page, the *Mischna* by treatise, chapter, and paragraph. From the *Midraschim* we have made use of: *Mechilta,* ed. Weiss, Vienna, 1846; *Sifra,* ed. Malbim, Bucharest, 1860; *Sifre,* ed. Friedmann, Vienna, 1864; *Pesikta des R. Kohana,* ed. Buber, Lyk, 1868. Besides this oldest *Midrasch* some other *Midraschim* have been used, the edition of which is later, but the essential contents of which rest on ancient synagogal traditions, namely, *Tanchuma,* ed. Buber, Wilna, 1885 (quoted by Parascha *et al.*), and several *Rabboth,* ed. Wünsche, Bibliotheca rabbinica, Leipzig, 1880. Concerning the *Torah,* see also Ricciotti, *op. cit.,* §§ 30–33, 34, 36, 494 *n.,* 537–538; F. Prat, *op. cit.,* I, 7–11; *Catholic Encyclopedia,* Vol. XIV.

was exaggerated more and more at the expense of the content of the Messianic revelation as proclaimed by the prophets. The rabbis not only caused the private religious life to become entirely bound up in devotion to the Law, with which prayer and sacrifice were not to be compared,[12] and not only did they make the reading of the *Torah* the central point of public worship and of the entire religious consciousness of the community,[13] but they taught that the book of the Law contained the whole of religion, and that the *Torah* was that religion in which God had included everything which he could in any way reveal through all eternity.[14] The Law existed even *before* the world,[15] and accordingly God circumcised Adam even before he breathed life into him.[16] Already Sem had a school for instruction in the Law,[17] while Esau and Jacob had a dispute on the interpretation of the Law in their mother's womb.[18] The prophetical and doctrinal books of the Old Testament not only came much later than the Law, but are included in Holy Scripture merely by chance and casually.[19] The books of the *Torah* will likewise exist eternally, while all the rest of revelation will at some future time lose force and validity.[20] God himself is strictly bound to the Law, and all his thought and will is directed to the Law. Just as on earth, so also in heaven there is a Sanhedrin and a whole hierarchy of rabbis, with Jahweh sitting in their midst, studying and disputing with them on the various paragraphs of the Law.[21] "Every day he occupies himself for three hours with the Law."[22] His dispositions and actions are likewise subject to the ordinances of the

---

[12] *Schabbath*, 10 a; *Jebamoth*, 105 a; *Wajjikra rabba*, 29.
[13] *Sifre*, 13 b, 40 a; *Schemoth rabba*, c. 34.
[14] *Debarim rabba*, c. 8, on Deut. 30:12; *Taanith*, 9 a.
[15] *Sebachim*, 116 a; *Schabbath*, 88 b; *Pirke aboth*, VI, 10; *Mechilta*, 64 b; *Bereschith rabba*, c. 1.
[16] *Tanchuma Parascha Noach*, 5.
[17] *Maccoth*, 23 b.
[18] *Bereschith rabba*, 63 b.
[19] *Nedarim*, 226; *Koheleth rabba*, on 1:13.
[20] *Schemoth rabba*, c. 33; jer. *Megilla*, I, 7.
[21] *Baba mezia*, 85 b, 86 a; *Bereschith rabba*, c. 49.
[22] *Targ. Jerusch.*, on 5 Mos. 32:4.

Law.[23] Despite his pressing labors he observes the Law,[24] attends his synagogue,[25] vests himself in the *Tallith* (prayer mantle),[26] puts on the phylacteries, that of the hand and of the head;[27] in one word: God is completely bound up in the Mosaic Law, in fact, in that Mosaic Law as it had been corrupted by the Pharisees with their countless trimmings and endless quibblings.

This frightful exaggeration destroyed the whole prophetic scheme of salvation. If the Mosaic Law, that is, the Law as interpreted by rabbinical and cabalistic exegesis, is the highest good, is the only thing which remains eternally and which in itself is everything, then *Mosaism* can no longer be merely a means to the fulfillment of Messianic redemption, no longer a transient institution; it is then in itself redemption and fulfillment.

In fact, it was regarded as such by rabbinical theology. According to the latter, Jahweh, by the promulgation of the Law on Sinai, offered to the chosen people his loving union[28] in order to repair Adam's fall, and Israel had acceded to the wooing of the divine Bridegroom by its acceptance of the Law.[29] Thus Judaism was redeemed on Sinai.[30] This act of redemption was to be the end of God's dealings, and to remain forever the nuptial relation,[31] which thereby had been brought into being between God and his people. Even though Israel had frustrated this plan of God by worshiping the golden calf,[32] yet this is certain, that all the revelation and all redemption cannot exceed that which was given on Sinai. The purpose, therefore, of the historical development of salvation is this:

---

[23] *Schemoth rabba*, c. 30.

[24] *Bereschith rabba*, c. 7.

[25] *Berachoth*, 7 a.

[26] *Rosch haschschana*, 17 b.

[27] *Berachoth*, 6 a, 7 a.

[28] *Bammidbar rabba*, cc. 5, 13.

[29] *Schir rabba*, on 1:2; *Schabbath*, 88 a; *Pesikta*, 124 b.

[30] *Schir rabba*, on 1:2 and 4:7; *Bammidbar rabba*, c. 16; *Schemoth rabba*, c. 32.

[31] *Debarim rabba*, c. 13; *Bammidbar rabba*, c. 2.

[32] *Pesikta*, 124 b; *Schabbath*, 88 a; *Schir rabba*, on 1:3.

to regain by the fulfillment of the Law what had been lost by the "episode of the golden calf" — the latter being a technical term of the *Talmud*.[33] There is, therefore, no longer a question of inward justification, of an atoning redemption from sin; sin, atonement, healing, and justification in the sense of Holy Scripture are unknown to rabbinical theology. The great *means of redemption* and the great *act of redemption* is *thoroughness and excellence in the observance of the Law* — that, and nothing else.

To accomplish this act of redemption, again, is *not* the work of the Messias. If justice and justification are conceived as mere legal notions, as the outward legal justice of the nation and of the individual, then nation and individual must in consequence also redeem itself and render itself just by a mathematically strict balance between credit and debit, between precepts of the Law and their fulfillment. Precepts and fulfillment are recorded day by day, added, credited, and balanced.[34] Wholly just is he whose legal performances numerically equal the sum of precepts;[35] relatively just is he whose daily as well as life balance shows at least an absolute majority of legal performances.[36]

It is only when the balance of all individuals and of the nation corresponds to the legal budget, in other words, when Israel has been justified and sanctified, that the Messias will appear.[37] It is true, a period of absolute lawlessness will precede his coming; the appearance of this era is like that of a mangy dog.[38] Elias, however, will come to create once more respect for the Law and thereby to justify and sanctify Israel fully for the Messias.[39] Then only does the Messias begin his work *by establishing*, or more correctly, *by re-establishing* the kingdom of God in that form in which, according to the rabbinical

---

[33] *Bammidbar rabba*, c. 17.

[34] *Wajjikra rabba*, c. 26; *Tanchuma, Wajjelech*, 2; *Aboda sara*, 2 a.

[35] *Schabbath*, 32 a.

[36] *Kidduschin*, 40 b; *Pesikta*, 176 a.

[37] *Sanhedrin*, 97 b; *Schabbath*, 118 a; *Schemoth rabba*, c. 25; *Wajjikra rabba*, c. 3.

[38] *Sotah*, IX, 15; *Sanhedrin*, 97 a; *Schir rabba*, on 2:13.

[39] *Pirke de Rabbi Elieser*, c. 43; cf. Mt. 17:10 ff.; Mk. 9:10 ff.; Lk. 1:16 f.

dream, it had already existed on Sinai, that is, as a worldly and very much secularized theocracy.

According to the rabbinical conception, the kingdom of heaven came down to earth with the Law on Sinai.[40] From then on politics and religion were one. To be subject to any other sovereign but Jahweh would mean denying the religious supremacy of God, and even religion itself. From the time that God had taken up his abode in the midst of his people, he alone was the people's King, and his dominion assured not only the supremacy of Israel over the Gentiles, who served him as his footstool, but it created paradisiac conditions of every kind. God's nearness banished all effects of original sin and restored the blissful primitive condition of the Garden of Eden in this terrestrial kingdom of heaven, until the earth itself should be merged into heaven, and time into eternity. Thus did nomism fancy the first kingdom of salvation on Sinai, and thus it logically fancied also its rehabilitation through the Messias.

On the first day that the entire nation observes the Law, the Messias will appear,[41] drive the Romans out of the country with a scourge, compel the Gentiles to observe the *Torah,* and establish the kingdom of God.[42] The latter is regarded as the continuation of the kingdom of David and Solomon,[43] which it will, however, far surpass in splendor, might, and happiness. Jerusalem, the capital of the kingdom, will at the same time be the metropolis of all the lands of the earth.[44] Its grandeur and magnificence will be immeasurable.[45] In the midst of the city God will pile up Carmel, Thabor, and Sinai, one on top of the other, and upon the summit he will erect the temple, visible to all the world.[46] From there the Messias will extend his scepter.

[40] *Mechilta,* 73 b; *Pesikta,* 16 b; *Schemoth rabba,* c. 23.
[41] *Pesikta,* 163 b; *Schemoth rabba,* c. 25.
[42] *Mechilta,* 59 b; *Pesikta,* 51 b; *Debarim rabba,* c. 1.
[43] *Pesachim,* 54 a.
[44] *Schir rabba,* on 1:5.
[45] *Baba bathra,* 75 a, b; *Sifre,* 65 a; *Pesikta,* 143 a, b.
[46] *Pesikta,* 144 b.

The Roman world-empire, which arose solely on account of Israel's sins, will lie crushed at his feet; the non-Roman pagan nations will be obliged to pay tribute to the Messianic kingdom as vassal states.[47] The sole purpose of the nations living outside of Palestine will be to serve the Jews in Palestine, but they will not participate in the Messianic blessings. The Messias will show himself as a beneficent king only to the children of Abraham and only in the Land of Promise.

There he will lavishly bestow upon them the blessings of the Messianic kingdom and era. All the fancied sensuous delights of the Israelitic kingdom of the *Torah* will again be realized: banishment of every kind of distress and sickness; wonderful physical beauty and vitality of the children of Israel; fabulous fertility of the soil and of trees.[48] Women will give birth to children daily.[49] Men will be twice as tall as Adam, who measured one hundred ells in height; even the dwarfs among them will reach to the pinnacle of the temple.[50] No bunch of grapes will yield less than thirty casks of wine, barley will attain the height of the palm tree and scatter the ground meal on demand without the necessity of harvesting.[51] If added to this one could fancy roasted pigeons flying into one's mouth, the measure of Messianic blessings would be full: a veritable fairy life in a veritable paradise!

Does all this mean that the rabbinical concept of the Messianic kingdom was merely earthly and political and not deeply *religious*? Far from it! To assume this would misconstrue it completely. Rabbinical Judaism never lost sight of the importance of the role it was to play in the scheme of salvation. The synagogue recognized the spiritual worth and essential character of the Messianic kingdom and era precisely in this: that the rule of the *Torah*, which was identical with the rule of

---

[47] *Tanchuma, Schophetim,* 19; *Schemoth rabba,* c. 35.
[48] *Bereschith rabba,* cc. 12, 26; *Schabbath,* 30 b; *Pesachim,* 68 a.
[49] *Schabbath,* 30 b.
[50] *Baba bathra,* 75 a.
[51] *Kethuboth,* 111 b.

God according to rabbinical interpretation, was to extend its force everywhere on earth. In this regard the pharisaic concept of the Messias was thoroughly religious, and religious even in a universal sense.

Not only in theory, but also in the practical conduct of life did the Jews show a great, in fact, an unheard-of zeal for the hoped-for kingdom of God. It must be admitted that under the leadership of the Pharisees they more than ever burned with zeal for the kingdom of God and sought to bring about its establishment not only through punctual observance of the precepts of the *Torah,* but also through the acceptance of the rabbinical interpretations of the Law. Not only in the gospel,[52] but also in the *Talmud,* the rabbinical observance of the Law is always designated as a "yoke" or "burden." Even a single precept was regarded as exceedingly difficult of fulfillment,[53] and such precepts were attached to all and sundry things.[54] Every article had to be handled according to definite regulations, every form of labor, for example, plowing, sowing, had to be performed according to definitely worded, casuistic precepts.[55] Precisely in order to increase the observance of the "yoke" and of the Law, and thus to usher in the kingdom of God more speedily, the Pharisees developed an intense missionary activity and went "round about the sea and the land to make one proselyte" (Mt. 23:15).

The colossal mistake, however, lay in the fact that this conception of the messiasship, practical as well as theoretical, was applied to a kingdom of God which had been transvaluated into one of a secular and national character. Everything that pharisaic Judaism hoped for, over and above the theocratic national supremacy, was purely incidental, a mere accompaniment. The *Talmud* often and expressly gives the assurance: "There is no other distinction between the present world and

---

[52] Cf. Mt. 23:4; Gal. 5:1.
[53] *Mechilta,* 110 a.
[54] *Sifre,* on Lev. 8:25.
[55] *Bammidbar rabba,* c. 17.

the days of the Messias than this one thing — the servitude imposed [on us] by the kingdoms [of the Gentiles]."[56]

It cannot be objected that this national and materialistic concept of the Messias possibly had begun to infiltrate Jewish theology only during the Christian era. Not even the *Psalms of Solomon,* which were composed half a century before Christ, and which give expression to the pharisaic concept of the kingdom of God in the most idealized form, rise above the level just described. According to their glowing description, the Messias will be a just King, taught by God and filled with the Holy Spirit, who will rule over a thoroughly just and holy people, that is, "just" by its exact observance of the legal precepts of the *Torah.*[57] He will gather under his rule even "the Gentiles, that they may serve him, and thus he will glorify Jahweh over the face of the whole earth."[58] The principal thing, however, the essential Messianic element in him is nevertheless his Davidic sovereignty, the secular might with which he will destroy the enemies of Israel, purify Jerusalem from the Gentiles, and confer blessedness on the chosen people.[59] Not a single non-Israelite shall live in the Messianic kingdom; strangers will be allowed merely to bring gifts to Palestine for the children of Israel and to be astounded and made envious by their grandeur.[60] The Messias is wholly a political sovereign, and the kingdom of the Messias a thoroughly secularized and nationalized "kingdom of heaven."[61]

That was also exactly the idea of the Jewish apocalyptic writers, who wrote shortly before and after Christ, and who were looked upon by the Rabbis among the Pharisees as sectarian dissenters.[62] The apocalyptic writings differed from the

---

[56] *Schabbath,* 63 a; *Pesachim,* 68 a.
[57] *Ps. Salom.,* XVII, 24–26.
[58] *Ibid.,* XVII, XVIII.
[59] *Ibid.,* XVII, 23–27.
[60] *Ibid.,* XI, XVII, XVIII.
[61] *Ibid.,* XVII, 30–34.
[62] The apocalyptic literature was in full sway from 160 B.C. to A.D. 120. Its more important productions, in so far as they concern the question

official concept of the Messias only in regard to the manner, the place, and the time of the establishment of the kingdom of heaven. The Pharisees were convinced that the kingdom of God would arise in this world and before the end of time. The older apocalyptic writers likewise held fast wholly or in part to the earthly, temporal kingdom of God and Messianic king of the synagogue. But when the prospects for the establishment of the Davidic-Messianic kingdom diminished after the downfall of the Machabees and following the rise of the Herodian rule, some zealots despaired of ever living to see it in a world so thoroughly corrupted. In consequence they clung narrowly and exclusively to the prophecy of Daniel regarding the Son of Man, who is to appear in transcendent power at the end of time, in order to place himself at the head of the postmundane kingdom of God. The terrestrial course of things must first be destroyed, the apocalyptic writers taught, before the supermundane, Messianic era of the kingdom of God could begin. But this eschatological element is the only point in which the apocalyptic concept of the Messianic kingdom differed from that of the Pharisees. The essential element regarding the Messias is on the part of both a glorious Jewish world supremacy on the basis of the *Torah* and under the leadership of the Messias.

The Jews in the Hellenic-Roman diaspora stressed this point just as emphatically as the members of their race in Palestine. According to Philo of Alexandria (born 20 B.C.), the Messias is to play a purely military role: a battle against the enemies of the rabbinic Mosaic Law and of the people of the Law; victory and eternal rule on the part of the latter, and in its wake

---

of the Messianic concept, are: *The Book of Henoch*, the fundamental composition of which dates from the time of the Machabees, and the most important parts of which, the metaphorical discourses, originated in the last decades before Christ; the *Book of Jubilees*, or *Little Genesis*, from the time of John Hyrcanus; the *Assumption of Moses*, written about six years after Christ; the *Apocalypse of Esdras* and of *Baruch*, completed only after the destruction of Jerusalem. Regarding these books and their conception of the messiasship, see Felder-Stoddard, *Christ and the Critics*, I, 163–170; Ricciotti, *The Life of Christ*, §§ 73, 75–77, 197, 201, 495.

luxury, riches, glory, physical vitality.[63] Flavius Josephus (born
A.D. 37–38) recognizes likewise only a King-Messias; in his
eagerness to flatter the emperor Vespasian he even hails the
latter as the hoped-for Messias.[64]

We need only to open the gospels in order to become convinced that the national-politic concept of the Messias held
full sway among the Jewish contemporaries of Jesus. The Saviour encountered it among the Pharisees and scribes as well as
among the masses, and it was difficult to persuade even his
own disciples to abandon it. The gospels, however, intimate
at the same time that there were circles of devout people whose
Messianic ideal drew its sustenance from the prophecies of the
Old Testament. We need only mention Mary and Joseph,
Zachary and Elizabeth, the aged Simeon in the temple, and
John the Baptist. These and similar exceptions, however, do not
detract from the fact that the official concept of the Messias on
the part of later Judaism was thoroughly and basically different
from that of the Old Testament. The kingdom of the Messias,
the activity of the Messias, and the person of the Messias as
conceived by the one and by the other stood in sharpest contrast.

The nationally restricted, materialistic world-power of the
pharisaic Messias-King was in direct opposition to the world-
embracing, spiritual, and religious kingdom of God or of the
Messias as presented by Sacred Scripture. It did indeed rest
on the religious fundamental Law of the *Torah* and possessed
a theocratic character; but essentially it was conceived as thoroughly earthly and political. This is evident from all that has
been said above.

The redeeming work of the Messias was conceived as being
in accordance with this Talmudic idea of the kingdom of God.
On the day that Israel became legally just, the rabbinical
Messias will automatically shatter every sort of foreign domina-

---

[63] Philo, *De praemiis*, XIV–XX; *De execrationibus*, VIII, IX, XIX. Cf.
Bréhier, *Les idées philosophiques et religieuses de Philon d'Alexandrie*,
Paris, 1908; Lagrange, *Le Messianisme chez les juifs*, Paris, 1909, 28–37.
[64] *Bellum judaicum*, VI, 5, 4.

tion, establish the might of the *Torah,* and in this kingdom of heaven raise up and perpetuate loyalty to the Law. Like the Pharisees, only more so, he will observe the *Torah* with all its bylaws, in all its niceties, with all the restrictions drawn round about it;[65] he will be "loaded down like a mill with fulfillments of the rabbinical precepts,"[66] and as a perfect scribe he will instruct the people in the *Torah.*[67] That is all! No inner rebirth of those sanctified by the Law, no religion which would transcend pure nomism, and least of all no vicarious redemption! The Jewish Messias will deliver the people from the Gentiles, not from sin! "The work of the Messias, the deliverance of Israel from foreign domination, the establishment of supremacy over all nations, the renewal of Israel as God's people — all this is accomplished, according to the ancient Palestinian theology of the Jews, without being interrupted by the atoning passion and death of the Messias. His might is not based, as the prophet teaches, on his atoning sacrifice, but on the personal justice which renders him worthy to accomplish the work of the Messias."[68] The figure of the "Servant of God" of the Old Testament no longer fitted into the frame of the pharisaic messiasship. Only rarely and timidly does a Rabbi dare to apply to the Messias the descriptions of the Psalms, of Isaias, and of the Book of Wisdom (2:12–20) relative to the sufferings of the "Just One." The *Targum of Jonathan,* composed during the second half of the first century after Christ, deals with the texts of Isaias concerning the suffering Servant of God, but extenuates and weakens them in such a way that they appear to say merely that "the Messias will expose his life to danger in the conflict with apostates."[69] The death of atonement on the part of the

---

[65] *Targ. Jonath.,* on Isa. 9:3.

[66] *Sanhedrin,* 93 b.

[67] *Targ. Jonath.,* on Isa. 53:5–10; *Schir rabba,* on 2:13.

[68] Ferd. Weber, *Jüdische Theologie auf Grund des Talmud und verwandter Schriften,* Leipzig, 1897, 362. See also Dalman, *Der leidende und sterbende Messias der Synagoge im ersten christlichen Jahrtausend,* Berlin, 1888; Lagrange, *Le Messianisme chez les juifs,* Paris, 1909, 236–251, 259 f.

[69] Jos. Felten, *Neutestamentliche Zeitgeschichte,* II, Regensburg, 1925, 193.

Saviour was for the Jews the greatest annoyance imaginable.[70]

From this point of view the person of the Messias is likewise purely human, both as to origin and nature.[71] The name of the Messias was indeed decreed from eternity, but only in this sense, "that it was God's will from eternity to create the Messias and to send him into the world, just as the fathers, who are spoken of as pre-existent with him, as well as the people of Israel and the temple were not actually present, but only in God's eternal plan of salvation."[72] Besides this nominal pre-existence of the soul of the Messias, Palestinian theology indeed also assumed an actual one, but this only in consequence of rabbinical anthropology, which regarded all human souls as being created before the world and stored in a warehouse of the seventh heaven until the moment of their union with the body.[73] Thus the Messias is in no other sense a pre-existent and transcendent being than the rest of men. The Rabbis no longer knew what to do with the "Son of man" of Daniel, not to mention the Messianic "Emmanuel." The Messias is begotten of men as man.[74] In vain did Jesus endeavor, arguing from Psalm 109, to convince the scribes that he was not merely an earthly descendant of David.[75] The Jew Tryphon, according to St. Justin, still very emphatically declared: "We all expect the Messias as a man, begotten of men and anointed by Elias, as soon as the latter should one day appear."[76] Only by his zeal for the Law does he rise above common humanity, just as Abraham, Moses, Job, Hiskia, and Hillel,[77] and thus render himself worthy to assume his role as sovereign. That was all which remained of the Messianic prophecies of the Old Testament: the "Son of David," purely terrestrial and political, the King of the Jews,

---

[70] Cf. 1 Cor. 1:23.
[71] *Targ. Jonath.*, on Isa. 11:1; *Schir rabba*, on 4:8.
[72] Weber, *loc. cit.*, 335.
[73] *Aboda sara*, 5 a.
[74] *Bereschith rabba*, c. 12; *Bammidbar rabba*, c. 13; *Pesikta*, 149 a.
[75] Cf. Mt. 22:42 f.; Mk. 12:35 f.; Lk. 20:41 f.
[76] St. Justin, *Dialogus cum Tryphone*, c. 49.
[77] *Bammidbar rabba*, c. 14; *Bereschith rabba*, c. 85.

who was to lead the nationalistic dominion of the *Torah* onward
to victory.[78]

There is a shocking element of tragedy in this Messianic
concept of later Judaism. Israel had suffered the loss of almost
everything else. Its liberty and independence were gone. From
the year 63 B.C. the city of Jerusalem was in the hands of the
Romans. Thirty-three years later the Idumean Herod ascended
the throne of David. The national sanctuary was under foreign
domination. Taxes and tribute were paid to pagan emperors, the
sons of God were pressed into service in pagan legions and
forced to defile themselves daily and to participate in abomina-
tions contrary to the Law. Matters stood no better as far as the
spirituality of religion was concerned. Rabbinical nomism, with
its countless and almost unbearable "traditions," had usurped
the place of the revelation of the Old Testament. There
remained only the hope of a Messias. This Messias, in whom
the fathers believed and whose figure the prophets had portrayed in ever more distinct lineaments, the Jews expected
with unswerving trust. Rabbinism had even increased this yearning with a mighty urge, but its great misfortune was that it
incited the hopes of Israel toward a mere phantom of the
Messias, guided its expectation on to false paths and interpreted
the person, the work, and the kingdom of the Messias according
to its own ideas and not according to the prophetic plans of
God. Hence, Rabbinism itself went astray and led others astray
regarding the Saviour.

---

[78] Regarding the Messianic concept in Judaism, see Ricciotti, *op. cit.*,
§§ 72–77, 187, 197, 201, 247–249, 252, 270–271, 304–305, 379, 400–403,
425–427, 495, 511–513, 534, 549, 667, 670.

Chapter 11. The Messianic Testimony of Jesus to Himself

ALL the Messianic prophecies reached the point of their fulfillment about the time of the reign of Augustus. The fullness of time had come. The New Testament writings, as well as the rabbinical synagogal literature, point to the eagerness with which the Messias was expected by the Jewish contemporaries of Jesus. The history of the Jewish war and of the destruction of Jerusalem is evidence of the fact that at this period every phantom of a Messias was eagerly pursued, so deeply was the nation penetrated with the thought of the nearness of the one so fervently desired and expected. But no matter how eager the search, the secularized Messias-King of the Jews did not appear.

The heavens, however, had opened and had wrought the miracle of the virginal birth as foretold by Isaias. The angel Gabriel declared unto Mary: "Behold thou shalt conceive in thy womb, and shalt bring forth a son; and thou shalt call his name Jesus. He shall be great, and shall be called the Son of the Most High; and the Lord God shall give unto him the throne of David his father; and he shall reign in the house of Jacob for ever. And of his kingdom there shall be no end. . . . The Holy Ghost shall come upon thee, and the power of the Most High shall overshadow thee. And therefore also the Holy which shall be born of thee shall be called the Son of God" (Lk. 1:31 ff.). To Joseph the angel said: "Joseph, son of David, fear not to take unto thee Mary thy wife, for that which is conceived in her, is of the Holy Ghost. And she shall bring forth a son: and thou shalt call his name Jesus. For he shall save his people from their sins." The evangelist adds: "Now all this was done that it might be fulfilled which the Lord spoke by the prophet, saying: Behold a virgin shall be with child, and bring forth a son, and they shall call his name Emmanuel, which being interpreted is, God with us" (Mt. 1:20 ff.).

In this manner the Old Testament teaching of the Messias became a reality: the pre-existent Son of God came down from heaven to earth, redeemed sinful humanity as the Servant of God, established the Davidic kingdom of God, and rules over it forever. The entire gospel story of the childhood of Jesus glows in the light of this sublime Messianic message.[1]

And yet the materialistic notion of the Messias, which haunted the minds of most of the people, cast its shadow upon the lofty scene. When Jesus was born in Bethlehem, behold, Wise Men came to Jerusalem from the East and inquired: "Where is he that is born king of the Jews? For we have seen his star in the east, and are come to adore him." When king Herod heard this he was frightened, and all Jerusalem with him. He assembled the chief priests and the scribes of the people, and inquired of them where the Messias should be born. When he was told that, according to the prophet Micheas, Bethlehem in Judea was to be the birthplace of the Messias, he "was exceeding angry; and sending killed all the men-children that were in Bethlehem, and in all the borders thereof, from two years old and under," in order to protect himself against the supposed pretender to the throne (cf. Mt. 2:1–23). This episode shows very clearly that every announcement of a Messias was interpreted by the Jews and the Romans in the country as of national-political significance, and as one which must of necessity lead to a catastrophe. Only from this point of view can one understand the Messianic testimony of Jesus to himself in its beginnings, its development, and its fulfillment.

I. THE BEGINNINGS OF THE MESSIANIC TES-TIMONY OF JESUS TO HIMSELF. Jesus veiled him-

---

[1] Cf. Mt., Chaps. 1 and 2; Lk., Chaps. 1 and 2.

self in secrecy — with the one exception of the episode of the twelve-year-old boy in the temple[2] — until the day when, according to the prophecy "the voice of one crying in the desert" (Isa. 40:3) proclaimed him. The appearance of the precursor John, his preaching of penance and his baptism pointed so clearly and so definitely to the nearness of the Messias,[3] that the multitudes surmised that the Baptist himself was the Christ, and the Sanhedrin approached him by means of an official delegation in order to learn the real facts of the case. "I am not the Christ, the Messias," John declared emphatically, "but there hath stood one in the midst of you, whom you know not. The same is he that shall come after me, who is preferred before me: the latchet of whose shoe I am not worthy to loose" (Jn. 1:19 ff.).

Soon afterward, Jesus presented himself for baptism. John recognized in him the one sent by God.[4] The heavens opened. The Spirit of God descended upon Jesus in the form of a dove, and from above the voice of the Father resounded clearly and distinctly: "This is my beloved Son, in whom I am well pleased."[5] There can be no doubt that Jesus himself regarded this occurrence as his Messianic consecration, as the recognition of himself as the Messias on the part of the heavenly Father.[6] It will be shown later that the term "Son of God" in its application to Jesus and in the mouth of Jesus himself denotes, if not always his divinity, at least always his messiasship.[7]

It has this connotation also in the episode of the temptation which immediately followed the baptism. The tempter surmised and feared that Jesus was the Messias, the Son of God. Yet he wished first to assure himself of this. "If thou art the

---

[2] For a complete study of this point, see P. J. Temple, *The Boyhood Consciousness of Christ* (New York: Macmillan Co., 1922).

[3] Cf. Mt. 3:1–12; Mk. 1:1–8; Lk. 3:1–18.

[4] Cf. Mt. 3:13–15; Jn. 1:29–34.

[5] Mt. 3:16–17; Mk. 1:10–11; Lk. 3:22.

[6] Cf. Lk. 4:18; Isa. 42:1–4; Acts 10:38.

[7] Cf. F. Prat, *Jesus Christ* (Milwaukee: The Bruce Publishing Co., 1950), I, 152–155; G. Ricciotti, *The Life of Christ* (Milwaukee: The Bruce Publishing Co., 1947), §§ 267–272; C. Fouard, *Christ the Son of God* (New York: Longmans, Green and Co., 1919), 110 ff., 129 ff.

Son of God [that is, at least the Messias], then prove thyself as such by thy works. The Saviour is proclaimed as a miracle-worker; work, then, his miracles! The Messias is predicted as the destroyer of the Satanic world-empire and as the founder of the all-embracing kingdom of God; receive, then, from my hands the kingdoms of the world!" That was, in substance, the language of the tempter. Jesus indignantly rejected the impostures of Satan. But the Messianic title "Son of God" he silently claimed for himself.[8]

The messiasship of Jesus formed, therefore, the focal point of the first episodes of his public life. John the Baptist announced and acknowledged Jesus as the Messias; heaven consecrated him audibly and visibly to the messiasship; the spirits feared him and testified to him as the Messias. Jesus himself in all this sustained within himself the calm consciousness of his Messianic dignity and mission.

At this point there began the first indications of the public announcement of his messiasship. At first "Jesus naturally observed a modest reserve about this mystery of his person, about this his sublime faith in himself."[9] Out of consideration for the capacity and the preconceived notions of those about him, he found it necessary, however, to forego the use of the name of Messias.

The name "Messias, Christ" was, in fact, not necessarily connected with the scheme of salvation as promised in the Old Testament. In consequence of their anointing, kings and priests from the beginning were given this name. And because the coming Saviour was to be priest and king in the fullest sense of the words, this connotation also fitted him in the highest sense. However, it is applied to him only three times in the Old Testament.[10] It was only shortly before the beginning of the Christian era,[11] and only conjointly with other appellations

---

[8] Cf. Mt. 4:1-11; Mk. 1:12-13; Lk. 4:1-13. Cf. also Ricciotti, *op. cit.*, § 276; Prat, *op. cit.*, I, 157 ff.

[9] H. Weinel, *Jesus im 19. Jahrhundert*, Tübingen, 1907, 109.

[10] Cf. 1 Kings 2:10; Ps. 2:2; Dan. 9:25 f.

[11] Ps. *Salom.*, XVII, 36; XVIII, 6, 8; *Apoc. Baruch*, 39:7; 40:1; 72:2.

("Son of David," "King of Israel"), that the term *Messias* was stamped as the official title of the hoped-for Deliverer. Precisely at this time there was coupled to the name Messias a concept which was equivalent to a surrender of the messiasship itself.

In the popular mind the Messias, as we already know, was in the first place *the political Deliverer*. As Son of David he was to break, by his mere appearance, the yoke of the Romans with one blow, re-establish the Jewish sovereignty, and as King of Israel lead the people of the Law and the observance of the Law to triumphant victory. With the masses in this state of mind, it needed but a breath of air to make the flame of national enthusiasm surge upward with mighty force. A rumor among the masses of the presence of the Messias, that is, of the national hero, would have sufficed to enkindle boundless political enthusiasm and to conjure up a general Messianic revolution.

Willingly or unwillingly Jesus would have been forced to head this movement if he had forthwith called himself the Messias. A disastrous conflict with the officials would have put a sudden end to his career, which had just begun, and would have frustrated his entire work. Jesus would have been condemned at once, as was finally the case, by the Jewish Sanhedrin as well as by the Roman courts — by the former on the charge that he had not been able to establish his claim to be the Messias-King, by the latter on the charge that he had wanted to make this claim. In order to avoid this premature catastrophe, he prevented the proclamation of his messiasship and himself abstained from assuming the name "Messias."

The first disciples, it is true, overpowered by the force of his words and of his personality, surmised that he was the Messias, and gave him this title. "We have found the Messias!" Andrew cried out to his brother Simon after his first meeting with Jesus (Jn. 1:41). "We have found him of whom Moses in the law, and the prophets did write!" Philip announced to Nathaniel (Jn. 1:45). Shortly after his meeting with Jesus, the latter also confessed: "Rabbi, thou art the Son of God, thou art the king of Israel!" (1:49.)

Even the demons sought to proclaim his messiasship through the mouths of those whom they possessed, for "they knew him"; "they knew that he was the Christ," "the Holy One of God," "the Anointed of God," "the Son of God," "the Son of the Most High God," who had "come to destroy" them.[12]

Jesus accepted with joy the confession of the first disciples, although it was, as it proved later, only the expression of a trustful hope that the Master would prove himself to be the Messias (cf. Jn. 1:50). However, he substitutes for the titles Messias, the Prophet, the King of Israel (in the mind of the Jews all these were of the same significance), the title "Son of man." Neither does he contradict the utterances of the demons, although he strictly forbids them to proclaim him publicly as the Messias.

Modern critics seriously misinterpret these prohibitions made by Jesus. From these Wellhausen and Wrede conclude that Jesus never felt himself to be the Messias, while other adherents of the liberal school contend that at least in the beginning of his career he had not yet believed in his messiasship.

Yet the very contrary is evident from the conduct of the Saviour in this regard. It was not because he considered the Messianic testimony of the demons to be false that he forbade its publication, but precisely because he considered it as true. The evangelists remark expressly: "He suffered them not to speak, because they knew him" (Mk. 1:34); "and rebuking them, he suffered them not to speak, for they knew that he was Christ" (Lk. 4:41); "he strictly charged them that they should not make him known" (Mk. 3:12). Consequently, it was not the *faith* in his messiasship that Jesus rebuked, but its *publication,* the spreading of a general report that he was the Messias in that sense in which the people had been expecting their Christ so long and so impatiently. It was by a quiet, intensive mode of education that Jesus sought to convince first of all his disciples and then the larger circle of his contemporaries of his messiasship, of his supernatural Messianic character, and of his

---

[12] Cf. Mt. 8:29; Mk. 1:24, 34; 3:12; 5:7; Lk. 4:34, 41; 8:28.

spiritual Messianic mission. The belief in him as the Messias was to be engendered and purified from within outward and on the basis of objective proofs. From his words, and above all from his works, the disciples and the masses were to come gradually to the conviction that he was the Messias, even if he did not inaugurate the hoped-for Messianic *coup d'état.*

In order to remove all misunderstanding on the part of his disciples and of the Jews, he replaced, as has been indicated above, the title of Messias with the title *Son of man.* He assumed this title with preference from the outset of his activity until his condemnation by the Sanhedrin.

The name "Son of man" occurs 32 times in Matthew, 14 times in Mark, 25 times in Luke, and 11 times in John. Outside of the gospels it is found only three times in the New Testament writings,[13] and even in the gospels it is only the Saviour who gives himself this title; he never receives it from his disciples.

This name did not have the political flavor which the other Messianic titles, Messias, Son of David, Prince of Peace, King of Israel, had acquired in the course of time. For that very reason it did not, as the others did, excite the national hopes and passions. It was thus best suited to become the conveyor of the Messianic views of Jesus, and the characteristic mark of his unobtrusive, gradual revelation of himself.

In the Aramaic mother tongue of Jesus *Son of man* indeed meant simply *man.* But ever since the prophecy of Daniel (7:13 f.), this term signified at the same time the Messias, heralded in the sacred writings of the Old Testament as the founder and prince of the kingdom of God, who was to come again one day in the clouds of heaven to judge the world.

Now, because Jesus called himself the Son of man in contrast to all other men, he evidently did not take the word in its first and simple meaning. It would have been senseless to assert all his life and solemnly that he was man. In fact, from the

---

[13] Cf. Acts 7:55; Apoc. 1:13; 14:14.

very first day he himself declared definitely that he applied the term "Son of man" to himself in the Messianic sense.[14] As his activity progressed he concentrated into this title, as we shall see, more and more of the dignity and character, rights and functions of the teaching, miracle-working, suffering, and glorified Messias. In fact, after deep research, Tillmann comes to the conclusion "that no passage referring to the Son of man is free from a Messianic interpretation, and that by far the greater number of them allow only this interpretation."[15] Proclaiming himself as the Son of man was, therefore, equivalent to testifying to himself as the Messias.

2. DEVELOPMENT OF CHRIST'S TESTIMONY TO HIMSELF AS THE MESSIAS. The sublime task of the Messias was the foundation of the kingdom of God, or of heaven. Jesus undertook this task from the first day of his public preaching. The forerunner John had pointed out the coming of the kingdom as directly imminent: "Do penance: for the kingdom of heaven is at hand!" (Mt. 3:2; Mk. 1:4; Lk. 3:3.) The Son of man proclaimed the same message: "Jesus came into Galilee, preaching the gospel of the kingdom of God, and saying: The time is accomplished and the kingdom of God is at hand: repent and believe the gospel!" (Mk. 1:14 f.; Mt. 4:17.) He sent out the twelve Apostles to spread the glad tidings: "And going, preach, saying: The kingdom of heaven is at hand!" (Mt. 10:7.) It had not as yet been established; but it had been approaching, and that very closely, since the Son of man had appeared. Every step that Jesus made meant an advance, an approach of the long-desired kingdom. The time of waiting and expecting, of prophecy and of hope was past. The kingdom stood before the door; the kingdom was there! That is the meaning of the message which followed upon the appearance of the Son of man.

---

[14] Compare Jn. 1:41, 45, 49, with 1:51.
[15] *Der Menschensohn*, Freiburg i.Br., 1907, 147. Cf. F. Prat, *op. cit.*, I, 186, 243, 295, 386, 418, 420; II, 154–157; K. Adam, *The Son of God* (London: Sheed and Ward, 1935), 179–183.

"The evangel of the kingdom of God" (Lk. 8:1), "the mystery of the kingdom of God" (Lk. 9:2), was from then on the burden of the message delivered by him day after day. In the cities and villages of Galilee, in the synagogues and in the market places, on the shores of the sea, and on the hillsides the message of the kingdom of God resounded. Jesus proclaimed his program: "The law and the prophets were until John: from that time the kingdom of God is preached" (Lk. 16:16). The lesser of those who received the gospel of the kingdom was, therefore, greater than John, who was but the forerunner of the kingdom (Mt. 11:11). Referring to his own person and to his gospel Jesus was able to assure the Pharisees: "The kingdom of God cometh not with observation; neither shall they say: Behold here, or behold there. For lo, the kingdom of God is within you" (Lk. 17:20 f.). The Pharisees, as well as the apocalyptics, thought that the fully established *Malkuth Jahweh* (kingdom of God) would descend suddenly and with great pomp from heaven to the earth, but while they eagerly awaited this momentous event, the kingdom of God had already come, like the dawn, quietly and unobtrusively.

To strengthen and seal his Messianic mission and preaching, the Son of man also performed the miraculous works which were prophesied of the Messias. He calmed the elements, healed the sick, delivered those possessed by devils, raised the dead to life, remitted sins, and worked new miracles to prove his authority to forgive sins.[16] The people surmised that this worker of miracles was the Messias-King. The Pharisees, however, ascribed his miraculous deeds to the power of Beelzebub. Jesus spoke the sublime words: "Every kingdom divided against itself shall be made desolate: and every city or house divided against itself shall not stand. And if Satan cast out Satan, he is divided against himself: how then shall his kingdom stand? . . . But if I by the Spirit of God cast out devils, then is the kingdom of God come upon you" (Mt. 12:25–28). He considered his

---

[16] Cf. Mt. 9:1–8; Mk. 2:1–12; Lk. 5:17–26.

victories over the devils, therefore, as blows against the kingdom of Satan and as evident triumphs of the kingdom which had arrived. In exactly the same manner he appealed to his other miracles as proofs for the presence of the kingdom of heaven (cf. Mt. 11:4–6).

It is true, he often sought to prevent the publication of these Messianic deeds,[17] no doubt in order to avoid every appearance of vanity and in order not to foment political enthusiasm. How well grounded this caution was became manifest on the occasion of the first multiplication of the loaves of bread (cf. Jn. 6:14 f.). In the working of miracles the important point was, on the one hand, not to endanger the Messianic cause by a storm of enthusiasm, on the other, to change the notions of the people by a constant, well-defined method of education, and to take possession, as it were, of one position after another (cf. Jn. 7:3–6). In this way the people gradually came to know him as a worker of miracles, and were able, with good will, to conclude from his works that he was the Christ, sent by God, although this Messias did not correspond to the national expectations of the masses.[18]

It is to this that Jesus called the attention also of the Baptist, who had sent the inquiry from his prison: "Art thou he that art to come, or wait we for another?" "Go and relate to John," Jesus replied, "what you have heard and seen. The blind see, the lame walk, the lepers are cleansed, the deaf hear, the dead rise again, the poor have the gospel preached to them" (Mt. 11:2–5; Lk. 7:18–23). In these words Jesus merely repeated the description which Isaias had given of the blessings of the Messianic period (cf. Isa. 29:18 ff.; 35:2 ff.; 61:1). The gist of the words of Jesus is this: "Compare what the prophets, especially Isaias, have foretold of the Messias, with what you see me do, and then decide for yourself whether or not I am the Messias." The proof is convincing and compelling for him who is acquainted with the prophets, recognizes them as true, and who has an open eye and ear. The Lord concluded the solemn testimony to his own person

---

17 Cf. Mt. 8:2 ff.; Mk. 1:43 ff.; 5:43; 7:36; 8:26; Lk. 5:12 f.; 8:56.
18 Cf. Jn. 5:36; 6:28 f.; 9:3 f.; 10:25–38; 14:10 f.; 15:24.

with the serious, momentous words: "And blessed is he who shall not be scandalized in me": blessed is he who does not take offense in the Messias, although he does not accomplish the expected, popular Messianic deeds, the national-political insurrection, and liberation. This alone was the stumbling block. All else was in agreement; he had furnished all the proofs of his messiasship. One thing alone was lacking — the political exploit which the narrow-mindedness and blindness of the Jews regarded as the real work of the Messias. But he could not execute this bold stroke without becoming a traitor to his spiritual Messianic dignity and mission. He could not declare himself the Messias in that sense in which the people wanted their Messias.

But in no other way could the masses be brought to recognize his messiasship. True, they praised God for his wonderful deeds and said: "A great prophet is risen up among us, and God hath visited his people" (Lk. 7:16). "A great prophet" — that was the general opinion held of him. Some said: "John [who had just been beheaded] is risen from the dead"; others: "Elias [who, according to the Jewish tradition, was to be the forerunner of the Messias] had appeared"; others again: "One of the old prophets is risen again" (Lk. 9:8 f., 19). Only occasionally did they ask in astonishment: "Is not this the Son of David?" (Mt. 12:23.) "Have mercy on us, O Son of David!" cried the blind men of Capharnaum and the Canaanite woman (Mt. 9:27; 15:22).

These voices from the people evidently show, too, that some groups were already close to believing in the messiasship of Jesus. In Samaria, where the political ideas of the Jews regarding the Messias were not shared, Jesus was able to declare himself expressly as Messias without danger of any kind, and found many who believed in him (cf. Jn. 4:39–41). Among his Jewish hearers also there were individuals and entire families who immediately joined his disciples (cf. Jn. 4:53). Under the influence of his miracles even large numbers of the populace for a time believed to have found in him the coming Christ (cf. 2:23), although those of his own kin refused to believe in him (cf. 7:5). After the multiplication of loaves at Bethsaida the people were raised to such a height of enthusiasm that they cried out: "This is of a truth the prophet that is to come into the world" — the Messias! And they wanted "to take him by force and make him king" (Jn. 6:15), that is, to proclaim him the national Messianic hero.[19]

Only on this condition, that he would carry out the decisive "Messianic" revolution, were the people ready to recognize his messiasship. How little reliance at the same time could be placed in the faith of the masses, and even of the larger circle of his disciples, became evident at the end of the Galilean period of his activity. As soon as Jesus put the coarse-minded notions of that wider circle to the test, most of them fell away. Only the twelve apostles survived the test and remained steadfast (cf. Jn. 6:67–69).

Among the twelve apostles faith in him had, in fact, taken root more and more deeply. The original disciples, as we have seen, had shown a disposition to believe from the beginning (cf. Jn. 1:37 ff.). It would indeed be absolutely unthinkable that they would have followed the Saviour without such a disposing faith. The first miracle at Cana confirmed them in their conviction (cf. Jn. 2:11).

Yet the realization of a positive, unchangeable faith in his messiasship was still far from being effected. The apostles were still in need of enlightenment regarding the messiasship, and only little by little did their minds open to the mysteries of the kingdom of God, which the Master made known to them frankly and confidentially, only in so far, however, as their powers of comprehension allowed.[20] There was need of the infinite patience of the Lord in order not to despair of their progress.[21] Nevertheless, their faith gradually grew stronger, nourished above all by the unbroken series of the miracles of

---

[19] Cf. Ricciotti, *op. cit.*, §§ 384–385; F. Prat, *op. cit.*, 363 f.; C. Fouard, *op. cit.*, I, 336–341.
[20] Cf. Mt. 13:10–12; Mk. 4:11; Lk. 8:10.
[21] Cf. Mk. 4:13, 40; 6:50 ff.; 7:18; 8:16 ff., etc.

Jesus. In their astonishment at the calming of the sea they fell at the feet of Jesus and cried out: "Indeed thou art the Son of God!" (Mt. 14:33.)

It was at Caesarea Philippi, before the conclusion of his Galilean activity, that Jesus put the searching question to them: "Whom do men say that the Son of man is?" They replied: "Some John the Baptist, and other some Elias, and others Jeremias, or one of the prophets." "But whom do you say that I am?" he inquired further. And for the first time he received from the lips of Peter the unequivocal answer: "Thou art Christ [the Messias], the Son of the living God." In his joy over this confession Jesus called him blessed: "Blessed art thou, Simon Bar-Jona; because flesh and blood hath not revealed it to thee, but my Father who is in heaven."[22]

Peter was not "scandalized" in the Messias, although he did not see him establish the materialistic Messianic kingdom. Hence the blessing. The other disciples, also, no doubt, had made progress in the faith (cf. Jn. 6:69 f.). They believed Jesus to be the Messias, the Son of the living God, although he was not the Messias-King as conceived by the Jews. But they were still firmly convinced that he would eventually become such and thus fulfill his essential task as Messias in the rabbinical sense.[23]

3. COMPLETION OF THE TESTIMONY OF JESUS TO HIS MESSIASSHIP. It was a most difficult task to rid the disciples of the idea that the Messias was to appear in the radiance of worldly power and splendor on the throne of David.

Hence, "from that time Jesus began to shew to his disciples, that he must go to Jerusalem, and suffer many things from the ancients and scribes and chief priests, and be put to death, and the third day rise again" (Mt. 16:21), and "so enter into his glory" (Lk. 24:26).

On previous occasions he had referred only casually and

---

[22] Mt. 16:13-17; Mk. 8:27-29; Lk. 9:18-20.

[23] Concerning the confession of Peter, see F. Prat, *op. cit.*, I, 379-380, 409-410; Ricciotti, *op. cit.*, §§ 402, 403.

figuratively to his vocation as a suffering Messias.[24] But now that the disciples believed in him, though they mistakenly regarded a brilliant political achievement to be his Messianic vocation, he taught them that the work of the Messias would consist essentially in suffering and dying and find its culmination in the glorification ensuing therefrom. This theme fills almost the whole last part of the gospels. Just as he held up the spiritual and suffering Messias in contrast to the political Messias, so he also set up, by word and deed (cf. Jn. 18:36), the religious and supernatural kingdom of God in contrast to the secularized kingdom of the Messias. The main objective in the teaching of Jesus to his disciples, from the day of Caesarea Philippi on, was the rectification of the Messianic belief and idea.

The success was not very pronounced. Even Peter, who on that day had distinguished himself so brilliantly, was the first who indignantly reproached the Saviour for his idea of suffering (cf. Mt. 16:22; Mk. 8:32), and even in the hour of the Passion thought the time had come to strike a blow for the political Messianic kingdom (cf. Lk. 22:49; Mk. 14:47, etc.). The two sons of Zebedee, James and John, even at a late hour in Christ's life, vied with one another for the most influential positions of honor in the Messianic kingdom (cf. Mk. 10:37, 45; Mt. 20:22, 28). Yes, even after the resurrection, the disciples did not understand the doctrine of the suffering Saviour (cf. Lk. 24:20–27), and the old rallying cry made its rounds among them: Now at last, and at once, must come the Messianic liberation from the Roman yoke (cf. Lk. 24:21) and the Messianic re-establishment of the kingdom of Israel (cf. Acts 1:6). Jesus had expounded to them clearly and forcibly the whole doctrine of his spiritual Messianic vocation and work; however, it was beyond their comprehension.

When we consider this frame of mind of the disciples, we also understand the corresponding attitude of Jesus toward the people after the conclusion of his Galilean activity. As wrong

---

[24] Cf. Mk. 2:19 f.; Mt. 9:15; Lk. 5:34 f.

as the impression may have been which the disciples had of the Messias, just so firm, with the exception of a few vacillations (cf. Jn. 16:30 f.), was their faith in his messiasship. But to the masses both faith and understanding were wanting now as well as before. Jesus was forced to take this into consideration if he did not wish to risk all before the proper time: if he had spoken openly of the suffering Messias and of his spiritual kingdom, all his hearers would have turned from him; if he had designated himself outright as the Messias, he would have been proclaimed triumphantly as the King of the Jews. After the confession of Peter, therefore, he again impressed upon his disciples the necessity of waiting a while before announcing him as the Messias (cf. Mt. 16:20). The Transfiguration on Mount Thabor and the testimony of the Father in the presence of the pillars of the Law and of the prophets, Moses and Elias, occurred soon after this. Nothing could have confirmed his disciples more in their faith in his Messianic mission, yet immediately Jesus repeated his positive command not to reveal this Messianic manifestation until the Son of man should have risen from the dead, that is, until he should have entered into his glory by his sufferings and humiliation, and thus should have proved unmistakably that he was the Messias and that only the spiritual concept of the Messias was the correct one.[25]

However, though it was still necessary to keep the title of Messias secret from the people, Jesus nevertheless preached his Messianic mission always more and more clearly during the last period of his public activity. Scarcely had Peter confessed the faith of the disciples in the messiasship at Caesarea Philippi, when Jesus called "the multitude together with his disciples" (Mk. 8:34) and addressed to "all" (Lk. 9:23) the stirring words: "Whosoever will save his life, shall lose it: and whosoever shall lose his life for my sake and the gospel, shall save it. . . . He that shall be ashamed of me and of my words in this

---

[25] Cf. Mt. 17:9; Mk. 9:9; Lk. 9:36. Cf. also Ricciotti, *op. cit.*, §§ 304–305, 342, 372–373, 402–403, 411, 600, 700; F. Prat, *op. cit.*, I, 306–307.

adulterous and sinful generation, the Son of man also will be ashamed of him, when he shall come in the glory of the Father with the holy angels" (Mk. 8:35–38). And another time, "when great multitudes stood about him, so that they trod one upon another," he said: "Whosoever shall confess me before men, him shall the Son of man also confess before the angels of God. But he that shall deny me before men, shall be denied before the angels of God" (Lk. 12:1, 8). In these and similar words he proclaimed himself openly and before all to be the One sent by God, declaring that on faith in him depended their eternal destiny.

The more plain, emphatic, and public his testimony to himself as the Messias became, the more openly did he render also the Messianic proof of miracles for the trustworthiness of his testimony. If previously he had set certain limits to the publication of his miracles, because "his time was not yet come" (Jn. 7:6), that is, the hour of his suffering and glorification (cf. Jn. 7:30; 12:23; 17:1), toward the end of his activity he more and more dispensed with the previous restrictions. No longer did he forbid to spread abroad the fame of his works. He performed his mighty deeds before great multitudes, before the priests, the scribes and Pharisees,[26] even in the temple at Jerusalem.[27] He constantly declared his miracles to be the proof of his having been sent by God, and demanded absolute faith in this.[28]

The eyewitness John continually observes the success with which this constant Messianic revelation was attended. "There was much murmuring among the multitude concerning him. For some said: He is a good man. And others said: No, but he seduceth the people. Yet no man spoke openly of him, for fear of the Jews [that is, of the scribes and Pharisees]. . . . But of the people many believed in him and said: When the Christ cometh, shall he do more miracles, than these which this man

---

[26] Cf. Mt. 21:12 f.; Mk. 11:15 ff.; Lk. 14:1 ff.; 19:45 f.; 22:49 ff.; Jn. 9:11.
[27] Cf. Mt. 12:12 f.; Mk. 11:15 ff.; Lk. 19:45.
[28] Cf. Jn. 9:3 f.; 10:25, 32, 37 f.; 14:10 f.; 15:24.

doth? The Pharisees heard the people murmuring these things concerning him: and the rulers and the Pharisees sent ministers to apprehend him" (Jn. 7:12 f., 31 f.). But Jesus, nevertheless, continued his impressive revelation, and the faith of the people increased. "Some said: This is the prophet indeed! Others said: This is the Christ! But some said: Doth the Christ come out of Galilee? . . . So there arose a dissension among the people because of him" (7:40–43). Yet the number of his adherents increased steadily (8:30). In vain did the Pharisees determine "that if any man should confess him to be Christ, he should be put out of the synagogue" (9:22). They were no longer able to stem the flood. In the Sanhedrin the high priests and the Pharisees gave vent to their feelings with a cry of terror: "What do we, for this man doth many miracles? If we let him alone so, all will believe in him!" (11:47 f.) In fact, Jesus was already quite commonly spoken of among the people as "Christ, the Messias" (Mt. 27:17, 22), and with each day the enthusiasm of his adherents grew.[29]

As the week of his passion approached, Jesus set about to correct publicly the popular Jewish notion of the Messias. The Son of man is not the longed-for Messias-King, his kingdom and his glory is not of this world. He "is not come to be ministered unto, but to minister, and to give his life a redemption for many" (Mk. 10:45). The way to the coming Messianic dominion leads through suffering, death, and the grave.[30] "For as the lightning that lighteneth from under heaven, shineth unto the parts that are under heaven, so shall the Son of man be in his day. But first he must suffer many things, and be rejected by this generation" (Lk. 17:24 f.).

But the people simply were deaf to such utterances (cf. Jn. 12:37). They persisted always more stubbornly in their idea

---

[29] Cf. Jn. 10:42; 11:27, 45. Concerning miracles as proof of his Messianic mission, see also K. Adam, *The Son of God*, 188 f.; F. Prat, *op. cit.*, I, 236–237; Devivier, *Christian Apologetics* (New York: J. Wagner, 1924), I, 414–428.

[30] Cf. Lk. 19:11–12; Mt. 26:10–12, etc.

that he was indeed the Messias, who would ascend the throne of David in the near future.[31]

Such was the popular sentiment under the influence of which the great Messianic demonstration was prepared and realized at the beginning of the holy week. On the eve of that week a miraculous event, coupled to the raising of Lazarus from the dead (cf. Jn. 12:17 f.), contributed the last impulse. Two blind men of Jericho hastened to meet Jesus, who was passing by surrounded by the multitude, with the cry: "O Lord, thou Son of David, have mercy on us!" And they regained their sight.[32]

When Jesus thereupon entered Jerusalem, the people met him with the joyous shouts of "Hosanna to the Son of David!" (Mt. 21:9.) "Blessed be the king who cometh in the name of the Lord!" (Lk. 19:38.) "Hosanna! Blessed is . . . the king of Israel!" (Jn. 12:13.) "Blessed be the kingdom of our father David that cometh: Hosanna in the highest!" (Mk. 11:10.) All joyous acclamations of the national Messias, whom they beheld in Jesus. This made the Pharisees furious and they said to one another: "Do you see that we prevail nothing? Behold the whole world is gone after him" (Jn. 12:19). And they resolved to destroy him without delay.

Some days later Jesus was brought before the highest tribunal of the Jews and of the Romans to answer for himself.

Before the Jewish Sanhedrin he was charged with declaring himself a spiritual Messias, with no political aspirations. The high priest commanded him to answer the question under oath: "I adjure thee by the living God, that thou tell us if thou be the Christ the Son of God." Jesus affirmed this, but he rejected every notion of a political messiaship: "Thou hast said it. Nevertheless I say to you, hereafter you shall see the Son of man sitting on the right hand of the power of God, and coming in the clouds of heaven." The high priest saw in this statement a

---

[31] See G. Ricciotti, op. cit., §§ 305, 407–408, 413, 506–507, 557.
[32] Cf. Mt. 20:30–31; Mk. 10:47–48.

blasphemous utterance, and for this Jesus was unanimously condemned to death by the judges of the court.[33]

Reversing their position, they accused him before the Roman governor as being a Messianic-political pretender to the throne: "We have found this man perverting our nation, and forbidding to give tribute to Caesar, and saying that he is Christ the king" (Lk. 23:2). But this charge was found to be baseless (cf. 23:3 ff.). For this reason they again fell back upon their real charge and demanded his death, because he had forfeited his life by his "blasphemous" claim to be the Messias and Son of God (cf. Jn. 19:7).

That was his alleged crime and that the cause of his death — that he wanted to be the Messias and Son of God in an entirely different sense from that held by his Jewish contemporaries.

---

[33] Cf. Mt. 26:63–66; Mk. 14:61–64.

Chapter 12. The Messiasship of Jesus

IN THE foregoing chapter we have demonstrated that Jesus not only testified to himself as the Messias all his life, but also that his conception of the messiasship was fundamentally different from that of his Jewish contemporaries. There remains but to describe this messiasship more exactly.

First of all, let us consider the idea of the *kingdom of God* as put forth by Jesus. We know that he declared emphatically up to the moment of his death: "My kingdom is not of this world." The kingdom of God, or of heaven, as he understood and realized it, is not a theocracy of a materialistic nature, neither in the rabbinical nor in the apocalyptic sense. Neither in its present beginnings nor in its future eternal state has this kingdom political elements of any sort. Jesus excludes with utmost decisiveness every thought of a subjugation of the Romans, and in general of the pagan world powers. His kingdom of God stands in opposition only to the kingdom of Satan. For Satan also, "the prince of this world" (Jn. 12:31, etc.), has a kingdom, a dominion on earth, a kingdom of sin and of enmity toward God (Mt. 12:26). In daily battle, with prayer and fasting, by precept and example, by exorcism, by threats and commands, he pursued Satan in all his strongholds. By his miraculous deeds, by the omnipotent power with which he drove out the demons, by the manifestations of divine might which proceeded from him, the dominion of Satan was driven back step by step. The downfall of the Satanic kingdom has been sealed: "The prince of this world is already judged" (Jn. 16:11); "now shall the prince of this world be cast out" (12:31).

Already Jesus saw "Satan like lightning falling from heaven" (Lk. 10:18). All this justifies his conclusion that now kingdom was set up against kingdom: "If I by the Spirit of God cast out devils, then is the kingdom of God come upon you" (Mt. 12:28).

He expounded the character and nature of the latter in his gospel, which is so truly the *Magna Charta* of the kingdom of heaven that it is called simply "the glad tidings of the kingdom of God" (Lk. 8:1), "the mystery of the kingdom of God" (Mk. 4:11), "the preaching of the kingdom of God" (Lk. 9:2). His objective is a spiritual, religious, and divine kingdom of truth and grace, of redemption and forgiveness of sins, of sanctity and blessedness. The fatherly rule of God within man and over man here on earth and one day in heaven, and again a childlike approach of man to God here below and an indissoluble union with God in the hereafter, and all that through the mediation of Jesus: that is the idea of the kingdom of God as expressed in the gospel.

The fundamental condition for admission into the kingdom is first of all belief and the acceptance of the gospel.[1] To this is added the spiritual rebirth "of water and the Holy Ghost"[2] for the forgiveness of sins, as well as a new manner of life by reason of this baptism and according to the precepts of the gospel.[3] Thus the kingdom of God presupposes a complete interior transformation in every individual, and demands, therefore, determination and a chivalrous, energetic disposition. Whoever does not prize and seek the "kingdom of God and its justice" above all things (cf. Mt. 6:33; Lk. 12:31), whoever puts his hand to the plough and looks back (cf. Lk. 9:62), whoever does not despise all things, and if necessary abandon all things (cf. Mt. 5:29 f.), whoever is not prepared to place even his own life at stake (cf. Mt. 10:39; Lk. 14:26) in order to gain the kingdom of heaven, is not fit for it.

---

[1] Cf. Mk. 10:16; Jn. 3:18, 36.
[2] Cf. Jn. 3:3, 5; Mt. 28:19; Mk. 16:15 f.
[3] Cf. Mt. 7:21; 19:18, 21; Mk. 10:17 ff.

One can, therefore, readily understand that the kingdom of God can extend itself only slowly and by constant efforts. It will not be established by a lightning-like *coup d'état* according to rabbinical interpretation, nor will it fall from heaven as a complete *Malkuth* in the apocalyptic sense (cf. Lk. 17:20 f.). As the grain quietly germinates, sends up its blades, blooms, and finally is garnered as fully ripe, so it is with the kingdom of God (cf. Mk. 4:26–29). In its beginnings it is like the tiny mustard seed, very small and inconspicuous, so that the great ones of the earth will pay no attention to it, but gradually it grows and becomes a tree; like the leaven it works from within outward, until it has transformed the whole world.[4]

Another characteristic trait of the kingdom of Jesus is that it is conceived as open to all the world, as all-embracing. Its founder has, indeed, been sent first of all to the lost sheep of the house of Israel (cf. Mt. 15:24); yet he has come to seek and to save all that which was lost (cf. Lk. 19:10; Mt. 18:11). Those sheep also who do not belong to the chosen fold of God's people he must bring into the kingdom of heaven (cf. Jn. 10:16). He poured out his blood for all men in order to redeem them and save them (cf. Mt. 26:28; Mk. 14:24). The kingdom of God is taken from the Jews and given to the Gentiles, who are more disposed to accept it (cf. Mt. 21:43). The parables of the wicked husbandmen (21:33 ff.) and of the marriage feast (22:1 ff.), the meeting of Jesus with the Samaritan woman and with the centurion of Capharnaum, as well as the coincident references on his part to the coming of a believing pagan world into the kingdom of heaven (8:5 ff.), are eloquent testimonies to the universality of the kingdom as conceived by Jesus.[5]

He did not, of course, live to see his kingdom extend itself over the whole world. His Church itself, which he expressly designates as the kingdom of heaven on earth (cf. Mt. 16:18 f.),

---

[4] Cf. Mt. 13:31–33; Mk. 4:30–32. Cf. Ricciotti, *The Life of Christ*, §§ 325 ff., 379 f., 461 f.; F. Prat, *Jesus Christ*, I, 315 ff.

[5] Cf. F. Prat, *op. cit.*, II, 216–217; Ricciotti, *op. cit.*, §§ 531 f., 460 ff.

was to strive to gain all nations and all souls. His command to convert the whole world, delivered to his own apostles and those of all times, is very definite: "Go ye into the whole world, and preach the gospel to every creature" (Mk. 16:15). "All power is given to me in heaven and on earth. Going, therefore, teach ye all nations; baptizing them in the name of the Father, and of the Son, and of the Holy Ghost, teaching them to observe all things whatsoever I have commanded you; and behold I am with you all days, even to the consummation of the world" (Mt. 28:18–20). "Unto all nations the gospel must first be preached" (Mk. 13:10). "The gospel of the kingdom shall be preached in the whole world, for a testimony to all nations, and then shall the consummation come" that is, the judgment (Mt. 24:14).

The *judgment* is the gate into the kingdom of God in the world to come. This gate is closed against the kingdom of Satan, who is condemned to the punishment of hell with those who on earth belonged to the kingdom of evil; on the other hand, it is opened to the children of God's kingdom, who finally and irrevocably take possession of the kingdom prepared for them from the foundation of the world (cf. Mt. 25:34). For the kingdom of God on earth is both in its entirety as well as in its application to the individual only the commencement, the preliminary step, the preparation for the everlasting kingdom of heaven in the next world. In its final consummation, there-fore, the kingdom is not yet complete. It is only approaching (cf. Lk. 19:22 ff.), and we must constantly pray for its coming: "Father . . . thy kingdom come!" (11:2.) As often as Jesus spoke of entering into the kingdom of God, he presupposed the kingdom in this sense as a future event (cf. Mt. 5:20; 7:21; Mk. 9:46). As often as he called the children of the kingdom of God on earth blessed, he promised them the future kingdom of God as reward: "For theirs is the kingdom of heaven. . . . For they shall see God. . . . Then shall the just shine as the sun, in the kingdom of their Father" (Mt. 5:3–12; 13:43).

Accordingly, the main feature and the completion of the

Messianic teaching of Jesus regarding the kingdom of heaven lies in the future, not in the present. Again and again he directs our mind and heart upward and forward, from the kingdom and life in it, both of which go forward here below under many difficulties, to the blessed perfection of the hereafter. Hope, expectation, and longing for the future and eternal kingdom of heaven — that is the fundamental character of the religion of Christ. But not exclusively. The establishment and the development of this kingdom are accomplished in this world. The contention of eschatological critics that Jesus, following the apocalyptic writers, had striven only for a postmundane Messianic kingdom, has been proved as untenable. The seed of the kingdom of God is cast into the earth, germinates therein, grows there, and ripens to maturity before it is gathered into the barns of heaven by the harvesting of the last judgment (cf. Mt. 13:36 ff.). In eternity will be harvested only what has been sown here below (cf. Gal. 6:7 f.). Time here on earth is for the sowing, eternity for the reaping, and between them the great day of judgment, when that which was sown and reaped will be judged and weighed according to merit. That which follows the judgment must have its basis and its development before the judgment. The future kingdom of heaven grows entirely out of the present kingdom of heaven on earth. In the mind of Jesus both form the one ideal of the kingdom of God.

In conformity with this he also interprets the term *Son of man*. In Daniel (7:13 f.) the Son of man appears only as supramundane judge of the world and prince of the postmundane kingdom of God. The Jewish apocalyptic writers adhered strictly to this eschatological prophecy, without considering that it was only a part of the whole prophetic idea of the messiasship. According to the eschatological critics of our day, the Man of Nazareth is supposed to have understood the title "Son of man" just as one-sidedly and narrowly and applied it thus to himself. The preceding elucidation, however, of the idea of the kingdom of God held by Jesus proves the contrary. He does, indeed, call himself the Son of man in the sense that he is to come again as judge of the world and to rule forever over the kingdom of God as Messias-King. But this is not the whole content of his doctrine regarding the Son of man. He extends this official Messianic name earthward and earthwide, and applies it to his whole life as Redeemer. As Son of man he has come down from heaven and will again return one day to heaven.[6] As Son of man he announces the glad tidings of the kingdom and accomplishes the work of redemption.[7] As Son of man he has the power to forgive sins,[8] and to set up against the Mosaic Law his own authority to teach and his own mode of conduct.[9] As Son of man he calls the sinners to the kingdom of God.[10] As Son of man he has not where to lay his head.[11] As Son of man he has come into this world to minister to others and to give his life a redemption for all men.[12] As Son of man he must be rejected by his people, be condemned by the scribes and chief priests, must die, and rise again on the third day.[13] Then only will he come again as the Son of man in the clouds of heaven, accompanied by the angels, in view of the whole earth, in order to judge the world, inflict the merited punishment of hell upon the wicked, and to bring home the good into the kingdom of his Father. Accordingly, Jesus does not assume the name and title of Son of man merely in the eschatological sense which it has in Daniel, but he extends it to include his whole Messianic vocation, his whole Messianic activity, his whole Messianic mission, which begins with the incarnation and is fully consummated only in eternity.

Thereby the Son of man takes the place of the *Son of David*. Everything of spiritual content which is true of this Messianic expression according to Old Testament prophecy, is carried over

---

[6] Cf. Jn. 3:13 ff.; 6:32 ff.
[7] Cf. Mt. 11:19; 12:32; 16:13; Lk. 7:34; 11:30; 12:10; 22:48.
[8] Cf. Mt. 9:6; Mk. 2:10; Lk. 5:24.
[9] Cf. Mt. 12:8; Mk. 2:28; Lk. 6:5.
[10] Cf. Mt. 9:13; Mk. 2:17; Lk. 5:32.
[11] Cf. Mt. 8:20; Lk. 9:58.
[12] Cf. Mt. 20:28; Mk. 10:45; Lk. 22:20.
[13] Cf. Mt. 12:40; 17:9, 12:20; 18; 26:2, 24, 45, etc.

by Jesus to the appellation "Son of man." The purely temporal, earthly, and political interpretation of the title "Son of David," as assumed by most of his contemporaries, had to be repudiated by the Saviour. In fact, in order to forestall a completely erroneous conception of his messiasship and not to become a traitor to himself and to his cause, Jesus saw himself forced to abandon in part the content of the term "Son of David," fixed though it was by the Old Testament.

God had from the beginning announced the Messianic salvation as a dominion and a kingdom and, correspondingly, the Messias as a ruler and a king. This was the best illustration which he could have chosen, one that fully corresponded to reality, in so far as it was interpreted in a spiritual and not in a material and earthly sense. In order to make it more acceptable to the chosen people, more intelligible and more popular, he announced the Saviour as King of Israel, and as a king from the illustrious dynastic family of David, who should rule forever and bring a superabundance of all blessings to both country and people. Although these promises for the most part appear in the lustrous garb of temporal pomp and power, yet evidently they were intended to be merely, or at least chiefly, the figurative shell and mold for the spiritual blessings and benefits of the Messianic period. Even in those passages of the Old Testament in which the messiasship assumes the most glowing national and materialistic coloring, the Son of David nevertheless appears as a worker of miracles, as priest and teacher of truth and justice, endowed with the choicest spiritual gifts of God, and sent for the salvation and welfare of all nations.

Unmistakably, however, the increasing tendency of the Jews to interpret the Messianic Kingdom and its Prince, the Son of David, more and more in a national, political sense, becomes noticeable in the Old Testament; and when Jesus appeared, the title "Son of David" was attached, for the most part, only to a racial, national hero of the Jews. Judaism had taken the shell for the kernel and the mold for the content of the Messianic prophecy.

Hence, Jesus was obliged to shatter the shell in order to preserve the true content of his Messianic person and mission. He merely tolerated the appellation "Son of David," but let the figure of the latter recede behind that of the Son of man, in fact, to disappear almost entirely.

It is true, he was announced by the angel as "the Son of the Most High," to whom "the Lord God shall give . . . the throne of David his father; and he shall reign in the house of Jacob for ever. And of his kingdom there shall be no end" (Lk. 1:32 f.). Yet there followed immediately the thoroughly spiritual interpretation of this dominion: "Thou shalt call his name Jesus, for he shall save his people from their sins" (Mt. 1:21). It is also true that the descent of Jesus from the house of David was constantly stressed (cf. Mt. 1:1–6; Lk. 1:27, 32, 69), for to abandon this lineage would not only mean to deny a historical fact, but also would have been equivalent to the abandonment of his messiasship, since the Messias had to come from the house of David (cf. Jn. 7:42). Even when the multitudes hailed him as the Son of David (cf. Mt. 21:9, 15, etc.), he could not refuse the ovation without denying his Messianic claims. And even when the blind and the distressed of every kind implored him as the Son of David for help,[14] he healed and helped them not only from the infinite tenderness of his heart, but because the Messias, according to the prophets, was to prove himself a worker of miracles.[15]

Yet he decidedly opposed the pharisaical supposition that the Messias was essentially only a natural descendant of David, and that his mission was merely to succeed David on a worldly throne,[16] and not once in his whole life did he call himself the Son of David, in order not to sanction the distorted rabbinical concept of the Messias.

Furthermore, the glorious title "Son of David" was less suitable to the Saviour for the reason that he was to be

---

[14] Cf. Mt. 21:9, 9:27, 15:22, 20:29 ff.; Mk. 10:46–47; Lk. 18:38.
[15] Cf. Isa. 29:18 ff.; 35:2 ff.; 61:1.
[16] Cf. Mt. 22:41 ff.; Mk. 12:35–37; Lk. 20:41–43.

before all else the *Servant of God,* the Redeemer and Saviour
of sinners in the truest sense of the word.[17]

Before he could enter upon his royal supremacy over the
kingdom of God, he first had to introduce it into the world and
rewin the individual, as well as humanity as such, for the
kingdom which had been destroyed through sin. First, Mediator
and Founder of the kingdom, then its King. Jesus, therefore,
is to be simply the Mediator, Redeemer, Saviour. As the Hellenic
world conferred these titles on its victorious hero kings, who
achieved its political deliverance, so also does Jesus claim for
himself the name "Saviour, Redeemer." He translates, in reference to himself, the word *Messias* by the other title, "Saviour
of the world" (cf. Jn. 4:25, 42). Yet in his case it is a spiritual
redemption from sin and guilt. Of him the angel had said:
"Thou shalt call his name Jesus [Saviour, Redeemer, Deliverer],
for he shall save his people from their sins" (Mt. 1:21). Jesus
himself confirmed this interpretation of his name, thereby
outlining the principal program of his Messianic mission as
that of redeeming from sin: "The Son of man is come to seek
and to save that which was lost" (Lk. 19:10).

No one who has read the gospels will be able to doubt that
the battle against sin and the return of sinful man to God
was the one great purpose of the life of Jesus. Not only was his
religious activity concentrated on this, even the physical blessings and the miracles wrought by him had always this *one*
aim: redemption from sin, forgiveness of sin. He healed the
paralytic at the pool of Bethsaida and admonished him: "Behold
thou art made whole: sin no more, lest some worse things
happen to thee" (Jn. 5:14). He freed the adulterous woman
from the hands of the pharisaical accusers and said: "Go, and
now sin no more" (Jn. 8:11). He took the sinful woman in the
house of Simon under his protection and gave her the comforting
assurance: "Thy sins are forgiven thee," and remarked to the
amazed Pharisees: "Many sins are forgiven her, because she

---

[17] Cf. F. Prat, *op. cit.,* I, 243, 418, 420.

has loved much" (Lk. 7:47). Before Jesus healed the paralytic he said to him: "Thy sins are forgiven thee." And since the Pharisees regarded this as an intrusion into the domain of God's power, and accordingly as an act of blasphemy, Jesus declared and proved that "the Son of man hath power on earth to forgive sins" (Mk. 2:1 ff.). The mission of the Saviour, by his very acts, has always the one aim: to effect the remission of sins through his mediation and to impart it himself.

But, above all, the aim of his mission is also to merit the remission of sins for men. We know that the Mediator is described in the book of Isaias as the Servant of God who takes upon himself the infirmities and sins of the people, and expiates them by his vicarious suffering. The gospel applies this prophecy of the Servant of God to Jesus. This is done in one passage of the first gospel in an especially remarkable way, when the evangelist says that the miracles of healing, which Jesus wrought in behalf of men, were performed for the purpose of fulfilling the prophecy of Isaias: "He hath borne our infirmities and carried our sorrows."[18] With profound truth the whole life of Jesus is again applied thereby to the central Messianic thought: vicarious atonement and redemption from sin and from its consequences.

Nevertheless, the suffering and death of Jesus remain the specific act of redemption. As has been demonstrated above, Jesus regarded his suffering, his death, and subsequent resurrection, before all else as his Messianic vocation. Even his teaching and all the rest of his Messianic pronouncements and activity give precedence to the momentous act of his suffering. At the same time he declared repeatedly that only thus can the Old Testament prophecy be fulfilled, according to which the Messias must suffer and die and so enter into his glory.[19] Consequently it is as the Servant of God in the sense of the Psalms and of the prophet Isaias that he atoned for the sins of humanity by his vicarious suffering and thus redeemed mankind.

---

[18] Mt. 8:17 (Isa. 53:4); cf. 1 Pet. 2:24.
[19] Cf. Mt. 16:21; Lk. 9:22–27.

Still more clearly does he state this purpose of his Messianic mission in the words of John's gospel: "As Moses lifted up the serpent in the desert, so must the Son of man be lifted up; that whosoever believeth in him, may not perish; but may have life everlasting. For God so loved the world, as to give his only begotten Son; that whosoever believeth in him, may not perish, but may have life everlasting. For God sent not his Son into the world, to judge the world, but that the world may be saved by him. . . . I am the good shepherd. The good shepherd giveth his life for his sheep" (3:14–17; 10:11). The answer which he gave, according to the synoptic gospels, to the sons of Zebedee, expresses exactly the same thought: "The Son of man is not come to be ministered unto, but to minister, and to give his life a redemption for many" (Mt. 20:28).

To this great declaration of the plan of salvation, into which he condensed the whole doctrine of redemption at the beginning of Passion Week, is joined the other, uttered immediately before his death. At the Last Supper he took bread, gave thanks, broke it and gave it to his disciples, saying: "This is my body, which is given for you." In like manner he took the chalice, after they had supped, and said: "Drink ye all of this. This is my blood of the new testament, which shall be shed for many unto the remission of sins. Do this for a commemoration of me."[20]

There is no need of explanation, and still less of proof, that Jesus by these words declared his death to be in atonement for the sins of mankind and as a redemption from sin. Atonement and redemptive death belong to the innermost substance of his Messianic mission, yes, they are the very core of his entire religion. Not content with delivering his own self once on the cross, he therefore changed bread and wine into his own flesh and blood, offered the latter to his Father in heaven as a sacrifice and to his disciples as food and drink, and commanded them to renew this eucharistic sacrifice and feast constantly in memory of his bloody death on the cross. "For as often as

---

[20] Mt. 20:26 f.; Mk. 14:22 f.; Lk. 22:19 f.; 1 Cor. 11:23–25.

you shall eat this bread," Paul adds in explanation, "you shall show the death of the Lord, until he come" (1 Cor. 11:26).

Whenever Jesus foretold his death, he at the same time foretold his resurrection from the dead. "The Son of man shall be betrayed into the hands of men: and they shall kill him, and the third day he shall rise again" (Mt. 17:21 f.). "The Son of man must suffer many things, and be rejected by the ancients, and by the high priests, and the scribes, and be killed: and after three days rise again" (Mk. 8:31). "The Son of man shall be betrayed to the chief priests and the scribes, and they shall condemn him to death. And shall deliver him to the Gentiles to be mocked, and scourged, and crucified, and the third day he shall rise again" (Mt. 20:18 f.). In these and similar words he constantly linked his resurrection with his redemptive death. The resurrection is not only the infallible proof of his messiasship and his divinity, it is the essential completion of our redemption, the real consummation of our salvation. Only the living Christ can be the pledge of our spiritual rebirth, of our own bodily resurrection, and of our everlasting glorification with him. In particular only the living, risen Christ can be the glorious Messias-King and Lord of the kingdom of God on earth and in heaven. Again and again, therefore, Jesus endeavored to bring his disciples to the understanding of these mysteries of his suffering and of his resurrection, and on the very day of his resurrection he rebuked them for not comprehending the one nor the other: "O foolish, and slow of heart to believe in all things which the prophets have spoken! Ought not Christ to have suffered these things, and so enter into his glory?" (Lk. 24:15 f.)[21]

Let us now sum up our conclusions and compare them with the conception of the messiasship of the Old Testament as well as of later Judaism. It is evident that the idea of the messiasship as held by Jesus was thoroughly alien to the Judaistic conception of his contemporaries. He had only one thing in common

---

[21] Cf. Ricciotti, *op. cit.*, §§ 305, 407, 408, 413, 506–507, 557; F. Prat, *op. cit.*, II, 169, 207.

with rabbinical and apocalyptic theology: the idea of the *parousia*, the prospect of his return at the end of the world. But he rejected in the most decided manner the national-political messiasship of whatever form and shape, and thereby he repudiated moreover the only thing which apparently still united him with contemporary Judaism — the doctrine of the *parousia*, conceived as it was by the latter as equally national and political.[22]

It is easy to understand, therefore, that Jesus as the Messias remained all the more incomprehensible to his people, the more the latter was committed, and remained so, to the later Jewish expectations of the Messias, so fundamentally different from those of the Old Testament. The Judaism of the synagogue could acknowledge as the Messias only a thoroughgoing Rabbi, whose work, words, conduct, and teaching confined themselves strictly to the narrow pale of Talmudic nomism, and whose Messianic kingdom was a world empire with a purely Jewish, provincial outlook. The Saviour, however, did not come borne on the shoulders of official rabbinism nor of an equally narrow Jewish eschatology, but he came standing on the divinely laid foundation of the Old Testament, repudiating that false messiasship which the later Jewish narrow-mindedness had misconstrued out of the Old Testament.

Nothing is more evident from the Messianic utterances of Jesus than this consciousness of the fact that he upheld the Old Testament idea of the messiasship in every respect. Whenever he spoke of his "having come" or "having been sent," and however he expressed himself regarding his Messianic beginning, whether he referred to his entry into this world, to his life, his activity as teacher, his miracles, his suffering, death, and resurrection, he always remained conscious that he was fulfilling the Old Testament prophecy of the Messias, completing it, perfecting and realizing it: "Do not think that I am come to destroy the law, or the prophets, I am not come

---

[22] Concerning the *parousia*, see F. Prat, *op. cit.*, I, 243, 386, 418, 420; II, 154–157, 239 ff., 337 ff.; Ricciotti, *op. cit.*, §§ 483, 513–514, 543–544.

to destroy, but to fulfill. For amen I say unto you, till heaven and earth pass, one jot or one tittle shall not pass of the law, till all be fulfilled" (Mt. 5:17 f.).

If we place the Messianic elements of the Old Testament, as we have presented them, side by side with the actual Messianic confession and the recorded events of the gospel, the essential unity of the Old Testament concept of the Messias with that of the gospel is at once evident. One can find many references to the Son of David, the Son of man, the suffering Servant of God, the Founder and King of the kingdom of God in this and the future world. Hence, Jesus was able to appeal constantly to the Old Testament in proof of his messiasship: "Search the scriptures . . . the same are they that give testimony of me" (Jn. 5:39). With such and similar words he sought to turn the Jews, who were offended at his Messianic activity (cf. Jn. 5:9-47), from their rabbinical legal pedantry to the real Messianic content of the Old Testament revelation.

Yet the notion of the Messias as put forth by Jesus is not wholly identical with that of the Old Testament. He *interpreted* prophecy concerning him in an entirely independent manner. It cannot be denied that, together with the spiritual, religious, universal, and supernatural upper current of Messianic prophecy, there flows also through the Old Testament an adjacent current, earthly, narrowly national, and very materialistic. Keen minds, it is true, might have come upon the interpretation that the latter was merely the shell and symbol of the former. But it was Jesus who was the first to free the notion of the Messias completely from the bonds of what was national, earthly, and sensual, and to declare with masterly decisiveness that every other conception of Messianic prophecy and expectation was absolutely false. This we have sufficiently proved.

Jesus *harmonized* the Old Testament concept of the Messias. It was by no means a simple thing, much less merely a matter of course, to understand that all Messianic prophecies referred to the one and the same person, and at the same time to see how they were to find their fulfillment in one and

the same person. Hence the songs of Isaias regarding the
Servant of God were never, until the time of Jesus, applied to
the Messias, at least as far as we can judge from the still extant
Jewish writings. To identify the Son of man in Daniel with
the Son of David, and to identify the kingdom of God,
which was to be built up with so much effort, with the
gloriously perfected one, appeared possible only to a very few.
But Jesus united all that in harmonious reality in his own
person and in his work. He is the thoroughly supernatural,
pre-existent Son of man of Daniel, but at the same time also
the truly incarnate, thoroughly human Son of man. Both
as Son of man and as Son of David he entered upon his
Messianic rule and power, but only after he had, as the humble
Servant of God, preached, suffered, and delivered himself to
death for the sins of the human race. By his teaching he enlisted
disciples for the kingdom of God, by his death he made possible
their entry into the kingdom of God, and by his resurrection
and glorification he took possession of the kingdom of God.
Thus with him and in him all prophecies, one after the other,
range together in most perfect harmony, and the whole Messianic idea of the Old Testament becomes one continuous
prophecy; and all this again does not form a mere theory with
so many paragraphs, but, is a living organism, embodied in the
one, truly living person of Jesus Christ himself.

Thereby Jesus also has *idealized* the Old Testament concept of the Messias. Nowhere did he endeavor merely to
copy prophecy letter for letter. In a masterful, sublime way he
fulfilled the prediction, without allowing himself to be narrowly
restricted by it. He showed himself as the Lord of the Old
Testament as well as of the New: "It was said to them of
old. . . . But I say to you. . . !" That is unmistakably the
language of majestic sovereignty. And he acted accordingly.
What the ancients neither surmised nor grasped, was elevated by
him to the chief commandment of his kingdom of God: Love.
What the ancients did not regard as feasible, he forthwith
made a fact: the proclamation of a gospel of grace in contrast

to the law of fear. What the ancients no doubt had expected as a matter of secondary importance, he placed in the foreground of his Messianic teaching and activity: redemption from sin and guilt through the vicarious suffering and death of the Messias. The Old Testament prophecy was a "light that shineth in a dark place" (2 Pet. 1:19). Through its fulfillment in Christ it was so far surpassed in brilliance and splendor, that it appeared less as a torch lighting up the future than as a shadow thrown back by Jesus upon the Old Testament.

This is the specifically *Christian* idea of the messiasship, of the mission, work, and person of the Messias, Jesus of Nazareth. Jesus fulfilled, interpreted, harmonized, and idealized the Old Testament conception of the messiasship; he corrected, opposed, and repudiated the Judaistic notion as held by most of his contemporaries, whether of rabbinical or of apocalyptic interpretation. With the modern idea as put forth by the liberal supercritics his messiasship has nothing whatever to do. This school of criticism claims Jesus to be merely a successful impersonator who adapted himself to the Judaistic expectations prevailing in his time. It assumes that he must have evolved either from the rabbinism of the Pharisees or from apocalyptic eschatology, and must have embodied now the one, now the other of these, though it admits that his was a strongly individual and gifted personality.[23] This is quite natural, since modern rationalism, for which no supernatural revelation exists but only purely natural evolution, cannot possibly solve the Messianic problem in any other way, although such a solution contradicts the facts of history and, in particular, as we have seen, contradicts the testimony of Jesus to himself as the Messias.

---

[23] Concerning rationalistic criticism on this point, see Ricciotti, *op. cit.*, §§ 187, 192, 194–199.

Part V
The Divinity of Christ

THE divinity of Jesus is the culminating point, the ultimate perfection of the messiasship; it is the very heart and soul of Christology, the cornerstone and the distinctive mark of Christianity. This has been self-evident to all Christians from the days of the apostles to the present time. Wilhelm Schnehen, although a pantheistic monist, observes correctly: "Even outside of Christianity such are always regarded as Christians who believe in the divinity of Christ and pray to him in this sense. Unchristian philosophy, in the person of its most prominent representatives, agrees thoroughly with the orthodox Churches in this concept, and the adherents of alien religions, as far as they know something of Christianity, also accept it; it has been reserved to the liberal, rationalistic theology of the last 150 years to invent for its own needs, an entirely new sort of Christianity."*

Rationalists of the liberal school of today do not, indeed, fail to recognize that the divinity of Jesus always and everywhere was regarded as the core, the very essence of Christianity, but they assert that Jesus, on the other hand, was of a different opinion, that at no time and nowhere in his life did he express a consciousness of his divinity. The idea of his divinity emerged only later and found its way into the belief of the primitive Church by degrees.

In contrast to this "Essence of Christianity" it can be proved that Jesus revealed himself as the God-Messias, as the Son of God, and as the Lord.

---

*Der moderne Jesuskultus, Frankfurt a. M., 1906, 7 f.

Chapter 13. Jesus, God-Messias

THE Old Testament prophecy, as we have seen, gave voice to the expectation of neither a mere man nor of a superman, but of the Emmanuel, "God with us," of the God-Messias. Later Judaism brought this expectation down to an earthly, nationalistic level, and for this reason it was unable to imagine the person of the Messias as more than a merely human one.[1] It never occurred, therefore, to any of the false pretenders to the messiasship to claim for themselves anything of a divine nature. Jesus of Nazareth, however, fulfilled in his person the unequivocal prophecy regarding the God-Messias and God-Man.

It is true, in the gospel his humanity comes to the foreground. In every respect and in every circumstance of life he is true man. In his body and soul, in his reason and will and conduct he is like to us other human beings, "in all things . . . made like unto his brethren" (Hebr. 2:17), "in all things like as we are, without sin" (4:15). So markedly and so completely did he make himself one with other human beings that liberal criticism concludes that he did not claim also to be God.

That this conclusion is false is quite evident. Whether Jesus was God or not, the human side of his being and of his person in either case would have had to manifest itself just as decidedly, not only precisely because he was really man, but because, presupposing his divinity, the divine nature revealed itself only in and through his human nature, because he was *God-Man, God incarnate.*

---

[1] See Chapter 10, pp. 172 ff., 176 ff.

An incarnate God thinks, wills, speaks, and acts as man, even when his thinking, willing, speaking, and acting cannot be explained merely from his humanity, but proceeds from the depths of divinity. A man who would lay aside the capacities, talents, and forces peculiar to his nature and, without further ado, claim to be God would also furnish the proof that he had an enormously poor understanding of his role, that he was simply an impostor. The incarnate God-Redeemer, whether he presented himself to his fellow men or to God, remained the Son of man, even when he gave testimony and proof in word and work of his pre-existence with the Father, of his supernatural being, of his equality with the Father, and of his divinity. Thus it is comprehensible, without the need of many words, that he not only had to express a decidedly human consciousness, but also that this consciousness was revealed with much greater clearness and decisiveness than the consciousness of his divine nature and being. Not only the theological, but also the purely psychological, evaluation of the person of Jesus forbids the overemphasizing of his clearly marked human consciousness to the detriment of the divine consciousness.

If, accordingly, the perfection of the human nature of Jesus does not argue against his divinity, conversely there is no possibility of explaining it completely without taking his divinity into account. This we have been able to establish repeatedly in the previous chapters. Human nature finds itself realized in him in such an absolutely noble and ideal form that everything points beyond the merely human, and even beyond the merely created, and reaches upward into the divine. The human appearance of Jesus, his prophetic spirit, his personal spiritual life, his association with men, and his relation to the Father break through all human limitations and give reason to assume that in Jesus of Nazareth God himself lived and walked among us. Very definitely also does Jesus express this.

In the first place, he expresses his divine consciousness by the *comparisons,* in which he sets himself apart from the created world, and identifies himself with God.

Despite his humility and modesty, he knows himself to be exalted above all created things. He is greater than Jonah and Solomon (cf. Mt. 12:41 f.; Lk. 11:30 f.); greater than Moses and Elias, the witnesses of his glorification (cf. Mt. 17:3; Lk. 9:30). In him his disciples beheld what prophets and kings desired to see (cf. Lk. 10:24). The lesser in his kingdom is greater than John the Baptist, who nevertheless was greater than any one born of woman until that time (cf. Mt. 11:9 f.). David, whose son the Messias was to be, looks up as a servant to Jesus, his Lord (cf. Mt. 22:45). Just as no man, so also can no angel stand comparison with him. He is served by angels (cf. Mt. 4:11; Mk. 1:13); one word from him would suffice for the Father to send twelve legions of angels (cf. Mt. 26:53). The angels are as much his angels as they are angels and servants of his Father (cf. Mt. 13:41; Mk. 13:27, etc.). On the day of judgment they will attend him as a retinue of honor, just as the royal household attends a king (cf. Mt. 16:27; Mk. 8:38; Lk. 9:36); at a wave of his hand they will assemble the whole world before his face (cf. Mt. 13:41; Mk. 13:27). He is more than men and angels. Exalted above both, he takes rank immediately next to the Father in heaven (cf. Mk. 13:32). He admonished the disciples forcibly that they were to call no one on earth Master or Father: "For one is your Father, who is in heaven; . . . one is your master: Christ . . . and all of you are brethren" (Mt. 23:8 f.). Jesus conceived both appellations, Father and Master, as parallel, applied the one to himself and the other to God the Father in heaven, and set in contrast with both all human beings, who are different from him as well as from the Father, but who among themselves are brethren.

If these comparisons which Jesus made between himself and the created world point not only to a supernatural mission, but also to a nature far superior to that of created things, then still more definitely do those utterances in which he compared himself directly with *God*. With admirable pedagogic wisdom he proceeded from the Old Testament idea of God and from the pre-Christian revelation of God, because these were intelligible to the disciples and were generally known. He applied to himself the utterances concerning Jahweh, the true God of the Old Testament. As Jahweh alone is the wedded Lord of Israel, so is Jesus also the bridegroom (cf. Mt. 22:1), and not merely the groomsman who is to lead the people to God. While the Old Testament is never called the congregation of one of the leaders sent by God, such as Moses or Joshua, but only that of Jahweh (Num. 16:3, etc.), Jesus calls the society of his believers exclusively *his* Church (cf. Mt. 16:18). As it was said of Jahweh in the Old Testament (cf. Isa. 31:5), Jesus wished to gather the children of Jerusalem to himself, as a hen gathers her chickens under her wings (cf. Mt. 23:37). With the same absolute and exclusive authority with which in the Old Testament God sent out the bearers of his revelation, Jesus also said: "I send to you prophets, and wise men, and scribes" (Mt. 23:34). As Jahweh gave to Moses the assurance for himself and his brother Aaron: "I will be in thy mouth, and in his mouth" (Exod. 4:15), so also Jesus encouraged the preachers of his gospel: "I will give you a mouth and wisdom, which all your adversaries shall not be able to resist and gainsay" (Lk. 21:15). Jesus never prefaced his discourses after the manner of the prophets: "Thus saith the Lord," but to the great amazement of his hearers he spoke like Jahweh himself, always in his own person, "as one having power" (Mk. 1:22). As Jahweh is the Lord of the Old Testament Law, and as this lordship forms his own personal and inalienable right, so Jesus declared himself to be the absolute Lord of this same Law. In opposition to all human authority he uttered his declaration of sovereignty: "The Son of man is lord even of the Sabbath" (Mt. 12:1–8). In other words, the Son of man not only interprets the Old Testament in virtue of his Messianic authority and mission, but he also stands above the Old Testament as its Lord, as its Lawgiver, as the one who revealed himself in the Old Testament by his own word and by his prophets. In the New Testament he draws near to humanity in the person of the Son of man. Jesus, therefore, applied the Old Testament utterances of Jahweh to himself without reservation and in solemn asseveration declared himself equal with the God of the Old Testament. Hence it is only a continuation and a further stressing of this thought when Jesus, as we shall soon see, removed all distinction of nature and being between himself and God the Father in heaven by his utterances concerning the Son of God.

Furthermore, Jesus expressed the consciousness of his divine nature in the *demands* which he made on mankind in reference to his person. Most remarkable is the *demand of faith*. This forms the basic theme of all his discourses and actions. What he sought among the Jews, but did not find in sufficient measure, is faith (cf. Mt. 8:10). That which qualifies the Gentiles to enter the kingdom of heaven before the Israelites, is their greater readiness to believe (cf. 8:10–12). To render the disciples strong in faith was the chief aim of his admonitions,[2] the most valuable fruit of his prayers (Lk. 22:32; Jn. 17:8, 20). In only two places do the synoptics inform us that Jesus was astonished, once at the faith and again at the unbelief manifested (cf. Mt. 8:10; Mk. 6:6). When contemplating his second coming the thought which concerned him the most was whether he "shall find faith on earth" (Lk. 18:8). One could, of course, easily understand his demand of faith in his words and his divine mission, even if he were really no more than a purely human Messias. However, his claim to faith refers not only to his words and his mission, but directly to his person: "Blessed is he that shall not be scandalized in me" (Mt. 11:6 ff.). Faith in the person of Jesus is the way to escape eternal ruin and to possess eternal life (cf. Jn. 3:15). Faith in him is the work demanded by God (cf. 6:29), and unbelief is the sin of the world (cf. 16:9). The disciples are to believe in him exactly in the same way as they believe in God (cf.

---

[2] Cf. Mt. 9:2, 22, 29; 15:28; 16:8; 17:19; 21:21; Mk. 4:40; 5:34; 10:52; 11:22; Lk. 7:50; 8:25, 48; 17:5 f., 19; 18:8, 42; Jn. 11:15, 25 ff., 40–48; 12:36–46; 14:1, 10 ff.

14:1); faith in the person of the Father and faith in the person of Jesus stand side by side. Still more, they merge into one: "He that believeth in me, doth not believe in me, but in him that sent me" (12:44). Whoever does not believe in Jesus, thereby proves his complete unbelief in God (cf. 5:37 f.). In a word, Jesus demands not only that men should believe in him and in his divine mission, but that they should accept him, his person, in faith. Judgment will be passed in the first place on unbelief in his person, and then only on unbelief in his teaching: "He that shall be ashamed of me, and my words, . . . the Son of man will also be ashamed of him, when he shall come in the glory of the Father with the holy angels" (Mk. 8:38). He declares himself to be the object and substance of faith. That would be outright idolatry if Jesus were mere man with a supernatural mission, but not true God, God-Man.

Together with the demand for faith Jesus also demands unlimited *love*. He reproached the Jews not only for their lack of faith, but also for their lack of love for his person (cf. Jn. 8:42). The disciples were constantly admonished to distinguish themselves through love of Jesus (cf. 8:42; 14:15, 21, 23). It is not, however, a purely natural love which he demands of his followers. On the contrary, every sort of mere natural love must be subordinated to the love of Jesus: "He that loveth father or mother more than me, is not worthy of me; and he that loveth son or daughter more than me, is not worthy of me" (Mt. 10:37). Yes, even the ties of the closest natural love must be torn asunder when love of Jesus would thereby be endangered: "If any man come to me, and hate not his father, and mother, and wife, and children, and brothers, and sisters, yea and his own life also, he cannot be my disciple" (Lk. 14:25 f.). No man, not even a man sent by God, may speak thus. The precept to love one's neighbor merely says: "Thou shalt love thy neighbor as thyself." Jesus demands much more: whoever does not love him more than himself, whoever does not love him above all else, cannot be his disciple. Jesus demands for himself the love of the whole heart, of the whole soul, and of the whole mind, that love and that manner of love which we owe to God alone. He demands that men fulfill toward his person the first and greatest commandment which is incumbent on them in respect to God. Whoever is wanting in this love of Jesus, is wanting also in the love of God (cf. Jn. 5:42). Whoever hates Jesus hates, thereby, God himself (cf. 15:23). Both are merged into one and both are alike — love of Jesus and love of God. That is an incisive claim to divine rights which affects life profoundly.

Again, Jesus allows *religious worship* to be offered him. We read repeatedly that friends of Jesus "fell down before him and adored him"; an act of homage which the Saviour not only accepted, but praised and rewarded with miracles. Now, the expression "fall down and adore" need not, of course, be taken outright as an expression of religious, divine worship. In itself it can mean merely the oriental *salaam*, the homage of deep reverence which the servant renders to his master and the subject to his king, and in which one falls on his knees and touches the ground with his forehead. The gospel has this conventional act of homage in mind when it says that the debtor "falling down [before his creditor], adored him,"[3] when the Wise Men from the East and Herod himself wished to adore the newborn King of the Jews (cf. Mt. 2:2, 8, 11), and when the Roman soldiers "bowing their knees, adored him" for the purpose of mocking Jesus as a pseudo-king of the Jews (cf. Mk. 15:19).

But whenever the expression "falling down and adoring" (*proskynesis*) is transferred from the profane to the religious sphere and hence becomes religious homage, it signifies, according to the usage of the gospels, in the highest sense the *latreutic adoration*, or worship which is paid to God alone. No man and no angel allows such an act of religious worship to be offered him. When the centurion Cornelius fell at Peter's feet and "adored him," the prince of the apostles reproved him with the words: "Arise, I myself also am a man" (Acts 10:25 f.).

---

[3] Mt. 18:26, according to the Greek original.

When St. John "fell down before his [the angel of the Apocalypse] feet to adore him," the latter said: "See thou do it not: I am thy fellow servant and of thy brethren. . . . Adore God" (Apoc. 19:10; 22:8, 9). To fall down and adore is that supreme act of worship which the believer paid to Jahweh in the temple at Jerusalem,[4] which the elect continually render at the throne of God,[5] and that "adoration in spirit and truth," which Jesus demands of "the true adorers of the Father" (Jn. 4:20–24), and of which he says: "The Lord thy God shalt thou adore, and him only shalt thou serve" (Mt. 4:10; Lk. 4:8).

Now Jesus allowed this form of adoration (*proskynesis*) to be offered him many times and on the most varied occasions. The question to be resolved is whether it was, on those occasions, a matter of religious adoration or merely of worldly homage. Leaving the concrete cases as they are recorded in the gospel out of consideration, it may be supposed that the Jews, with their secular and political ideal of the Messias, might have adored the Saviour as the expected Master Rabbi and national Deliverer and, consequently, might have paid homage to the Messias-King, the destroyer of the Romans, according to the secular manner of a court. However, the gospel contains not a single instance of worship of this kind, as far as we can see. Jesus would have refused it just as decidedly as he refused the title and name of an earthly Messias-King, and would have protested against being addressed and honored as Lord and Master after the manner of the Rabbis. Just as he conceived his whole work and the significance of his person to be exclusively religious, so he could approve the worship offered him only as religious homage.

Yet not only did he himself consider it as such, in the subjective feelings of his worshipers the homage offered him is always of a religious nature, although in a varying degree. It so happens that people who honored the Saviour as the

[4] Cf. Jn. 4:20–22; 12:20; Acts 8:27; 24:11.
[5] Cf. Apoc. 4:10; 5:14; 7:11; 11:16; 19:4.

possessor of supernatural, miraculous powers fell down before him in spontaneous religious awe and hope, without being aware in any way of his messiasship, and still less of his divinity. That may have been true of the pagan woman who "came and adored him saying: Lord, help me!" (Mt. 15:25), and perhaps also of the leper who "came and adored him, saying: Lord, if thou wilt, thou canst make me clean" (8:2). In other instances worshipers fell down before Jesus because, overwhelmed by the power of his teaching, of his person, and of his miraculous deeds, they beheld in him the Messias in the true, religious sense, sent by God and endowed with divine wisdom and power, without, however, positively regarding and acknowledging him on that account as God, and then only momentarily. Such was the case with the man born blind, who, on being healed and instructed by Jesus, proclaimed him as the Son of God, "and falling down, adored him" (Jn. 9:35-39). Apparently Jairus also, the leader of the synagogue, was animated by the same religious sentiment, when he "adored him" and pleaded for the resuscitation of his dead daughter (cf. Mt. 9:18); likewise the man of Gerasa with the unclean spirit who cried to him for help as "the Son of the most high God" (Mk. 5:6 f.); the disciples, who, after the calming of the storm on the sea and the walking of Jesus on the water, "adored him, saying: Indeed thou art the Son of God!" (Mt. 14:33.)

Jesus could not allow such acts of homage, which under the circumstances were purely religious, to be paid him if we suppose that he knew himself *not* to be God. On this supposition this homage would be superstition in so far as it was directed to something divine or even to a momentarily excited faith in his genuine divinity. In so far, however, as it was directed only to the Messias as the religious ambassador of God it was an act of misconduct, which Jesus, the jealous defender of the rights of his Father, would be forced to reject as decidedly as Peter and the angel of the Apocalypse rejected the religious adoration offered them. If Jesus does not reject it and allows himself to be adored as the Messias, then he thereby manifested his consciousness of being truly the incarnate God. This is all the more true of those instances in which, as we shall see later, it is a matter of adoring Jesus as the Son of God in the strict Christological sense of the word. So it was with the women and the disciples after the Lord's resurrection (cf. Mt. 28:9, 17; Lk. 24:52). It is clear that Jesus confessed himself to be true God by accepting this adoration.[6]

A third series of revelations of a divine consciousness of Jesus points to his works of almightiness. Omnipotence is the most convincing attribute of God and the most palpable proof of divinity. Jesus himself sees therein the manifestation of divinity, since he declared that with God, in contrast to men, all things are possible (cf. Mt. 19:26). Now, whoever considers the portrait of Jesus as given in the gospels impartially, undoubtedly receives the impression that Jesus was omnipotent. Neither men, nor conditions, nor the powers of nature are able to interfere with his life and conduct. He was never compelled to omit something which he had resolved to do, nor did he ever suffer or experience anything which he himself had not willed. Never and nowhere, as happened occasionally to the disciples (cf. Mk. 9:17 f., 27), did the power fail him to perform at will even the most difficult task, surpassing the powers of a mere creature.

His *miraculous deeds* bear witness to this. With unique, divine omnipotence he healed every kind of affliction and disease of humanity, raised the dead to life, commanded evil spirits, and compelled the forces of nature to obey. All attempts to expunge the miracles of Jesus from the gospels or to explain them as natural occurrences have broken down completely.[7]

[6] Cf. K. Adam, *The Son of God*, 157–206; F. Prat, *Jesus Christ*, I, 190, 385 f., 389; II, 17, 74, 291 ff.; W. Devivier, *Christian Apologetics*, 542–551.

[7] For the proofs, see Felder-Stoddard, *Christ and the Critics*, II, 227–432; Ricciotti, *The Life of Christ*, §§ 179–216; Devivier, *op. cit.*, 430 ff.; P. Batiffol, *The Credibility of the Gospel* (New York: Longmans, Green and Co., 1912), 184–195.

His miracles form the granite foundation of his life and teaching, of his divine mission, and of his divinity. He himself always accorded to his miracles this stupendous significance. He pointed to his miracles as a legitimation of himself in his answer to the disciples of John: "Go and relate to John what you have heard and seen. The blind see, the lame walk, the lepers are cleansed, the deaf hear, the dead rise again, the poor have the gospel preached them. And blessed is he that shall not be scandalized in me" (Mt. 11:4 f.; Lk. 7:23). He repeatedly scored the unbelief of the Jews by appealing to the concrete actuality of his miracles: "The works which the Father hath given me to perfect, the works themselves which I do, give testimony of me. . . . If I do not the works of my Father believe me not. But if I do, though you will not believe me, believe the works; that you may know and believe that the Father is in me, and I in the Father" (Jn. 5:36; 10:37 f.). The miracles give testimony of him so irrefutably that unbelief no longer can resort to subterfuge and no longer finds excuse: "If I had not done among them the works that no other man hath done, they would not have sin; but now they have both seen and hated both me and my Father" (Jn. 15:24). On the day of judgment "it shall be more tolerable" for the inhabitants of Tyre and Sidon than for those who have not believed in spite of the miracles (cf. Mt. 11:21). Nothing is more obvious than this significance of the miracles of Jesus, for a miracle is the voice of God, before which all human folly is struck dumb; it is the finger of God, which confounds every design of creatures; it is the work of God, which surpasses all power and might of the world; it is the seal of God, which he places on his word and on his ambassadors in order to authenticate infallibly their supernatural character. If, then, the Almighty imparts to the Saviour, Jesus of Nazareth, the power of working miracles in verification of his gospel and of his consciousness of being incarnate God, he thereby proclaims him as the divine Redeemer, sent by God. If, still more, Jesus shows that the power of working miracles is essentially and personally proper to him, he thereby directly proves himself to be the Lord of nature and of the world, proves himself to be God almighty.

Now, Jesus actually worked his miracles from his own inherent power. If at times he designated them as the works of the Father,[8] performed by the power of the Spirit of God (cf. Mt. 12:28), he nevertheless identified this power as his own and claimed for himself the essential plenitude of divine miraculous power. This proceeded from him as his own personal power and as essentially proper to his being. Whoever came near to him, felt this. The power to perform miracles is every moment at his disposal; he may use it when, how, and as often as he wills. A single word is sufficient to accomplish the most miraculous deed. Miracles appear as a perfectly natural expression of an innate power. They flow from his hands as from a limitless, inexhaustible fountain, without exhausting it or diminishing it in the least. He possesses this ever fresh source of divine omnipotence so independently and so personally, that he imparted also to the disciples the unlimited power to work miracles in his name and by his authority: "Heal the sick, raise the dead, cleanse the lepers, cast out devils: freely have you received, freely give."[9] With these words he sent his disciples into the world, and their deeds were in accordance with the assurances given them. The twelve apostles drove out devils and healed every manner of infirmity and of disease (cf. Mk. 6:13; Lk. 9:6). They were able to affirm joyfully: "Lord, the devils also are subject to us in thy name" (Lk. 10:17). After the death of their Master the apostles continued to heal the sick, to cast out devils, and to raise the dead "in the name of the Lord Jesus of Nazareth."[10]

More astounding even than the physical miracles is the spiritual power exercised by Christ of *forgiving sins*. No prophet had ever done that. At most the prophets announced

---

[8] Cf. Mk. 5:19; Lk. 8:39; Jn. 5:19, 20, 36; 11:41; 14:10.

[9] Cf. Mt. 10:1, 8; Mk. 3:15; 16:17; Lk. 9:1 f.

[10] Cf. Acts 3:6–16; 4:10, 30; 9:34–42; 16:18. See Steinmueller-Sullivan, *A Companion to the New Testament* (New York: J. Wagner, 1944), 102–104; K. Adam, *op. cit.*, 188–189; Devivier, *op. cit.*, 414–443.

forgiveness in the name of Jahweh (2 Kings 12:13). Everywhere in the Old Testament the forgiveness of sins is reserved
to God alone, just as he alone can judge sinners. Judaism did
not ascribe the power to forgive sins even to the expected
Messias.[11] The Pharisees at the time of Jesus thought the
same, and denounced the arrogance of a man forgiving sins as
downright blasphemy,[12] and Jesus silently confirmed this
opinion. But in order to show that the Messias was more than
man and claimed divine sovereign powers, he not only forgave
sins,[13] but expressly ascribed to himself the right to forgive
sins, and by a miracle proved that he possessed this absolute
power in his own person.[14] In fact, he even transferred this
divine right of forgiving sins in his name to his disciples:
"Whose sins you forgive, they are forgiven them; and whose
sins you shall retain, they are retained" (Jn. 20:23). "Amen I
say to you, whatsoever you shall bind upon earth, shall be bound
also in heaven; and whatsoever you shall loose upon earth, it
shall be loosed also in heaven" (Mt. 18:18).

The power to forgive sins arises solely from the Messianic
vocation of Jesus *as the Redeemer, Saviour of sinners.*[15] Jesus
came to seek and to save that which was lost (cf. Lk. 19:10).
This saving consists in rescuing men from the state of damnation, that state in which man finds himself in consequence of
the guilt of sin. It is, however, by no means accomplished merely
by having God announce to the sinner that his sins are forgiven
and then forgiving them; rather is this forgiveness and remission
of sin inherently bound up with the sacrifice of the life of Jesus.
He declared expressly that his "life is a redemption for many"
(Mt. 20:28), that his blood is the price for the remission of
sins (cf. 26:28). Jesus, therefore, has the full consciousness
that his life, his blood, and his person have such value that

---

[11] G. Dalman, *Die Worte Jesu*, I, Leipzig, 1898, 215.

[12] Cf. Mt. 9:3; Mk. 2:7; Lk. 5:21.

[13] Cf. Mt. 9:2 ff.; Mk. 2:3 ff.; Lk. 5:18 ff.; 7:47 ff.

[14] Cf. Mt. 9:5-7; Mk. 2:10-12; Lk. 5:24 f. See also Seitz, *Das Evangelium vom Gottessohn*, Freiburg, 1908, 422-429.

[15] See above, p. 175 f.

their sacrifice is complete satisfaction for the offense against
the majesty of God which is inherent in sin. It would be
madness and blasphemy if a mere man, and for that matter if
any creature, would ascribe to himself such importance. "The
man who fulfills the promise that God will redeem his people
from all their sins, the man who personally steps into the breach
which yawns between God and the world, the man who
claims his life to be of such value that it is satisfaction
for the infinitely great shortcomings of humanity, and whose
importance for the world is like that of God: that man is the
embodiment in a human person of God's decree of salvation,"[16]
he is the God-Redeemer in human form.

With the right to forgive sins and with the work of redemption by which sin is destroyed there is directly and logically
connected the right which Jesus reserved to himself, that is, to
pronounce final judgment one day on the living and the dead,
as *the Judge of the world.* He appeared in humility and poverty
to redeem the world; he will come again at the end of time to
judge the world "in his majesty, and that of his Father, and
of the holy angels" (Lk. 9:26). He will not only take part in
the judgment, like the angels, the apostles, and the just, but
he, and he alone, in his own person will carry out the judgment
with divine, absolute authority (cf. Mt. 7:23). The judgment
and the final sentence are so exclusively his own that even
the heavenly Father will not participate in it: "For neither
doth the Father judge any man; but hath given all judgment
to the Son, that all men may honor the Son, as they honor
the Father" (Jn. 5:22 f.).

If Jesus, as Judge of the world, merits the same divine
honor and adoration that is due to God the Father, then
evidently that Judge is not a merely human representative
of God, but God himself, like to the Father. Divine honor
and adoration can be conferred upon no creature, not even
upon a merely human representative of God. As man, even as

---

[16] Joh. Steinbeck, *Das göttliche Selbstbewusstsein Jesu nach dem Zeugniss
der Synoptiker,* Leipzig, 1908, 55.

the Messianic Son of man, viewed as merely human, Jesus would be at most capable only of carrying out the sentence pronounced by God as Judge in the name and by the authority of God. Christ, on the contrary, will search heart and reins and judge with omniscient penetration;[17] he will judge men not only according to their external works, but also their innermost thoughts and sentiments, known to God alone (cf. Mt. 12:36; Lk. 13:25 ff.), and he will apportion to each with independent, absolute sovereignty either eternal life or eternal punishment, according to the measure of his deserts or of his guilt (cf. Mt. 7:23; 16:27; 26:64). Only the all-knowing, all-just, and almighty God can thus judge the world.

In fact, the entire Old Testament proclaims that Jahweh, the Lord, the true God, would execute the judgment of the world in his own person. The day of judgment is "the great and dreadful day of the Lord" (Mal. 4:5). In "the glory of his majesty . . . he shall rise up" for judgment (Isa. 2:19). The Lord "will gather them together with all nations and tongues," that they may behold the glory of his judgment (66:18). "And the Lord God shall come [to judgment], and all the saints with him" (Zach. 14:5). "The God of gods, the Lord . . . shall come manifestly: and the heavens shall declare his justice: for God is judge" (Ps. 49:1-6). "The Lord shall judge the ends of the earth" (1 Kings 2:10). "He cometh to judge the earth, he shall judge the world with justice, and the people with his truth" (Ps. 95:12; 97:8 f.). There can be no doubt that Jahweh, the Lord God, is the one who, according to the Old Testament, is to execute the judgment of the world in person. Since Jesus, therefore, confirmed the Old Testament teaching of the judgment, applied it to himself and represented himself as the sole Judge of the world, he just as unequivocally proclaimed himself to be God.[18]

This testimony to himself as being God, as we have so far considered it, is most intimately connected with his messiasship.

---

[17] Cf. Mt. 10:26; Mk. 4:22; Lk. 8:17.
[18] See K. Adam, *op. cit.*, 171–179; F. Prat, *op. cit.*, 246–249.

He made all his utterances of his supernatural consciousness in his character as Messias. No one who studies them carefully can doubt this. Even liberal critics agree with us on this point. On the other hand, they assert that Jesus, as the Messias, reveals therein no consciousness of divine being, but merely the consciousness of a divine calling. Jesus, they assert, was fully conscious that he was by nature mere man; only he imagined to have received a Messianic vocation from God. From this Messianic role can be explained all that was of an extraordinary and supernatural nature, which Jesus thought and asserted of himself.

But such an explanation, as we have seen repeatedly, does not answer its purpose, especially if the Messianic mission of Jesus is looked upon from the purely Jewish point of view, as does the liberal school, that is, if the Saviour is made to proclaim himself as Messias only in the sense of contemporary Judaism. Every other conception of the messiasship also, unless it holds firmly to the God-Redeemer, fails to do justice to the superhuman consciousness of Jesus. The *comparisons* by which Jesus distinctly set himself apart from the world of creation, as well as identifying himself with the Divinity; the *demands*, which he made upon the faith, love, and worship of men; the *proofs* of his divinity which he furnished by his deeds of omnipotence as worker of miracles, as forgiver and destroyer of sin, as Judge of the world, all point not only to the consciousness of a *divine vocation*, but also to the consciousness of *divine being* in the fullest extent. Jesus not only lifted the Messianic conception of his time and environment from the low level of Jewish national-political notions, but at the same time he gave us the certainty that he as the Messias, and precisely as the Messias, must be God and actually is God. His Messianic consciousness is, therefore, the consciousness of being God; his Messianic revelation is the revelation of God, and the Son of man is the God-Messias, the Son of God.

Chapter 14. Jesus, the Son of God

THE Old Testament prophecy of the God-Messias ends on the jubilant note that his relationship is that of Son to God the Father, he is the Son of God.[1] This was indeed very puzzling and unintelligible to Jewish monotheism. It was only through the fulfillment of this prophecy in Jesus of Nazareth that everything became clear. Even the most radical critics almost unanimously concede the fact that Christ's designation of himself as the Son of God goes back not only to the disciples, but to the Saviour himself. It is only the meaning of this designation which is questioned. Did Jesus intend to represent himself as the Son of God by nature and being, or did he understand this term in another, subordinate meaning?

Taking our own manner of thought and speech as a guide, this question would easily be solved. In the West the term *son* is applied only to the one who is begotten by his father. With the Oriental, especially with the Semite, the name *son* has a more extensive application. It is used to express every close connection and kinship, every physical or moral communion or relation which in any way resembles the relationship between son and father. Sacred Scripture adheres throughout to this linguistic usage. Whosoever has been anointed with oil is called a "son of oil" (cf. Zach. 4:14); whoever merits death or has been condemned to death, is called a "son of death."[2] The term *son* is also transferred to the physical relations of inanimate things. Thus the arrow is the "son of the bow" or "daughter of

---

[1] See above, Chapter 10, pp. 169–176.
[2] Cf. 1 Kings 20:31; 2 Kings 12:5; Ps. 78:11.

the quiver" (Lam. 3:13), the threshed-out grain is the "son of the [threshing] floor" (Isa. 21:10). In a moral respect the pupils of the prophets are the "sons of the prophets,"[3] evil men are the "sons of Belial,"[4] "sons of perdition" (Jn. 17:12), the damned are the "sons of hell" (Mt. 23:15), the enemies of Jesus "sons of the devil" (Jn. 8:44), while Jesus himself calls the apostles "my sons [children]" (Mk. 10:24).

Similarly, and in an analogous sense, is found the expression "son of God," or "sons of God." Above all, it was natural to call the angels "sons of God" in consequence of their close connection with God.[5] For the same reason just men and loyal servants of the Most High receive the title "sons of God."[6] Therefore it was only proper to give to the Israelites the distinguishing name "sons of God," and to the people of Israel the name "son of God."[7] With even greater propriety the name "son of God" was conferred on the representative of Jahweh among the chosen people, that is, on the king who was anointed in the name of God (cf. 2 Kings 7:14). Occasionally the kings and judges of peoples in general received this title (Ps. 81:6).

It is obvious, therefore, that the Messias, the King of kings, the Anointed of the Lord in the highest sense of the word, deserved to be called the "Son of God." Though he appears in the Old Testament only occasionally under this title, nevertheless this designation was known and used as a Messianic title at the time of Christ. The Book of Henoch and the Fourth Book of Esdras plainly testify to this fact,[8] as do the

---

[3] Cf. 3 Kings 20:35; 4 Kings 2:3, 5, 7; 4:38.
[4] Cf. Deut. 13:13; Judges 19:22; 1 Kings 2:12.
[5] Cf. Job 1:6; 2:1; 38:7; Ps. 88:7.
[6] Cf. Wisd. 2:13; Ecclus. 4:11.
[7] Cf. Exod. 4:22; Deut. 14:1; Isa. 1:2; 45:11; 63:8; Jer. 3:22; Osee 2:1. Similarly in the New Testament, the disciples and believers: Mt. 5:9, 45; Lk. 6:35; Jn. 1:12; 11:52; 1 Jn. 3:1; 5:2.
[8] Cf. Henoch 105:2; 4 Esdr. 7:28 f; 13:32, 37, 52; 14:9. Also in the Sibylline Books (III, 776) the Messias is called "Son of the great God." This passage, however, may be a Christian interpolation. See Geffken, "Die Oracula Sibyllina," Die griechischen Schriftsteller der ersten drei Jahrhunderte, Leipzig, 1902, 87. For the Book of Henoch, see G. Ricciotti, The Life of Christ, § 85 f.; J. Lebreton, History of the Dogma of the

gospels.[9] By no means was it always the divine Saviour, the Founder and Ruler of the world-wide, spiritual, and religious kingdom of God who was understood by the term "Messias, Son of God," but often merely a human being, called by Jahweh and endowed by him with heavenly grace, who was to establish and rule over the national-political Messianic kingdom of which the Jews dreamed.

Consequently there arises the momentous question: In what sense did Jesus know and confess himself to be the Son of God? Does he claim to be the Son of God in a sense wholly transcending the limitations of earth, of humanity and creation, or does he in no wise elevate the significance of the term *Son of God* above the limits of a purely human relation to the Father in heaven, however intimate this may be? Does he stand in the relation to the Father as Son by nature and being, or only in a moral and religious sense? Is he the begotten Son of God, or the Son of God only by adoption?

The answer to this most important alternative in the history of the world is, after all, contained in the proofs given above that Jesus is the God-Redeemer. If, namely, the divine sonship claimed by him is simply synonymous with his messiasship, then it is certain that the former, as well as the latter, exceeds all limitations of the merely created. However, the utterances regarding his divine sonship evidently do not refer merely to the messiasship and to his person as Messias — they actually express his relation as Son to God the Father. This relation, therefore, must be examined more closely.

A mere cursory and general examination of these utterances of Jesus regarding his divine sonship affords us the conviction that he is conscious of being the Son of God in a sense entirely different from that in which all men are or can be the children of God. Whenever he spoke of his relation to the Father

---

Trinity (New York: Benziger Bros., 1939), 128–132, Vol. I. Concerning the apocryphal books, see also *Catholic Encyclopedia,* Vol. I, "Apocrypha"; Vol. XIII, "Sibylline Books."

[9] Cf. Mt. 4:1 ff.; 16:16; Mk. 3:12; Lk. 4:3, 9, 41; Jn. 1:49.

he used, without exception, the expression, "My Father," and whenever he called the attention of the disciples to their God as his children, he used the equally definite expression, "Your Father." At no time did he place himself on a level with the disciples and other human beings by using the quite natural expression, "Our Father." In the Lord's prayer he indeed taught the apostles to say: "Our Father, who art in heaven" (Mt. 6:9), yet he only put this prayer in the mouth of the disciples; he himself did not pray thus. This is evident from the clear injunction: "Thus therefore shall you pray," as well as from the added reference to the forgiveness of sins, in which again the words, "Your Father," are repeated: "For if you will forgive men their offenses, your heavenly Father will forgive you also your offenses" (6:14). Even on these occasions when Jesus united himself with his disciples in a relationship to God, when it certainly could be expected that he would use the collective expression, "Our Father," he nevertheless chose the expression "My Father": "And I say to you, I will not drink from henceforth of this fruit of the vine, until the day when I shall drink it with you new in the kingdom of my Father" (26:29). "Come, ye blessed of my Father, possess you the kingdom prepared for you from the foundation of the world" (25:34). "And I send the promise of my Father upon you" (Lk. 24:49).

In these and similar words Jesus distinguished sharply and unequivocally between his divine sonship and that of the disciples and of men in general. Gustav Dalman, who is thoroughly acquainted with the Aramaic tongue spoken by Jesus, sees himself forced to admit: "Nowhere do we find that Jesus proclaimed himself to be the Son of God in such a way that merely a religious and ethical relation is meant, such as others also could and should actually possess. . . . Jesus has made it unmistakably plain, that he is not only *a* but *the* Son of God."[10] By examining the most important utterances of

---

[10] *Die Worte Jesu*, I, Leipzig, 1898, 230, 235.

Jesus regarding his divine sonship separately, this conviction will be strengthened.

His first revelation regarding this point, made in the temple, proves this. At the age of twelve Jesus made his first Passover journey to Jerusalem with Mary and Joseph. At the close of the seven days' festival the boy remained behind in the temple, where his anxious parents, disconsolate over his absence, found him after a three-day search. In the agitation of her tender mother's heart, Mary uttered the mild reproach: "Son, why hast thou done so to us? Behold thy father and I have sought thee sorrowing." Thereupon came the remarkable reply of this unusual child: "How is it that you sought me? Did you not know, that I must be about my Father's business?" St. Luke adds the remark: "And they understood not the word that he spoke unto them" (2:48–50).

In fact, Jesus reveals in these first words which have been preserved of him a superhuman, wholly divine relation of himself to the Father in heaven. He claims to be the Son of God precisely in that physical sense in which he was regarded as the son of Joseph by the world at large. In contrast to the definite words of Mary: "Thy father and I," he placed the equally definite words: "My Father" in heaven. The *tertium comparationis* is not an ethical, but a physical fatherhood. For this very reason, and only for the reason that God is the Father of the Child Jesus in the real sense, this Child is exalted above the mere sonship proper to creatures and the sonship which connects him with Joseph and Mary. As a creature Jesus was obliged to spare his mother and his foster father the anxiety and trouble which he caused them by remaining in the temple. If he were not the true Son of God by nature and being, but only a human child, his words would be as unchildlike as improper and meaningless: "How is it that you sought me? Did you not know that I must be about my Father's business?" Even thoroughgoing liberal critics must admit: "When twelve years old he had in a unique sense felt Himself to be the Son of God."[11]

Because of this it is certain that this consciousness of divine sonship is not the result of a gradual, psychological development. Jesus did not come to the conviction that he was the Son of God in a unique sense by gradual stages, by progressive knowledge of God, and continued conduct pleasing to God. Even less than inward reflection did outward circumstances, such as perhaps the eager Messianic expectations of his contemporaries, help to awaken and develop his consciousness of divine sonship. No, even before such a development could begin, the consciousness of divine sonship is complete. As a boy of twelve, who had grown up in the poorest, most common and secluded circumstances, he knows himself to be the real, true Son of God and this with innate knowledge. Such a consciousness, however, evidently cannot be acquired or instilled: it is inborn and proper to him by nature and being.[12]

After this scene in the temple almost twenty years elapsed before Jesus further revealed himself. But after the Baptist had proclaimed him publicly as the Son of God (Jn. 1:34); after the voice from heaven had spoken: "This is my beloved Son, in whom I am well pleased" (Mt. 3:17; Mk. 1:11; Lk. 3:22); after the tempter had surmised in him the Son of God (Mt. 4:3, 6; Lk. 4:3, 9); after those possessed of devils had proclaimed him the Son of God (Mk. 3:12; Lk. 4:41), and after the first disciples had joyously hailed him as such (cf. Jn. 1:49), although they did not grasp the full significance of this expression — then Jesus began to unveil his divine sonship.

He revealed himself first of all in his conversation with the Pharisee Nicodemus (cf. Jn. 3:1-21). By reason of his benevolent disposition and greater education, this honored master was

---

[11] Bernhard Weiss, *Leben Jesu*, I, Stuttgart, 1902, 279 f. English tr. by J. W. Hope (Edinburgh: T. and T. Clark, 1894), I, 302.

[12] For an exhaustive treatment, see P. J. Temple, *The Boyhood Consciousness of Jesus* (New York: Macmillan, 1922); F. Prat, *Jesus Christ*, I, 119-124; Ricciotti, *The Life of Christ*, §§ 262-264.

worthy and capable of gaining a deeper insight into the personality of Jesus than was the case even with the apostles.

In the first place, Nicodemus frankly acknowledged his viewpoint and that of a similarly minded group in regard to the Saviour: "Rabbi, we know that thou art come a teacher from God; for no man can do these signs which thou dost, unless God be with him" (Jn. 3:2). Accordingly, he saw in Jesus a teacher sent by God, *a prophet*. Jesus availed himself of this confession as a starting point in order to lead his questioner, by means of a didactic dialogue adapted to the scholastic method of the Rabbis, to the heights of the revelation of his divine sonship.

Recognized as a prophet, he guided the conversation directly to the central idea of the Old Testament conception of the messiasship and to the final aim of all doctrinal effort in Israel: the kingdom of God. To the astonished Rabbi he unfolded the basic features of the establishment of the Messianic kingdom and the fundamental requisites for entering into the kingdom of heaven, and thereby always more definitely claimed to be the Messias of the world, sent by God.

After this had been set forth, he then prepared the way for the proper knowledge of his Messianic person. In contrast with the hybrid idea of the Rabbis, who expected in the Messias merely a man enlightened and favored by Jahweh, Jesus declared that he is a transcendental, supramundane, and heavenly being. The doctrine which he imparts to men is drawn by him from his own, personal knowledge, and not from a knowledge infused by God: "Amen, amen, I say to thee, that we speak what we know, and we testify what we have seen" (Jn. 3:11).

Whoever thus knows heaven, with a personal and direct knowledge, and knows everything pertaining to it, evidently must have been there. In fact, Jesus declared, by using the prophecy of Daniel regarding the Son of man as a starting point, that he was in heaven before he lived on earth, and that he would return again to heaven — in a word, that he is a heavenly being: "No man hath ascended into heaven, but he that hath descended from heaven, the Son of man who is in heaven" (Jn. 3:13). However, he proceeded a step further and laid the keystone of the gradually ascending revelation. After having elevated his knowledge and being above everything merely human and mundane, he now raised himself above everything created in general and affirmed his essential, metaphysical sonship of God. In the plainest terms he declared the Son of man to be the "only begotten Son of the Father," whom the Father has sent into the world, that the world may believe in him and be saved through him: "As Moses lifted up the serpent in the desert, so must the Son of man be lifted up: that whosoever believeth in him, may not perish; but may have life everlasting. For God so loved the world, as to give his only begotten Son; that whosoever believeth in him, may not perish, but may have life everlasting. For God sent not his Son into the world to judge the world, but that the world may be saved by him. He that believeth in him is not judged. But he that doth not believe, is already judged: because he believeth not in the name of the only begotten Son of God" (Jn. 3:14–18). It would be sheer blasphemy if a purely human ambassador of God, were he ever so endowed with grace, would use such language. Only the essential Son of God can speak thus.[13]

Closely connected, both as to time and content, with this sublime conversation between Jesus and Nicodemus, is the revelation imparted by Jesus to seventy-two disciples on their return from their first missionary effort (cf. Lk. 10:17 ff.). The messengers of the gospel joyfully related the miracles which they had wrought in his name. Then Jesus rejoiced in spirit and broke out into a lofty hymn of prayer, in which he praised the Father because he had hid the miraculous deeds and mysteries of the kingdom of God from the wise and prudent of the world, but had revealed them to little ones (cf. 10:21).

---

[13] Cf. Ricciotti, *op. cit.*, §§ 290–293; F. Prat, *op. cit.*, I, 184–187; C. Fouard, *Christ the Son of God*, I, 169.

Then he added the following words, which are identical in Matthew and Luke with only a slight variation: "All things are delivered to me by my Father. And no one knoweth the Son, but the Father; neither doth any one know the Father, but the Son, and he to whom it shall please the Son to reveal him" (Mt. 11:27). "All things are delivered to me by my Father; and no one knoweth who the Son is, but the Father; and who the Father is, but the Son, and to whom the Son will reveal him" (Lk. 10:22).

This exultant utterance of Jesus gives us a surprisingly deep insight into his consciousness of divine sonship, and his most intimate relations with the Father. "All things are delivered to me by my Father." Evidently Jesus thought first of the power which he received from the Father to work miracles and to overthrow the kingdom of Satan. For he himself had shortly before given this power to the disciples, and now the seventy-two return with the joyful tidings that they had actually, in his name, been able to exercise power over sickness, death, and the devils. The Master took occasion from this to lead his disciples a step further and to declare to them that the Father had given to him not only divine power, for this had just been proved, but simply divine *omnipotence*: "All things are delivered to me by my Father," or, as he expressed himself later on: "All power is given to me in heaven and in earth" (Mt. 28:18).

But this does not fully exhaust the significance of the words of Jesus. Among "all things" which are delivered to the Son by the Father, is found, besides omnipotent power, also *omniscience*, absolutely divine knowledge. Not only because he said in general terms and without reservation, "all things," but because he added expressly: "No one knoweth the Son, but the Father; neither doth any one know the Father, but the Son, and he to whom it shall please the Son to reveal him." The knowledge and the essence of the Son is so infinite that only the Father can fathom it: "No one knoweth the Son, but the Father." On the other hand, the knowledge of the Son is so perfect that he, and he alone, comprehends the divine knowledge and essence of the Father, and that all knowledge of God and all perception of him on the part of creatures flows from the divine knowledge of the Son as from an inexhaustible source: "Neither doth any one know the Father, but the Son, and he to whom it shall please the Son to reveal him." The fundamental idea is the same as that expressed in the passage of the gospel of John: "No man hath seen God at any time: the only begotten Son, who is in the bosom of the Father, he hath declared him" (1:18). In a word, the Son has a Godlike, divine knowledge of the Father, just as the Father has a divine knowledge of the Son. The knowledge of both, that of the Father and that of the Son, is identical, both are equally divine and equally infinite, two infinite suns, mutually illumining each other.

Jesus, therefore, is conscious of possessing the two qualities of being and operation which belong to God alone and in which the being, the operation, and the life of God consists: omniscience of intellect and perception, and omnipotence of will and power. Consequently it is out of the question to speak of him as being merely a man whom God has endowed more richly, from pure grace and mercy, than other human beings. The divine knowledge and the divine power of the Son can have its root only in the divine nature of the Son of God, and only therein can it find its full explanation.

This is made still clearer by the complete *equality* which exists between Father and Son. There is no further need of explanation and proof, but merely of an unprejudiced examination of the words of Jesus in order to gain the positive impression that Jesus is conscious of the fact that the Father is as the Son, and the Son as the Father, with the sole exception of the relations resulting from fatherhood and sonship. In other words, between Jesus and the Father there exists in the strictest sense that relation which exists between the Father and his only-begotten Son: equality as to nature, distinction as to person. Jesus detracted nothing from this when he declared: "All things are delivered to me by my Father." On the contrary, every

son must speak so of his father. He has received from his father
all things, his nature as well as that personal relationship which
distinguishes him from the father, and at the same time unites
him to the father. Thus there is found in this hymn of praise
and jubilation, as recorded by the synoptics, the complete confession of the genuine, divine sonship of Jesus.[14]

Toward the close of his Galilean activity Jesus endeavored
to initiate the great masses of the people into the mystery of
his teaching regarding himself as the Messias and Son of God.
The people at this time possessed about the same degree of
knowledge as Nicodemus when he approached the Master.
They regarded the teacher and worker of miracles from Nazareth as a prophet. Some saw in him John the Baptist returned
to life, or one of those men who were to be the forerunners of
the Messias.[15] Occasionally the multitudes allowed themselves
to be carried away and hailed him as the expected national
Deliverer.[16] The enthusiasm of the masses found expression in
an especially drastic manner after the miraculous multiplication of the loaves at Bethsaida, when the people wanted to proclaim him the Messias-King with the jubilant cry: "This is
of a truth the prophet, that is to come into the world!" (Jn.
6:14 f.)

In a magnificent discourse Jesus took this occasion to impart
to the people instructions similar to those he had given to the
seventy-two disciples and to Nicodemus, who held the same
viewpoint as the people. He made it clear to them that he was
not a mere man, but a supramundane being, pre-existent in
heaven, who saved mankind by his own power, and who was the
salvation of men in his own person — the Messias; sent by
God and true Son of God. "This is the work of God, that you
believe in him whom he hath sent. . . . My Father giveth you
the true bread from heaven. For the bread of God is that which
cometh down from heaven, and giveth life to the world. . . . I

---

[14] Cf. F. Prat, op. cit., II, 14–18; Ricciotti, op. cit., § 441 f.
[15] Cf. Mt. 16:13 f.; Mk. 8:27 f.; Lk. 9:18 f.
[16] Cf. Mt. 9:27; 12:23; 15:22.

am the bread of life. . . . I came down from heaven. . . . Now this is the will of the Father who sent me: that of all that he hath given me, I should lose nothing; but should raise it up again in the last day. And this is the will of my Father that sent me: that every one that seeth the Son and believeth in him, may have life everlasting, and I will raise him up in the last day. . . . Amen, amen I say unto you: he that believeth in me, hath everlasting life. I am the bread of life . . . the living bread which came down from heaven. If any man eat of this bread, he shall live forever; and the bread that I will give, is my flesh, for the life of the world. . . . He that eateth my flesh, and drinketh my blood, abideth in me, and I in him. As the living Father hath sent me, and I live by the Father; so he that eateth me, the same also shall live by me" (Jn. 6:29–58).

These words, embodying as they did the Eucharistic prophecy as well as the self-revelation of Jesus as Messias and Son of God, were too exalted for the people, and even for the majority of the disciples. Their faith foundered on this rock, so that the eyewitness John is forced to add: "After this, many of his disciples went back, and walked no more with him" (6:67). Only the Twelve remained. When Jesus asked: "Will you also go away?" Simon Peter answered: "Lord, to whom shall we go? thou hast the words of eternal life. And we have believed, and have known, that thou art the Christ, the Son of God" (Jn. 6:67–69). To the further question of the Master: "Whom do you say that I am?" Peter answered with the equally definite declaration: "Thou art Christ, the Son of the living God." And Jesus made this testimony of Peter his own by attributing it to a special illumination of God and praising him for it (cf. Mt. 16:15 ff.). It is quite certain that Peter may have laid greater stress on the testimony to the messiasship than to the sonship of God;[17] his later conduct showed that his ideas about the messiasship as well as about the divine sonship of the Master were decidedly faulty. There was still a long way to

[17] In Mk. 8:29 and Lk. 9:20 reference is made only to the messiasship.

his confession of faith in "Jesus Christ, our God and Saviour"
(2 Pet. 1:1).

Jesus, therefore, all the more diligently made use of the
Judean period of his activity, which began now, in order to
make clear his divine mission and divine sonship to the disciples,
the people, and the Pharisees. He now presented the practical,
perceptible and therefore more comprehensible side of Christology, proving by miracles that he is equal to the Father in
power and operation, and that, consequently, he is the divine
Son of the divine Father. "Amen, amen I say unto you . . .
what things soever he [the Father] doth, these the Son also
doth in like manner. For the Father loveth the Son, and showeth
him all things which he himself doth. . . . For as the Father
raiseth up the dead, and giveth life, so the Son also giveth
life to whom he will. . . . Amen, amen I say unto you, that
the hour cometh, and now is, when the dead shall hear the voice
of the Son of God, and they that hear shall live. For as the
Father hath life in himself, so he hath given to the Son also
to have life in himself" (Jn. 5:19–26).

The Son does all that the Father does, even the Father's
works of omnipotence; he does all according to his own will,
like the Father, as he has seen it and because he has seen it
while with the Father, and he is able to do all this because
he has life in himself like the Father. This declaration, found
in the gospel of John and repeated again and again by Jesus
in various forms, is only a variation of that revelation of his
divinity made to the seventy-two disciples and which is found
in the synoptic gospels: "All things are delivered to me by my
Father; and no one knoweth the Son but the Father, and no
one knoweth the Father but the Son, and he to whom it shall
please the Son to reveal him" (Lk. 10:22; Mt. 11:27).

There is the same power, the same might, proceeding from
the same inward-divine source of life which is inherent in the
Son as in the Father: divinity of the Son as well as of the
Father. His hearers were fully aware that Jesus declared himself to be the essential Son of God in this sense: "Hereupon

therefore the Jews sought the more to kill him, because he did not only break the Sabbath [by healing the paralytic], but also said God was his Father, making himself equal to God" (Jn. 5:18).

In fact, from this day on the agitation which had begun to ferment among the people and the increasing enmity of its leaders pressed ever more onward to a catastrophe. Yet this was not to happen before Jesus had given a still more complete and irrefutable proof for the divinity of his mission and of his nature. He took the occasion of the most brilliant annual festival at Jerusalem to resume his teaching on this point. In several momentous discussions he presented further testimony regarding his person during the days of the Feast of the Tabernacles in the temple. While constantly affirming his equality with God, he now at the same time promoted the doctrinal knowledge of his *metaphysical divine sonship*.

During the discourse the Pharisees put to him the definite question: "Who art thou?" (Jn. 8:25.) Jesus explained his supramundane origin, his coming forth from the Father, his being sent by his Father in heaven, and then added: "Abraham your father rejoiced that he might see my day: he saw it and was very glad." They replied sneeringly: "Thou art not yet fifty years old, and hast thou seen Abraham?" Jesus answered: "Amen, amen I say to you: before Abraham was made, I am" (8:56-58). Now, if he who was not yet fifty years old existed before Abraham, that is, thousands of years ago, then obviously he must have had another existence before his human mode of existence. And when he said in regard to this existence: "I am," and not, "I was," or, "I was made," as Abraham was, does not this mean that for him time does not exist, that he is *from eternity*? Does he not thereby say of himself what God has said of himself and what he alone can say of himself: "I am who am" (Exod. 3:14): he who eternally is? The Jews actually understood him to mean this, for they tried to inflict on him the punishment of stoning, decreed for blasphemers (cf. Jn. 8:59).[18]

---

[18] Cf. F. Prat, *op. cit.*, II, 39-45.

In order to remove all doubt regarding the correctness of this assumption, he announced himself to the people as the *light of the world:* "I am the light of the world. He that followeth me, walketh not in darkness, but shall have the light of life" (Jn. 8:2–12). Jesus spoke thus at the close of the Feast of the Tabernacles, which recalled the miraculous leading of Israel through the desert and the revelation of Jahweh in the cloud of light. For God is light. As the sun furnishes material light, so God is the original abode and the fountainhead of spiritual light: truth. In many passages of the Old and New Testaments, as well as in non-Biblical literature, the essence of God is represented as light.[19] Exactly so does Jesus conceive his nature and his work in behalf of the world. He is the essential, living, and life-giving source from which all salvation flows and in which all salvation exists. Again and again he impressed this truth upon the Jews, and presented it concretely by imparting, immediately following his declaration, bodily light to the one born blind, as a symbol of that light which is spiritual and divine (cf. Jn., ch. 9). In connection with this miracle he added the solemn warning to the blind masses of the people and to their blind guides: "Whilst you have the light, believe in the light, that you may be the children of light. . . . He that believeth in me, doth not believe in me, but in him that sent me. . . . I am come a light into the world; that whosoever believeth in me, may not remain in darkness" (Jn. 12:36, 44, 46). No man, no prophet sent by God, may characterize himself as the light of the world, nor declare that he dispenses light from his own essential plenitude. Whoever does this must know himself to be God.

Light is *life* and imparts life. In Biblical revelation and, above all, in the words of the Saviour, light appears as the effect and as the cause of life. Because God is the supreme and sole possessor of life-force, he is called simply "the life," "the Living

---

[19] For the proofs, see Julius Grill, *Untersuchungen über die Entstehung des vierten Evangeliums,* Tübingen, 1902, I, 259–271, 308–312; F. Prat, *op. cit.,* II, 51–54.

One." In contrast to the lifeless idols of the pagans and to creatures who are in need of life, the true God is defined in all Sacred Scripture as the essential Life, and as the Life-giver.[20] To speak of the "living" God was the most unequivocal way of expressing the monotheistic idea of God. Jesus also called his Father "the living Father," who "hath life in himself." But he added directly that the Son also is a "Living One" like God, and that he has life in himself like the Father: "As the Father hath life in himself, so he hath given to the Son also to have life in himself" (Jn. 5:26). Henceforth this doctrine occurs again and again in the most varied forms, and is illustrated by numerous metaphors and examples. It is finally cast into the most pithy and concise Christological form: "I am the way, the truth, and the life" (14:6). In these words Jesus ascribed to himself the best known and the most convincing attribute of divinity — absolute Being and Life.

He is, moreover, *absolute Dispenser* of life. As his Father is the omnipotent Lord of natural life and the infinitely loving Author of the supernatural life of salvation, so the Son also is the personal source of life and salvation for mankind. He proclaimed himself as the fountain of "living water . . . springing up into life everlasting" (Jn. 4:10, 14); as the vine, from which lasting life-force flows into the branches, that is, into the faithful united to him (cf. 15:1–6); as the "bread of life" (6:35, 48), "the living bread which came down from heaven" (6:51, 59) and which "giveth life to the world" (6:33). He is able to give the divine assurance: "Amen, amen I say to you: if any man keep my word, he shall not see death for ever. . . . I give them [my sheep] life everlasting; and they shall not perish for ever, and no man shall pluck them out of my hand" (8:51; 10:28).

As proof that he is the principle and source of the spiritual life of mankind, he awakened Lazarus from physical death and, turning to Martha, expressly stated: "I am the resurrection and the life; he that believeth in me, although he be dead, shall live:

---

[20] See Grill, *loc. cit.*, 225–259; F. Prat, *op. cit.*, II, 47–51.

and every one that liveth, and believeth in me, shall not die
for ever. Believest thou this? She saith to him: Yea, Lord, I
have believed that thou art the Christ the Son of the living
God, who art come into this world" (Jn. 11:25–27). In fact,
this is the only possible answer to the Saviour's question. Whoever of himself creates physical life, and from himself dispenses
eternal, spiritual life, and within himself possesses essential life,
cannot be a mere creature.

Eternal Light and Life like the Father — therefore *consubstantial* and *one in essence* with the Father. "I and the father are
one" (Jn. 10:30). With these words the Christological doctrine of Jesus imparted to the people reached its climax. Through
these words we are given to understand that not only does a
moral unity exist between Father and Son, but the consubstantiality of both. Father and Son are one in that essence from
which springs in equal measure the divine operation of the
Father and of the Son (cf. 10:25, 37 f.); they are one in the
full metaphysical sense, so that Jesus can affirm: "The Father
is in me, and I in the Father" (10:38). The oneness of essence
and consubstantiality is expressed so clearly thereby that the
Jews were shocked and exclaimed: "For a good work we stone
thee not, but for blasphemy; and because that thou, being a
man, makest thyself God" (10:33). The common people also
understood the Saviour to claim to be God by nature — God in
the same sense in which his Father in heaven is God, in contrast to everything created. And Jesus affirmed that this is the
sense of his words (10:33–39).

In view of his imminent death Jesus related to the Jews, at
the beginning of the Passion Week, the parable of the vineyard
and the husbandmen: "There was a man a householder, who
planted a vineyard, and made a hedge round about it, and dug
in it a press, and built a tower, and let it out to husbandmen;
and went into a strange country. And when the time of the
fruits drew nigh, he sent his servants to the husbandmen, that
they might receive the fruits thereof. And the husbandmen lay-
ing hands on his servants, beat one, and killed another, and

stoned another. Again he sent other servants more than the former; and they did to them in like manner. And last of all he sent to them his son, saying: They will reverence my son. But the husbandmen seeing the son, said among themselves: This is the heir: come let us kill him, and we shall have his inheritance. And taking him, they cast him forth out of the vineyard, and killed him" (Mt. 21:33–39).

No one could fail to understand this parable. By the house-holder is understood God, by the vineyard, Israel, by the hus-bandmen the Jewish people, by the servants the series of prophets, by the son, "the only son, most dear to him," Jesus himself. In contrast to the prophets, therefore, he is not a servant, but the Son of God, and indeed "the only, beloved Son." If he were a merely human Messias, that is, the Son of God in a figurative sense, then he would be only the greatest in the ascending series of prophets; the contrast drawn between the servants and "the only, dearly beloved son" would then simply be absurd.

The rights pertaining to the Son reveal this still more clearly. "The position of son is . . . considered as a legal position, which confers the right to the entire family estate. In the case of the Son of God there can be question only of a dominion over the world, and indeed such a dominion as no Jewish ruler could exercise, but as God exercises it."[21] Human be-ings, even the most favored, such as the prophets, have only duties as servants and no rights of dominion; the Son, how-ever, by reason of his nature, his origin, and generation, enters upon the absolute, divine dominion and coregency of the world. Evidently there is here no question of an adoptive relation, but of the divine sonship of Jesus in the full metaphysical sense of the word.

The high priests and Pharisees, in fact, felt themselves so painfully struck by this parable of the husbandmen that they resolved to put the Saviour to death at once.[22] Jesus thereupon

---

[21] Dalman, Die Worte Jesu, I, 230 f.
[22] Cf. Mt. 21:45 f.; Mk. 12:12; Lk. 20:19.

confronted them with fearless candor and again put to them the decisive question: *"What think ye of Christ? Whose son is he?"* They replied: "David's." Again he asked: "How then doth David in spirit call him Lord, saying: The Lord said to my Lord, Sit on my right hand, until I make thy enemies thy footstool? [Ps. 109:1.] If David then called him Lord, how is he his son?"[23] It would never have occurred to a Jew to doubt that the Messias was to be a descendant of David, for this had been prophesied too often and too clearly as a characteristic mark of the Saviour.[24] Jesus himself also firmly upheld his Davidic descent;[25] but just as decidedly did he proclaim his origin and his dignity as Son of God as supernatural and as transcending his physical descent from David. The former is to be understood as the actual and essential divine sonship just as plainly as the latter is to be understood as the actual and essential Davidic sonship. This, and no other, is the meaning of the disputation of Jesus with the Pharisees. As the Son of God he is the "Lord" of David, his progenitor; as Son of God he sits at the right hand of Jahweh and rules with divine power and majesty. And it is only in his character as Son of God that he is capable of being the Messias, that is, David's son. "For him who reads the words of Jesus without dogmatic prejudice, no other meaning can result than that the Messias is in reality the Son of a Higher One than David, that is, of God."[26] This fact appeared so evident in the question put by Jesus to the Pharisees that the evangelist adds: "No man was able to answer him a word; neither durst any man from that day forth ask him any more questions" (Mt. 22:46).

In the last hours before his death Jesus addressed himself exclusively to the narrower circle of his faithful disciples. The basic thought of the touching farewell discourses and of the high-priestly prayer is again the furtherance of the disciples' knowledge regarding his divine sonship. So decisively did he

---

[23] Cf. Mt. 22:41–45; Mk. 12:35–37; Lk. 20:41–44.

[24] See Chapter 10, p. 169 f.

[25] See Chapter 12, p. 213 f.

[26] Dalman, *loc. cit.*, 234; cf. Ricciotti, *op. cit.*, §§ 531–533.

advance this knowledge in his last solemn hour that he could declare, placing the previous and the present knowledge of the disciples in strong contrast: "If you had known me, you would without doubt have known my Father also: and from henceforth you shall know him, and you have seen him" (Jn. 14:7). With ray on ray and flash on flash Jesus illuminated for them the truth that in the Son they perceive and behold the Father himself, and the divinity of the Father in the divinity of the Son: "He that seeth me, seeth the Father also" (14:9) — oneness of nature and consubstantiality of the Father and the Son; "I am in the Father and the Father in me" (14:11) — unity and permeation of essential being; "All things whatsoever he hath, are mine" (16:15; 17:10) — community and reciprocity of essential being. The Son does the works of the Father, who abides in him; whoever does not perceive and see the Father in and from the works of the Son, hates the Father as well as the Son (14:10; 15:24 f.) — community and reciprocity of operation: "He that hateth me, hateth my Father also" (15:23); whoever loves the Son, is loved also by the Father (cf. 16:27) — complete merging of the interests of the Son in those of the Father, and vice versa. Jesus could not have expressed his true divinity as Son of God in more unmistakable and more forcible terms.

And now, after he had revealed himself completely to his disciples and had made known to them the full consciousness of his inward-divine life with the Father and in the Father, he was filled with an infinite longing to return to the glory of the Father: "And now glorify thou me, O Father, with thyself, with the glory which I had, before the world was, with thee" (Jn. 17:5). Only by voluntary self-humiliation did the Son "empty himself" of his majesty in the Incarnation (cf. Phil. 2:6 ff.); his earthly life and passion cast only a veil over his divine glory. Now he returns to the Father after his earthly pilgrimage, in order, as God and man, to enter once more into the possession of divine glory, and thereby to render also his faithful disciples blessed: "That they all may be one, as thou,

Father, in me, and I in thee; that they also may be one in us; that the world may believe that thou hast sent me. . . . Father, I will that where I am, they also whom thou hast given me may be with me; that they may see my glory which thou hast given me, because thou hast loved me before the creation of the world" (17:21, 24).

The disciples were still under the impact of this complete Christological and Soteriological revelation when Jesus came before the judges of the Sanhedrin, and gave the final testimony to himself. Not as if he could have let these judges see into the depths of his divine being, just revealed; he could only let fall upon them the shadow of his divine-human personality. Yet there was light enough in this shadow to convince them that he claimed to be the true Messias of the world and the true, metaphysical Son of God.

For a long time the members of the Sanhedrin had been trying to destroy this obnoxious man from Nazareth (cf. Jn. 7:44 ff.; 8:59; 10:31, 39). Their attempts, however, were without success because the hour of Jesus had not yet come (cf. 8:20). After he had raised Lazarus from the dead, their agitation rose to such a pitch that the High Council passed a formal resolution to put him to death (cf. 11:47–53). Not much time was to elapse before they succeeded in taking him into custody. With all speed he was placed before the high priest Caiphas and the quickly assembled Council. After the testimony of many suborned witnesses was proved to be false, the high priest rose, placed the accused under oath, and directed to him the solemn question: "I adjure thee by the living God, that thou tell us if thou be the Christ, the Son of God." Jesus answered: "Thou hast said it. Nevertheless I say to you, hereafter you shall see the Son of man sitting on the right hand of the power of God, and coming in the clouds of heaven." Then the high priest rent his garments and cried: "He hath blasphemed; what further need have we of witnesses? Behold, now you have heard the blasphemy: what think you?" "He is guilty of death!" they replied (cf. Mt. 26:63–66; Mk. 14:61–64).

Jesus, accordingly, answered directly the question as to his messiasship and divine sonship. But, in order to preclude any misunderstanding and to obviate the idea that he was the Messias and Son of God of merely human origin and nature, he added that "hereafter he would sit at the right hand of the power of God and come in the clouds of heaven." This revelation stirred up enormous agitation, so much so that the Councilors, together with Caiphas, found him guilty of blasphemy and condemned him to death. It would not have been blasphemy to lay claim to the title of Messias and Son of God as understood by the Jews; it would have been the case only if a curse or insult had been uttered against Jahweh.[27] In the eyes of the members of the Council, however, Jesus made himself guilty of such a revilement, punishable with death, when he arrogated to himself the privilege to sit at the right hand of the Almighty and to judge the world from his throne in the clouds. That meant arrogating to himself divine attributes and rights, which was just as much an act of insolence as the arrogant utterance of the Babylonian king: "I will ascend above the height of the clouds, I will be like the Most High" (Isa. 14:14). In making this statement, and that under oath, Jesus raised himself above the Jewish conception of the messiasship and sonship of God and characterized himself as the real and actual God-Messias and Son of God, and because of this claim he was sentenced to death.

All this took place in an extraordinary night session of the Sanhedrin. But, since in criminal cases the death sentence became legal only a day after the beginning of the trial, the procedure against Jesus was repeated at daybreak. The judges now merely asked for a statement: "If thou be the Christ, tell us." Jesus answered: "If I shall tell you, you will not believe me. And if I shall also ask you [in order to lead you to the knowl-

---

[27] H. J. Holtzmann, in *Lehrbuch der neutestamtl. Theologie*, I, 265 f.; *Das messianische Bewusstsein Jesu*, 31 ff., stands alone in his opinion that the claim to the messiasship in itself was a blasphemy. "However, he merely proves thereby his own ignorance regarding Jewish legal thought," Dalman pertinently remarks (*Die Worte Jesu*, 257).

edge of the real facts], you will not answer me, nor let me go. But hereafter the Son of man shall be sitting on the right hand of the power of God." They readily understood that once again he declared himself to be the God-Messias, and they interrupted him by saying: "Art thou then the Son of God?" "You say that I am," he replied. From the night session, which had been conducted only a few hours before, they knew that he wished his divine sonship as well as his divine messiasship to be taken in a literal sense, and therefore they all cried out: "What need have we of further testimony? for we ourselves have heard it from his mouth" (cf. Lk. 22:66–71).

Then the Councilors arose and led him to Pilate (cf. Mt. 27:2), in order that the latter might confirm and carry out the sentence as the final court of appeals. Fully aware of the fact that the Roman procurator cared little about the religious crime alleged against Jesus, they brought forward a charge of *lèse majesté* and of rebellion against Caesar, ostensibly committed by Jesus: "We have found this man perverting our nation, and forbidding to give tribute to Caesar, and saying that he is Christ the king" (Lk. 23:2). When this charge, however, proved groundless (cf. 23:3 ff.) they reverted to the real charge on which they already had condemned him: "We have a law; and according to the law he ought to die, because he made himself the Son of God" (Jn. 19:7). The juridical status is here sharply defined: on account of his confessing himself to be the Son of God, Jesus must die in virtue of the Mosaic law. This law ordained: "He that blasphemeth the name of the Lord, dying let him die: all the multitude shall stone him whether he be a native or a stranger" (Lev. 24:16). Jesus incurs the penalty provided by this law without further process "because he made himself the Son of God." The procurator could understand this in no other sense than that the Nazarene had claimed actual divine sonship; a mere adoptive sonship of God would have been incomprehensible to the Roman. The members of the Council on their part had heard the words spoken by the accused that he would "hereafter sit at the right hand of the power of God and come in the clouds of heaven." Thus, in the eyes of the Councilors as of Pilate, the fact of a *gidduf*, a blasphemy, had been established; Jesus is condemned to death because he confessed himself to be the God-Messias and metaphysical Son of God under solemn oath and before the highest religious as well as political officials of the land.[28]

---

[28] See Ricciotti, *op. cit.*, §§ 594–602; F. Prat, *op. cit.*, II, 327–339. For a summary of the testimonies of Jesus to his divinity, see Devivier, *Catholic Apologetics*, I, 542–551.

Chapter 15. Jesus, God the Lord

THE condemnation and death of Jesus proved a most distressing ordeal for the faith of the disciples.

Despite the constant instruction of the Master, they had not yet risen above the rabbinical misconception of a Messias who was to deliver Palestine from the yoke of the Romans, re-establish the earthly throne of David, and rule over Israel as a theocratic king. The idea of Jesus succumbing to his sufferings naturally could not be reconciled with this conception of the messiasship. It was precisely his most loyal followers who were scandalized the most when again and again they heard him declare that the Son of man must be rejected by his own people, condemned by the scribes and high priests, and delivered to death by the Gentiles. It was of no avail that Jesus added that on the third day he would rise again, for the disciples were by no means susceptible to such a pronouncement. Their whole endeavor was directed to persuade the Master to abandon his idea of suffering. At the very time that Peter had confessed so candidly: "Thou art the Christ, the Son of the living God," he had rebuked the Master for speaking of his suffering: "Lord, be it far from thee, this shall not be unto thee!" (Mt. 16:22.)

And now they were horribly disappointed to see Jesus allow himself to be taken captive, dragged before the judges, and declare in the most solemn manner: "My kingdom is not of this world. If my kingdom were of this world, my servants would certainly strive that I should not be delivered to the Jews: but now my kingdom is not from hence" (Jn. 18:36). According to their view, this meant the final renunciation of the messiasship. The subsequent catastrophe of his passion and death actually filled them with the fear that they had been deceived regarding the Master, and that now everything was over. Nothing shows their wavering state of mind more clearly than the plaint of the disciples journeying to Emmaus, when they said to the risen Master: "Jesus of Nazareth . . . was a prophet, mighty in work and word before God and all the people. . . . Our chief priests and princes delivered him to be condemned to death, and crucified him. But we hoped, that it was he that should have redeemed Israel: and now besides all this, today is the third day since these things were done" (Lk. 24:19–21).

From this critical ordeal for the belief in his messiasship we may conclude how much severer a test the passion and death of Jesus proved for the disciples' belief in his divinity. This precisely had always been the most difficult point of doctrine for them. The prophecy of Isaias that God himself was to come as the Redeemer had for the longest time found no place, as we know, in the popular concept of the messiasship. But that the Messias was actually the Son of God seemed irreconcilable with the Jewish concept of God. The first duty, and at the same time the greatest privilege, of the chosen people, was the exact observance of the precept of the Law: "Hear, O Israel, the Lord our God is *one* Lord!" (Deut. 6:4.) How, then, could God have a Son equal to him! How could Jesus, who so decisively stressed the doctrine regarding the *oneness* of God (cf. Mt. 4:10; Lk. 4:8), justify himself as the Son of God in the true and proper sense? It was only after much wavering and with great difficulty that the apostles arrived at this knowledge. How often was Jesus forced to complain of their unbelief! Even at the Last Supper he uttered the reproach: "Have I been so long a time with you, and you have not known me? Philip . . . believe you not that I am in the Father, and the Father in me? Otherwise believe for the very works' sake" (Jn. 14:9, 11 f.). Shortly after he again asked: "Do you now believe?" Then, in view of his passion which was about to commence and of their weak faith, he added: "Behold, the hour cometh, and it is now come, that you shall be scattered every man to his own, and shall leave me alone" (16:32). On the way to the Garden of Olives he declared sorrowfully: "All you shall be scandalized in me this night" (Mt. 26:31). And turning to Simon Peter, he said: "Simon, Simon, behold Satan hath desired to have you, that he may sift you as wheat: but I have prayed for thee, that thy faith fail not: and thou, being once converted, confirm thy brethren" (Lk. 22:31 f.). Only a few hours later Simon "began to curse and to swear that he knew not the man" (Mt. 26:74). The other disciples also, with the exception of John (cf. Jn. 18:15-17; 19:25-27), abandoned him and fled (cf. Mk. 14:50). Not as if they had deliberately renounced their faith; they were unable to solve the dreadful puzzle how he could be the Son of God who let himself be condemned and crucified as a blasphemer of God.

Only the resurrection could solve this puzzle and bring light into the darkness of their doubting. However, they definitely rejected the thought that their Master would rise again to a new life and prove himself to be the Lord over death and the grave, and hence they sank into the depths of perplexity and disconsolateness. The devout women arrived at the grave early in the morning of the third day after the crucifixion, in order to give the body of Jesus the final embalming. They were utterly dismayed on hearing the angel's message: "Why seek you the living with the dead? He is not here, but is risen. Remember how he spoke unto you, when he was yet in Galilee, saying: The Son of man must be delivered into the hands of sinful men, and be crucified, and the third day rise again" (Lk. 24: 5-7). When the Eleven heard this message of the women, "these words seemed to them as idle tales; and they did not believe them" (24:8-11). The risen Saviour himself sent Mary Magdalen to the apostles with the announcement: "Go to my brethren, and say to them: I ascend to my Father, and to your Father, to my God and to your God" (Jn. 20:11-17). Mary found the disciples "mourning and weeping," but they "did not believe" (Mk. 16:10 f.). Peter hastened to the sepulcher and found "the linen cloths laid by themselves, and went away wondering in himself" (Lk. 24:12), "for as yet they knew not the scripture, that he must rise again from the dead" (Jn. 20:9). Cleophas and his companion told their unknown fellow traveler, who was Jesus himself, of the "fright" which the news of the resurrection, brought by the women, had caused in them; from the lips of Jesus they then heard the Old Testament prophecies regarding the suffering and resurrection of the Messias, yet they did not understand him (cf. Lk. 24:13–27). Jesus came in person into the midst of his apostles and gave them the greeting of peace; "but they, being troubled and frightened, supposed that they saw a spirit" (24:36 f.). Thus, the time from Good Friday until Easter proved a critical one for the faith of the disciples, because not a single ray of hope, radiating from his resurrection, penetrated their soul.

It was only through the visible, palpable, evident demonstration of his resurrection that Jesus rescued them from the night of spiritual darkness and led them into the bright sunlight of Christological faith. He did not, of course, stand before them in his previous earthly corporeality, but with a glorified body, which was able to pass through closed doors, appear and disappear suddenly, and in general had retained so little of a coarse-grained nature that its identity with its previous form was not recognized immediately and with certainty. But despite this transfiguration, complete, living, and concrete corporeality was inherent in it. It was not merely a phantom which the disciples saw. Jesus spoke with them, explained Scripture to them (cf. Lk. 24:17–27), and rebuked them for their unbelief (cf. Mk. 16:14; Jn. 20:29). He journeyed with them, entered the house with them and let himself be constrained to stay (cf. Lk. 24:14 ff.). He requested food, sat at table with them, blessed the food, and broke the bread (24:30, 39–43). He showed his hands and feet, pierced by the nails, to the Eleven, as well as his side, opened by the lance, offered the marks of the wounds to be touched, and said: "Why are you troubled, and why do thoughts arise in your hearts?

See my hands and feet, that it is I myself: handle, and see: for a spirit hath not flesh and bones, as you see me to have" (24:38–40). With these and "many other proofs" he demonstrated to them in a graphic and realistic manner that he was alive (cf. Acts 1:3). Thus from the evening of Easter day, faith made its triumphant and lasting entry into their hearts.

Only one still hesitated, Thomas, the perfect critic among the apostles. He had not been present at the first appearances of the risen Saviour, and remained skeptical of the reports of his companions: "Except I shall see in his hands the print of the nails, and put my finger into the place of the nails, and put my hand into his side, I will not believe." Eight days later the disciples were again assembled, and Thomas was with them. Jesus appeared, the doors being shut, stood in the midst and said: "Peace be to you!" Then he said to Thomas: "Put in thy finger hither, and see my hands; and bring hither thy hand and put it into my side; and be not faithless, but believing!" Thomas cried out: "My Lord and my God!" Jesus said to him: "Because thou hast seen me, Thomas, thou hast believed: blessed are they that have not seen, and have believed!" (Jn. 20:24–29.)[1]

This episode reflects, with a flashlike illumination, the faith of the disciples from the evening of Easter day to the day on which Jesus "was taken up into heaven" to sit "at the right hand of God" (Mk. 16:19). There is no doubt that this profession of faith on the part of Thomas was shared by the other disciples, for surely we cannot assume that the "faithless" one was more believing than the believing brethren. They, however, did not clothe their belief in the divinity of Jesus perhaps quite so generally in the solemn doxology, "My Lord and my God," as used by Thomas, but simply in the form, "Lord, my Lord, our Lord." In the closing paragraphs of the gospels, Jesus is no longer called by them Rabbi, Master, but always *Mari, Marana,* that is, *my Lord, our Lord.*[2] Accordingly, their attitude was no

---

[1] See F. Prat, *Jesus Christ,* II, 433–436; K. Adam, *The Son of God,* 207–262.

[2] Cf. Mk. 16:19–20; Lk. 24:34; Jn. 21:7, 12, 15, 17, 20, 21; also Acts 1:6.

longer that of pupils toward the Master, but that of servants toward their divine Lord. When the risen Saviour appeared to them on the shores of the sea of Tiberias, "none of them . . . durst ask him: Who art thou?" (Jn. 21:12.) When Jesus thrice asked Peter: "Simon, lovest thou me?" the latter was deeply grieved, but not a word of displeasure passed Peter's lips, only the expression of profound faith: "Lord, thou knowest all things: thou knowest that I love thee" (Jn. 21:17). Never before had the apostles called him "Lord and God" and never had they, in a body, worshiped him on their knees, even if they had previously rendered the homage of prostrate adoration (*proskynesis*) on many occasions. But when he rose up to heaven on a cloud, to the throne of God (cf. Acts 1:9), they adored him profoundly (cf. Lk. 24:52). In the following chapter it will be shown that the divine appellation "Lord" was used outright as a proper name of Jesus from the day of Pentecost. The belief in the "Lord" Jesus must, therefore, have become firmly fixed between Easter and Pentecost. Thus it becomes all the more important to ascertain in what sense and for what reason Jesus was accepted as the "Lord" by the community of the faithful after the resurrection.

In itself the word *Lord* is a form of address which denotes nothing superhuman or even extraordinary. Exactly as is the case in Western languages, it could be used by the Semites as a polite address of an equal or as an expression of reverence toward a superior. Jesus himself was often called "Lord" by the disciples before they believed in his divinity. But that they called him "Lord" in an entirely different sense and even with a meaning implying his divinity since the resurrection is evident not only from Thomas' exclamation, "My Lord and my God," but also from the fact that they ascribed omniscience to the "Lord" Jesus (cf. Jn. 21:17), that they declared that the "Lord" Jesus sits "at the right hand of God" (cf. Mk. 16:19), and that already from the day of Pentecost they make the confession of Jesus as "the Lord" the cardinal point of Christian belief. With this confession they simply applied to Jesus the name and conception of God, as it was familiar to them and as it was applied in the Old Testament.

The divine Being is called *Elohim* and *Jahweh* in the Old Testament. *Elohim* signifies the divinity in general. It was usually understood of the true God, but under certain circumstances it could be applied also to the gods of the pagans. The danger of misunderstanding was obviated if the expression *Jahweh* was used instead of, or with the word, *Elohim. Jahweh* is the exclusively proper name of the only true God of the Israelites. The fixed designation of its meaning and significance goes back to the revelation made by God to Moses. When the latter inquired after the name of the divine Being, who had called him unto the deliverance of Israel from the bondage of the Egyptians, he received the answer: "I AM WHO AM. . . . Thus shalt thou say to the children of Israel: He who is, hath sent me to you. . . . The Lord God (*Jahweh Elohim*) of your fathers, the God of Abraham, the God of Isaac, and the God of Jacob, hath sent me to you: This (*Jahweh*) is my name for ever, and this is my memorial unto all generations" (Exod. 3:13–15). Jahweh, therefore, is: He who is, the God who has being, in contrast to the false pagan gods who have no being, but who are "nothings." It was self-evident that the recognition and glorification of Jahweh had always to be the supreme prerogative of the chosen people. For this reason the revelation was made anew to Isaias: "I the Lord, this is my name: I will not give my glory to another, nor my praise to graven things" (42:8). Not only the nature, but the mere name of Jahweh filled every Israelite with reverential awe. Already in Deuteronomy (28:58) he was enjoined to "fear his glorious and terrible name: that is, The Lord thy God." Blasphemy against this name was to be punished with death (cf. Lev. 24:16), and every vain use of it was a penal offense (cf. Exod. 20:7).

The result of this was that the use of the expression Jahweh became rare and finally was avoided altogether.[3] This custom

---

[3] For the following exposition, see the thorough investigation of Wolf Wilhelm Graf Baudissin, *Kyrios als Gottesname im Judentum und seine*

set in after the Babylonian captivity and reached its height at the time of Jesus. We note that the later books of the Old Testament, in particular the *Elohim Psalms* (42 and 83), *Kohelet, Daniel,* and the *Books of the Machabees,* seek to avoid as much as possible the Tetragrammaton, that is, the symbol for the word Jahweh, and to employ other names for God. At the time of Philo of Alexandria, *Jahweh* was already regarded as the "unutterable name," that is, it was no longer to be pronounced, nor was it known just how it was to be pronounced. It was replaced by an abbreviated form, or instead of it, general terms were used in speaking and writing, such as "the Holy One," "the Sublime One," "the Supreme One," "the Merciful One," "the King of kings," "the Great Majesty," "the Heavens." In fact, even much more cautious and unimaginative terms were used, such as "the Voice, the Height, the Place."[4] Jesus himself indicated (cf. Mt. 5:34 f.; 23:16–22) that it was customary not to mention the name of God when taking an oath, but the name of heaven, of Jerusalem, of the temple, of the altar, of the sacrifice, of one's own head; he deemed it better not to swear at all than to name Jahweh when swearing. He himself seldom used the name of God, be that for the purpose of accommodating himself to the popular custom, or because God was his Father and was always called Father by him.

In quoting and reading Scripture the name of Jahweh could not, of course, be simply omitted. It occurred countless times in the Sacred Books and evidently could not be deleted or avoided. However, the difficulty was solved by using a substitute wherever *Jahweh* occurred, and thus the word *Adonai, Lord* soon came into almost universal usage. This usage began about the third century before Christ and gradually became a general custom.[5] Later on, the Masoretic collaborators of the

---

Stellung in der Religionsgeschichte, Giessen, 1929, II, 168–239. Cf. also F. Prat, *The Theology of St. Paul* (Westminster, Md.: Newman Book Shop, 1927), II, 437–438.

[4] See Dalman, *Die Worte Jesu,* Leipzig, 1898, 159–191; G. Hollmann, *Welche Religion hatten die Juden als Jesus auftrat?,* Halle, 1905, 26 f.

[5] According to Dalman (*Der Gottesname Adonai und seine Geschichte,*

Hebrew bible text went still further, allowing the consonants of the word Jahweh to stand, but inserting into it the vowels of the word *Adonai*. Henceforth the word was always written *Jahweh-Adonai*, but only the word *Adonai* was pronounced. *Adonai — the Lord* was, therefore, the substitute and had exactly the same meaning as *Jahweh*, the name proper to the true God. The term *Adonai* was all the more fitting, since it emphasized just that which Sacred Scripture, in hundreds of ways and in a thousand places, repeatedly stresses as the most essential prerogative of God: lordship, dominion, sovereign power of God over the world and mankind, and, on the other hand, the recognition of God's divine lordship and sovereign rights on the part of the world and of mankind. This appellation and worship of God as the Lord did not remain limited to the reading of Scripture and to the official cult, but in the private exercises of religion as well the word *Lord* was used in place of the name *Jahweh*.

This is the case in the most striking manner in the so-called *Schmone Esre*. In this chief prayer, which every Israelite, including women, children, and slaves, had to perform three times a day, that is, in the morning, in the afternoon (at the time of the *Mincha* sacrifice), and in the evening, the designation of God as the *Lord* is found no less than thirty times. It is actually touching to hear invocations such as the following: "Praised be thou, Lord, our God and the God of our fathers, God of Abraham, God of Isaac, and God of Jacob, great, mighty, and terrible God, most high God, who dispensest copious grace and createst all things and art mindful of the blessed promises of the fathers and sendest a Saviour to their children's children for the sake of thy name out of love. . . . Praised be thou, Lord Redeemer of Israel . . . Ruler over us, thou only God, in blessing and mercy. . . . We bless thee, for thou art the Lord,

---

78 f.), the custom of reading *Adonai* instead of *Jahweh* had been universally established since the second century before Christ, while Baudissin (*loc. cit.*, 188 f.) assumes that it reached its final stage of development at the earliest toward the end of the first century. Cf. *Catholic Encyclopedia*, Vol. IX, "Jehovah."

our God, and the God of our fathers forever, the rock of our life, the shield of our salvation . . . thou art our King, the Lord of all salvation."[6] In other prayers also, the devout Israelite addresses God as "our Lord," "our heavenly Lord," or he invokes him directly as "My God and my Lord!"[7]

We are now able to better understand what was implied when the early community of believers called Jesus *Lord* after the resurrection and in the still more solemn confession of Thomas, "My Lord and my God." The community gave to Jesus the Aramaic name *Mari — my Lord,* which corresponded exactly to the Hebrew word *Adonai,* and the latter, as we have seen, was merely the substitute for Jahweh, the proper name of the true God. Thus the first Christians adored Jesus as the true God after his resurrection. Thomas called Jesus in his Aramaic mother tongue *Mari Eloi,* "My Lord and my God," which just as exactly corresponded to the Hebrew *Jahweh-Elohim,* which occurs many times in Sacred Scripture, and which is the twofold name with which the one, true God of Israel was adored in an especially emphatic manner.[8] The content of the Christological confessions of the disciples after the resurrection can, therefore, be interpreted only in this sense: Jesus is God, the Lord of heaven and earth, to whom all sovereignty and lordship is due, in whose kingdom and by whose kingly grace we are all saved.

But how can it be explained that the disciples, since the resur-

---

[6] E. Schürer, *A History of the Jewish People,* II, 85 ff. (*Geschichte des jüdischen Volkes,* II, 460–464).

[7] Dalman, *Die Worte Jesu,* 147.

[8] According to the lingual usage of Palestine (cf. Dalman, *loc. cit.,* 268) the word *Mar,* "Lord," was never used alone, but always with the pronominal prefix, thus *Mari,* "my Lord," *Marana,* "our Lord." Just as Thomas cried out: *Mari Eloi,* so does the daughter of Sion cry out in the prayer quoted above, with inversion of the double name: *Eloi Umari,* "my God and my Lord." This invocation expressed the thought that the "Lord God" belonged to the supplicant and also to the whole community of the Israelite people as "lordly" Protector and Redeemer (cf. Baudissin, *Kyrios,* III, 639–641). In the course of time the suffix *my* and *our* in the above-mentioned and similar forms of speech became almost meaningless, just as with the modern forms of address *monsieur, monseigneur.*

rection, not only believed decisively in the messiasship and divinity of Jesus, but also confessed him as the "Lord"? Without any doubt, the reason for this is found primarily in the resurrection itself. We shall see directly that the resurrection henceforth is appealed to by the disciples as the main proof that Jesus is the Messias and the Lord.[9] It is self-evident that they could never have come to the conviction that a man who remained dead in the grave could be the Messias and Lord of the world. For this reason all hope had disappeared from the hearts of the disciples at the death of the Master, to return only on the day of the resurrection. Whoever claimed to be the Messias and Lord had to demonstrate in himself his power over death and the world. Only the resurrection became the infallible pledge that the kingdom of God was triumphant and that the Lord directed the machinations of men toward the execution of his decrees. Furthermore, Jesus himself offered his resurrection as the proof of his personal revelation, and had granted his opponents the right to refuse belief if he would not perform this miracle of miracles. When they asked him for a sign from heaven, he said to them: "An evil and adulterous generation seeketh a sign: and a sign shall not be given it, but the sign of Jonas the prophet. For as Jonas was in the whale's belly three days and three nights: so shall the Son of man be in the heart of the earth three days and three nights" (Mt. 12:38 f.). When he drove out the traffickers and money-changers from the temple, the Jews remonstrated: "What sign dost thou show unto us, seeing thou dost these things?" Jesus answered: "Destroy this temple, and in three days I will raise it up." But he spoke of the temple of his body (cf. Jn. 2:18–22). After the crucifixion his enemies actually affirmed that they understood this prophecy of the resurrection correctly, and for this reason they demanded of Pilate: "Sir, we have remembered that that seducer said, while he was yet alive: After three days I will rise again. Command, therefore, the sepulchre to be

---

[9] Cf. Acts 2:24, 32; 3:15; 4:10, 40; 13:30–31; 17:31; 1 Cor. 15:12 ff.; 1 Pet. 1:3; etc.

guarded until the third day" (Mt. 27:63 f.). On another occasion also he foretold that he would rise from the dead by his own power and in virtue of his sovereignty: "Therefore doth the Father love me: because I lay down my life, that I may take it again. No man taketh it away from me: but I lay it down of myself, and I have power to lay it down: and I have power to take it up again" (Jn. 10:17 f.).

And now he had performed this miracle of omnipotence. No longer could it be denied. The disciples saw it with their own eyes and touched it with their own hands. Jesus had furnished the actual proof that he was the victor over the mighty power of death, that he was the Creator of life, in a word, that he was God the Lord. Therefore the triumphant and jubilant cry of the witnesses of the resurrection: "The Lord is risen indeed!" (Lk. 24:34.)[10]

The scales had now fallen from their eyes and at last they understood that long ago he had proclaimed himself the Lord, yes, that *his entire self-revelation represented an ever increasing revelation of his lordship.* In the first place, this was true of his Messianic self-revelation. As we have seen in the foregoing pages, all the threads of the Old Testament expectations unite in the one thought that the Saviour, as the spiritual Founder and Prince of the kingdom of God, would rule over the whole world, that he would be the Lord. Spiritual dominion and divine power over the world, redemption, and judgment of the world; these are the great achievements and the sovereign prerogatives of the Messias-King. Isaias, having attained that height of prophecy, then also announced: "God himself will come and will save you" (35:4). Jesus repeatedly stressed that he fulfills this prophetic concept of the Messias to the last iota. In constantly new forms of expression he identified himself with Jahweh, the Lord, who had revealed himself in the Old Testament.[11] Then he performed, as an overwhelming, practical

---

[10] Cf. Devivier, *Christian Apologetics*, I, 419–433.

[11] See Chapter 13, p. 227.

method of instruction, the lordly deeds of God in a long, ever increasing series: healing the sick, driving out devils, raising the dead to life, commanding the elements, forgiving sins. At the same time he developed his divine consciousness of being the Lord, which, immediately before his death, he clothed in the prayer: "And now glorify thou me, O Father, with thyself, with the glory which I had, before the world was, with thee. . . . Father, I will that where I am, they also whom thou hast given me may be with me; that they may see my glory" (Jn. 17:5, 24). Accordingly, just as the faith of the disciples in his divinity after the resurrection traces its origin from the impression made by his personality and from the revelation of himself before his death, so also the special form in which the faith of the disciples now appears, that is, their belief in him as the Lord, stems from the vital instruction given by the Saviour himself.

After the resurrection also, the Christological instructions of Jesus visibly have but one aim, to convince the disciples of his essential divinity, and this preferably in the form of divine "lordship." St. Luke calls attention to the fact that the risen Saviour "showed himself . . . for forty days appearing to them, and speaking of the kingdom of God" (Acts 1:3), that is, of his divine kingship on earth.

The consciousness of being God and Lord pervades the message delivered to Mary Magdalen at the first Easter appearance: "Go to my brethren, and say to them: I ascend to *my* Father and to your Father, to *my* God and your God" (Jn. 20:17). He who proclaims himself the Son of God in a totally unique manner, one contrasting with that of his brethren, and who has the consciousness of being able to ascend to the Father in heaven by his own personal power and sovereignty, must himself be God and Lord.

It was again this consciousness of being God and Lord in which, on Easter day, he refers to the entire divinely revealed Messianic prophecy of the Old Testament as fulfilled in himself in the presence of the two disciples on the way to Emmaus:

"O foolish, and slow of heart to believe in all things which the prophets have spoken! Ought not Christ to have suffered these things, and so enter into his *glory?*" (Lk. 24:25 f.)

He revealed himself as God and Lord in the evening of Easter day when he ascribes to himself the power to forgive sins, the supreme, divine power inherent in his sovereignty, and transmits it, again in virtue of his personal sovereignty, to the apostles with the words: "As the Father hath sent me, I also send you. . . . Receive ye the Holy Ghost. Whose sins you shall forgive, they are forgiven them; and whose sins you shall retain, they are retained" (Jn. 20:19–23).

Eight days later he demanded and obtained the profession of faith in his person as God and Lord from the doubting Thomas: "Put in thy finger hither, and see my hands; and bring hither thy hand, and put it into my side; and be not faithless, but believing! . . . My Lord and my God! . . . Because thou hast seen me, Thomas, thou hast believed: blessed are they that have not seen, and have believed!" (Jn. 20:26–29.)

He elicited the confession of his divinity and sovereign lordship from the disciples at the sea of Tiberias, on the occasion of the miraculous draught of fishes, in consequence of which they exclaimed: "It is the Lord!" He then demanded from Peter the thrice repeated confession of love, such as only God the Lord can demand; he afforded the prince of the apostles the opportunity of confessing his omniscience, and conferred upon him the office of shepherd over the lambs and the sheep, that is over the kingdom of God on earth, the Church (cf. Jn. 21:1–17).

Jesus acted as God and Lord when he transmitted his own power of working miracles to the believers: "These signs shall follow them that believe: In my name they shall cast out devils: they shall speak with new tongues. They shall take up serpents: and if they shall drink any deadly thing, it shall not hurt them: they shall lay their hands upon the sick, and they shall recover" (Mk. 16:17 f.).

In virtue of his divinity and sovereign lordship he also sent the Holy Ghost upon the disciples. He had promised this at the Last Supper: "It is expedient to you that I go: for if I go not, the Paraclete will not come to you; but if I go, I will send him to you. . . . I have yet many things to say to you: but you cannot bear them now. But when he, the Spirit of truth, is come, he will teach you all truth. . . . He shall glorify me; because he shall receive of mine, and shall show it to you" (Jn. 16:7, 12–14). Now he declared, in virtue of his divine omnipotence and omniscience, that the coming of the Holy Ghost was directly imminent: "I send the promise of my Father upon you: but stay in the city till you be endued with power from on high" (Lk. 24:49 f.).

Finally, in the hour of his ascension, there streamed forth from the consciousness of his divinity and sovereign lordship words of august majesty: "All power is given to me in heaven and in earth. Going, therefore, teach ye all nations, baptizing them in the name of the Father, and of the Son, and of the Holy Ghost. Teaching them to observe all things whatsoever I have commanded you. And behold, I am with you all days even to the consummation of the world" (Mt. 28:18–20).

Jesus is the possessor and bearer of all power, of all dominion, of all lordship in heaven and on earth: that is precisely the most commonly known and at the same time the most theologically correct meaning of the idea: "God and Lord," a meaning which was familiar and intelligible to every Israelite, and, in particular, to everyone acquainted with the Old Testament. And when Jesus closed his earthly existence and completed the revelation of himself as the Lord "in the name of the Father, and of the Son, and of the Holy Ghost," he placed himself *on a level* with God the Father and the Holy Ghost. He made himself one with the Father and the Holy Ghost in the *one* mysterious Trinity, whose distinct Persons possess the same divine majesty, being, and operation, and for this very reason are one in divine unity: "In the name [not in the *names*] of the Father, and of the Son, and of the Holy Ghost." And when he declared, at the moment of ascending into heaven on the throne of a cloud and "sitting on the right hand of God" (Mk. 16:19), that he would never-theless remain with his own on earth for all time, it becomes evident that he is exalted above time and space, that he is eternal and omnipresent, and that he has, in his divinity, existed from all eternity in the bosom of the Most Holy Trinity, to which he now returns in his divinity and humanity.

Part VI
Jesus in the Early Church

IN THE foregoing pages we have considered the testimony which Jesus gave of himself. In the following chapters the message of his disciples regarding him will be presented. This presentation does not break the lines of our treatise, but continues them. The message of the disciples is nothing but the echo of all that which the Master had taught them and had commanded them to teach.

In accordance with the objective arrangement of thought, as well as with the historical development of events, we shall consider first the *gospel of Jesus in the early Christian Church,* then the *Pauline Christology,* and finally the *Johannine theology.*

Chapter 16. The Gospel of Jesus in the Early Christian Church

THE final injunction of Jesus to his disciples was very definite and emphatic: "Go ye into the whole world, and preach the gospel to every creature. . . . Going therefore, teach ye all nations; baptizing them in the name of the Father, and of the Son, and of the Holy Ghost. Teaching them to observe all things whatsoever I have commanded you: and behold I am with you all days, even to the consummation of the world" (Mk. 16:15; Mt. 28:19 f.). The preaching of the gospel of Jesus and of his kingdom was, therefore, not to be limited as to place, time, or content. However, the immediate objective could only be to preach the gospel in Palestine, the home country of the Israelites, and then, spreading out as from a central point, to preach it to the Jewish and pagan Hellenists scattered throughout the Roman empire, which extended to the boundaries of the then known world. Furthermore, the early preachers had to stress first of all the fundamental truths, and only later, and by gradual steps, could they initiate the neophytes into the full content of the doctrine of salvation.

This was the mind of the Saviour, as he himself indicated plainly. Though his teaching was all-embracing, yet he placed the main emphasis at all times on his suffering and his resurrection. His vicarious suffering and his glorious resurrection constitute the essence of his work of redemption,[1] just as the Old Testament prophecy is fulfilled in the atoning death and subsequent glorification of the Messianic Servant of God. It

---

[1] See Chapters 12 (p. 216 ff.); 13 (p. 239 ff.); 15 (p. 270 ff.).

is precisely for this reason that Jesus constantly, and in the most varied forms, referred to this fact: "All things shall be accomplished which were written by the prophets concerning the Son of man. For he shall be delivered to the Gentiles, and shall be mocked, and scourged, and spit upon: and after they have scourged him, they will put him to death; and on the third day he shall rise again" (Lk. 18:31–33). However, it was just this which the disciples, enmeshed as they were in the rabbinical conception of the messiasship, did not want to grasp, so much so that Jesus had to rebuke them even after his resurrection: "O foolish, and slow of heart to believe in all things which the prophets have spoken. Ought not Christ to have suffered these things, and so to enter into his glory?" (24:25 f.) On the day of his ascension he gave them the final instruction: "These are the words which I spoke to you, while I was yet with you, that all things must needs be fulfilled which are written in the law of Moses and in the prophets, and in the psalms, concerning me." Then he enlightened their minds that they might understand Scripture. And he said to them: "Thus it is written, and thus it behooved Christ to suffer, and to rise again from the dead, the third day: and that penance and remission of sins should be preached in his name, unto all nations, beginning at Jerusalem. And you are witnesses of these things" (24:44–47). The early Christian preaching was *to bear witness*, therefore, first of all to the fact that by his suffering and resurrection Jesus had given proof of being the Messias, promised by the prophets.

Even now the disciples did not comprehend this without being influenced strongly by their Jewish nationalism. They asked: "Lord, wilt thou at this time restore again the kingdom of Israel?" But he replied: "It is not for you to know the times or moments, which the Father hath put in his own power: but you shall receive the power of the Holy Ghost, coming upon you, and you shall be witnesses unto me in Jerusalem, and in all Judea, and Samaria, and even to the uttermost part of the earth" (Acts 1:6–8).

The physician and evangelist Luke relates, in his *Acts of the Apostles,* how the disciples carried out this commission.

A typical example of their missionary activity among the Israelites "in Jerusalem, and in all Judea and in Samaria" are the catecheses which Peter delivered, beginning with the feast of Pentecost. On this day he spoke to an immense gathering of Jews who lived in Jerusalem or who had come to Jerusalem from all parts of the earth for the feast: "Ye men of Israel, hear these words: Jesus of Nazareth, a man approved of God among you by miracles, and wonders, and signs, which God did by him, in the midst of you, as you also know: this same being delivered up, by the determinate counsel and foreknowledge of God, you by the hands of wicked men have crucified and slain. Whom God hath raised up, having loosed the sorrows of hell, as it was impossible that he should be holden by it. . . . This Jesus hath God raised again, whereof all we are witnesses. Being exalted therefore by the right hand of God, and having received of the Father the promise of the Holy Ghost, he hath poured forth this which you see and hear" (Acts 2:22–24, 32 f.). In the porch of Solomon Peter repeated the same testimony: "The God of Abraham, and the God of Isaac, and the God of Jacob, the God of our fathers, hath glorified his Son Jesus, whom you indeed delivered up and denied before the face of Pilate, when he judged he should be released. But you denied the Holy One and the Just, and desired a murderer to be granted to you. But the author of life you killed, whom God hath raised from the dead, of which we are witnesses" (3:13–15). When taken to account for the healing of the lame man at the gate of the temple, called the Beautiful, Peter addressed the members of the High Council with the words: "Ye princes of the people, and ancients, hear: if we this day are examined concerning the good deed done to the infirm man, by what means he hath been made whole: be it known to you all, and to all the people of Israel, that by the name of our Lord Jesus Christ of Nazareth, whom you crucified, whom God hath raised from the dead, even by him this man standeth here before you whole. This is the stone which was rejected by you the builders, which is become the head of the corner. Neither is there salvation in any other. For there is no other name under heaven given to men, whereby we must be saved" (4:8–12). Cast into prison, and again brought before the Council, Peter stood by his testimony: "The God of our fathers hath raised up Jesus, whom you put to death, hanging him upon a tree. Him hath God exalted with his right hand, to be Prince and Saviour, to give repentance to Israel, and remission of sins. And we are witnesses of these things and the Holy Ghost, whom God hath given to all that obey him" (5:30–32).

The essential points of the earliest gospel message are, therefore, the miraculous deeds of Jesus, his death on the cross, and the resurrection. Among them the resurrection occupies such a prominent place that the apostles henceforth, and with emphasis, called themselves witnesses of the resurrection, yes, they even declared that to be an apostle means simply to be "a witness of the resurrection" (Acts 1:21 f.). For though the miracles and the death of Jesus were known to all the people, yet the risen Saviour had appeared only to his own disciples, and only they could therefore give testimony of him. Furthermore, the resurrection, together with the ascension and the descent of the Holy Spirit, was the most evident and palpable proof that Jesus was the Lord and Messias.

However, the earliest preachers of the gospel not only testified to the reality of the miracles, suffering, and resurrection of Jesus, they also declared that this was foretold by the prophets.[2] They saw therein the fulfillment in particular of the prophecies of Isaias concerning the Servant of God, who suffers and dies for the sins of humanity, rises again from the dead, and so enters into his glory.[3] The Jews were reminded continually that Jesus is this suffering, atoning, and glorified Servant of God,[4] and that he who ascended into heaven is the Lord, to whom

---

[2] Cf. Acts 2:16–21, 25–35; 3:18–25; 7:2–53.
[3] See Chapter 10, p. 169 ff.
[4] Cf. Acts 3:13, 26; 4:27, 30.

Jahweh says, according to the psalmist: "The Lord said to my Lord, sit thou on my right hand, until I make thy enemies thy footstool" (Acts 2:34 f.; Ps. 109:1).

Hence the conclusive argument of the early catechesis: "Therefore let all the house of Israel know most certainly, that God hath made both Lord and Christ, this same Jesus, whom you crucified" (Acts 2:36). Hereby "it is not said that he had not yet been the Christ or the Lord during his lifetime, but merely, that God had now raised him to a position, and had transfigured him into a living form, wherein he could prove himself to his community as the Lord and the Christ, which he had already been before."[5] It was not only the resurrection on which the belief in Jesus as the Lord and Messias was founded, but the resurrection in union with the definite declaration of Jesus that he was the Lord and Messias. The belief of the disciples had its root not only in the events accompanying the resurrection; it went back beyond Golgotha to the self-revelation of the Master as God and Messias. With this self-revelation as a basis, however, the resurrection and its finale, the ascension, became the irrefutable proof that Jesus was truly the Lord and Messias.

The messiasship and the lordship of Jesus were in fact so firmly anchored in the catechesis of the disciples and in the belief of the community from the very beginning, that these two predicates were applied to him outright as proper names. Precisely in the same manner as he had heretofore been called "Jesus," he was called henceforth simply *Jesus Messias = Jesus Christ*,[6] or *the Lord, the Lord Jesus, our Lord Jesus Christ*.[7]

Before the close of the Palestinian period of the early preaching of the gospel, the call went out from Jesus to the highly educated Pharisee and most violent persecutor, Saul.[8] When he

---

[5] Th. Zahn, *Skizzen aus dem Leben der alten Kirche*, Leipzig, 1908, 294 f.

[6] For the first time in Acts 2:38, also 3:6, 20; 4:10; 5:42; 8:12, 37, etc.

[7] For the first time at the election of Matthias: Acts 1:21 ("the Lord Jesus"), also 4:33; 7:58; 8:16; 9:17, 34, etc.

[8] Acts 9:1-19. At the latest his conversion took place three to five

had become Paul, he "increased much more in strength, and confounded the Jews who dwelt at Damascus, affirming that he is the Christ" (Acts 9:22). Soon he also preached in Jerusalem, "dealing confidently in the name of the Lord" (9:28). Upon his shoulders fell the burden of performing the principal role in the forthcoming mission among the Jewish and pagan Hellenists in the world-wide Roman empire. The Lord himself made the revelation regarding him: "This man is to me a vessel of election, to carry my name before the Gentiles, and kings, and the children of Israel. For I will shew him how great things he must suffer for my name's sake" (9:15 f.).

The impetus to this mission to the Gentiles was given directly by the Lord. In a vision he showed Peter that the non-Israelites also were called to the kingdom of God, and Peter led the centurion Cornelius of Caesarea and his household into the Church as the first neophytes (Acts 10:1–48). This occurrence seemed almost incomprehensible to the earliest Jewish disciples. They "contended" with Peter, saying: "Why didst thou go in to men uncircumcised, and didst eat with them?" (11:1–3.) It was only when he pointed out that the Lord himself had taken a hand in the matter that they were quieted, so that they exclaimed: "God then hath also to the Gentiles given repentance unto life!" (11:18.)

At the same time all the missionaries were conscious of the fact that Israel was the chosen people, and that the Gentiles were the second-born children of God. How impressive are the words of the apostle of the Gentiles on this point, as found in the ninth to the eleventh chapter of his epistle to the Romans! Among others, Paul penned the following sentences: "I wished myself to be an anathema from Christ, for my brethren, who are my kinsmen according to the flesh, who are Israelites: to whom

---

years after the death of the Saviour; according to Harnack (*Geschichte der altchristl. Literatur*, II, 1, Leipzig, 1897, 237), it is to be placed as early as "the year 30, i.e., either in the year of the death of Christ or the following year."

belongeth the adoption as of children and the glory and the testament and the giving of the law and the service of God and the promises: whose are the fathers and of whom is Christ, according to the flesh, who is over all things, God blessed for ever" (9:3-5). On the other hand, he also admits: "If thou confess with thy mouth the Lord Jesus and believe in thy heart that God hath raised him up from the dead, thou shalt be saved. . . . For there is no distinction of the Jew and the Greek: for the same Lord is over all, rich unto all who call upon him" (10:9, 12).

Accordingly, the messengers of the gospel addressed themselves first to the "Jews among the Gentiles" (Acts 21:21), wherever they encountered them. In Antioch, where "the disciples were first called Christians" (11:26), the disciples at first spoke "the word to none, but to the Jews only," but later on also to the Gentiles, "preaching the Lord Jesus" (11:19 f.). In Ephesus Apollo preached "boldly in the synagogue" (18:26), and in Achaia also "he convinced the Jews openly, showing by Scripture, that Jesus is the Christ" (18:28). Paul and Barnabas "preached the word of God in the synagogues of the Jews" at Salamina (13:5). At Iconium "they entered together into the synagogue of the Jews, and so spoke that a very great multitude both of the Jews and of the Greeks did believe" (14:1). At Thessalonica "Paul, according to his custom, went in unto them: and for three sabbath days he reasoned with them out of the scriptures: declaring and insinuating that the Christ was to suffer, and to rise again from the dead; and that this is Jesus Christ, whom I preach to you. And some of them believed and were associated to Paul and Silas: and of those that served God and of the Gentiles a great multitude: and of noble women not a few" (17:1-4). At Corinth Paul "reasoned in the synagogue every sabbath, bringing in the name of the Lord Jesus; and he persuaded the Jews and the Greeks" (18:4). At Ephesus, "entering into the synagogue, he spoke boldly for the space of three months, disputing and exhorting concerning the kingdom of God. But when some were hardened and believed not, speaking evil of the way of the Lord before the multitude, departing from them, he separated the disciples, disputing daily in the school of one Tyrannus. And this continued for the space of two years, so that all who dwelt in Asia, heard the word of the Lord, both Jews and Gentiles" (19:8–10). We observe the same everywhere: the early preachers direct their message first to the Jews; at the same time they seek to gain the Gentiles present in the synagogues, but it is only when the children of Israel become hardened against the faith that the words of condemnation are uttered against them: "To you it behooved us first to speak the word of God: but because you reject it and judge yourselves unworthy of eternal life, behold we turn to the Gentiles. For so the Lord hath commanded us: I have set thee to be the light of the Gentiles; that thou mayest be for salvation unto the utmost part of the earth" (13:46 f.). Paul acted in the same manner at Corinth. He "was earnest in preaching, testifying to the Jews, that Jesus is the Christ. But they gainsaying and blaspheming, he shook his garments, and said to them: Your blood be upon your own heads: I am clean: from henceforth I will go unto the Gentiles" (18:5 f.).

Among the Hellenistic Jews the preaching of the Lord Jesus was always linked to the Messianic prophecies of the Old Testament, and reached its high point in the proof that Jesus of Nazareth was the promised Messias. A typical example of this method of procedure is the address of Paul in the synagogue at Antioch. He sets forth that Jahweh had chosen the people of Israel and had promised them a Saviour from the house of David, who had now appeared in the person of Jesus (Acts 13:16–25). Then the apostle adds:

> Men, brethren, children of the stock of Abraham, and whosoever among you fear God, to you the word of this salvation is sent. For they that inhabited Jerusalem, and the rulers thereof, not knowing him, nor the voices of the prophets, which are read every sabbath, judging him have fulfilled them. And finding no cause of death in him, they desired of Pilate, that they might

kill him. And when they had fulfilled all things that were written of him, taking him down from the tree, they laid him in a sepulchre. But God raised him up from the dead the third day: who was seen for many days, by them who came up with him from Galilee to Jerusalem, who to this present are his witnesses to the people. And we declare unto you, that the promise which was made to our fathers, this same God hath fulfilled to our children, raising up Jesus, as in the second psalm also is written: Thou art my Son, this day have I begotten thee. And to show that he raised him up from the dead, not to return now any more to corruption, he said thus: I will give you the holy things of David faithful [Isa. 55:3]. And therefore, in another place also, he saith: Thou shalt not suffer thy holy one to see corruption [Ps. 15:10]. For David, when he had served in his generation, according to the will of God, slept: and was laid unto his fathers, and saw corruption. But he whom God hath raised from the dead, saw no corruption. Be it known therefore to you, men, brethren, that through him forgiveness of sin is preached to you . . . (13:26–38).

As can be seen, this preaching, and all the catecheses directed to the Jewish Hellenists, aim first of all at proving that Jesus is the Messias. That the Messias Jesus is the "Lord" followed naturally from his resurrection, and Peter accordingly already on Pentecost drew therefrom the following conclusion: "Therefore let all the house of Israel know most certainly, that God hath made both Lord and Christ, this same Jesus, whom you have crucified" (Acts 2:36).

The Gentile Hellenists were acquainted neither with the Messianic prophecies, nor with the monotheism of the Old Testament. For this reason, when Paul "preached to them Jesus and the resurrection" at Athens (Acts 17:18), he had to speak to the Areopagites first of the "unknown God" (17:22–31). It was only after the foundation of the belief in God had been laid that it was possible to "preach Jesus" and to call attention to the fact that the prophets had spoken of him. Significant in this regard is the discourse of the prince of the apostles in the house of Cornelius the centurion:

God sent the word to the children of Israel, preaching peace by

Jesus Christ: (he is Lord of all). You know the word which hath been published through all Judea: for it began from Galilee, after the baptism which John preached, Jesus of Nazareth: how God anointed him with the Holy Ghost, and with power, who went about doing good and healing all that were oppressed by the devil, for God was with him. And we are witnesses of all things that he did in the land of the Jews and in Jerusalem, whom they killed, hanging him upon a tree. Him God raised up on the third day: and gave him to be made manifest, not to all the people, but to witnesses preordained by God, even to us, who did eat and drink with him, after he arose again from the dead; and he commanded us to preach to the people, and to testify that it is he who was appointed by God to be the judge of the living and the dead. To him all the prophets give testimony, that by his name all receive remission of sins, who believe in him (10:36–43).

The content of this "preaching Jesus" to the Gentiles was the same as of that addressed to the Jews, with the exception that the main emphasis was no longer placed on his messiasship, but on the fact that he was "the Lord of all." Not as if the confession of the messiasship had been abandoned; on the contrary, this always remained one of the principal dogmas of Christianity. The conviction that Jesus was the Messias was so deeply embedded, as we know, that he was called *Christ* as well as Jesus as a matter of course, the Greek word being used for the Hebraic term. However, the word *Christ* was applied, precisely as the word *Jesus,* more as a proper name than as a designation of office.

On the other hand, whatever the early Church wished to say of Jesus Christ, was by preference linked to the name "Lord," "our Lord," "our Lord Jesus Christ." To become a Christian meant simply "to believe in the Lord Jesus Christ" (Acts 11:17) or "to become converted to the Lord" (11:21). The gospel of Jesus in its entirety is called "the word of the Lord" (12:24; 13:48; 15:36) or "the doctrine of the Lord" (13:12; 28:31). The first messengers of the gospel preached simply "the Lord Jesus" (11:20). They are "men that have given their lives for the name of our Lord Jesus Christ" (15:26).

Any manner of doubt concerning the meaning of this confession is inadmissible. We have seen in the foregoing pages that Jesus revealed himself to them as God the Lord, and that ever since the day of the resurrection they adored him definitely as God the Lord. If then they, from the day of Pentecost, began to preach the gospel of the Lord Jesus to the whole world, they obviously also wished to preach him as God the Lord. The correctness of this statement will be proved specifically later on by means of the Acts. Just now we wish merely to emphasize that the confession of the divinity of Jesus was linked to the expression "Lord" in a manner which was actually providential. In the religious idiom of the Gentile Hellenists as well as of the Jews in the diaspora and in Palestine, this word long since bore a meaning which supported the Christian belief and brought it into strong relief.[9]

"It can be said with certainty that at the time when Christianity originated, 'Lord' was a divine predicate intelligible to the whole Eastern world."[10] The use of this divine title most probably appeared first in Syria, spread from there to Egypt, and was simply taken over by the polytheistic religions of the Greco-Roman world of culture. Its signification, likewise, remained the same everywhere in the pagan world. The term *God* merely designated the divine Being; the word *Lord* denoted the divinity in its relation to its worshipers. The tutelary god stood in relation to his clients as a lord in relation to his servants. Whenever the latter prayed to him, they were aware that they belonged entirely to him and that he belonged entirely to them. They were subject to him as bondsmen, and his duty was to provide for them, as a benevolent feudal lord for his vassals. He was, in the fullest sense, *their* lord, and they were

---

[9] Regarding the profane use of the word *Lord*, a brief but excellent explanation is given by E. von Dobschütz: "Κύριος Ἰησοῦς," *Zeitschrift für neutestamentl. Wissenschaft*, 30 (1931), 107–112.

[10] Adolf Deissmann, *Licht vom Osten*, Tübingen, 1909, 263. English tr. by Lionel R. M. Strachan, *Light From the Ancient East* (New York: George H. Doran Co., 1927), p. 350.

his household. Naturally, there were many "lords," just as there were many gods. Every district, every city, every person had a "lord" who was not the lord of the others.[11] This polytheistic use of the divine predicate *Lord* was a deplorable error, but in a certain way it was, nevertheless, a preparation of Gentile Hellenism for the reception of the gospel of the Lord Jesus. The popular appellation for the gods as lords helped the Gentiles to understand the Christian message, the chief point of which was that Jesus is not one of many lords, but "the Lord of all" (Acts 10:36), "the same Lord over all, rich unto all who call upon him" (Rom. 10:12).

The Hellenist Jews were better prepared for this doctrine of the Lord Jesus Christ. Supported by the lingual usage of the title *Kyrios,* but in contrast to its signification among the pagans, the Hellenist Jews designated the *one,* true God as the "Lord." This is made evident especially by the Septuagint, the Greek translation of the Old Testament, which was begun in the third century before Christ, and which took the place of the Hebrew Bible text among the Jews in the diaspora. The collaborators of the Septuagint translate the Tetragrammaton JHVH (Jahweh) throughout with *Kyrios* (Lord), precisely in the same manner as they translate *Elohim* with *Theos* (God). The divine appellation *Kyrios* is found about 8000 times in the Greek Old Testament, the word *Theos* 4200 times. In 995 passages the two words are joined in the emphatic formula

---

[11] Cf. Lagrange, *Études sur les réligions sémitiques,* Paris, 1905, 83–109; Werner Foerster, *Herr ist Jesus, Herkunft und Bedeutung des urchristlichen Kyrios-Bekenntnisses,* Gütersloh, 1924, 69–98; W. W. Graf Baudissin, *Kyrios als Gottesname im Judentum und seine Stelle in der Religionsgeschichte,* Giessen, 1929, 264–286. Baudissin's investigations confirm the opinion of W. Bousset (*Kyrios Christos,* Göttingen, 1913, 112–118) that the name *lord* was applied to gods undoubtedly first in the religions of Syro-Phoenicia, then of Asia Minor, and finally of Greece and Rome. On the other hand, the main thesis of Bousset, namely, that Christianity had simply transferred the Syro-Phoenician name of, and belief in, the gods, and even the Roman cult of the Caesars, to Jesus Christ, has been proved false. On this point, cf. Foerster, *loc. cit.,* 12 ff.; E. v. Dobschütz, *loc. cit.,* 105 f.; Karl Prümm, S.J., *Der christliche Glaube und die altheidnische Welt,* Leipzig, 1935, I, 176–227; F. Prat, *Jesus Christ,* II, 435, n. 30.

Kyrios ho Theos (the Lord God) in translating the Hebraic *Jahweh Elohim*.[12] But even outside of the Septuagint *Kyrios* is found as a substitute for *Jahweh* already in the first Christian century, thus in the *Psalms of Solomon* and in the *Assumptio Mosis*. Philo, likewise, makes *Kyrios* and *Jahweh* identical; moreover, he is of the opinion that God himself had given the word *Kyrios* to men for the correct and proper pronunciation of his "unutterable name."[13] Wherever, in general, the word *Kyrios* occurs in the ritual language of Hellenistic Judaism, "it is used only of the *one*, true God."[14] If, then, the early messengers of the gospel of Jesus preached him as "the Lord," every Jew in the diaspora was aware that they regarded him as being the same as the one, true God.

This was just as self-evident to the Jews in Palestine. We have shown in the preceding chapter that in the reading of Scripture, as well as in their prayers, they replaced the divine appellation *Jahweh* with the Hebraic *Adonai*, respectively with the Aramaic *Mari* (my Lord). *Adonai-Mari* was equivalent to *Kyrios*, with the result that the Septuagint took over this Greek appellation of God.[15] The mere use of the sacral expression

---

[12] Baudissin furnishes every desirable proof and full explanation in his monumental work, *Kyrios als Gottesnamen im Judentum*. Cf. Dobschütz, *loc. cit.*, 98.

[13] Cf. Foerster, *loc. cit.*, 1181–20; Baudissin, II, 12–15, 179–181.

[14] Baudissin, III, 698.

[15] Formerly it was commonly thought that *Adonai* as pronunciation for *Jahweh* was of earlier date than the use of *Kyrios* as a substitute for the same name. Recently Baudissin endeavored to establish by painstaking investigation "that the use of *Adonai* as a proper name dates from a later period, that the Greek translators . . . had not found it in their [Hebrew] original texts and that apparently they were not acquainted with the expression *Adonai* in place of *Jahweh*, consequently, that the word *Kyrios* of the Septuagint is not a translation of *Adonai*" (*loc. cit.*, II, 236). However, the reasons brought forward by Baudissin do not appear conclusive and were refuted by the expert investigations of E. v. Dobschütz, *loc. cit.*, 102 ff., and especially by those of Lucien Cerfaux, "Le Nom divin Kyrios dans la Bible grecque" and "Adonai et Kyrios" (*Revue des sciences philosophiques et théologiques XX année*, Paris, 1931, 27–51, 417–452). The traditional assumption stands, therefore, that *Kyrios* in the Septuagint is simply a translation of *Adonai*, which the Hebraistic Rabbis commonly substituted for JHVH in their scriptural readings.

Adonai-Mari for Jesus was an unequivocal affirmation of his divinity.[16] It was the firmly established and express repetition of the confession of Thomas: "My Lord and my God."

The Acts allow no doubt to remain that the earliest preachers, and with them the whole primitive Church, confessed Jesus in this sense as the Lord. The latter designation is used mostly of Jesus (84 times), but occasionally also of God (15 times). At times it is difficult to decide whether the name *Lord* refers to God or to Jesus or to both, since the reference passes imperceptibly from one to the other.[17] Precisely this is a plain indication that the Lord Jesus was regarded as being identical with the Lord God.

Furthermore, in several passages the suggestion is expressly made by means of additional terms that Jesus bears the title *Lord* as an absolutely divine proper name. The Lord Jesus strikes down Saul and converts him.[18] In the name and by the power of the Lord Jesus the disciples work all their miracles.[19] In the name of the Lord Jesus they baptize unto remission of sins.[20] The belief in the Lord Jesus and the grace of the Lord Jesus works unto salvation.[21] The disciples give their life for the name of the Lord Jesus.[22] The Lord Jesus is the "author of life" (Acts 3:15), "the judge of the living and the dead" (10:42). In these and similar expressions are set forth purely divine attributes. They contain precisely what was regarded as the attribute of the true divinity in the Old and the New Testaments: sovereign dominion over heaven and earth. They prove irrefutably that Jesus Christ was placed from the very first hour on a level with God. "There is no gospel of Jesus Christ which has not proclaimed him as heavenly Lord and King. The same men who sailed the sea of Galilee with Jesus

---

[16] Cf. Chapter 15, p. 274 ff.
[17] Cf. Acts 2:47; 8:22; 9:28, 31.
[18] Cf. Acts 9:5–27.
[19] Cf. Acts 3:6–12 ff.; 4:7–12; 9:34; 12:11, 17; 16:18; 19:11–15.
[20] Cf. Acts 2:38; 8:12; 10:48; 19:5.
[21] Cf. Acts 11:17; 15:11; 16:31; 20:20 f.; 28:28.
[22] Cf. Acts 15:26; 21:13.

and who ate and drank with him, have, with death-defying courage and irrepressible joy, proclaimed this same Jesus as the Lord, exalted to the right hand of the Father, who has given divine powers and divine life to his own, and has made them certain of the heavenly consummation. The speeches of Peter in the first part of the Acts give eloquent testimony to the fact that the earliest apostolic portrait of Christ also radiated divine splendor."[23] Even though the individual features and the more exact delineation of the divine portrait of Jesus may have been still rather obscure for many, and even though the theological and speculative study of this portrait may have occupied the first Christians but little, their belief in the divinity of the "Lord" was already complete on Pentecost day, and with that feast it set out on its triumphant march through the world.

This is evident also from another most important viewpoint, that is, the position occupied by the "Lord" in the religious life and cult of the early Christians. Without detracting from the adoration due to the Father — for this was identical with the adoration due to the Son — the early Christians passed from the Old Testament cult of Jahweh to the cult of the "Lord" Jesus. While at Jerusalem, the Apostles indeed still participated in the divine cult of the Jews and visited the temple at the customary prayer hours in order to pray to the God of their fathers with and for the people (Acts 3:1; 22:17). But besides this common bond which still united the Christians with the Jews, the former gave expression, in an unequivocal manner, to their own belief in their religious rites. This was done by the adoration and invocation of the Lord Jesus. From the very first, this occupied a central position in the specifically Christian creed and religious practice.

At his conversion Saul is enjoined by the disciple Ananias to call upon the name of the Lord Jesus, as a fundamental condition for baptism and the remission of sin (Acts 22:16). And even before Saul had been converted, the Christians of

---

23 Paul Feine, *Paulus als Theologe*, Gr. Lichterfelde-Berlin, 1906, 44.

Damascus, as well as of Jerusalem, called upon the name of the Lord Jesus, in fact, the community of the believers were simply called people who invoked the name of the Lord Jesus (9:14, 21). Even earlier than this, the dying Stephen prays for himself and for his murderers to the Lord Jesus, in the same manner as Jesus on the cross had prayed to his Father: "Lord Jesus, receive my spirit! . . . Lord, lay not this sin to their charge!" (7:58 f.)[24] On Pentecost day Peter applied to Jesus the words of the prophet Joel: "Whosoever shall call upon the name of the Lord, shall be saved," for this discourse, which the prince of the apostles linked to this prophetic text, concludes with the one thought that Jesus Christ is the Lord, in whose name all mankind obtains remission of sin and salvation (2:21–38).

The early Christians, therefore, did not stop at the enthusiastic veneration and glorification of their Master. They transferred to him the real invocation which is due to God alone and is offered to him only. They prayed to the Lord Jesus and expected from him a favorable hearing, grace, forgiveness, eternal happiness. Even liberal critics are convinced that this was the central and absolutely divine position occupied by the Lord Jesus in the religious cult and life of the earliest Christians. Johannes Weiss, to mention only one, makes the following statement on this point:

> In the formula, *our Lord Jesus Christ,* the primitive Christian religion is contained in a nutshell. Obedient submission, reverence, and holy fear of offending him, the sense of absolute dependence on him in all things . . . gratitude and love, trust, in a word, everything which man can feel in relation to the divinity, all this comes to expression in this name. . . . This regarding God and Christ as being equal, which is fully equivalent to their coregency, is characteristic of the piety of the primitive Christians. As the Christians cry *Abba, Father,* and pray to him, so undoubtedly have they also prayed to Christ in the most literal sense of the word, not only in worshipful adoration, but also in the form of

---

[24] "Father, forgive them, for they know not what they do! . . . Father, into thy hands I commend my spirit!" (Lk. 23:34, 46.)

petition. . . . The Christians actually stood in the same relation to Christ as to God. . . . The historian must say that from the earliest beginnings Christianity has put into practice, together with the belief in God the Father, also the worship of Christ as the form of religion perfectly natural to it.[25]

The belief in God the Father, however, and the worship of Christ was usually expressed in a manner distinguishing one from the other. A study of the Acts concerning this point shows that Jesus is never called *God,* but exclusively *the Lord,* while the Father only occasionally is called *the Lord,* mostly always *God.* Even within the period which is described in the Acts, this terminology had so far developed that Paul is able to write: "To us there is but one God, the Father, of whom are all things, and we unto him; and one Lord Jesus Christ, by whom are all things, and we by him" (1 Cor. 8:6). The lingual usage of the Christians followed the Old Testament custom of using the twofold name for the supreme Being: Jahweh (= *Adonai*) *Elohim, Kyrios ho Theos,* the Lord God. Both terms had essentially the same signification, only the viewpoint was different. "God" as such, without further modification, denoted the divine Being in itself, as we already know, while "Lord" expresses this Being rather in its relation to the world.[26] By applying the first of the two names, *Lord God,* to Jesus, and the second to the Father, the true divinity and the essential unity of both, as well as their distinction as to Person, was expressed unequivocally. The monotheism of the Jews, and no less the Christian belief in the Trinity, was accorded full recognition by including also the Holy Spirit in this belief.[27] This juxtaposition was never thought of as belief

---

[25] J. Weiss, *Christus,* Tübingen, 1909, 24 f. Similarly Gustav Dalman (*Die Worte Jesu,* 271 f.); G. B. Stevens (*The Theology of the New Testament,* London, 1901, 266 f.); B. Weiss (*Lehrbuch der bibl. Theologie des N. Test.,* Berlin, 1903, 133); K. Müller ("Unser Herr," *Bibl. Zeit- und Streitfragen,* 1906, 133); Ed. v. Hartmann (*Das Christentum des N. Test.,* 1905, 178). See also the treatise of Th. Zahn, *Skizzen aus dem Leben der alten Kirche,* Leipzig, 1908, 271–308.

[26] Cf. Baudissin, *Kyrios,* I, 18, 27 f.; 50; II, 273, 277.

[27] Cf. Acts 1:16; 2:4; 8:18; 10:44; 13:2; 19:2, 6; 20:23, 28. In Acts 8:39, he is called "the Spirit of the Lord," in Acts 16:7, "the Spirit of Jesus."

in three Gods, but as belief in three divine Persons, in the sense of the formula of baptism as given by Jesus and as always customary in the Church: "In the name of the Father, and of the Son, and of the Holy Ghost."

However, as appropriate and comprehensive as was the term *Lord* for Jesus, there was nevertheless a need for a supplementary name as soon as the expression "Lord *and* Messias" was no longer used. In a certain sense, indeed, the messiasship also found suitable expression in the name *Lord*. According to our previous statements, all the threads of the Old Testament expectations of the Messias come together in the one thought, that the one so ardently hoped for would rule over mankind as Founder and King of the kingdom of God, and that through him all men would become members and heirs of God's kingdom. The name *Lord*, therefore, was the most strikingly apt expression for the Messias-King, who was to be the sovereign head of this kingdom. However, in the title *Lord* the resplendent and felicitous glory of Jesus Christ stood out more prominently, while there was merely an indication in it that he had suffered vicariously for the sins of mankind, had made atonement and thereby had merited the Messianic dominion and glory. The work of salvation, the real essence of his messiasship, was not expressed with sufficient clearness in the name and title of Lord. For this reason the confession of the *Kyrios-Lord* was supplemented by the confession of the *Soter-Saviour,* the Redeemer, Deliverer.

The meaning of the name *Jesus* had been indicated by the angel: "Thou shalt call his name Jesus, for he shall save his people from their sins" (Mt. 1:21). But from the beginning Jesus was merely a proper name, and, furthermore, the signification of this Hebrew word, precisely like that of Messias, in a short time would not have been understood in those parts where the Greek language was in use. The peculiar work of the Lord, that is, of *saving,* had to be characterized in some other manner. In fact, Peter immediately stated, in his sermon on Pentecost day, that in Jesus Christ the promise of the prophet

Joel had been fulfilled: "Whosoever shall call upon the name of the Lord, shall be *saved*" (Acts 2:21). Soon after, there followed the still more definite declaration: "Neither is there *salvation* in any other [name]. For there is no other name under heaven given to men, whereby we must be *saved*" (Acts 4:12). At the Apostolic Council the dogma was enunciated that "by the grace of the Lord Jesus Christ" the Gentiles and Jews "are to be *saved*" (15:11). Paul designated the gospel of Jesus simply as "the word of *salvation*" and Jesus as the "Saviour" (13:23, 26).[28] St. Peter, when brought before the assembled High Court of the Jews, coined the expression "Prince and Saviour," just as he shortly before, on the feast of Pentecost, coined the expression "Lord and Messias": "Him hath God exalted with his right hand, to be Prince and *Saviour*, to give repentance to Israel and remission of sins" (5:31). At the time the second Petrine epistle was written, the expression "our Lord and Saviour Jesus Christ" had already become a fixed formula of belief. It was not strange to speak of the "everlasting kingdom of our Lord and Saviour Jesus Christ" (2 Pet. 1:11), of "the precepts of the Lord and Saviour" (3:2), of "the grace and knowledge of our Lord and Saviour Jesus Christ" (3:18), of "the justice of our God and Saviour Jesus Christ" (1:1).

From these and similar passages of the New Testament[29] it becomes clear that the "preaching of Jesus" in the earliest apostolic Church is identical with the Christological belief of the Church of our days: Jesus Christ is our Lord and Saviour, God the Lord, and God the Saviour.

---

[28] That the name given to Jesus, *the Saviour,* had nothing in common with the same title given to Hellenic kings, is irrefutably proved by K. Prümm, *loc. cit.,* 195–201.

[29] Cf. Jn. 4:42; 2 Tim. 1:10; Titus 1:4; 2:13; 3:6; 1 Jn. 4:14.

Chapter 17. The Pauline Christology

IN EXAMINING the Christology of the early Church, as presented by the *Acts of the Apostles,* we have come upon an outline of Paul's teaching concerning Christ. However, this appears in its complete fullness and clearness only in the epistles of the teacher of the Gentiles. In the *Acts* it was a matter of a short, preparatory instruction for the purpose of leading Jew and Gentile to the faith; in the epistles we have a more advanced and practical instruction of the Christians after their admission to the Church. Closely bound up with this instruction is found the development of Christology itself. Whatever Jesus had revealed regarding himself and had delivered as doctrine to his disciples, St. Paul presents, expands, and develops in his incomparable epistles. In the present chapter our attention will be devoted to this Pauline Christology. It can be summed up in four titles: *the doctrine of Jesus Christ the Saviour, Jesus Christ the Lord, Jesus Christ God, and Jesus Christ the Son of God.*

Jesus Christ the Saviour. The doctrine of salvation occupies such a prominent place in the Pauline epistles that it can be dealt with fittingly before the others. In the first place, Paul constantly gives expression to the fundamental truth that Jesus Christ has redeemed the human race from sin, and has merited for it all blessings of salvation: "A faithful saying and worthy of all acceptation: that Jesus Christ came into this world to save sinners [1 Tim. 1:15]. . . . When the fulness of the time was come, God sent his Son . . . that we might receive the adoption of sons [Gal. 4:4 f.]. . . . In whom we have redemp-

tion through his blood, the remission of sins [Col. 1:14]. . . .
The law of the spirit and life, in Christ Jesus, hath delivered
me from the law of sin and of death. For what the [Mosaic]
law could not do, in that it was weak through the flesh; God,
sending his own Son in the likeness of sinful flesh and of sin,
hath condemned sin in the flesh. . . . If Christ be in you,
the body indeed is dead, because of sin; but the spirit liveth,
because of justification [Rom. 8:2 f., 10]. . . . We were by
nature children of wrath, even as the rest: but God (who is
rich in mercy), for his exceeding charity wherewith he loved
us, even when we were dead in sins, hath quickened us together
in Christ, (by whose grace we are saved,) and hath raised us
up together, and hath made us sit together in the heavenly
places, through Christ Jesus. That he might shew in the ages
to come the abundant riches of his grace, in his bounty towards
us in Christ Jesus" (Eph. 2:3–7). Jesus Christ is the source of
grace and sanctification (cf. 2 Thess. 2:12), of supernatural life
and eternal glory; he is, in a word, "the author of our salvation."[1]

The whole life of Jesus on earth was consecrated to our
salvation; however, he accomplished the actual work of redemption by his bloody death on the cross. "In whom we have
redemption through his blood, the remission of sins [Eph. 1:7].
. . . You, who some time were afar off [from God], are made
nigh by the blood of Christ" [2:13]; he wished "to reconcile
both to God in one body by the cross, killing the enmities in
himself [2:16]. . . . It hath well pleased the Father . . . through
him to reconcile all things unto himself, making peace through
the blood of his cross, both as to the things that are on earth
and the things that are in heaven [Col. 1:19 f.]. . . . God
hath not appointed us unto wrath, but unto the purchasing of
salvation by our Lord Jesus Christ, who died for us: that,
whether we watch or sleep, we may live together with him
[1 Thess. 5:9 f.]. . . . Jesus also, that he might sanctify the
people by his own blood, suffered [Hebr. 13:12]. . . . He hath

[1] Col. 1:27; 2 Tim. 2:10; 4:18; Hebr. 2:10 f.; 4:14; 5:1–7; 7:24; 9:7,
15, 24; 10:12; 12:2, 24; 13:12.

quickened you . . . forgiving you all offences: blotting out the handwriting of the decree that was against us, which was contrary to us. And he hath taken the same out of the way, fastening it to the cross [Col. 3:14]. . . . For why did Christ, when as yet we were weak, according to the time, die for the ungodly? . . . But God commendeth his charity towards us: because when as yet we were sinners according to the time, Christ died for us. Much more, therefore, being now justified by his blood, shall we be saved from wrath through him. For if, when we were enemies, we were reconciled to God by the death of his Son: much more, being reconciled, shall we be saved by his life" (Rom. 5:6–10). It is actually touching to read with what conviction, warmth, and devotion St. Paul expects all salvation from the blood and the death of the Crucified. "The death on the cross was indeed for all Christians of the greatest moment, but for Paul it was simply *the* deed and *the* work of Christ. . . . His preaching was the announcement of salvation, accomplished through the cross and the resurrection. This afforded him such an inexhaustible source of consolation and instruction, that before it all else sank into the background."[2]

According to Paul, the pre-eminent importance of the death of the cross consisted in the fact that it was the infinitely precious sacrifice of atonement for our salvation. Jesus Christ himself became *the victim* on the cross, through whom our sins are blotted out and by whom our justification is accomplished: "Who was delivered up for our sins, and rose again for our justification" (Rom. 4:25). He is the true paschal lamb, the sacrifice of the New Covenant, the real and eternal sacrifice of reconciliation: "Christ our pasch is sacrificed [1 Cor. 5:7]. . . . This chalice is the new testament in my blood [11:25]. . . . For all have sinned and do need the glory of God. Being

---

justified freely by his grace, through the redemption that is in Christ Jesus, whom God hath proposed to be a propitiation" (Rom. 3:23–25). Just as he was the victim on the cross, so also is he the *sacrificial priest* who delivered himself for us of his own free will: "Who gave himself for our sins, that he might deliver us . . . according to the will of God and our Father [Gal. 1:4]. . . . Who gave himself for us, that he might redeem us from all iniquity and might cleanse to himself a people acceptable, a pursuer of good works [Titus 2:14]. . . . The blood of Christ, who by the Holy Ghost offered himself unspotted unto God, shall cleanse our conscience from dead works, to serve the living God. . . . He hath appeared for the destruction of sin by the sacrifice of himself [Hebr. 9:14 f., 26]. . . . For there is one God: and one mediator of God and men, the man Christ Jesus who gave himself a redemption for all" [1 Tim. 2:5 f.]. What is of supreme importance, however, is that Jesus Christ sacrificed himself on the cross *out of pure love for us:* "Christ also hath loved us and hath delivered himself for us, an oblation and a sacrifice to God for an odor of sweetness [Eph. 5:2]. . . . Christ also loved the Church and delivered himself up for it [5:25]. . . . I live now in the flesh: I live in the faith of the Son of God, who loved me, and delivered himself for me" (Gal. 2:20).

Those are the main points of Paul's teaching concerning the Saviour. They are repeated so often and so clearly in his writings that any controversy on this point is not possible. All the more diligently, therefore, do eschatological critics endeavor to stamp Paul as the innovator and author of this doctrine of the atoning sacrifice of Jesus. They claim that it was due to his writings and to his powerful influence, that the early Church had soon conformed to this soteriological dogma, which had been unknown before. However, Paul does not propose the doctrine of the redeeming death of Jesus as his own opinion, which first would have to contend for the approval of the early Church. On the contrary, everywhere he presupposes that it is known and current among the churches to whom he writes, and that it constitutes a fundamental part of apostolic teaching. He states emphatically and expressly: "I delivered unto you first of all, which I also received: how that Christ died for our sins, according to the scriptures" (1 Cor. 15:3). This cardinal point of doctrine in the Pauline gospel is, therefore, pre-Pauline. Paul, indeed, reduced the doctrine of redemption to a completely developed synthesis; the dogma of redemption as such, however, was embedded in the early apostolic tradition.

A glance at the non-Pauline writings of the New Testament proves this convincingly: "The blood of Jesus Christ his Son cleanseth us from all sin" (1 Jn. 1:7). "You were not redeemed with corruptible things as gold or silver, from your vain conversation of the tradition of your fathers: but with the precious blood of Christ, as of a lamb unspotted and undefiled" (1 Pet. 1:18 f.). In this and similar manner the writings of the early disciples voice this doctrine. What we know from the *Acts* regarding the original preaching of the gospel of Jesus amounts precisely to this, that in Christ alone is there salvation. Even Harnack admits:

> The name of Jesus Christ of Nazareth . . . neither is there salvation in any other: for there is no other name under heaven given among men, whereby we may be saved. Such is the creed of the Christian Church. With this creed she began; in the faith of it her martyrs died; and today, as eighteen hundred years ago, it is from this creed that she derives her strength. The whole substance and meaning of religion — life in God, the forgiveness of sins, consolation in suffering — she couples with Christ's person.[3]

And in another place: "That these positions [death and resurrection for our sins] were of capital importance for the primitive community has never been doubted: even Strauss did not dispute it; and the great critic, Ferdinand Christian Baur acknowledged that it was on the belief of them that the earliest Christian communion was built up."[4] Indeed, Christianity never knew any other gospel.

[3] *Das Christentum und die Geschichte*, Leipzig, 1904, 3.
[4] Harnack-Saunders, *What Is Christianity?*, 168.

We must go even farther. The Christians of the first days had received this gospel of redemption from Jesus Christ himself. From his lips it passed into the synoptic writings.[5] Paul also traces it directly to Jesus: "I have received of the Lord that which I also delivered unto you, that the Lord Jesus, the same night in which he was betrayed, took bread, and giving thanks, broke and said: Take ye, and eat: this is my body, which shall be delivered for you: this do for the commemoration of me. In like manner also the chalice, after he had supped, saying: This chalice is the new testament in my blood: this do ye, as often as you shall drink, for the commemoration of me. For as often as you shall eat this bread, and drink the chalice, you shall shew the death of the Lord, until he come" (2 Cor. 11:23–26). In his account of the Last Supper Paul indeed has in mind directly the sacrifice of the altar, and only indirectly the sacrifice of the cross. However, the former is offered only in remembrance of the latter; both are one, for in both the flesh and blood of Christ is offered for our salvation, and both have their origin in Jesus Christ.[6]

Jesus Christ the Lord. Just as Jesus was believed from the beginning to be the Saviour, so also was he believed to be the Lord. This has been shown in detail in the previous chapter on the early Christian gospel, especially by means of the *Acts.* The Pauline epistles, however, make it still clearer that the Christians in his day with preference and most commonly summed up their creed in the name: *The Lord, our Lord, our Lord Jesus Christ.* Significant in this regard is the one invocation: *Maranatha* — "Come, Lord!" The Aramaic form of this invocation proves that it originated in the earliest community of Christians. In later years and to later generations it appeared so typical and so venerable that it was retained also by those Christians and those communities who were not acquainted with the Aramaic tongue, and used on solemn occasions, both

---

[5] See above, Chapter 12.
[6] Cf. F. Prat, *The Theology of St. Paul*, II, 180–223.

at divine service and otherwise.[7] The confession of Jesus as the
Lord was accounted as one of the most sacred acts: "No man can
say: the Lord Jesus, but by the Holy Ghost" (1 Cor. 12:3).
This belief is the necessary condition for salvation: "If thou
confess with thy mouth the Lord Jesus, and believe in thy
heart that God hath raised him up from the dead, thou shalt
be saved" (Rom. 10:9). For this reason this confession should
be on the lips of everyone: "In the name of Jesus every knee
should bow, of those that are in heaven, on earth, and under the
earth: and every tongue should confess that the Lord Jesus
Christ is in the glory of the Father" (Phil. 2:10 f.).

This alone proves that with the name *Lord* evidently was to
be expressed all that was supreme. In fact, we know that *Kyrios*
was equivalent to *Jahweh, Adonai,* the only true God, in the
eyes of Paul's coreligionists, Judaistic as well as Hellenistic.[8]
Moreover, it can be proved definitely that Paul understands the
name *Kyrios* in this and no other sense.

He does not hesitate a moment, in quoting the Old Testament, to apply the title *Kyrios,* therein referred to Jahweh,
unreservedly to Jesus Christ (1 Cor. 1:31; cf. Jer. 9:24).
Jahweh, who led the Israelites out of Egypt and through the
desert, is no other than Jesus Christ according to Pauline
teaching (1 Cor. 10:4). The saying of the prophet Joel 2:32:
"Whosoever shall call upon the name of the Lord Jahweh, shall
be saved," Paul understands directly of Jesus Christ (Rom.
10:12 f.). It is written of Christ the Lord in Psalm 101:26:
"Thou in the beginning, O Lord, didst found the earth: and
the works of thy hands are the heavens" (Hebr. 1:10). Yes,
Paul refers the Old Testament passage: "Who hath known the
mind of the Lord?" (cf. Isa. 40:13) at one time to God, and
at another expressly to Christ (1 Cor. 2:16).

If, therefore, *Kyrios Christ* is one with the Old Testament
Jahweh, he then also takes his place beside God in the New

---

[7] Cf. 1 Cor. 16:22; Apoc. 22:20; Didache, X, 6.
[8] See preceding chapter, p. 296 f.

Testament; according to Paul's exposition, he is equal to God
and one with him.

This can be seen in the most concrete and certain manner
from the religious worship and invocation of the Lord on the
part of Christian believers. In contrast with the pagans, who
worshiped many gods and many lords, the Christians worship
only the one God, the Father, and the one Lord, Jesus Christ
(1 Cor. 8:5 f.). Hereby "is expressed the position of Christ as
being equal to God, and the worship offered him as being
equal to that of God."[9]

This divine worship of Christ as the *Lord,* was, at the time
when Paul wrote his great epistles, that is, about twenty to
twenty-five years after the death of Jesus, the distinguishing
mark and the uniting bond of all Christians. Paul addresses
the Christians of Corinth as "called to be saints, with all that
invoke the name of our Lord Jesus Christ in every place of
theirs and ours" (1 Cor. 1:2). Many things separated the Jewish
Christians in Palestine, whose piety was still somewhat bound
up with the Mosaic law, from the Gentile Christians living
throughout the empire, to whom the Jewish forms of religious
life were alien. But all are one and united in the worship of
the Lord Jesus Christ: "There is no distinction of the Jew
and the Greek: for the same is Lord over all, rich unto all that
call upon him" (Rom. 10:12).

The invocation of the Lord Jesus is made not only for the
purpose of adoration and of the recognition of his sovereignty,
but also for the purpose of *petition* and of *prayer.* Paul and his
fellow Christians expect from the Lord Jesus grace, help, and
mercy. The apostle wishes, and prays for, grace and peace from
God the Father and the Lord Jesus Christ in behalf of the
churches (cf. Rom 1:7, etc.). Through the personal mercy of
Jesus the Christians are endowed with grace (1 Tim. 1:12 ff.).
All will obtain salvation through his mercy (cf. 2 Tim. 1:16,
18; 4:17 f.). The Lord Jesus Christ is the eternal High Priest,

---

[9] J. Weiss, *Christus,* Tübingen, 1909, 26.

who, by reason of his own life upon earth, knows how to have compassion with the faithful in all conditions and needs, and who actually has compassion. Everyone should, therefore, approach the throne of grace and mercy and prayerfully call upon his God and his coreigning Lord and High Priest Jesus for a favorable hearing and for assistance (cf. Hebr. 2:17 f.; 4:15 f.; 10:19 ff.).

Paul commends himself to the Lord Jesus even in temporal needs and bodily infirmity (cf. 2 Cor. 12:7–9; Gal. 4:13 f.). He is aware that all fortunes and events in nature and life depend on the Lord Jesus, and are the result of his dispositions (cf. 1 Cor. 4:19). This postulates the belief that the *Lord* is the fountainhead of all grace, that he possesses divine knowledge and divine power, that there exists no sphere of human and divine life over which absolute sovereignty is not his by right. In accordance with the creed of the early Church, Paul sums up this belief in the absolute participation of Jesus in the dominion over the world in the words: "Sitting at the right hand of God."[10]

In the moral sphere also, Paul knows himself to be completely dependent on the Lord Jesus Christ as the supreme and divine authority. The word and the precept of the Lord is the standard and the binding norm for all moral action and thought (cf. 1 Cor. 7:10, 12, 25). The Christian must seek the Lord in all things: "None of us liveth to himself: and no man dieth to himself. Whether we live, we live unto the Lord; or whether we die, we die unto the Lord" (Rom. 14:7 f.).

It is not a positive theologian, but the very liberal professor J. Weiss, who epitomizes the whole relation of Paul and of the Pauline churches to the *Lord* in the words:

> To Paul Jesus is an object not only of belief, but also of religious veneration. A man who asks for "grace and peace" not only "from God our Father" but also "from our Lord Jesus Christ," must regard Christ as co-equal with God. . . . The practical faith

---

[10] Rom. 8:34; Col. 3:1; Hebr. 1:3; 8:1; 10:12; 12:2; cf. Acts 2:33 f.; 7:55 f.; 1 Pet. 3:22; Apoc. 5:6.

of Paul and his congregations expects no less from Christ than from God — guidance, help, and blessing. Their prayers as well as their praises are offered to him. To the apostle Jesus is not merely a mediator, guide, and example, but he is also the object of religious veneration.[11]

Now we understand why St. Paul, in reference to the name *Kyrios*, glories that "God hath also exalted him [Christ], and hath given him a name which is above all names: that in the name of Jesus every knee should bow, of those that are in heaven, on earth, and under the earth: and that every tongue should confess that the Lord Jesus Christ is in the glory of God the Father" (Phil. 2:9–11). The name *Lord* is therefore the highest name, exalted above all names, a name which surpasses every created name and gives claim to supreme, unqualified worship on the part of all creatures: *Kyrios, Adonai, Jahweh.* Undoubtedly, Paul here has in mind the passages of Scripture, such as Isaias 48:2, and 45:22 ff., and applies to Christ what God there says of himself: "I the Lord, this is my name: I will not give my glory to another. . . . Every knee shall be bowed to me, and every tongue shall swear. Therefore shall he say: In the Lord are my justices and empire." Even J. Weiss remarks, in reference to the import of the name *Lord* in the epistle to the Philippians: "Christ is thereby raised not only to an abstract divine sphere, he occupies outright the place of almighty God. *Kyrios,* therefore, cannot in any event here have a lesser import than *Theos.*"[12] Eduard v. Hartmann admits tersely: "The expression *Lord,* in the Pauline gospel, is not merely a polite form of address, it denotes the Lord of the universe, to whom all things are subject, except the one who has subjected all things to him. . . . Paul uses the word *Lord* alternately for God and for Christ."[13]

The latter statement, of course, must be modified in so far that Paul applies the word *Lord* in most cases to Jesus Christ,

---

[11] *Paulus und Jesus*, Berlin, 1909, 3, 72. English tr., *Paul and Jesus*, trans. by H. J. Chaytor (New York: Harper and Brothers, 1909), 4, 130.

[12] *Christus*, 28.

[13] *Das Christentum des Neuen Testamentes*, 1905, 178.

and only exceptionally to the Father. In the Pauline epistles this designation is applied to Jesus Christ 203 times, but only 12 times to the Father. Moreover, it is noteworthy that in these 12 passages the Father is not mentioned directly, but only in Old Testament quotations (7 times) or allusions (5 times).[14] Hence, Christianity is very truly the religion of *God the Father* and of the *Lord Jesus Christ*. The Father is conceived therein as the Godhead in itself, in so far as it is the principle, the source, and the end of all existence, while by the *Lord* the Godhead is understood in its relation to us, in so far, namely, as Jesus Christ belongs to us as Creator, Redeemer, Mediator, and Saviour, and in so far as we are his bondsmen, his servants and clients.[15]

Jesus Christ God. Since the expression *Lord,* as is evident from the foregoing, in itself denotes the genuine divinity of Jesus Christ, it is almost of no consequence whether St. Paul, in his epistles, applies the name *God* to him. Paul, however, separates the Old Testament double name *Jahweh Elohim* = *Kyrios ho Theos* = *the Lord God,* in such a way that Jesus Christ is called *the Lord,* while the Father is called *God.* God the Father and the Lord Jesus Christ, therefore, on the one hand, are distinguished one from the other; on the other, they are placed on a level of equality. Especially significant is Paul's word of greeting: "Grace to you, and peace from God our Father, and from the Lord Jesus Christ" (Rom. 1:7, etc.). Both, indeed, are mentioned separately, yet they are joined together by the one conjunctive word.

In exceptional cases, however, Jesus Christ is also given the name *God.* Thus we read in the epistle to the Hebrews: "But to the Son; Thy throne, O God, is for ever and ever: a sceptre of justice is the sceptre of thy kingdom" (1:8; cf. Ps. 44:7). What the psalmist here says directly of the one, true God, Paul

---

[14] For a list of these passages, see E. v. Dobschütz, *loc. cit.,* 122.

[15] In this sense the word *Lord* in the Pauline epistles has still the same underlying meaning as originally in the Syro-Egyptian, and later in the Greco-Roman religions. See above, Chapter 16, p. 295 ff. Cf. also F. Prat, *The Theology of St. Paul,* II, 117–119, 124–132, 138–140, 437–438.

refers expressly to the Son. In the Greek original, the latter is called, with the addition of the definite article, *the God,* therefore the one, true God, and since his sovereign dominion is also stressed, he is given in substance the twofold name: *the Lord God.*

In the epistle to Titus (written about the year 65), Paul admonishes: "Servants [are] to be obedient to their masters . . . in all things shewing fidelity, that they may adorn the doctrine of God our Saviour in all things: for the grace of God our Saviour hath appeared to all men; instructing us, that, denying ungodliness and worldly desires, we should live soberly and justly and godly in this world, looking for the blessed hope and coming of the glory of the great God and our Saviour Jesus Christ" (2:9–13). In this passage, the Saviour Jesus Christ is called God three times, each time with the definite article; *the God,* and the last time also with the added word, *the great God,* while at the same time emphasis is laid on his office as Saviour and on his sovereign glory.

Almost simultaneously Paul speaks, in the first epistle to Timothy (1:17), "of the glory of the blessed God, Jesus Christ," and adds: "To the king of ages, immortal, invisible, the only God, be honor and glory for ever and ever!" A more emphatic and more solemn confession of the divinity of Jesus Christ cannot be imagined.

In essentially the same strain Paul had already written (about 58) to the community of Christians at Rome "of the love of God, which is in Christ Jesus our Lord . . . who is over all things, God blessed for ever" (Rom. 8:39; 9:5). This testimony is all the more important since Paul writes to believers whom he had not instructed himself, but who had already received the gospel from Peter (about ten years after the death of Christ). Accordingly, the divinity of Christ was preached from the very beginning; it was a matter of dogma, universally admitted, and regarding which a difference of opinion among the Christians was not thinkable. Of course, the title *God* was usually given to the Father; if it was occasionally referred to

Jesus Christ, it was implied thereby that he was the Son of God.[16]

Jesus Christ the Son of God. The epistle to the Galatians contains sentences which are as incisive as if hewn in stone: "When the fulness of time was come, God sent his Son, made of a woman, made under the law: that he might redeem them who were under the law: that we might receive the adoption of sons. And because you are sons, God hath sent the Spirit of his Son into your hearts, crying: Abba Father!" (4:4 f.) St. Paul here alludes to the incarnation and the human nature of the Son, as well as to his mission and to salvation through him. There is no need of dealing with this point here, nor of enlarging upon it. However, Paul also mentions the divine nature of the Son and his inward-divine relation to the Father and to the Holy Spirit. This is wholly within the scope of the present chapter.

Unquestionably, Paul understands the designation of Christ as Son of God in the metaphysical, and not in a moral sense. To him the Son of God, Jesus Christ, is by no means a mere man, particularly beloved of the Father, merely a child of the Father by adoption or by grace. At the first glance it is striking that the apostle applies the title *Son of God* to Jesus Christ in the most solemn passages of his epistle and in the most sublime utterances. Whenever he desires to stress the infinite love of the Father, and the immeasurable humility and condescension of Jesus, which form the foundation for the incarnation (cf. Rom. 1:1–5; 8:3); whenever he wishes to extol in jubilant notes the certainty and divine blessedness of the reconciliation and redemption through Jesus Christ (cf. Rom. 5:10; 8:1 ff.; Gal. 4:6 f.); whenever he is urged to emphasize strikingly the whole might and greatness of the Saviour Jesus Christ (cf. Rom. 1:4; Phil. 2:9; Hebr. 1:2 ff.); whenever he summons all to believe in Jesus Christ (cf. Gal. 2:16, 20) and to invoke his name in every place (cf. 1 Cor. 1:1–9) — he prefers to call Christ the

---

[16] Cf. F. Prat, *op. cit.,* II, 124–132.

Son of God. And, accordingly, in the most solemn moments and by analogous expressions, he likewise calls God "the God and Father of our Lord Jesus Christ" (cf. Rom. 15:6; 2 Cor. 1:3; 11:31). All this evidently points to relations of the Son of God to the Father in heaven, which go beyond a mere adoptive relation, and which transcend the idea of an extraordinary child of grace, of a mere human being beloved by God.

Paul, indeed, expressly gives prominence to the love of the Father for his Son (e.g., Rom. 8:32). However, even H. Weinel admits without reservation that nevertheless "very often the word [Son of God], even without such a note of sentiment, stands purely as the name for the divine nature of the Messias."[17] And J. Weiss states that it is an error to explain the passages in which the love of God for the Son is strongly emphasized, "in such a way, that sonship is but another word for love: because God so loved this being, therefore he is the Son of God. The contrary is true: Because he is the Son, therefore God loves him. . . . Here [in the Pauline epistles] *Son* signifies, not a relationship of love or of trust, not adoption and not an allegorical phrasing of a moral or natural resemblance of being, but what the word usually designates, that is, generation by God. . . . His premundane being has its origin in God, and this in a unique manner."[18]

In fact, Paul proceeds from the standpoint that the Son of God had being with the Father in heaven previous to his earthly, human manner of being, and that he was sent by him into the world (cf. Gal. 4:4). He constantly reverts to this doctrine of the pre-existence of the Son of God.[19] However, far from having a merely created pre-existence, it is the Son who called the entire created world into existence. Even skeptical critics do not dare to deny that Paul ascribes the *work of creation* to the pre-existent Son of God. They assert, however, that he, under the influence of Neo-Platonism and the pagan-Jewish theory concerning

---

[17] *Paulus*, Tübingen, 1904, 252.
[18] *Christus*, Tübingen, 1909, 35.
[19] Cf. Rom. 8:3; 2 Cor. 8:9; 1 Tim. 1:15; 3:16.

spirits, considers his Christ merely as the builder of the world, as demiurge, as an intermediary being, through whom God had organized the world. According to them, Christ is "the most prominent among the intermediary powers, the one through whom the universe was brought forth from God into separate existence;"[20] his character is only that of "intermediary in the creation of the world,"[21] "a cosmic role of intermediary" in so far as "God first created the heavenly man [Christ], and then through his mediate agency created the earthly man."[22]

The above authors misunderstand Paul completely. Paul, on the contrary, teaches: "The Son of his love . . . who is the image of the invisible God, the firstborn of every creature; for in him were all things created in heaven and on earth, visible and invisible, whether thrones, or dominations, or principalities, or powers: all things were created by him and in him. And he is before all, and by him all things consist" (Col. 1:13–17). The Son of God "made the world . . . upholding all things by the word of his power" (Hebr. 1:2 f.). Consequently, the Son of God is not only the world-builder, a spiritual being who performs the role of an intermediary; rather is he the world-creator, begotten by God before all creation. He is not only the instrument employed by God in the creation of the world, he himself "made the world," "all things were created by him and in him," "he upholds all things by the word of his power." And just as the world owes its origin to him, so is he also the divine preserver and the final end of the world: "All things were created in him" and "by him all things consist." In another place Paul affirms precisely the same of God the Father: "To us there is but one God, the Father, of whom are all things, and we unto him; and one Lord Jesus Christ, by whom are all things, and we by him" (1 Cor. 8:6).

---

[20] Adolf Jülicher, "Die Religion Jesu," *Kultur der Gegenwart*, I, 1906, 87.
[21] Bernh. Weiss, *Lehrbuch der bibl. Theologie*, Berlin, 1895, 301.
[22] H. J. Holtzmann, *Neutestamentliche Theologie*, I, Freiburg and Leipzig, 1897, 83 ff., 91 f.

However, divine omnipotence is but *one* of the divine attributes which Paul ascribes to the Son of God. Just as emphatically does he extol his *omniscience*. Jesus Christ is for him "the power of God and the wisdom of God" (1 Cor. 1:24). "In him are hid all the treasures of wisdom and knowledge" (Col. 2:3). Here is set forth in essence the Johannine doctrine of the Logos, which reaches its summit in the belief that Jesus is the knowledge, wisdom, and Word of God. As such the Son of God, according to Paul, naturally has not only existed in the bosom of the Father previous to his earthly existence, he has simply existence without beginning: *eternity*. He is begotten by God before all time as "the Son of his love . . . the image of the invisible God, the firstborn of every creature" (Col. 1:13, 15). And since he created all things, and time also was created by him, the succession of periods of time and the transitoriness of created things becomes actually the gauge of the eternity and immutability of the Son. What was said in the Old Testament of Jahweh, Paul says of the Son of God: "Thy throne, O God, is for ever and ever. . . . Thou in the beginning, O Lord, didst found the earth: and the works of thy hands are the heavens. They shall perish: but thou shalt continue. And they shall all grow old as a garment. And as a vesture shalt thou change them, and they shall be changed: but thou art always the selfsame, and thy years shall not fail" (Hebr. 1:8, 10–12; cf. Ps. 44:7; 101:26–28). Just as in the Sacred Books God is extolled as the imperishable, immutable and therefore eternal Being, so in like manner is it said of the Son of God: "Jesus Christ, yesterday and today; and the same for ever" (Hebr. 13:8).

It is evident from the above that Paul ascribes to the Son of God those three attributes which, whether viewed scientifically or from the standpoint of popular notion, completely express and describe the divine Being as to essence and nature: omnipotence, omniscience, and eternity. Consequently, the Son also possesses a *divine nature*. Paul specifically affirms this when he extols the Son as "the image of God" (2 Cor. 4:4), "the

image of the invisible God" (Col. 1:15), "the brightness of his
glory, and the figure of his substance" (Hebr. 1:3). The Son
is not merely made *"according to* the image and likeness of
God" as man is (Gen. 1:26), he is *the* image of God by reason
of his own nature and being, a divine self-likeness. Thereby he
is elevated above all spheres of created things; the consubstantial
image of God can be only a divine being. And, indeed, he
possesses not only a part, a ray of this being, as the Gnostic doctrine of emanation asserted of the world-builder; rather does he
possess the entire, undivided being and essence of God: "In
him dwelleth all the fulness of the Godhead corporeally" (Col.
2:9).

It was purely from condescending love for us that he
assumed a human form, though he existed with the Father in
divine essence, and even in the human form of a servant he
remained conscious of his equality with God and of his right
to divine honor: "Being in the form of God, [he] thought it
not robbery to be equal with God: but emptied himself, taking
the form of a servant, being made in the likeness of men, and
in habit found as man. He humbled himself, becoming obedient
unto death, even to the death of the cross. For which cause
God also hath exalted him, and given him a name which is
above all names: that in the name of Jesus every knee should
bow, of those that are in heaven, on earth, and under the earth"
(Phil. 2:6–11). Even extremely liberal critics are forced to
admit that, according to this classical passage in the epistle to
the Philippians, "Jesus Christ existed from all eternity in the
essence of God, in a nature equal to God,"[23] that he is "a divine
pre-existent being,"[24] "a divine being of power . . . a divine
being."[25]

There remains but to refer briefly to the *Trinitarian relation*
of the Son to the Father and to the Holy Spirit. Our observa-

---

[23] H. v. Soden, *Der Brief des Apostels Paulus an die Philipper*, Tübingen,
1906, 45; Ad. Jülicher, *Die Religion Jesu, loc. cit.*, 86.

[24] Gustav Krüger, *Dreieinigkeit und Gottmenschheit*, Tübingen, 1905, 86.

[25] Weinel, *Paulus*, Tübingen, 1904, 245 f.

tions on this point are based on a number of statistical facts. In
the opening, respectively the closing, verses of the Pauline
epistles *Jesus Christ* alone is mentioned once (cf. Philem. 1),
and five times *the Lord,* or *our Lord Jesus Christ.*[26] Twelve
times Paul mentions *God the Father and our Lord Jesus
Christ,*[27] once *God and Jesus Christ* (cf. Rom. 16:27), and
once *God and his first-born Son* (cf. Hebr. 1:1 f.). Twice the
three terms occur together, that is, *God, his Son, the Son of God
in power, and his Holy Spirit* (cf. Rom. 1:1–6), respectively,
the Lord, God and the Holy Ghost (cf. 2 Cor. 13:13). In the
epistles themselves, however, the three Persons are mentioned
together about forty times.[28] The order of enumeration is not
always the same; it is transposed at will, according to the trend
of thought. However, it becomes clear from the context that
for Paul the Trinitarian formula was: God, respectively, the
Father, or also God the Father — the Lord, respectively, the
Son — the Holy Spirit. These are the actual facts of the case.

If we now direct our attention to the content of the Trinitarian confession, it is made clear by the foregoing exposition,
first of all, that, according to Pauline Christology, Jesus stands
in relation to the Father as Son. He is the first-born and the
only begotten of the Father; he is begotten by the Father from
all eternity, in such wise that he has his divine nature from
him and shares it with him. The Father is, therefore, the
divine source of being for the Son, and for this very reason is
called with preference God the Father, or simply God. But in
the Holy Spirit also there is inherent a relation, of divine
essence and operation, to the Father and the Son. He is the
Spirit of the Father[29] and of the Son.[30] He is the author of grace,

---

[26] Cf. 1 Cor. 16:23; Gal. 6:18; Phil. 4:23; 1 Thess. 5:28; 2 Thess. 3:18.
[27] Cf. 1 Cor. 1:3; 2 Cor. 1:2; Gal. 1:1 f.; Eph. 1:2; 6:23 f.; Phil. 1:2;
Col. 1:3; 1 Thess. 1:1; 2 Thess. 1:2; 1 Tim. 1:2; 2 Tim. 1:2.
[28] These Trinitarian texts are compiled and explained in F. Prat, S.J.,
La théologie de Saint Paul, Paris, 1923, II, 158–165, 518–521. English,
The Theology of St. Paul, tr. by John L. Stoddard (Westminster, Md.:
Newman Book Shop), II, 132–147, 431–434. Cf. C. J. Callan, *The Epistles of
St. Paul* (New York: J. Wagner, 1931), I, 337, 629; II, 49, 357 f.
[29] Cf. Rom. 8:9, 14; 1 Cor. 2:11, etc. [30] Cf. Rom. 8:9; 2 Cor. 3:17, etc.

as is the Father and the Son.[31] The faithful are the temples of the Holy Spirit as well as of God.[32] The Father, Son, and Holy Spirit accomplish our justification in baptism, and dwell in us through sanctifying grace.[33] In the Father, Son, and Holy Spirit we are made children of God, heirs of God, and joint heirs with Christ.[34] God the Father will one day raise us up from the dead through Jesus Christ and through his Spirit, who dwells in us.[35] The extraordinary gifts of God also proceed at once from the Father and the Son and the Holy Spirit: "There are diversities of graces, but the same *Spirit*. And there are diversities of ministries, but the same *Lord;* and there are diversities of operations, but the same *God,* who worketh all in all" (1 Cor. 12:4–6). Hence, Paul has no more ardent wish in behalf of his faithful than that they may be confirmed in the Father, and the Son, and the Holy Spirit: "The grace of our Lord Jesus Christ, and the charity of God, and the communication of the Holy Ghost be with you all!" (2 Cor. 13:13.)

In these and similar passages the extremely clear statement is made that the Father, Son, and Holy Spirit are one as to divine essence and being, and that nevertheless they have three distinct forms of existence. F. Prat, to whom we owe the best work on Pauline theology, justly remarks:

> If we do not look in St. Paul for the technical terms of present theology: "nature, substance, person" and still less "subsistence, consubstantiality, circuminsession," we find in him a fund of ideas and mutual relations, destined, one day, to render the uniform adoption of all those terms necessary. . . . In order to express this constant phenomenon of relative opposition and mutual interpenetration and to make it consistent with the strict monotheism which, as all concede, predominates in the writings of St. Paul, only one exact formula is possible: Trinity in Unity.[36]

---

[31] Cf. 1 Cor. 12:11, etc.
[32] Cf. 1 Cor. 6:19; 3:16.
[33] Cf. 1 Cor. 6:11; Titus 3:4–6.
[34] Cf. Rom. 8:14–17.
[35] Cf. Rom. 8:11; 1 Cor. 15:21.
[36] *Loc. cit.,* 132, 138.

This formula is, for that matter, identical with the Pauline confession of God the Father, of his Son and our Lord, and of the Holy Spirit. The Trinitarian confession of Paul, on the other hand, is based on the words of Jesus Christ himself: "Going therefore, teach ye all nations; baptizing them in the name of the Father, and of the Son, and of the Holy Ghost" (Mt. 28:18 f.).

Chapter 18. The Johannine Theology

WHAT the Pauline epistles were soon after the middle of the first century, the writings of John were toward the close of this century — landmarks of the development and the fixation of Christological dogma. Between Paul and John stand the synoptics, Matthew, Mark, and Luke. Their gospels cannot be valued too highly. They take hold of the earliest Christian tradition at its source and present it in undimmed purity, without, as it were, adding a word of their own. What Jesus Christ had done and taught and testified regarding himself is recorded in the earliest gospels on the basis of the threefold, yet one, source of the primitive catechesis. This is of incalculable value for us, and yet it does not represent a new source of knowledge concerning Christology. St. Paul, however, with his powerful mind plumbed, by abstract speculation, the traditions of the early "eyewitnesses and ministers of the word" (Lk. 1:1 f.), and also gave them their practical application, and now John, as the last of the Apostles and an eyewitness to the life of Jesus, enriches these traditions definitely and conclusively, defends them against rising heresy, and renders them acceptable to the Hellenic world of culture. This *Johannine theology* now remains to be examined. However, our attention is not directed to what it has in common with Pauline and synoptic theology, but to that which is peculiar to it alone, which must be regarded as special and proper to John. We are concerned, therefore, with John's doctrine of Jesus Christ as the incarnate *Son of God* and as the *Logos of God*.

The first thing which strikes one who reads the writings of

John is the express and forcible emphasis placed on the divine
Sonship of Jesus. Not as if the doctrine of the divinity of the
Son of God owed its origin to the beloved disciple; on the
contrary, it traces its origin to the Saviour himself, who all his
life proclaimed himself the Messias and Son of God. These
specific and fundamental truths were the undisputed property
of all Christian communities and believers of the earliest days,
Jewish as well as Gentile. We have been able to gain this
conviction from the *Acts of the Apostles* and from the Pauline
epistles, and this conviction is strengthened by the synoptic
gospels. Even liberal critics must admit with Wilhelm Bousset:
Already the earliest gospel "was written from the viewpoint of
faith [in the divinity of Jesus]: already for Mark Jesus is not
only the Messias of the Jewish race, but the wonderful, eternal
Son of God, whose glory shone forth in this world. And it
has been rightly stressed that in this respect our three gospels
differ from the fourth only in degree."[1] In fact, Mark merely
sets forth the main content of his gospel, and of the gospels
in general, when he prefaces the story of the Master with the
words: "The beginning of the gospel of Jesus Christ, the Son of
God" (1:1). There is no possibility of a doubt that Mark, as
well as Matthew and Luke, "regarded the Son of God as the
one begotten by God,"[2] that they obtained this conviction from
the revelation of Jesus, and that they regarded their presentation as absolute proof for the divine consciousness of the
Saviour.

Nevertheless, the divinity of Jesus is taught by the synoptics
more indirectly than directly, more mediately than immediately,
more by suggestion than outspokenly. They simply relate, as
remarked above, the life of the Master, without setting off those
things in which his divinity was manifested in an especially
characteristic manner, and without any special emphasis on the
fact that, and in how far, he proved himself the true Son of
God by his words and deeds. They did not feel themselves

---

[1] *Was wissen wir von Jesus?*, Halle, 1904, 30 f.
[2] Gustav Dalman, *Die Worte Jesu*, Leipzig, 1898, 236.

called upon to speak of the divinity of Jesus in a thematic manner, precisely because this truth stood out plainly enough from the simple narration of facts, and because at that time no one would have thought of doubting or denying it.

Matters stood different, however, a few decades later. After the first enthusiasm had passed, a reaction became noticeable among some Christians, occasionally even a relapse into previous Jewish and pagan ideas from which they had just been converted. Some of them, as is easily understood, had not been able to rid themselves entirely of the former ideas inherent in the Greek popular philosophy of which they had been fond; many Jewish Christians were again attracted by the theology of the synagogue, above all by the rabbinical and apocalyptic concept of the Messias, which previously had kept the majority of their race from believing in Jesus Christ, and which again drew even those who had become believers with great force into the depths of the inherited national-Jewish ideas. After the judgment of God on Jerusalem had come to pass (A.D. 70), and the visible center of the nation had disappeared, the Judaists clung all the more tenaciously to the idealistic nucleus, to the nationalistically colored portrait of the Messias, while the Gentile Christians, to a great extent, mixed Jewish and Greco-Alexandrian elements into their Christianity. In this way the Jewish-Gnostic sects originated, who either questioned the true divinity of Jesus, or bluntly denied it.

John wrote his gospel, according to the unanimous testimony of tradition, to counteract these sects.[3] His purpose was to strengthen the Christian churches of Asia Minor in their faith by portraying the divine-human life of Jesus as authentic witness of it, and by setting vividly and forcibly the divine-human self-authentication of Jesus before their eyes.

John expresses himself very definitely regarding this purpose

---

[3] Irenaeus, *Adv. Haeres.*, III, 11, 1 f.; Epiphanius, *Haeres.*, L. I, 2, 12; Hieronymus, *De viris illustr.*, 9. Cf. C. Fouard, *St. John and the Close of the Apostolic Age* (New York: Longmans, Green and Co., 1905), IX to XIX, 155–175; J. Lebreton-J. Zeiller, *The History of the Primitive Church,* tr. by E. J. Messenger (New York: Macmillan Co., 1949), II, 617–640.

of his gospel. He tells his readers that it has been "written, that you may believe that Jesus is the Christ the Son of God: and that believing, you may have life in his name" (Jn. 20:31).

True to this purpose, the evangelist, as will be shown later, in the *prologue* to his gospel unfolds the whole ground plan of Christian teaching concerning the God-Man in pithy and striking sentences. He then shows how this teaching is developed throughout the entire life of Jesus. Witness thereto is, first of all, John the Baptist, who proclaimed the pre-existence of Jesus and his eternal being with the Father (cf. Jn. 1:15, 27, 30), his heavenly origin (3:31 f.), his divine sonship (1:34), and his divine-human work as Saviour (1:29). Jesus commended the forerunner for his Christology and affirmed that "he gave testimony to the truth" (5:33–36).

Continuing from this point, Jesus himself proclaimed the truth of his divine sonship in a constantly ascending degree and with ever-increasing emphasis. His mission from God forms the ever recurring subject of his conversations with the disciples and of his public discourses to the people (cf. Jn. 5:38, 43; 7:16, 29; 8:42; 12:49). After he had thus granted his hearers a flashing glimpse of his supernatural nature, he explained to them his relation to the Father: he had personal existence in God before he came into this world (8:58); he will return again to God, as soon as he has accomplished his task on earth, the redemption of mankind (8:42; 16:28); he is the Son of God, the only Son, begotten of the essence of God, and in consequence like in nature to the Father (1:14, 18; 3:16, 18); he is God like the Father (5:18; 10:30–36; 20:28). On the unity of being and nature of Father and Son is grounded the divine origin and character of his teaching: what he himself heard and saw while in the bosom of the Father, he speaks and proclaims to the world (3:11; 8:26; 15:15). From the same unity of being and nature of Father and Son proceeds also the unity of operation (10:30, 38; 14:9–11; 17:21); the Son does nothing that the Father does not, just as he, on the other hand, performs all the works of the Father (5:19).

It is precisely these works which give to the utterances of Jesus regarding his divinity their decisive proof. He considers his miraculous deeds as motivation for belief in him (cf. Jn. 10:25, 37 f.; 14:12 f.). They are the unmistakable seal of his mission (2:23; 3:2); they demonstrate in Jesus, who performs them, the presence of a higher, supernatural, divine power, they point to his relation to the Father as Son (5:36; 10:38), and are symbols of invisible processes and truths. Thus the miraculous multiplication of the loaves was a symbol of the power to impart life and spiritual nourishment, common to both the Father and the Son (6:26), the healing of the one born blind a symbol of Jesus as the light of the world, as the spiritual illumination of mankind (9:1 ff.). The cure of the man who had been sick for thirty-eight years, on the Sabbath, is not only proof of his wonder-working power, but is a symbol of the truth that his works are in complete harmony with those of the Father, and thus authenticate his claims as Son (5:17).

To the testimony of Jesus to his divinity, given by word and work, John adds his own experiences and that of his fellow apostles and believers. Step by step they had been brought to believe in the Master solely in virtue of the enlightenment produced by his words and deeds, overwhelmed as they were by the evidence of the proofs which had been presented. At the time of John there still lived, in his own vicinity in Asia Minor, a number of disciples of Jesus, who were hearers of his doctrine in which he proclaimed his divinity, and witnesses of the miracles wrought in proof of it, and who asserted that the Christology of John was a true echo of the teaching of Christ (cf. Jn. 21:24). But with greater reason than the others John could point to the fact that his account, as that of an eyewitness, concerning Jesus, his life, his humanity, his messiasship and divinity, was grounded on truth and reality: "He that saw it hath given testimony: and his testimony is true. And he knoweth that he saith true; that you also may believe . . . that Jesus is the Christ, the Son of God: and that believing, you may have life in his name" (19:35; 20:31).

Hence the fourth gospel is an incisive and solidly founded confession of the true divinity of Jesus, in its opening and closing lines as well as in its whole content. The first words of this marvelous book avow the divinity of Christ in striking, clear-cut sentences; the same doctrine forms the keynote which dominates the whole work and ends on the final, trumpet note, that on this earth it is the belief in Jesus as the Messias and the Son of God which makes a Christian truly a Christian, and which is the unfailing pledge of eternal life in the world to come. The confession of the metaphysical divine sonship of Jesus is so much the very core of the gospel of John that even unbelieving critics confess that the bitter fight which has been waged about it for more than a hundred years centers, in fact, merely on the divinity of Christ, expressed so clearly therein.[4]

Simultaneously with presenting the gospel of the divinity of Jesus to the churches in Asia Minor, John wrote an accompanying letter in which he again very decisively inculcates the same fundamental Christian truth. The authenticity of this first epistle of St. John is proved, according to general opinion, along with the authenticity of the fourth gospel. Those critics who deny the Johannine authorship of the fourth gospel nevertheless find themselves forced to admit that the latter, as well as the three epistles of John and the Apocalypse, "belong to the same school . . . the Johannine school."[5]

According to the first epistle of John, the Son of God, who gave his life for us, is true God, and his mission from the Father and his work of redemption is, therefore, the supreme manifestation of God's love for us: "By this hath the charity of God appeared towards us, because God hath sent his only begotten Son into the world, that we may live by him [1 Jn. 4:9]. . . . He is the propitiation for our sins: and not for ours only, but also for those of the whole world [2:2]. . . . The blood

---

[4] Otto Schmiedel, Die Hauptprobleme der Leben-Jesu-Forschung, Tübingen, 1906, 17. Cf. J. Steinmueller-K. Sullivan, A Companion to the New Testament (New York: J. Wagner, 1944), 221–223.

[5] Ed. v. Hartmann, Das Christentum des Neuen Testaments, 1905, 246 f. Cf. C. Fouard, op. cit., 201–212.

of Jesus Christ his Son cleanseth us from all sin [1:7]. . . . In
this we have known the charity of God, because he hath laid
down his life for us" (3:16).

Belief in the divinity of the Son and love for him are a
divine precept and the supreme proof of faith in the Father and
of love for the Father: "This is his [God's] commandment: that
we should believe in the name of his Son Jesus Christ [1 Jn.
3:23]. . . . Every one who loveth him who begot, loveth him
also who is born of him" (5:1). Belief in the divinity of the
Son leads to victory over the world and confers eternal life:
"Who is he that overcometh the world, but he that believeth
that Jesus is the Son of God? [5:5]. . . . He that believeth in
the Son of God, hath the testimony of God in himself [5:10].
. . . These things I write to you, that you may know that you
have eternal life: you who believe in the name of the Son of
God" (5:13). But whoever denies the divinity of the Son,
accuses God the Father of giving false testimony: "He that
believeth not the Son, maketh him a liar: because he believeth
not the testimony which God hath testified of his Son. And
this is the testimony that God hath given to us eternal life. And
this life is in his Son. He that hath the Son, hath life. He
that hath not the Son, hath not life. . . . We know that the Son
of God is come: and he hath given us understanding that we
may know the true God, and may be in his true Son. This is the
true God and life eternal" (5:10–12, 20).

According to John, this doctrine of the divine sonship of
Jesus agrees fully with the primitive teaching of Christianity,
and is based on the testimony of the apostle himself as eye- and
earwitness: "He that confesseth the Son, hath the Father also. As
for you, let that which you have heard from the beginning, abide
in you. If that abide in you, which you have heard from the
beginning, you also shall abide in the Son, and in the Father
[1 Jn. 2:23 f.]. . . . That which we have seen and have heard,
we declare unto you, that you also may have fellowship with
us, and our fellowship may be with the Father, and with his
Son Jesus Christ [1:3]. . . . We know that the Son of God is

come: and he hath given us understanding that we may know the true God, and may be in his true Son. This is the true God and life eternal" (5:20).

The divinity of Jesus is declared by John just as emphatically in the *Apocalypse,* that book in which even liberal critics "always believed to have discovered the most genuine expressions of the early Christian belief, such as has perhaps become alien to us,"[6] a belief which protested against any sort of apotheosis and adoration of created things (cf. 19:10; 22:9). According to this book, Christ is the beginning of creation (cf. 3:14). He conquers the world (cf. Chap. 6). He is the Lamb of God, slain for the sins of the world, and redeeming the world from sin (cf. 5:6, 8, 12; 7:17). He sits in glory on a throne set up in heaven (cf. 4:2 ff.; 5:1). What Jahweh, the true God of Israel, had himself testified by the prophets, and what the same Book of Revelation declares of the heavenly Father (cf. 1:8; 21:6), that Christ can also say of himself: "I am Alpha and Omega, the First and the Last, the beginning and the end. . . . I am living for ever and ever, and have the keys of death and of hell" (1:18; 2:8; 22:13). To him is due the same honor and adoration as to God on the part of all creatures in heaven and on earth. The Seer of Patmos, who once had rested trustfully on the bosom of Jesus, now falls down like dead before the throne of God and at the feet of the Son of God (cf. 1:17). Thereupon he describes the glory he had seen with a trembling hand: "And I beheld, and I heard the voice of many angels round about the throne, and the living creatures, and the ancients; and the number of them was thousands and thousands, saying with a loud voice: The Lamb that was slain is worthy to receive power, and divinity, and wisdom, and strength, and honor, and glory, and benediction. And every creature, which is in heaven and on the earth, and under the earth, and such as are in the sea, and all that are in them: I heard all saying: To him that sitteth on the throne, and to the Lamb, benediction, and

---

[6] Karl Müller, "Unser Herr," *Biblische Zeit- und Streitfragen,* 1906, 8.

honor, and glory, and power, for ever and ever. . . . And they cried with a loud voice, saying: Salvation to our God, who sitteth upon the throne, and to the Lamb" (5:11–13; 7:10).

John, therefore, sets forth the divinity of Jesus in the clearest and most decisive manner conceivable in his gospel, his first epistle, and in the Apocalypse. This mode of presentation stands out in strong relief when compared with that of the synoptics, who, it is true, present the testimony of Jesus to himself as God, and who give expression to their unconditional belief in his divinity, without, however, making the doctrine of Christ's divinity the sharply defined and clearly outspoken theme and chief purpose of their writings.[7]

The second difference which we discern between the synoptic and the Johannine doctrine concerning Jesus, is the fact that the beloved disciple sums up this doctrine in the one title of the *Logos of God*.

The oldest passage in the writings of John, in fact, of the New Testament, in which we encounter the expression *Logos (Word)* in reference to the person of Jesus, is found in the nineteenth chapter of the Apocalypse. Therein is described the victory of Christ over the powers of Satan. The victor sets out, sitting on a white horse, accompanied by the heavenly hosts, who follow him sitting likewise on white horses and clothed in resplendently white linen. Christ is designated the King of kings and Lord of lords. He strikes down his enemies with a rod of iron. His eyes, flames of fire, penetrate all things; on his head he bears many diadems, "and his name is called, the Word [*Logos*] of God" (19:13). It is obvious that the name *Logos of God*, which is here given to the glorified Christ, is to be referred to the person of Jesus in general, just as it appears in the whole Apocalypse as the Son of God, Messias, and Man.

Nevertheless, we are greatly amazed to read the remarkable, wholly unique sentences in the opening verses of the fourth gospel: "In the beginning was the Word, and the Word was

---

[7] Concerning the *Apocalypse* and the divinity of Christ, see C. Fouard, *op. cit.*, 96–116; Steinmueller-Sullivan, *op. cit.*, 234–268.

with God, and the Word was God. The same was in the beginning with God. All things were made by him: and without him was made nothing that was made. In him was life, and the life was the light of men. And the light shineth in darkness, and the darkness did not comprehend it. . . . That was the true light, which enlighteneth every man that cometh into this world. He was in the world, and the world was made by him, and the world knew him not. He came into his own, and his own received him not. But as many as received him, he gave them power to be made the sons of God, to them that believe in his name. Who are born, not of blood, nor of the will of the flesh, nor of the will of man, but of God. And the Word was made flesh, and dwelt among us, (and we saw his glory, the glory as it were of the only begotten of the Father,) full of grace and truth" (Jn. 1:1–5, 9–14).

Before John proceeds to the narration of the human-divine history of the earthly life and activity of Jesus, he wishes to characterize the pre-existent personality of the *Logos*, and, before all else, the *nature* of the *Logos* in itself (v. 1–2). The *Logos* had a pretemporal existence; to him belong *beginning before all things and eternity.* "In the beginning," when God had not yet created the world, the *Logos* was with God.[8] It is not a matter of the *Logos* being merely outwardly with and beside God, but of an inward relation of being: the *Logos* is a being equal to God, he is himself a personal divine being, is himself God (v. 1). Only as a personal divine being could the *Logos* be with God from eternity (v. 2).

Divine *operation* also corresponds to this divine essence (v. 3–5). The creation of the whole world is the work of the *Logos*, and, in fact, this creation of all things out of nothing is so exclusively his work that not a single thing was made except by him (v. 3). Every kind of dualism for explaining creation,

---

[8] In the words: "In the beginning . . . the Logos was with God," there is the idea "primarily of simple existence before the world; in the background, however, is the idea of eternity as such, as it is included in the idea of God" (Julius Grill, *Untersuchungen über die Entstehung des vierten Evangeliums,* I, Tübingen, 1920, 90 *n.*).

every thought of a creative intermediary, therefore, is at once excluded. To the act of creation is joined that of revelation on the part of the *Logos*. Just as he is the cause and first principle of material light and life, so also is he the cause as well as the dispenser of spiritual and supernatural life and light (for the most part not recognized by men), wherever it shines (v. 4–5).

Having revealed himself outwardly and mediately by his pretemporal activity as Creator as well as by his pre-Christian revelation, in the fullness of time the *Logos* appeared immediately and personally in Jesus Christ, became man and lived among men in order to accomplish the revelation of God and the redemption of mankind (v. 9–14). Whoever believes in the *Logos* becomes spiritually united to him and, in consequence, is adopted as a child of God (v. 12–13). This climax of revelation and redemption, however, could be attained only by the *Logos*, the only-begotten, the metaphysical Son of God, assuming a human nature, pouring out, as the true God-Man Jesus Christ, the fullness of his grace and truth upon humanity, and visibly revealing to men his divine glory (v. 14–18).

How this revelation of divine glory, of divine truth and grace, of the divine essence and person of the *Logos*, unfolded itself harmoniously in the life of Jesus, in his works, his teaching, in his testimony to himself, of this John now begins to tell. His gospel is but a continuous commentary on the prologue of the *Logos*, or rather, the prologue is merely the concisely drawn ground plan of the fourth gospel, based on the words and works of Jesus. The term *Logos* does not, indeed, occur again in the gospel. John is aware that Jesus never applied this title to himself, and for this reason he does not introduce it again in the historical narration of the life of Jesus. The fundamental ideas of the prologue however — the pre-existence and eternity of the *Logos*; the operation *ad extra* of creation and revelation, the incarnation, the divine sonship, and the divinity of the *Logos*; the *Logos* as the essentially divine light and life, the visible glory and the personified grace of God — all this forms the very essence of the fourth gospel. By means of the prologue the reader of the gospel of John is carried by natural degrees from the eternity of the *Logos* through the period before time, before his pretemporal activity, into the present time, from which the evangelist draws his account of the appearance of the Saviour, on the strength of his own (John's) experience. The result of this account is in every respect in harmony with this prologue: Jesus Christ proves himself to be the light, grace, and truth by his words, his deeds, and his life; he proves himself to be the Son of God, who became flesh for us, redeemed us through his suffering, and who leads us, through his glory, to eternal light and life.

That John wishes his whole gospel, all that he tells of Jesus in virtue of his own experience as eye- and earwitness, to be regarded as the doctrine of the *Logos,* he himself declares in his *first epistle.* In its very beginning he remarks, obviously referring to his gospel and with a view to the following content of his epistle: "That which was from the beginning, which we have heard, which we have seen with our eyes, which we have looked upon, and our hands have handled, of the word of life . . . we . . . declare unto you" (1 Jn. 1:1 f.).

St. John, therefore, purposely and preferably employs the term peculiar to him only, in order to give expression to his belief in Jesus Christ: *the Logos, the Word.* Not as if he deprecated the expressions otherwise commonly employed, such as, the Son of David, Son of man, Messias, Son of God, God. All these expressions are found in his gospel more often than the term *Logos.* But what all other expressions convey in meaning, is reduced by him to the one designation, peculiar solely to him: the *Logos of God,* the *Logos of life,* the *Logos of Light, the Logos. Logos* to him is the sum total of all Christology.

How did this come to pass, and *why* does John give it such importance? That is one of the most interesting problems in the history of early Christian literature and dogma.

In the first place it is clear that the linguistic expression *Logos,* as referred to Christ, was already known to the readers of the Johannine writings. The apostle applies this term to the

Saviour without giving any sort of explanation. He employs it in the first verse of his gospel, in the middle of the accompanying epistle and toward the end of the Apocalypse, as a name for Christ which was familiar to all. Thereby he gives reason to surmise that the Hellenistic Christians, to whom they were directed, were acquainted with a *certain doctrine* of the *Logos*, against which the Johannine writings are very outspokenly directed. What was this false doctrine of the Logos?[9]

In Ephesus, where the gospel of John originated, the *Logos* was, ever since Heraclitus "the Obscure" (about 500 B.C.), understood to be the firelike primordial reason which forms and activates the world. The Stoics took over this pantheistic-materialistic idea of the *Logos*, but idealized it in so far that their *Logos* possessed intelligence, and was identified only with the finer elements (air and fire) and not with the coarser (earth and water). The theistic counterpart thereto is the *Logos* idea of the Alexandrian-Jewish philosophy of religion.

While the Jews of Palestine kept themselves aloof as much as possible from Grecian thought and teaching, the members of their race in the diaspora saw themselves drawn into the Hellenic-Alexandrian world of thought. Partly for apologetic reasons, partly from enthusiasm, they sought to unite Mosaic theology and Hellenic philosophy, or at least to shed light upon them through mutual contact and to render them scientifically more profound. A copious theological-philosophical, as well as devotional, literature affords proof of this. One needs only to mention the Alexandrian books of Sacred Scripture, as well as

---

[9] Concerning the following discussion of the Hellenistic-Alexandrian doctrine of the *Logos*, see the more extensive treatment in my work, *Christ and the Critics* (tr. by John L. Stoddard [London: Burns, Oates and Washburne, 1933], I, 386–405). To the references mentioned therein should be added: E. Krebs, "Der Logos als Heiland im ersten christlichen Jahrhundert" (*Freiburger theol. Studien*, 2), 1910; J. Lebreton, *Histoire du Dogme de la Trinité*, Paris, 1927, I, 56–84, 490–508 (an English edition of this work appeared under the title: *History of the Dogma of the Trinity*, tr. Algar Thorold [New York: Benziger Brothers, 1939], I, 52–80, 440–443, 447–450); K. Prümm, *Der christliche Glaube und die altheidnische Welt*, Leipzig, 1935, I, 227–252; C. Fouard, *St. John and the Close of the Apostolic Age*, 158–174; also *Catholic Encyclopedia*, Vol. IX, under *Logos*.

the Old Testament apocrypha and pseudo-epigrapha. Philo, in particular (about 20 B.C. to A.D. 40), devoted himself to this more than dangerous reconciliation of the Jewish faith with Grecian culture. In doing so he took from pagan philosophy not only form and figure, but only too often also matter and ideas, whereby the revealed truth was lost in pagan speculation. This was particularly true of the fundamental teaching regarding the universe.

The monotheistic view of the universe was for Philo not merely an inviolable truth, but emphatically *the* truth, in opposition to Hellenic pantheism and materialism. In fact, with a view of excluding as far as possible the pantheistic-materialistic idea of God, Philo conceived God — entirely in harmony with the contemporary theology of the synagogue — not only as an absolutely one, spiritual, personal, and supernatural being, but as a being so exalted above everything earthly and material that there existed between this being and the world an absolute contrast. God is not only different, but absolutely separate, from matter. The latter existed from eternity as a second principle together with God.[10] When the world was to be formed out of it, or when, respectively, matter was to be formed and organized, God had to make use of a countless number of *intermediary beings*, called *Logoi*, for this purpose. These *Logoi*, standing between God and the world, have their origin and find their unity in the one and true *Logos*, which is the sum total of the divine ideas, according to which the universe was to be formed; consequently it is the rational world-plan of God. By the fact that God expressed in words this ideal world-plan or world-thought, the *Logos* came forth from God and entered into a union with matter. Through the union of both the actual world came into being. Thereby the *Logos* has become the *world-builder*, and for all time remains the instrument through which God brings forth the actual things of the world, preserves, and governs them.

---

[10] Philo does not see that with this dualistic view he surrenders his monotheism.

With Philo, of course, there can be no question of the *divinity* of the *Logos,* although at times he calls the *Logos* the second God, or the older Son of God, in distinction from the younger, that is, from the world formed through him. In the Philonian system there is, in fact, only room for the *Logos,* and only thereby is he capable of acting as world-builder and world-ruler, if and because he is not of divine essence. He is the barrier between God and the world. Nothing else. Even the identification of the *Logos* with the *Word* and the *Wisdom* of God has no significance. On the contrary, Philo conceives these two Old Testament ideas directly as intermediate beings who stand above the world and below God.

Just as little as there is room for God and divine creation of the world in the *Logos*-system of Philo, so little also does the *incarnation* fit into its framework. According to Philo, it is barred for the very reason that his *Logos* is not a person, but a pure abstraction, precisely as in the world philosophy of Heraclitus and of the Stoics. With such a supposition it was simply impossible to arrive at the idea of the incarnation of the *Logos.* Philo barred the way thereto with his teaching that all matter was corrupt and that it was impossible for God to enter into a direct union with it. Just as he was not able, by virtue of his dualism, to accept a creation of the world by God, just so little could he accept an incarnate God.

The *redemption* also could not be fitted into the *Logos*-theory of Philo. Philo, indeed, occupies himself a great deal with the idea of virtue, but he understands by this term only the one which man can attain by the study of philosophy. And just as he does not recognize virtue as a moral good, he does not recognize sin as a moral evil. He knows nothing of the fallen and corrupt state of human nature. Consequently, the idea of redemption from sin, or moral evil, is alien to his philosophy. Of course, the Alexandrian philosopher completely shares the Messianic hopes of his race, above all the national-political hopes. In rich, glowing colors he describes the Messias and those Messianic expectations which we have represented as the rabbinic-pharisaic conception of the Messias (Chap. 10). Yet there is no mention of the *Logos*. As stated above, Philo, of course, sought to make his *Logos* rhyme with the *Word of God* and with the *Wisdom* of the Old Testament, so that one is led to believe that he will arrive at a Messias-*Logos* from this point. However, he connects the ideas *Word-Logos* (Word of God) and *Reason-Logos* (Wisdom of God), which in the Old Testament context certainly belong to the content of Messianic prophecy, only as a supplement to his *Logos* theory. His *Logos* is merely pasted on, so to say, to the Old Testament. According to origin and essence, his *Logos* is merely a product of Greek philosophy; it is, as mentioned above, identical with the *Logos* of Heraclitus, of the Stoics, and of Plato, as the *world-soul, world-idea, world-reason.*

Thus the *Logos* theory of Philo and Christology were opposed to each other as fire and water. The former became all the more a serious danger for the latter since the Hellenistic-Alexandrian religious philosophy exerted a strong fascination on wide circles of the educated classes, as well as of the common people. It threatened, in particular, the churches of Asia Minor, and above all the Christian community of Ephesus, the birthplace of the older Greek doctrine of the *Logos,* the center of the newer Hellenic culture, and at the same time the place of origin of the fourth gospel. That alone would explain why John made his the gospel of the *Logos.*

However, he did so for a much more direct reason. Philo's Greek doctrine of the *Logos* had already given birth to a heresy within the bosom of Christianity, which disquieted the church of Ephesus, and which threatened to become a focus of infection for all the churches of Asia Minor. John himself writes of this in his first and second epistle, and the earliest Fathers supplement his statements.[11]

Referring to his doctrine of the *Logos* of God, the apostle

---

[11] Concerning the *Logos of Philo,* see Ricciotti, *The Life of Christ,* § 152; J. Lebreton, *History of the Dogma of the Trinity,* Vol. I, pp. XIV–XVIII, 157–188.

warns his readers against the forerunners of the Antichrist: "Even now there are become many Antichrists. . . . They went out from us, but they were not of us. For if they had been of us, they would no doubt have remained with us; but that they may be manifest, that they are not all of us. . . . Dearly beloved, believe not every spirit, but try the spirits if they be of God: because many false prophets are gone out into the world" (1 Jn. 2:18 f.; 4:1; cf. 2 Jn. 8). These false prophets, therefore, in spite of their name as Christians, have never belonged inwardly to Christianity. John regards them, as Paul did the pharisaical Jew Christians, as "false brethren" (cf. Gal. 2:4; 2 Cor. 11:26). From the fact that there were many it must not be concluded that there existed many forms of heresy, but only that there were many adherents of the one kind of heresy. After they had been expelled from the legitimate Church (cf. 1 Jn. 2:19; 4:4), they still sought to exert a seductive influence and, as Christian brethren, to find friendship and a hospitable reception in the houses of the members of the Church (cf. 2 Jn. 10 f.). Association with them was all the more infectious, because they based their Christology on the un-Christian wisdom of the world (cf. 1 Jn. 4:5), a plain reference to Grecian-Philonian influences.

In fact, the head of this sect was Cerinthus, a Jewish-Christian Gnostic from Egypt. He received his education in Greek and Philonian philosophy at Alexandria,[12] and came to the province of Asia, by way of Jerusalem, Caesarea, and Antioch, opening a school where he spread his false doctrine with such success that he was looked upon as a veritable pestilence.[13] This explains the exclamation of John when he encountered Cerinthus in the Baths of Ephesus: "Away! Lest the baths collapse, for Cerinthus is within, the enemy of truth!"[14] Cerinthus attempted to apply the Grecian-Philonian theory of the *Reason-Logos* to Christianity. He assumes two eternal princi-

---

[12] Epiphanius, *Haeres.*, XXXVIII, 2. Cf. C. Fouard, *op. cit.*, 158 ff.
[13] Irenaeus, *Contra Haeres.*, I, 26, 1; Epiphanius, *Haeres.*, XXVIII, 1-4.
[14] Related by Polycarp, the disciple of John, Epiphanius, *Haeres.*, III, 28.

ples, God as the active, and matter as the passive, principle. The formation of the world out of the eternal, primordial matter was not done by God, but by subordinate, intermediary beings.[15] Jesus is not the Creator of the world. He is mere man, though an extraordinary one, born according to nature of Mary and Joseph. He is not the same person as the Messias-Christ. The latter was not incarnate in and with Jesus; he merely united himself to him outwardly at the baptism and left him again before the passion. Consequently, redemption is out of the question, because a mere man could not render full satisfaction for the sins of humanity. As far as Cerinthus is concerned, there is simply no idea of the divinity and true divine sonship of Jesus.[16]

In opposition to this Cerinthian caricature, and indirectly also to its Greco-Philonian model, John sets forth the genuine, Christian doctrine of the *Logos*. Ample proof has been given above that his *Logos* is not an intermediate being, standing between God and the world; that he is the Christ, the Messianic Saviour of the world, and that the Son of God-Messias became flesh, that is, that in the one historical person of Jesus there has been effected a real and lasting union of the divine *Logos* with the corporal-spiritual nature of a human individual. It need only be added how decisively the point of this *Logos* doctrine is directed against those heretical phantasies which denied the divinity, the messiasship and the incarnation of the *Logos* Jesus. Sharp as steel are the antitheses of John against Cerinthus and his adherents: "That which we have seen and have heard, we declare unto you, that . . . our fellowship may be with the Father, and with *his Son Jesus Christ*" (1 Jn. 1:3). "That is Antichrist, who denieth the Father and the Son. Whosoever denieth the Son, the same hath not the Father. He that confesseth the Son, hath the Father also. As for you, let that which

---

[15] Irenaeus, *Contra Haeres.*, I, 26, 1; Hippolytus, *Philosoph.*, VII, 5, 53.
[16] Irenaeus, *Contra Haeres.*, I, 26, 1; III, 11, 1–4; Hippolytus, *Philosoph.*, VII, 5, 33; Tertullian, *Praescript.*, 48; Epiphanius, *Haeres.*, XXVIII, 1–6; Philastrius, *Haer.*, 36; Augustine, *Haer.*, 8; Theodoret, *Haeret, fabul.*, II, 3.

you have heard from the beginning, abide in you. If that abide in you, which you have heard from the beginning, you also shall abide in the Son, and in the Father" (2:22–24). And again: "Who is a liar but he who denieth that *Jesus is the Christ?*" (2:22.) "Whosoever believeth that Jesus is the Christ, is born of God" (5:1). Furthermore: "Every spirit which confesseth that *Jesus Christ is come in the flesh,* is of God: and every spirit that dissolveth Jesus, is not of God: and this is Antichrist, of whom you have heard that he cometh, and he is now already in the world" (4:2–3). "Many seducers are gone out into the world, who confess not that Jesus Christ is come in the flesh: this is a seducer and an antichrist" (2 Jn. 7). Finally, the apostle adjures his followers to hold fast to the entire Christian *Logos* doctrine with utmost fidelity, but to repudiate the teaching of Cerinthus: "Look to yourselves, that you lose not the things which you have wrought: but that you may receive a full reward. Whosoever revolteth, and continueth not in the doctrine of Christ, hath not God. He that continueth in the doctrine, the same hath both the Father and the Son. If any man come to you, and bring not this doctrine, receive him not into the house, nor say to him, God speed you. For he that saith unto him, God speed you, communicateth with his wicked work" (2 Jn. 8–11).

In view of this decisive repudiation of the Greco-Philonian errors, and in particular of those of Cerinthus, it must appear astonishing that John retains the shell employed by them, by using the same term *Logos,* and by dealing with the essentially same problems of the *Logos.* Evidently he did this primarily because these had become familiar for hundreds of years in his Hellenic surroundings. By appropriating them the evangelist was able to popularize the doctrine of the true *Logos,* Jesus Christ, and thus win many converts among the contemporary educated classes. Furthermore — and this is the determining factor — the traditional shell of the opposing *Logos* philosophy was eminently suited to the reception of the Christian *Logos* doctrine. After John had purified it of all the dross which had

remained therein as a result of pagan philosophy, Jewish theo-
sophy, and pseudo-Christian speculation, he poured into this
mold, providentially prepared, the pure and extremely sublime
content of the revealed, genuine *Logos* doctrine.

Just as emphatically as John repudiates the false theories of
the *Logos,* just so deliberately does he follow the *Logos* ideas
of historical revelation. This must be forcibly stressed in order
to answer fully the question now occupying us. The words of
John: "In the beginning was the Word," plainly refer to the
Mosaic expression: "In the beginning God created heaven and
earth." Thereupon the evangelist follows the *Logos* everywhere
on Biblical paths. The twofold meaning of the Greek word
Logos: reason (thought) and *speech* (word), offered a point of
connection with the Old Testament doctrine of *the divine
Word,* or *the Word of God.* In most cases where reference is
made in the Old Testament to the word or speech of God, the
corresponding Hebraic expression (*dabar*) of the original text
is represented in the Septuagint by *Logos.* The *Logos,* the Word
of God, according to the Old Testament, performs a very
prominent role in the natural creation, preservation, and government of the world, as well as in the supernatural revelation
and in the dispensing of divine salvation; in fact, in some
passages the *Logos* of God seems to appear as an individual,
a person. In the doctrinal books of Holy Scripture, *Sophia,* the
Wisdom of God, appears even more distinctly not only as an
attribute of Jahweh, but forthright as the supreme, personal
principle of the creation, rule, and government of the world,
as well as of all divine revelation made to the world. In the
Book of Proverbs is described the eternity of Wisdom, its union
with God, and its blessed activity in behalf of humanity (Chap.
8). The son of Sirach relates how wisdom, which came forth
from the mouth of God, was active in the creation and in
behalf of the people of God (Ecclus., Chap. 24). Solomon extols
the absolutely supernatural qualities of Wisdom (Wisd. 7:22–
24); it is "a vapour of the power of God, and a certain pure
emanation of the glory of the almighty God . . . the brightness

of eternal light, and the unspotted mirror of God's majesty, and the image of his goodness" (7:25 f.); it "reacheth from end to end mightily, and ordereth all things" (8:1). Furthermore, this Wisdom is expressly called *Logos* (9:1; 16:12; 18:15).

St. Paul does not use the term *Logos,* but, on the other hand, he does avail himself of the Old Testament idea of *Wisdom.* He finds this idea personified in Jesus Christ and sets it in contrast to the pagan-Hellenic speculations on *Wisdom.* In the first epistle to the Corinthians, one of his earliest writings, he says: "The Greeks seek after wisdom: but we preach Christ crucified, unto the Jews indeed a stumbling block, and unto the Gentiles foolishness: but unto them that are called, both Jews and Greeks, Christ the power of God, and the wisdom of God" (1:22–24). According to Paul, therefore, the incarnate Son of God is the personal Wisdom of God. In his later writings, particularly in the epistles to the Ephesians, Philippians, Colossians, and Hebrews, he expounds his relation to the Father, his eternal pre-existence, his creative activity, his incarnation, and redemption — a Christology which is essentially the same as that of John (see above, Chap. 17).

But John is the first and the only one who combines the various elements of this *Logos* Christology and casts it into its final form. Already in the prologue he presents it in pithy conciseness and clarity. Nowhere in all Sacred Scripture is there found a series of dogmatic pronouncements of such weight and profundity. The writer sets them down with an amazing matter-of-factness and erects them as a barrier against the raging sea of pagan-Jewish and pseudo-Christian *Logos* speculations. His *Logos* commentary, as his whole gospel proves itself to be, is just as clear and incomparably complete. The beloved disciple describes not only the external events in the life of his Master; he sees hidden under the human form of Jesus the sublimity and majesty of the God-*Logos;* he penetrates within the innermost nature, the unfathomable being, the heart and soul of the incarnate Word, with whom he had lived in such

HOLY GHOST FATHERS
FERNDALE
NORWALK, CONN.

close association during his life on earth, and in whom he had become completely absorbed in consequence of deepest contemplation, continued over a period of many decades. By means of his first epistle the aged apostle wishes to infuse into his followers the same knowledge of the *Logos,* and to inflame them with the same love to the *Logos,* and to protect them against the false *Logos* doctrine. In the Apocalypse he beholds the *Logos* in the glory of heaven and hears all creation sing to him in jubilation, and adore him forever and ever (cf. 5:9–14; 19:11 ff.). Hence it will be readily understood that John presented the doctrine of the Son of God and *Logos* of God in all its completeness.

In putting forth this doctrine of the *Logos* in general, John also unfolded the exact relation in which the Son of God stands to the Father. This must be stressed in particular, because it is the culmination of Johannine Christology. Essentially, the mere name *Son of God* as such conveys the truth that he possesses divine nature by virtue of a spiritual generation from the Father. The term *Logos,* however, defined the manner of generation of the Son from a peculiar aspect. The Greek expression *Logos* denotes, as we know, primarily the inner word, thought, cognition, but then, too, its outward expression in speech. When John calls the Son *Logos,* he teaches that the latter was begotten of the inner-divine cognition of the Father, and in time became outwardly visible by means of the incarnation. The Son of a spiritual being, of a pure intellect, is precisely his cognition, his knowledge, his thought, and, by assuming a human nature, this thought became the outwardly expressed Word of God. Thereby John struck the keynote of what is the ultimate and the most profound concept possible to a created mind of the divine sonship and the inner-divine life of God. For this very reason he has been called, from the first centuries on, the theologian among the evangelists. His *Logos*-idea became the starting point and the guiding star of the incipient development of the Trinitarian-Christological dogma. With a firm hand he fixed the subsequent theology in the definitions of the complete equality of essence and of the distinction as to Persons of the Father and the Son. Every deviation from the Johannine *Logos*-doctrine at all times led to Subordination or Arian heresy. On the other hand, the great Fathers of the Church, Irenaeus, Athanasius, Gregory of Nazianzus, Augustine, developed with utmost certainty the doctrine of the Trinity by closely adhering to John. We cannot but admire the ways of Providence which led the fourth evangelist to choose the incomparable term *Logos,* and to fix firmly that unique idea of the *Logos,* in which our faith and our knowledge of the greatest mysteries of the Christian creed are safely guarded.

The most important point, however, is the fact that the entire *Logos* doctrine of St. John is built up on the granite foundation of *historical, divine revelation.* He knows and carefully examines all New Testament records concerning Christ. He approves them and supplements them as the witness of the first and of the last hour. He is conscious of repudiating every legend, every inaccuracy, every false statement concerning the *Logos:* "That which was from the beginning, which we have heard, which we have seen with our eyes, which we have looked upon, and our hands have handled, of the word of life . . . we bear witness and we declare unto you" (1 Jn. 1:1 f.). And at the end of the prologue, the source of the unfathomable, and for us incomprehensible, knowledge of the *Logos,* he leads us to that pure spring whence flows all knowledge of creatures concerning the Son of God and the Word of God: "No man hath seen God at any time: The only begotten Son who is in the bosom of the Father, he hath declared him" (Jn. 1:18).

Index

347

3 5282 00078 2311